By the same author

The First Day on the Somme
The Nuremberg Raid
Convoy
Battleship (with Patrick Mahoney)
The Kaiser's Battle

Martin Middlebrook

The Battle of Hamburg

Allied Bomber Forces against
a German City in 1943

CHARLES SCRIBNER'S SONS
New York

First U.S. edition published by Charles Scribner's Sons, 1981
Copyright © 1980 Martin Middlebrook

Library of Congress Cataloging in Publication Data

Middlebrook, Martin, 1932–
    The Battle of Hamburg.

    Bibliography: p.
    Includes index.
    1. Hamburg—Bombardment, 1943. I. Title.
D757.9.H3M53   940.54′21   80-27329
ISBN 0-684-16727-1

1 3 5 7 9 11 13 15 17 19 Q/C 20 18 16 14 12 8 6 4 2

Printed in the United States of America

Contents

List of Plates

List of Maps

*Maps by Reginald Piggott from preliminary drawings
by Mary Middlebrook*

Introduction

At approximately 8.30 a.m. on Saturday, 24 July 1943, Air Chief Marshal Sir Arthur Harris ordered that the maximum strength of heavy bombers in Royal Air Force Bomber Command would attack the German city of Hamburg that night. Harris's morning conference soon broke up and the staff officers who had been attending departed to finalize the detailed plan for this attack. At exactly fifty-seven minutes past midnight, three bombers of the Pathfinder Force released their loads accurately over the centre of Hamburg. Nine nights later, in the early hours of 3 August, a Wellington bomber from an Australian squadron released its load on what its crew hoped was Hamburg (but, because of severe weather conditions, it might have been anywhere within a thirty-mile radius of the city). Six major air raids – four by the R.A.F. and two by American bombers – and three small harassing ones had taken place between the dropping of these first and last bombs. Allied historians later named this period of sustained bombing against one city 'The Battle of Hamburg'. The citizens and city historians of Hamburg called it '*die Katastrophe*'.

I have deliberately chosen the historical phrase, 'The Battle of Hamburg', as the title for this book. It will present a study, in as much detail as possible, of one round in what I call 'the bombing war', or what formal historians call the 'Strategic Bombing Offensive'. What happened to Hamburg may have been an extreme example of Allied success but the results obtained were the results that were hoped for every time the Allied heavy-bomber forces set out for Germany. The raids in the prolonged bombing-war campaign were, indeed, 'battles' – bloody contests between the bomber forces and the German cities.

Some years ago I wrote a book called *The Nuremberg Raid*. This described a Bomber Command raid on the night of 30–31 March 1944 in which the R.A.F. crews involved were opposed by a successful German night-fighter defence and some bad luck with the weather. Ninety-five bombers and their crews – more than 13 per cent of those that had taken off – were lost. Nuremberg was scarcely damaged. It was a clear failure, the R.A.F.'s greatest disaster of the war. I have sometimes been criticized by reviewers and by professional service officers for producing a one-sided view of wartime events by describing too many British disasters. This may be fair criticism, although I would like to state that it is often through a close study of such setbacks that the finer points of strategy and tactics can be highlighted and, also, it is in such actions that the finest examples of human endeavour and courage can be found. However, for once, here is a clear-cut Allied success. The raids on Hamburg in July and August 1943 were immediately recognized and have since been confirmed by historians as being an outstanding Allied victory in the bombing war.

So, as a contrast to the British failure of Nuremberg eight months later, I present this study of the Battle of Hamburg. Ironically, I am again likely to be criticized – in fact I have already been so criticized by some ex-R.A.F. officers – for choosing a series of raids which produced such extremes of horror on the ground. But I must point out that a large proportion of the raids carried out by R.A.F. Bomber Command in the Second World War were devoted to this type of bombing. What happened at Hamburg was what happened when Bomber Command 'got everything right'. I can understand the distaste that ex-bomber men might show when they see one of their achievements described in such detail but I will attempt to set their war in the fuller context of the war as a whole.

There is an added bonus in this book in that units of the United States Eighth Army Air Force, which were stationed in England at that time, took part in the Battle of Hamburg, mounting two major daylight raids. This has provided me with the interesting opportunity to study and compare the methods of the two air forces in such areas as strategic policy, target selection and tactical methods, and to look at the experiences and attitudes of the men of both bomber forces. Indeed, such comparisons are a major purpose of this book. I hope the reader will find them as interesting as I have done.

The book will be a complex one because there were so many participants in the Battle of Hamburg: the R.A.F. and U.S.A.A.F. heavy-bomber units, some British light bombers and fighters, the Luftwaffe's night-fighter, day-fighter, anti-aircraft and radar units, the municipal authorities, the industrial element, the civil-defence units and, above all, the civilians of Hamburg. Some of these participants rarely met others who took part and many survivors still have only vague notions of the experiences of the other actors. I have attempted in my research to cover every aspect of the Battle of Hamburg and the book will attempt to describe all the elements and events in the battle. The scenes of action will constantly shift and it is possible that enthusiasts and specialist readers may not find enough of their favourite subjects and I realize that only the most dedicated reader will be equally interested in every section of the book. In particular, I must warn that events in the air may appear to be given less prominence than events on the ground but, unlike the Nuremberg raid, what happened in the target city was more significant than what happened on the way to it. For aviation enthusiasts, however, there is much previously unpublished reference material in the Appendixes.

Although I happen to be an Englishman, I have attempted to write my story impartially. There will be no 'us' and no 'them'. After more than thirty years, wartime passions should have dampened; the patriotism and ideals, the courage and suffering of all can surely be recorded, although the villainy and deceit of some must never be forgotten.

Let me explain the technique that will be used. Every effort will be made to bring to life what happened in the Battle of Hamburg by using the personal reminiscences of the ordinary people involved. My search for survivors was spread over every group taking part in the battle and, as far as the passage of years allows, covered every level from the most eminent to the most humble. I eventually received contributions from over 500 people who had taken part. Much of the material received was as a result of correspondence but several interviewing trips in Britain and one each to Germany and the United States brought rich results. I regret that there will be one gap in this personal coverage. The Luftwaffe day-fighter force suffered such severe attrition after 1943 that I had great difficulty finding survivors of the units that faced the American bombers flying to Hamburg.

Before this personal material could be used, however, it was essential to establish a sound framework from documentary sources and the main research effort was devoted to this purpose. A mass of prime source documents was discovered and there will be no difficulty in providing the bare bones of most aspects of the Battle of Hamburg. The records of the R.A.F. and U.S.A.A.F. units are mostly in a complete and reliable condition. R.A.F. operations are recorded right down to individual crew level. The American units, being mostly in their first months of active war conditions, had not yet settled down to an established system. 'We were still learning in this as in other things', as one American officer said, but their records sometimes contain interesting items of a kind not recorded in a more orthodox system.

The situation concerning German documents can be summarized by stating that the civil side of the action is well covered but not the Luftwaffe side. The very detailed report of the Hamburg Chief of Police and its appendixes survived the war intact and, fortunately for an Englishman with a poor knowledge of German, was fully translated into English (or 'American' to be more precise) after the war.* A modest outlay secured copies of these translations. Unfortunately, nearly all the Luftwaffe documents were destroyed at the end of the war to avoid capture. This has created a gap in the firm knowledge of any operation in which the Luftwaffe was involved, although a limited coverage can be provided by piecing together fragments of information from the small selection of documents that have survived.

* The title held by the senior police officer in Hamburg was that of *Polizeipräsident*. I do not think that the literal translation of 'Police President' is the best one for an English-speaking readership and prefer the expression 'Chief of Police'.

1

The Road to Hamburg

In some ways, history will see the First and Second World Wars as one struggle fought in two stages. In no aspect of that war is this more true than in the case of strategic bombing, defined in the dictionary as 'designed to disorganize the enemy's internal economy and to destroy morale'.*[1] Every element in the bombing of the Second World War, except the use of the atomic bomb, had been seen in the first war, albeit often on the smallest of scales. A short examination of the events of 1914–18 will reveal the origins of what happened in Hamburg a quarter of a century later.

There had been talk of war between England and Germany for several years before 1914. It is almost as though a death wish existed that these two proud and powerful nations should test their strength against each other. The long run-up to the actual conflict had caused some thought to be given to the use of the newly invented flying machine in the event of war. It was taken for granted that aeroplanes and airships would be used over the battlefield and sea in support of armies and navies, but such tactical uses are not the subject of this book. The revolutionary forecast that bombs might actually be carried from one country to another and dropped on cities proved remarkably prophetic. What would be the purpose of such bombing and what effect would it have? In 1912 a German naval officer, lecturing to his colleagues at Kiel, summed up the intention. The bombing of England would cause serious material damage but it would also 'strike at the morale of the people'.[2] So here, two years before the First World War, can be seen the two aims of strategic air bombardment: industrial or material destruction and the demoralization of civilian populations never before touched directly by war. These two aims have been pursued, with changing emphasis on one or the other, from that day to this.

German Zeppelin airships were first off the mark. Flying by night from their bases in Germany and, later, from Belgium,

* Numbered notes are printed at the end of the chapter.

they started bombing industrial cities and towns in the Midlands and north of England in 1915. Two aspects of aerial bombing were immediately revealed. The Zeppelin captains tried to aim their bombs at factories, bridges and railways but often found it difficult to do so accurately and many bombs hit private houses. It was not indiscriminate bombing but civilians were killed without discrimination. It was found, too, that civilian morale was badly shaken, sometimes becoming almost hysterical in the face of attacks that, by later standards, were mere pin-pricks.

The Zeppelin raids diminished when the British defences became more effective but they were replaced by a new weapon – the daylight bomber. In the summer of 1917, a single squadron of twin-engined Gotha bombers, which never exceeded an operational strength of twenty-one planes, started operating from airfields in Belgium. The Gothas made three raids on southern England, two of which reached London. The sensational effects of these raids have been well covered in other works; it is sufficient here to summarize their results. The Gothas carried out a total of sixty-three flights, killing 322 people and wounding 872 others, mostly in London where there was once again much panic. Amidst the almost universal condemnation of this latest German 'barbarity', one man, Lord Montagu, voiced the opinion that London, with its many war factories, was a legitimate target for the German bombing. He received little support for this brave view. But the British defence became more effective and the Gotha raids gradually ceased.

Several German cities were very vulnerable to retaliatory attack by British and French bombers based in France. Airfields in the Verdun and Nancy areas were less than 200 miles from cities such as Stuttgart, Mannheim, Cologne and those of the Ruhr, and French bombers had been raiding Germany since the summer of 1916. The French policy was one of strict selectivity; the German chemical industry was judged to be particularly vulnerable to air attack and to be a vital factor in the manufacture of the shells which the armies on the Western Front demanded in such huge quantities. So the French airmen, flying by day, concentrated very carefully on the German chemical factories. The last thing that the French wanted was to allow their bombing to become indiscriminate and to bring German retaliation on Paris. In October 1916, the French were joined by squadrons of the Royal Naval Air Service which had always been to the fore in British long-range bombing.

Events during the rest of the war can be described quickly. It was a tale of wild dreams but modest achievement. As early as October 1917, the British Admiral E. F. Kerr was asking for the production of 2,000 long-range British strategic bombers! Such proposals were bitterly opposed by the Army, which insisted that its air support on the Western Front should not be reduced. The British and French squadrons attacking Germany found that the German defences were becoming too strong and daylight raids had to be abandoned. The airmen tried their best to carry out the night raids that followed but with only modest results and at the cost of increased losses. The war ended before a large force of four-engined bombers based in England with the intention of mounting heavy raids deep into Germany could be used. Berlin and Hamburg had been mentioned as targets for this force.

Much effort had been devoted in the past four years to this new form of warfare. Although some material damage and much panic had been caused, the dream of the more dedicated strategic air leaders had not been achieved. No bottleneck shortages had been created in industry. There had been some panic but no widespread civil disorder. The truth is that long-range bombing had hardly affected the outcome of the war. It had been the long-suffering soldiers on the Western Front and the silent naval blockade that had brought victory to the Allies. But the appetites of the airmen had been whetted. More and better aircraft, heavier bomb-loads, priorities in resources, determination – all these might achieve the dream of a bomber victory in a future war.

Let us draw up a list of the main points that emerged from that first use of the bomber aircraft; they were all to be seen again in the Second World War: the vulnerability of civilians when airmen attempted to bomb industrial targets in poor bomb-aiming conditions; the effect on civilian morale and the apparent conclusion that this would quickly break under sufficiently heavy attack; the belief that concentration on one particular type of industry would cause a more widespread industrial collapse; the myth of the self-defending daylight-bomber formation and the inevitable turning to less efficient bombing by night; the controversy over when a city was a legitimate target; the increasing diversions of manpower from the fighting fronts by both attackers and defenders; and the dreams of whole fleets of bombers that must prove decisive. For those who looked ahead to the use of the bomber in the next war, all the signs were there in the one just ended.

The next twenty years can be passed over quickly. The large air forces of 1918 were rapidly run down and the following years were spent in philosophizing, experimenting and planning. When it became obvious that Europe was heading for war again, the nations started to rearm and the plans and aspirations of air leaders took on new significance. It was obvious that air power was going to play a major part. The conventionalists still saw the aeroplane mainly as a tactical weapon to be used in direct support of armies and navies. The Germans and French supported this philosophy. Germany's fine new Luftwaffe was designed as a short- and medium-range force to prepare the way for fast-moving armoured ground forces. *Blitzkrieg!* Lightning war! The French Air Force was also designed purely as a supporting force for their army; fear of German retaliation on vulnerable French cities forbade anything bolder.

In Britain, the Army and Royal Navy would have liked to have had control of air power in the same way but the R.A.F. had managed to break free. It had become a truly independent service and was now dominated by strategic-bomber men. They realized that some effort would have to be devoted to the support of the Army and Navy and their defensive force, Fighter Command, must be maintained at sufficient strength to protect the United Kingdom, but the main weapon and the priority for production was for heavy, long-range bombers. These would fly to Germany, by day it was assumed, and destroy the industrial capacity of that country, rendering Germany unable to continue the fight. This was the bomber dream – no more 1914-style continental land battles for Britain! The driving force behind this philosophy was Air Marshal Sir Hugh Trenchard who had led the R.A.F. throughout the inter-war years. American air officers called Trenchard 'the patron saint of air power' and the description is a fitting one. But the ageing Trenchard would not be in command when the war came. His disciples would have to put into effect his plan and try to achieve his hopes. He would, however, live through the Second World War and continue to press his influence.

There was even a dark school of thought that the most profitable target was the morale of civilians. No one had forgotten the panic and hysteria caused by bombing in the First World War. It was widely thought that the heavier scale of bombing now possible would produce a greater effect. The morale of civilian populations was judged to have a low breaking point. Although the Washington Treaty of 1922 had forbidden the use of bombing intended to terrorize civilian populations or to destroy non-military or non-industrial property, similar provisions had not been incorporated into the Geneva Convention which was accepted by the European nations as providing the guiding principles in the conduct of war. However, it was still almost universally agreed that 'terror' bombing intended to produce civilian disorder should not be employed. But some R.A.F. leaders could not give up the conviction that it was here that the most efficient use of the bomber lay. The British official historians attribute these thoughts to Trenchard:

> Sir Hugh Trenchard had not only insisted on the maintenance of the offence at all costs and the reduction of the defensive force to the lowest possible number, but also had implied that the war could be won by producing such morale effect on the civilian population of the enemy that its government would have to sue for peace. This was never stated quite explicitly and the advantage of destroying military installations and factories was recognised, but the essence of the theory was that it was easier to overcome the will to resist among the workers than to destroy the means to resist. Morale effect, it had continually been said, was as to material effect as twenty to one. Thus, the war could be won without the use of large armies.[3]

However, this policy was not at that time blessed either by public opinion or by the British Government, which was several times asked to pass judgement on the subject. As late as 14 September 1939, after the outbreak of war, Prime Minister Neville Chamberlain told the House of Commons:

> Whatever the lengths to which others may go, His Majesty's

Government will never resort to the deliberate attack on women and children and other civilians for purposes of mere terrorism.

The only relevant nation not yet mentioned is the United States. It would be more than two years before the Americans joined the conflict but their thinking was well advanced. They were strategic-bombing purists. Heavy bombers, used by daylight to guarantee accurate bombing, should be used only in precision attacks on industrial and other legitimate targets of war. There was no hankering by the Americans to pursue an attack on civilian morale. Of all the air forces mentioned here, only the Americans were to stick to their philosophy from beginning to end – at least in Europe.

It was going to be an interesting war for airmen but the civilians of many countries would have to depend on the goodwill of their enemies for the safety of their property and lives.

The first eight months of the war were an anti-climax. The Luftwaffe carried out its part in the German invasion of Poland with fierce efficiency and many Polish communities were bombed in the name of tactical bombing, the yardstick being that, if a town stood in the way of the Wehrmacht, it was bombed. The rest of the world was horrified but no retaliation on Germany took place. France dared not, for fear of counter retaliation on her vulnerable cities, and Britain would not, partly out of deference to the wishes of the French, partly out of a fear of provoking a general outbreak of bombing in western Europe for which the R.A.F. was not yet prepared. Britain's air rearmament had not yet produced much result. The R.A.F. only had 280 bombers of what might be called 'intermediate' types – twin-engined planes with limited bomb-carrying capacity; the first of the four-engined 'heavies' would not be ready until 1941. The R.A.F. bombers had already suffered a severe setback when sent out in a series of modest daylight raids on German naval targets in September and December 1939. The supposedly self-defending bomber formations had been badly mauled by German fighters, twenty-nine bombers having been lost out of 159 taking part! The importance of this setback cannot be exaggerated. The whole concept of British strategic bombing had been that the bombers would operate by daylight, beat off fighter attack, and bomb accurately in good visibility. The much-used pre-war claim that 'the bomber will always get through' had been proved false.

It was clear that operations which led to losses of almost 20 per cent even before the German mainland was penetrated could not be continued. The decision was swiftly taken that Bomber Command would convert itself into a night-bombing force. It was a solution that could be put into effect within months – any other would have taken years – but it was an unsatisfactory compromise and Bomber Command would have to operate under severely unfavourable conditions for the majority of the war. This change of policy was a major step on the road to Hamburg.

The winter of 1939–40 passed with only a few small-scale night raids being made on German island and coastal targets; some long-range flights were made over German cities but only propaganda leaflets were dropped. The Luftwaffe showed similar restraint in the West. Then, on 10 May 1940, the Germans invaded France and the neutral countries of Holland and Belgium. The bombing scenes of Poland were repeated, a particularly severe attack on Rotterdam doing more harm to Germany's reputation in the world than any good it did the Wehrmacht. Winston Churchill was now Britain's Prime Minister and he immediately sanctioned the R.A.F.'s request to commence the attack on German industrial centres that had been put off for so long. The resulting raids were the first strategic-bombing operations of the Second World War.

This new phase in the bombing war lasted for just over a year and a half, from May 1940 to the end of 1941. Flying almost exclusively by night, Bomber Command maintained its offensive against those German industrial cities that could be reached within the various seasonal lengths of darkness. It was a period of 'pure' strategic bombing in that the bomber crews were instructed only to bomb industrial targets, each crew actually being given an individual factory or installation to bomb. The R.A.F. commanders persevered with this policy and the aircrews pressed home their attacks with much fortitude. Bomber Command flew 43,774 sorties and dropped 44,592 tons of bombs in this period; 1,019 aircraft and their crews never returned. It had never been expected that this eighteen-month campaign, with a force that never exceeded 430 night bombers of limited bomb-carrying capacity, would prove decisive. This was merely the opening of what was realized would be a prolonged campaign but one which would have a cumulative and, hopefully, overwhelming effect in future years. In the meantime, it was believed that much damage was being done to German industry.

During this period the Luftwaffe bombers had fought the Battle of Britain but, even though escorted by fighters, they had suffered heavy loss and had inevitably turned to night operations. The German bombers then raided London and many other cities in what the British called 'the Blitz'. Like their R.A.F. counterparts, the Luftwaffe crews were ordered to bomb industrial targets and they made some effort to do so. The British observed several interesting aspects of these German raids. It was found that the worst damage was caused by fire and not by high-explosive bombs. The German bombing accuracy was poor and their bombs often fell into civilian areas and many casualties occurred there. Much contempt was shown for the Germans' lack of accuracy and much anger was officially aroused at what was termed indiscriminate bombing. A surprising aspect of the effects of the German bombing was the discovery that civilian morale stood up remarkably well to the bombing. There were even signs that bombing in civilian areas was counter-productive. It increased the determination of beleaguered and isolated Britain to hold out and the national attitude to the war was certainly strengthened. In the growing up of just one generation, mankind had learned to live with the phenomenon of aerial bombing.

However, the R.A.F. raids on Germany were not proving as effective as had been thought. The results had been very similar to the Luftwaffe bombing of England. Very few of the British bombs had hit their targets and the effect on industrial production had been slight. The German civilians had shown no sign of panic at the effect of those bombs that had landed in residential areas. There was one difference between the English and the German attitudes. While British propaganda made the most of the German bombing of English cities, the German authorities mostly kept a discreet silence about bombs falling on Germany. At a time when German arms were everywhere triumphant, it was embarrassing to admit that the Luftwaffe was not able to defend its homeland. Had not Reichsmarschall Hermann Goering somewhat jokingly declared that he would change his name to 'Hermann Meier' if his Luftwaffe ever allowed the R.A.F. to bomb German cities?

This phase of the bombing war came to an end in the middle of November 1941. In August, the British had ordered a survey to be made of the evidence available on the results of the bombing in this first phase. The investigation was ordered by the War Cabinet, not by the R.A.F., and it was carried out by a civil servant, Mr D. M. Butt. The Butt Report presented the results of an examination made of the flash-lit photographs of the ground taken at the moment of bombing by 4,065 aircraft in a hundred raids. The results were a bitter disappointment. Only the best crews had cameras fitted to their aircraft and, for raids against Germany, *only one in four* of those crews which had claimed to have bombed their targets had been *within five miles of that target*. Against targets in the industrial Ruhr, the proportion of bombs dropped within five miles only reached one in ten of those crews reporting success. Better results had been achieved on moonlit nights but it was on these nights that the German defence was most effective. This disastrous news for the R.A.F. coincided with a worsening casualty rate as the German defences became more skilled. On 13 November 1941, Bomber Command was ordered to cease long-range operations for the time being.

In any study of strategic bombing in the Second World War there appear a number of distinct turning points. The British strategic-bombing offensive now stood at the second major turning point. The first had been the failure of the self-defending daylight bomber to operate safely in late 1939. The solution chosen then – to use the same aircraft to bomb by night – now appeared to be equally unsuccessful.

One of the easiest solutions to this latest problem would have been to admit that it was unlikely that the policy of strategic bombing could be made to work and that the manpower and industrial resources required for the heavy bomber force be deployed elsewhere. There were plenty of claimants. The arguments which followed took up most of the mid-winter months but the air leaders won. The bomber dream was kept alive. On 14 February 1942, the Air Ministry sent a new directive to the headquarters of R.A.F. Bomber Command. The restraint on distant operations that had been imposed in November 1941 was lifted and Bomber Command was ordered to recommence intensive night operations against Germany whenever weather conditions were favourable. The answer to the problem of target finding by night was to be found in yet another major concession to pre-war concepts. No longer were individual industrial targets chosen for attack but much larger areas of German industrial cities were now to be the target. Because bombs could not be guaranteed to hit targets such as factories or railway yards, then the Aiming Points would be chosen so that they would be certain to hit at least some part of the target city. The reader will easily recognize that such bombing represented a departure from the strict principles of attacking only 'legitimate' war targets and that residential and cultural areas of cities were likely to be hit. The Air Ministry directive made no attempt to hide this departure from previous policy and, in fact, made a virtue out of the necessity.

A review has been made ... and it has been decided that the primary object of your operations should now be focussed on the morale of the enemy civilian population and, in particular, of the industrial workers. With this aim in view, a list of selected area targets ... is attached.[4]

The new method was known as 'Area Bombing'. The intention was to stop the life of German cities by devastating large areas of those cities. Instead of blowing off the roof of an armaments factory and destroying the machinery inside the factory, the city's power and water supplies were to be cut off, its transportation system disorganized, the postal, telephone and civic services disrupted. But, above all, the easiest target, the thing that a bomber could hardly miss when attacking a large city, was the workers' housing areas. Such bombing would severely disrupt industrial production, even if the factories themselves remained untouched. But the directive did not even give industrial disruption equal priority with civilian morale. 'The primary object', the directive had stated, was 'the morale of the enemy civil population.'

The directive never spelled out just what was expected to happen to the inhabitants of the German cities. Just that one sentence summed up the new policy; the rest of the document dealt with a new navigational device called Gee, the weather, and the German cities to which priority was to be given. But it must have been obvious to the senior officers concerned that the German civilians were to be bombed, their homes and belongings destroyed, and, if they were not evacuated or given adequate air-raid shelters, they would be killed, burnt and mutilated in large numbers. On the face of it, this was a callous, cruel and inhuman way to wage war but I must ask the reader to withhold his opinion on this until he has read some views presented later in the book after the bombing of Hamburg, the supreme example of Area Bombing, has been described in later chapters.

It is often suggested that the primary reason for the British bomber offensive during these middle years of the war was to placate Russian demands for an invasion in the West during a period when the British and Americans were not ready for such an invasion. It is true that the bombing of German cities did provide Churchill with a useful counter to Stalin's demands and that he ensured that Bomber Command received most of the resources it asked for during this period, but investing the bomber offensive with the status of a substitute Second Front was never more than a useful by-product of the main aim. The bombing between early 1942 and the invasion in mid-1944 was a campaign in its own right, a natural development of the long-held policy of the R.A.F.'s leaders, the 'bomber barons' as they were sometimes called.

So the decision was made. The strategic bomber was given yet another lease of life and a new role that would allow it greater freedom of destruction and, it was hoped, greater opportunity to bring the war more quickly to a victorious conclusion for the Allies. But the German city dwellers were sentenced to face an ever-growing assault on their homes and on their very lives. The long agony of the German civilian population was about to begin.

But the climax of the trial of strength between the R.A.F. bombers and Germany was yet again to be delayed. When

Sir Arthur Harris took over the leadership of Bomber Command in February 1942, his force consisted of only 400 operational night bombers because several bomber squadrons had been detached for service in the Middle East or with Coastal Command. Harris made every effort to stop this depletion of his command but it was to continue for some time. Using this modest force of bombers and the new navigational device, Gee,* Harris now set out to implement the Area Bombing Directive. In the post-war dispatch that Harris prepared on his tenure of command, he called the next twelve-month period the 'Preliminary Phase'. There were many disappointments during this year's operations but there were three important developments: the fire attack on the Baltic coastal port of Lübeck in March, the successful Thousand-Bomber Raid on Cologne in May – many of the aircraft used being borrowed from training units – and the formation of the Pathfinder Force in August. It was the target finding and marking of the Pathfinders, combined with the bomber-stream tactic developed at Cologne and the fire-raising technique first proved at Lübeck, that would be the methods relied upon by the R.A.F. for their attacks on German cities during the rest of the war.

On 17 August 1942, just one day before the first Pathfinder-led R.A.F. operation, to the German port of Flensburg near the Danish border, there had been an event of greater significance 500 miles to the south. A formation of twelve American Boeing bombers – 'B-17s' to their crew members, 'Flying Fortresses' to the press and public – flew across the French coast in clear daylight, penetrated thirty miles inland, and bombed a railway marshalling yard near Rouen. The Fortresses were escorted by four squadrons of R.A.F. Spitfires and all returned safely to their airfields in England. A surprised German fighter controller broadcast that 'twelve Lancasters'

* The device code-named Gee had recently started to be fitted to R.A.F. bombers. It enabled a bomber navigator to plot his position by receiving a series of radio pulses emitted from ground stations in England, but its range was limited by the curvature of the earth. Cities in the Ruhr and Rhineland areas and some of the North German ports could be reached on Gee but the bombers had to manage without the use of the new device beyond that range. It was expected that Gee would remain free from German jamming for no more than six months

were carrying out the raid but he was soon to get used to the idea of American bombers flying into his air space.

The Americans were enthusiastic in their desire to join the R.A.F. in the plan to cripple Germany by strategic bombing and, with the vital energy and massive industrial resources of their country, the first operational unit of these heavy bombers had been able to carry out this raid at Rouen less than nine months after the American entry into the war. The Americans were purists in their attitude to strategic bombing in that they steadfastly intended to concentrate on the accurate bombing of targets that were universally acknowledged to be legitimate ones for aerial bombardment. There were to be no compromises for the Americans. Their bombing would always be by daylight and they had no intention of getting mixed up with an attack on the morale of the German people by the general bombing of city areas, although they occasionally did bomb blindly when their primary targets and all possible alternatives were found to be cloud covered. It was with these high principles that the American bomber men entered the European war. American officers privately described R.A.F. area-bombing methods as 'agricultural bombing' or 'potato farming'.

The British, who had tried daylight bombing in 1939, forecast that the Americans would not succeed in their policy and suggested, sometimes forcefully, that the American bombers join the R.A.F. in the night offensive. The Americans declined. Their bombers flew in tight formation and were heavily armed; each carried at least ten heavy-calibre 0·5-inch machine-guns. Although these were the identical methods with which the R.A.F. had failed in 1939, the Americans still believed that their formations could beat off German fighter attack. Their bombs would be aimed carefully with their brilliant new Norden bomb-sight in good daylight visibility. General Ira C. Eaker, the commander of the first American bombers in England, claimed that his bombardiers would soon work up to a bomb-aiming accuracy that would result in 90 per cent of their bombs falling within a mile of a target, 40 per cent within 500 yards, 25 per cent within 250 yards and 10 per cent 'dead on' any building 100 yards square. These results were sometimes achieved, but only under favourable conditions.

The Americans were forced to make only a slow start. For the remainder of 1942, they carried out raids only on France, Holland and Belgium. Their targets were airfields, shipyards, railways, aircraft factories and U-boat bases. On most raids, the bombers flew under the escort of Allied fighters but, when attacking the more distant U-boat bases in Brittany, they had to fly the last part of each raid without such cover. Losses on such targets rose but were never severe and it seemed that the American claim that their so-called Flying Fortresses could look after themselves could be a valid one. The real test, however, would come in attacks on the heavily defended targets of Germany. These would have to wait until well into 1943 while the American bomber force gradually added to its strength and gained experience. A lot of people – American, British and German – were watching with great interest to see how the American version of strategic bombing developed.

With the coming of 1943, we are only seven months away from the Battle of Hamburg. This year was destined to be one of the most interesting in the bombing war. It was to be the year in which both the R.A.F. and the U.S.A.A.F. saw a big increase in the strength of their bomber forces, the combined weight of which should become sufficient to make a significant impression on the enemy for the first time in this or any war. The bomber dream was to be put to a serious test at last. Not only were increased numbers of bombers to become available but valuable technical aids, some of which were the result of years of experiment, were also to appear. The year 1943 was also to be the last full one before the invasion of Europe.

The bomber force available to Harris at the opening of 1943 was only slightly greater on paper than the one he had inherited a year earlier. His night-bomber strength still numbered only 483, but most of the older types had been phased out and 70 per cent of the bombers were now four-engined types with much improved range and bomb-carrying capacity. Bomber Command was also receiving a few of the fast, new, twin-engined Mosquito bombers which could be put to such versatile use. Equally valuable reinforcements were appearing in the shape of two new navigational and target-finding devices code-named Oboe and H2S.

Oboe was a blind-bombing device which depended upon

signals transmitted from ground stations in England. It was extremely accurate but only one bomber could use a pair of Oboe stations at any one time and the range of the device was limited by the curvature of the earth. It was only fitted to Mosquito bombers, which used it to produce either very accurate target marking for forces of heavy bombers or to carry out precision bombing on their own. The Germans never succeeded in jamming Oboe and within its limited range it remained a most useful device for the remainder of the war.

H2S was an early example of a radar set fitted into an aircraft. A small screen produced a rough radar picture of the ground over which the aircraft was flying. The first H2S sets were fitted in Pathfinder heavy bombers, in which they could be used both as a navigational aid and, although not as accurate as Oboe, as a blind-bombing or marking device. The great advantage of H2S was that, being carried in the aircraft, there was no limit to its operational range. Unfortunately, the Germans obtained an almost intact example of H2S from a shot-down bomber soon after the device was first used. Although H2S could not be jammed, the Germans soon produced tracking devices which were able to follow a force of bombers using H2S and even help a night fighter to home on to individual bombers. Even so, H2S was to be the mainstay of Bomber Command operations beyond the range of Oboe and it will play a major part in the Hamburg story.

These devices were available early in March 1943 when Bomber Command opened what Sir Arthur Harris's post-war dispatch called the 'Main Offensive'. The months of spring and early summer saw his bombers operating on as many nights as the weather and the state of the moon would permit. This period became known as the Battle of the Ruhr. This was the first time that the term 'Battle' was used for a series of raids and it should be explained. It was well known that a single raid, however successful, was unlikely to knock out a large city target, still less the sprawling complex of cities that made up the Ruhr. To cripple such targets effectively needed a series of raids in a concentrated time period. The Battle of the Ruhr opened in the evening of 5 March, with a highly successful Oboe-marked raid on Essen, and it lasted until mid-July. One-third of the raids in this period were on targets well away from the Ruhr – targets as far apart as Nuremberg,

Kiel, Berlin, and even Pilsen, in Czechoslovakia. These widespread targets were attacked to prevent the Germans concentrating their defences at the Ruhr. Few of these distant raids achieved much success – mainly because they were beyond the range of Oboe – and some had been expensive in bombers and crews lost. The real success had come in those raids that had concentrated on the Ruhr targets. The short routes meant heavier bomb loads and the Oboe marking was always accurate. The bomber crews at last felt they were being successful and they pressed home their attacks determinedly against these heavily defended targets.

For the first time in the war, German cities suffered severe damage and heavy casualties; approximately 32,000 German civilians were killed during this period. Thanks to photographic reconnaissance, the R.A.F. soon knew the results and Harris, with some justification, wrote to Portal: 'If we can keep this up, it cannot fail to be lethal within a period of time which, in my view, will be surprisingly short.' The next months would prove vital. Could the R.A.F. keep it up and inflict similar damage on more distant targets without the use of Oboe and without suffering too heavy casualties? The cost of the Battle of the Ruhr had been heavy. A total of 872 bombers and crews had been lost – 4·7 per cent of those dispatched!

The Americans were having to wait for their successes. Partly because of political and inter-service pressures to send more American bombers to the Pacific than had been planned and partly because one of their aircraft had made a disappointing start in Europe and had been sent to North Africa, there had been a much slower build-up than expected in England. It had been decided that a minimum of 300 bombers was to be considered essential to protect themselves on deep raids into German-defended territory without fighter escort. The turn of the year had found the Americans with only 100 heavy bombers available; the figure of 200 was reached in May 1943 but that important number of 300 did not become available until just before the Hamburg raids in July. (The eventual plan was to build up to a force of 2,700 bombers!) Tentative raids on Germany did commence in January but the Americans rarely ventured further than the German coast during this period. In the interval, the Americans built up valuable experience and their precision bombing certainly caused significant damage to important objectives.

This chapter has taken the story of the bombing war to mid-July 1943. R.A.F. Bomber Command, with the triumph of the Battle of the Ruhr behind it, stood powerful and ready for its next contest. The nights of midsummer started to lengthen and the British bombers could start reaching out again to more distant targets. The Americans, with their 300 B-17s at last, were looking to bomb targets of the highest importance deep in Germany and put their particular dream of success through the self-defending daylight-bomber formation to its true test.

It is a convenient time to pause and look more intimately at the men and women in the forces ranged against each other in the next round of this deadly game.

NOTES

1. *The Concise Oxford Dictionary of Current English.*
2. These details are recorded in Neville Jones, *The Origins of Strategic Bombing*, 1973, p. 40.
3. Sir Charles Webster and Noble Frankland, *The Strategic Air Offensive against Germany 1939–1945*, 1961, Vol. 1, p. 86. This work will be referred to as the 'British Official History'.
4. British Official History, Vol. IV, p. 144.

The Attackers – British

When the British bombers took off from their airfields on the evening of 24 July 1943 and headed out over the North Sea towards Hamburg, R.A.F. Bomber Command had been flying and fighting for almost four years and not only the half-way mark but also the two-thirds mark of its long war against Germany had passed. July 1943 saw Bomber Command far from being at the height of its strength but certainly approaching the most important phase of its campaign of strategic bombing. This chapter will examine Bomber Command on the eve of the Battle of Hamburg. This short study will cover the commander-in-chief, the aircraft available to him and the men who flew those aircraft.

Air Chief Marshal Sir Arthur Harris had impressed his formidable personality firmly on Bomber Command during the year and a half that he had led it. His name was known to every man and woman who served under him and he was given unstinted loyalty by them. To his close associates he was 'Bert' and to the Press and public he was 'Bomber Harris', but the operational personnel of Bomber Command all called him 'Butch' – short for 'the Butcher' – a nickname reflecting the wry admiration of Harris's men both for his hard-driving methods in directing Bomber Command's operations and for the punishment he obviously loved meting out to the Germans.

Harris was to become and will remain a controversial figure in the history of the air war but, in the context of that war and the form it took from early 1942 onwards, no one should ever belittle Harris's achievements in the first period of his command. He had inspired a dispirited force, giving it a renewed pride and self-confidence that would carry it right through to the end of the war. All this was achieved in remarkable fashion because he rarely left his headquarters and not one person in a hundred in Bomber Command ever saw him. But the power of his personality and leadership somehow flowed out from those offices at High Wycombe to every corner of every unit of Bomber Command. He was one of the great leaders of men of his time.

Harris had been lucky to come to Bomber Command when improved types of aircraft and better equipment were becoming available and when the mistakes of earlier years were being rectified, but he made brilliant use of this advantage. The tactical advances that he introduced in 1942 – the bomber-stream, the fire technique, the use of Pathfinders – all made the bombing of his crews more effective. But his greatest achievement at this time was that he put Bomber Command 'on the map'; he ensured that public and political opinion would back him in the vital years ahead.

As for the Germans, Harris had for them a simple, un-questioning, enduring hatred for what they had done to Europe in two world wars and he was perfectly happy to put into effect the policy of attack on Germany's industrial cities by Area Bombing. He resisted to the utmost all outside attempts to divert Bomber Command from this purpose. Every bomber, every bomb, must be directed on to a target in Germany on every night that the weather and moon conditions permitted it. That was Harris's simple policy.

One disadvantage that Bomber Command had to struggle with for most of the war was the multiplicity of aircraft types that it had to operate at any one period and the high proportion of those types that were always obsolete and unsuitable but which had to be employed until better types became available. There had been worse examples of this situation than existed in the summer of 1943 but the force which was to fight the Battle of Hamburg was typical of it.

The twin-engined, medium Wellington was the only old faithful left from the pre-war period. Its steady performance and sound construction had served Bomber Command well and it had been popular with its crews. But its general obsolescence and particularly its limited bomb-carrying capacity were the causes of its being withdrawn from service as quickly as more advanced replacements could be found. The four-engined types introduced since the war began had a distinct order of usefulness. The factors of height and bomb-carrying capacity were vital ones. The Stirling had the worst operational height and smallest bomb load, the Lancaster the best, with the Halifax coming between the two. The Stirling would disappear from Bomber Command's order of battle in 1944 but the Halifax would fly on to the end of the war.

Bomber Command was just starting to receive significant numbers of the new, twin-engined Mosquito, which was to prove such a versatile and useful aircraft in the remaining years of the war. The Mosquito – of mainly wooden construction – flew high and fast, needed no defensive armament and carried a good bomb-load for its size. Its height made it a particularly useful Oboe-controlled Pathfinder marker aircraft and its recent use as such in the Battle of the Ruhr would prove to be one of the most significant developments in the bombing war. Fighter Command versions of the Mosquito also flew on low-level 'Intruder' operations to German airfields in support of the bombers. The Intruder successes were not dramatic but they contributed to a steady attrition in the German night-fighter force and they often had a disruptive effect on a carefully prepared German defence plan when an Intruder appeared over a German airfield just when night fighters were taking off or landing.

Bomber Command had only contained 483 night bombers at the beginning of 1943 but a big expansion in the early months of the year had enabled a peak of 826 bombers to be achieved in May. This increase had taken place entirely in the four-engined types, all three of which had roughly doubled their operational strength. Since the May peak, the overall numbers involved had fallen slightly, partly because of the heavier losses towards the end of the Battle of the Ruhr but more because the Wellington element was being deliberately phased out of front-line service.*

More than any other British service, the R.A.F. represented the British Empire at war. In Bomber Command, the commander-in-chief was an Englishman who had spent his youth in Rhodesia and only two of the six group commanders were English; the remainder were from Canada, Australia, New Zealand and South Africa. This mixture of Empire nationalities permeated Bomber Command. The intermingling went right down to the level of individual bomber

* Appendix 1 gives the order of battle of R.A.F. Bomber Command and of the Fighter Command Intruder squadrons at 24 July 1943.

crews; there were usually at least two nationalities in every crew. This was all the result of a deliberate policy to foster a Bomber Command spirit which would override any narrow national loyalty and the policy certainly succeeded.

Men from the United Kingdom always formed a majority in Bomber Command, approximately 70 per cent of the total. Harris, in his memoirs, says that such men were as brave as any and more effective than most due to their being better educated than overseas aircrew. The phlegmatic British character and the desire to avenge German bombing of British cities earlier in the war certainly gave them an extra dedication. But, as the war progressed, Britain's manpower was stretched to the limit and the overseas elements in Bomber Command increased steadily.

The Canadians were the most numerous of the Empire men, providing up to 20 per cent of aircrew.

What did it feel like to be a Canadian airman flying bombers from England? In Canada I was a flying instructor on the single-engined Harvard and I personally found it to be a terrific challenge in converting over to the heavy stuff with those four beautiful Rolls-Royce engines and a crew of my own, two of whom were English. We all got along magnificently and we Canadians thought England and the English had fantastic spunk and we were really quite proud to be there.

Nearly all the Canadian crews had one or more English members and this seemed to meld the two national systems together and we were really English–Canadians or Canadian–English. (Flying Officer J. A. Westland, 419 Squadron)*

The Canadians were a carefree bunch of airmen who enjoyed themselves to the limit when not on operations and swept many a girl off her feet wherever they were based. Canadian pilots were not always noted for their flying discipline but airmen from other countries sometimes say that the Canadian air gunners had the sharpest eyesight. The Canadians had their own bomber group, 6 Group, based on airfields in North Yorkshire, but 6 Group was still new in 1943 and some way from the peak of its efficiency. There was also a Canadian

---

* All quotations by Allied or German contributors who were involved in the Battle of Hamburg are the result of correspondence or interviews with the author, unless other sources are given. Ranks and units for service

Pathfinder squadron – 405 – which had come to the Pathfinders straight from Coastal Command operations in the Bay
of Biscay and was now led by a legendary bomber pilot, Wing
Commander John Fauquier. The stories told about the
unorthodox Fauquier and his style of command are legion.

Australians and New Zealanders provided about one man
in ten of the bomber crews. Bomber Command contained
three squadrons of the Royal Australian Air Force at this time
and an R.A.F. squadron that bore the title 'New Zealand' and
to which many New Zealand airmen were posted. It appears
that the Australian Government was pressing that their
squadrons should become, as far as possible, only Australian
crewed.

Perhaps one of the most remarkable facts of that time was the
manner in which young people such as myself could adjust to a
totally alien way of life. Flying over Europe, risking one's life,
became the normal rather than the abnormal. Personal pride, I
believe, was perhaps the greatest single factor that prompted many
of us to do our best – the thought that we had to live with ourselves.
Another factor was the mixed-crew concept. I was the only Australian
in my crew. Although we did not think in terms of nationalities
within a squadron, I believe that the friendly rivalries in a mixed
squadron produced an infinitely better spirit both at the squadron
and at the crew level.

When my own squadron became more than just a nominally
Australian squadron, many of us were disappointed. We felt that
we had lost something that was irreplaceable. What was worse, the
changeover was, I believe, purely a political move to keep people
back home happy. No consideration was given to the crews themselves or to squadron efficiency. Such is the way of politicians!
(Pilot Officer J. H. Whiting, 467 Squadron)

I do not have a handy quotation for the New Zealanders
but both New Zealanders and Australians made particularly
reliable bomber pilots and many went on from the Main
Force squadrons to distinguish themselves in the Pathfinders.

Individual airmen came from many other parts of the world
to fly with Bomber Command – Rhodesians, a few South
Africans – although their government had a policy of not

---

personnel are those of 24 July 1943. German and American names are
printed with Christian names, following their national custom.

allowing any of her armed forces units to leave the continent of Africa, West Indians, Indians, a surprisingly large number of men from the British communities in South America and several from the United States who had joined the Royal Canadian Air Force before Pearl Harbor and were completing their tours of operations with Bomber Command before transferring to the U.S.A.A.F.

The most dedicated airmen in Bomber Command were undoubtedly those who had escaped from the Occupied Countries. The largest body of these were the Poles, who provided the crews for two Wellington squadrons which were an exception to the mixed-nationality squadron rule in that every crew was made up only of Poles, although some dilution took place later. The Poles were fanatical in their hatred of the Germans for what had been done to their country. This is how Group Captain H. I. Cozens, their English station commander, remembers the Poles:

> Their language was a very difficult one, being an eastern, non-Roman language. They were very serious about their religion and were more Catholic than the Pope.* They were very charming and debonair and an absolute menace to any girl in the area. Some had been so hungry in their various journeys from Poland that they used to eat everything in sight and took away any food left over after a meal. They couldn't get used to the idea that there would be food there tomorrow.
>
> The Polish aircrew were every bit as good as English crews. They had a double loyalty. They flew for the honour of Poland firstly, and only then for that of the R.A.F. The ground crew staff were skilled and ingenious mechanics. When you were about to give any of them a rocket, they would do something quite charming and disarm you. It was very infuriating.

The Poles were to experience many disappointments and were never to achieve their greatest dream which was to fly their planes back to a free Poland. A recent sorrow was the death of General Sikorski, leader of the Free Polish Forces, who had been killed in an air crash at Gibraltar on 4 July. His body was buried in the Polish cemetery at Newark on 16 July and many men from the two Polish bomber squadrons attended the funeral ceremony.

* This interesting remark was made before the election of a Polish Pope in 1978.

The airmen from the other Occupied Countries were so few in number that they could not make up their own squadrons and had to serve in R.A.F. squadrons, although two Free French squadrons were formed later. The only significant group at the time of the Hamburg raids was a number of Norwegians who flew Halifaxes with the crews of 76 Squadron. The Norwegians served with the same determination as the Poles.

I only flew with one of the Norwegians; he was my skipper and was one of the coolest, calmest men I have ever known in action. If Lief had a fault, it was his desire to smash the Nazi regime, so much so that, on bombing the target, I have known him go round three times before bombing. (Sergeant E. Freeman, 76 Squadron)

Second Lieutenant Leif Hulthin was killed during a raid on Cassel in October 1943.

All R.A.F. aircrew were volunteers, although the men who flew with Bomber Command had not specifically volunteered to fly heavy bombers. The R.A.F. directed trained aircrew wherever they were needed, and Bomber Command needed about 1,000 new aircrew members every week at this time! The men arriving at the Operational Training Units of Bomber Command had first to form themselves into crews. This was usually done by assembling the required number of men in a hangar and then leaving them to sort themselves out. These crews then went through a final phase of training before being posted to their squadrons. There, usually after the new pilots had flown one or two operational flights as 'second dickeys' with experienced crews, the new men were ready to commence their first tour of operations.

The first tour for Bomber Command aircrew on Main Force squadrons was thirty operational flights. It was well known that new crews were at their most vulnerable during the first part of a tour and those who managed to complete the first five operations safely were considered to have some chance of surviving the remainder. If losses had been particularly heavy, a squadron commander could allow a crew to finish before reaching thirty completed operations to bolster the morale of other crews on that squadron. For those fortunate enough to survive their first tour, there came a rest from operational flying, usually spent as an instructor at a training unit, and then a return to a squadron for a second tour of twenty operations. If this was completed successfully, the aircrew member could not be asked to fly heavy bombers again and he was posted out of Bomber Command.

The standard Pathfinder tour was forty-five operations, any earlier operations flown with the Main Force to count towards this total. This prolonged Pathfinder tour was insisted upon to get the full benefit of the skill in marking targets that was not achieved until well into the tour. If a Pathfinder man survived this tour, he could either rest and come back for a normal second tour or he could continue flying without a break to complete a tour of sixty operations. This extended tour counted as two tours and such a man need not be called back for further Bomber Command operations. Men could volunteer for a third tour but such men were only allowed to fly with the Pathfinders or with 617 (Dambuster) Squadron which was now being used as a specialist precision-bombing unit. A few individuals managed to defy the odds and fly more than 100 operations. These were mostly United Kingdom men because the Empire governments insisted that any of their men who reached sixty flights be returned home.

The casualty rate in Bomber Command was the heaviest of any British service in the Second World War. The British Official History contains monthly returns for operational losses for the whole war. These show that the average casualty rate for the year of 1943 was 3·6 per cent of all aircraft that took off for operations, the second highest rate for those years in which major operations were flown.[1] From these figures it can be calculated that 33 per cent of the crews which flew in 1943 could survive their first tour and only 16 per cent would survive both first and second tours.* No separate statistics exist for Pathfinder squadrons and it is not known what effect their longer tour had on their aircrews' chances of survival. The expertise they built up must have helped them but the exposed position over a target of those Pathfinders who led an attack must have cancelled out some of this advantage. It is probable that slightly fewer Pathfinders survived their tours than men in Main Force squadrons.

* For help in calculating these figures I am grateful to M. H. Field, F.I.A., and Geoff Marriott of the Phoenix Assurance Co. Ltd.

In mid-July 1943, Bomber Command had just finished fighting the rugged Battle of the Ruhr and was about to embark on the Battle of Hamburg. Immediately after this, the commander-in-chief intended to commence what would become known as the Battle of Berlin, which would turn out to be the supreme test for Bomber Command. Morale in large forces of men about to enter a major battle is always a subject of interest and some effort has been devoted to identifying the state of the morale of the British airmen who were about to fight the Battle of Hamburg.

Morale in Bomber Command depended on many factors: leadership, results believed to have been achieved in recent raids and the casualty rate experienced in those raids, personal fatigue, the provision of good aircraft and equipment. There is no need to say much about leadership. Sir Arthur Harris had by now established his personality throughout Bomber Command and his men had a confidence in him that was near absolute. Good leadership also existed at group level and, more important, at squadron level. The best of the survivors of the earlier years of the war were now squadron and flight commanders. Such men still had to fly on operations, although over an extended period, and these officers, with few exceptions, gave the best of examples by selecting themselves to fly against difficult targets.

There is also no doubt that the results of the recent raids on the Ruhr had provided a great uplift to morale. The bomber crews had seen the accurate marking and the concentrated bombing. Then they had seen the daylight photographs taken by the high-flying reconnaissance aircraft which revealed the smoking ruins of the Ruhr cities. All this had persuaded the bomber crews that, for the first time since the start of strategic bombing, they were able to carry out a prolonged series of effective raids against heavily defended German targets. Many may not have realized that most of this success was due to the Oboe device, which would not be available for the accurate marking of the more distant targets that would have to be raided in the lengthening nights to come, but what they had seen happening to the Ruhr left them with every hope that their success could be maintained and that all their efforts, and the losses of their comrades, were becoming worth while.

It is true that casualties in the Battle of the Ruhr had been heavy, but the survivors had not been badly affected by these. Each crew did not mix much with other crews and the men who had 'got the chop' had often been strangers, new crews who had not been on a squadron for long. An airman often saw a bomber caught in a cone of searchlights and shot down in flames but he never saw the charred or smashed bodies of the men inside that bomber – scenes that might have shaken his morale severely. These optimistic young men were mostly buoyed along by the spirit of 'it can never happen to me'. A further factor was fatigue. Bomber Command was now receiving a plentiful supply of fresh aircrew and there was rarely the necessity to press the men on the squadrons too hard. Individual crews who had been through a hard time could be rested for a few days and a week's leave came round once every six weeks – a far more generous allowance than for any other serviceman. The recent period of midsummer had also seen a slackening off of operations. The full strength of Bomber Command had only been to Germany once in the first three weeks of July – although smaller forces had carried out German raids – and some of the operations flown recently had been to targets in northern Italy, long flights but relatively free from danger.*

It is true that many men were flying aircraft that were known to be less efficient than others. The distinct pecking order of the four-engined types – the Lancaster, the Halifax, then the Stirling – was well known but men on Halifax and Stirling squadrons were never able to make direct comparisons between their aircraft and the Lancasters and the British character was such that Halifax or Stirling men took a perverse and defiant pride in flying their particular aircraft. This pride was usually genuine and deep. Provided such aircrew did not belong to a squadron which had suffered a run of heavy casualties, their morale was likely to be as good as that of the Lancaster men. It should be remembered, too, that any four-engined bomber was a novelty in 1943. Such aircraft had only been in service for eighteen months and it

---

* A notable exception to the comparative safety of these Italian raids was the loss of the commander of 44 (Rhodesia) Squadron, Wing Commander John Nettleton, V.C., the leader of the famous daylight raid on Augsburg of 17 April 1942. Nettleton and his crew were shot down into the Channel while returning from Turin on 13 July 1943.

was a source of pride to be flying to Germany in any kind of these large aircraft which had so captured the imagination of the wartime public. As for the few men still flying Wellingtons, this much-loved old type was quite acceptable to their crews and was no drawback to morale.

It is quite clear that the average level of morale in Bomber Command at this time was good and, in many squadrons, excellent. The great majority of the men in Bomber Command were in sound heart and quite ready to carry out the orders of their commander-in-chief in the next round of his offensive. Let some of the men who were soon to fly to Hamburg speak for themselves.

I do not wish to pontificate on the morale of the squadron but will speak for my own crew. They were a motley lot, God bless them, endowed with their fair share of apprehension – so was I – but they were always able to joke about it and were always prepared – if not dashing – to go on the next trip. (Pilot Officer J. H. Ratcliff, 103 Squadron)

Those Ruhr raids! When we saw the extent of the damage shown on the target maps, we felt the Germans couldn't last more than a few more months. When you saw a couple of thousand tons going down on a Ruhr city in half an hour – that was fantastic!

Another good boost to morale were the Italian trips we were doing at that time. They were very popular for two reasons. There was the nice view of the Alps in moonlight – a nice view of the Alps was better than a picture of forty searchlights over a German target. Then, when you reached the target, the Italians had no stomach for fighting. I saw an Italian night fighter once and it shot off into the darkness as fast as it could. Those Italian trips were very reassuring. (Pilot Officer D. A. Duncan, 50 Squadron)

Certainly the Halifax crews were envious of the Lancaster crews but, at the same time, we felt superior to the Stirling crews. I do not recall that there was ever a comparison of losses between the various types of aircraft and, naturally, they were not available at the time anyway. It was not until a long time afterwards that I recalled that, in over four months of continuous flying, I do not remember a single crew completing a tour of operations on 51 Squadron.

A certain amount of derisory comment was heard about the aircraft itself. It was called 'The Flying Coffin' et cetera but this was more with a sense of pride and bravado than dejection. (Sergeant T. Nelson, 51 Squadron)

The R.A.F. were very good at morale boosting and, as I remember, we on the Stirling squadrons were always made to feel that we were the only ones that mattered – the Rolls-Royce squadrons, as opposed to the mass-produced ranks of Lancs and Halifaxes and, as we were usually timed into targets at lower levels and at closer times to the Pathfinders than the rest of the Main Force, we were always – 90 Squadron anyway – made to feel that we were back-up support to the Pathfinders. This sense of pride and achievement was a great morale booster. (Sergeant C. N. Searle, 90 Squadron)

In a year spent on 90 Squadron, I have only recollections of excellent morale. The 'press-on spirit' was rife and I never heard any moans from my pals on 149 and 218 Squadrons near by. Summing up, I feel that 3 Group always had their tails up and, to us, the Stirling was a good aircraft. I preferred 14,000 feet to 24,000 feet in any case – it was too bloody cold higher up. (Sergeant K. G. Forester, 90 Squadron)

On 115 Squadron we had our brand-new Lancaster IIs and our loss rate – though not negligible – was vastly superior to the surrounding 3 Group squadrons, equipped as they were with the inferior Stirlings. With our fine aircraft, we were able to penetrate to the most distant as well as the most heavily defended targets with a man-sized bomb-load and come back with good photographic evidence.

I need not expand upon the sublime confidence we had at this time in the planning of operations by the Command Staff and its legendary Chief. (Warrant Officer E. H. Noxon, 115 Squadron)

NOTE

1. These figures are contained in the British Official History, Vol. IV, pp. 429–39.

3

The Attackers — American

The American airmen who flew heavy bombers from England were as proud to serve in what they called 'the Eighth Air Force' as the British bomber men were to serve in R.A.F. Bomber Command. The Americans were actually in VIII Bomber Command which was one of the main components of the United States Eighth Army Air Force.* VIII Bomber Command had its own commander, mounted all its own operations and kept its own records but its title was rarely used in conversation by the men who served in it. Their loyalty was to the Eighth Air Force and, although this chapter is about VIII Bomber Command, the title of its better-known parent will often be used.

Before proceeding further it is necessary to explain the basic organization of the American bomber units at that time, since every one of the American terms used had different meanings to similar terms in use in the R.A.F. This was the American heavy-bomber chain of command that existed in July 1943:

EIGHTH AIR FORCE
|
VIII BOMBER COMMAND
|
BOMBARDMENT WINGS
|
BOMBARDMENT GROUPS
|
BOMBARDMENT SQUADRONS

There was no exact equivalent in the home-based R.A.F. of the Eighth Air Force. VIII Bomber Command was a similar

* The American Air Force had still not achieved its independence from the United States Army, unlike the R.A.F. which had been independent since 1918. In fact the U.S. Army Air Force had until recently been merely the U.S. Army Air Corps and it would not become free of its links with the Army until 1947. But the links with the Army were very loose ones and, by 1943, the U.S.A.A.F. had as much freedom in conducting its operations as had the R.A.F.

organization to R.A.F. Bomber Command although not yet as large. An American bombardment wing was almost equivalent to an R.A.F. bomber group and it performed a similar function in the American chain of command. There were three heavy-bomber bombardment wings in the Eighth Air Force in 1943. The 1st and 4th Bombardment Wings operated B-17 Fortresses and the 2nd had B-24 Liberators.* The bomb group, of which there was no fixed number in a bombardment wing, was the basic combat-bomber unit, always based on one airfield and directly equivalent to an R.A.F. squadron, although slightly stronger in its number of aircraft. The American bomb squadron was roughly equivalent to an R.A.F. flight. The two air forces could hardly have chosen a more confusing set of unit titles, often being so similar in name but always differing in composition.

I apologize to the reader for starting this chapter with what may appear to be a tedious exposition of the chain of command of the American bomber units but an understanding of it will make it more easy for the reader to follow much of the material in the remainder of this chapter and certainly in the later action chapters which involve the American bombers. The more important points for the reader to remember are that it was at the headquarters of VIII Bomber Command that raids were ordered and targets chosen and that these orders were eventually carried out by the operational bomb groups.

Major-General Carl Spaatz had originally set up and commanded the Eighth Air Force in England but he had departed at the end of 1942 to take command of the combined Allied air forces in North Africa. His place had been taken by Major-General Ira C. Eaker who, under Spaatz, had built

---

* Appendix 2 shows the Order of Battle of VIII Bomber Command on 24 July 1943. There had been a 3rd Bombardment Wing, made up of B-26 Marauder medium bombers, but this wing had been temporarily transformed into the VIII Air Support Command and would soon leave the Eighth Air Force, being transferred in October 1943 to the U.S. Ninth Air Force in North Africa. The bombardment wings were soon to be retitled 'air divisions'. The cumbersome adjective 'bombardment' which was contained in the wing, group and squadron titles, was rarely used in conversation at group or squadron level and these units are referred to here by the more commonly used terms 'bomb group' and 'bomb squadron'.

up the bomber part of the Eighth Air Force and had been the first commander of VIII Bomber Command. Ira Eaker had flown in a B-17 on the very first American raid to Rouen. He was a dedicated bomber man and the bomber part of his command would receive his absolute support as long as he had any influence on its affairs. A new commander for VIII Bomber Command was appointed on 1 July 1943. The new man was Brigadier-General Frederick L. Anderson Jr, known to all as Fred Anderson.

This officer will be of particular interest to the Hamburg story for several reasons. Not only was he the commanding general of the American bombers that would attack Hamburg but he was also to become involved in one of the raids and actually to fly over that German city in most unconventional circumstances. This young American general was only thirty-seven years old, compared to the fifty-one years of Sir Arthur Harris, his R.A.F. equivalent. One of Anderson's staff officers has described him as 'having a natural ebullience that possibly made him look even younger than his years. He was an energetic, impulsive person.' Another officer has said that Anderson had been 'one of Hap Arnold's "wonder boys", a group of five or so very promising professional Air Corps officers – one of that small group of pilots who had grown up as long-range strategic bomber enthusiasts'. Fred Anderson was also a brave man. He had once been flying a plane over San Francisco when his engine caught fire but he had stayed at the controls to prevent the plane crashing on the city. In doing so, he had badly scorched his lungs and this injury permanently affected his health.

Brigadier-General Anderson had come straight to Europe from the post of Director of Bombardment at the newly built Pentagon. He had commanded the B-17 groups in the 4th Bombardment Wing for a mere two months before being moved up to lead VIII Bomber Command only three weeks before the Battle of Hamburg. His headquarters were at Wycombe Abbey Girls' School, only a short distance from those of Sir Arthur Harris, and Anderson regularly attended Harris's morning conferences. It could never be said that it was a meeting of equals. Anderson had to visit Harris. The relationship was almost that of a promising young nephew visiting his wise uncle, although the friendly Anderson was always treated with a great deal of respect by the R.A.F.

By the time of the Hamburg raids, Anderson had two strong wings of B-17s under his command. The 1st Wing was the original B-17 force which had been flying since August 1942. Its commander in July 1943 was Brigadier-General Frank A. Armstrong who had been commander of a bomb group for most of the past year and had personally led the first American raids both on France and, more recently, on Germany. The 4th Bombardment Wing, which had only been in existence for two months, was equipped with a long-range version of the B-17. These planes carried extra fuel tanks – called Tokyo tanks – in their outer wing sections to give longer range. These tanks were so named because it was hoped that this version of the B-17 might one day be based near enough to Japan to bomb Tokyo (an ambition which was to be fulfilled by a more modern plane, the B-29 Superfortress). The commander of the 4th Bombardment Wing was Colonel Curtis LeMay, a brilliant ex-bomb-group commander who had thought out and developed in action many of the formation flying and bombing procedures now used by the American bomber units.

The whole command set-up of the Americans was in a state of flux at this stage of the war, with promising young officers receiving rapid promotion in the ever-growing American air forces. Of these three senior officers who would command during the period of the Battle of Hamburg – Fred Anderson Frank Armstrong and Curtis LeMay – not one had been in his present position five weeks earlier! Armstrong and LeMay were both to become famous after the war. Curtis LeMay commanded the units that dropped the first atomic bombs on Japan and, after the war, pioneered the formation of the Strategic Air Command and led it through the worst of the Cold War years. Frank Armstrong got himself into trouble for making a famous speech in Norfolk, Virginia, a naval city, in which he disparaged the policies of both the U.S. Navy and the Marines during the period of inter-service controversy leading up to the government decision finally to give the Air Force its independence from the Army.

There was, in theory, one more wing of heavy bombers. This was the 2nd Bombardment Wing with the four-engined B-24 Liberator. Although it was faster than the B-17 and could carry a larger bomb load, the B-24 had not had a happy introduction to the European war. It carried much extra weight in its radio and navigational fittings because it had been designed as a 'double-standard' bomber, capable of serving both with the U.S.A.A.F. and the R.A.F. This, and a badly designed wing, caused this large aircraft to have a lower ceiling than the B-17 and to be a poor formation keeper. In their first few raids to Germany the B-24 groups had suffered heavily; in particular, their extensive interior hydraulic lines caused them to blow up or burn quickly when damaged. One B-17 man says that 'we liked it when we knew the B-24s were flying. They were our best diversion.' Another says that, when in a German prison camp, 'we could spot which type of aircraft incoming prisoners had flown by the bandages on burned B-24 crews'. The 2nd Bombardment Wing only had two B-24 groups under command in July 1943. These were the 44th and 93rd Groups but neither was in England at that time. They had been sent to North Africa to support the Allied invasion of Sicily and to prepare for a raid on a Romanian oil-refinery town – Ploesti.

As stated before, this book is not a technical one and, just as the main features of the famous Lancaster are well known, so there is no need for a lengthy description of the equally famous B-17 Flying Fortress. The main operational features of this bomber were that it could fly fully loaded at a height of 28,000 feet – 6,000 feet above the average Lancaster's best height – and, therefore, was that much more difficult for the German Flak (anti-aircraft guns) to hit, that it was a beautiful aircraft for its pilots to fly and was easy to keep in formation, and that it was of tough construction that could withstand much battle damage and was not prone to catching fire. The Americans were lucky in that they had two years longer than the R.A.F. to prepare for their war and were able to test and develop their main heavy bomber at leisure and then put it into mass production. The basic B-17 served the Eighth Air Force in Europe from beginning to end without any major modification. This allowed a rapid build-up in the American bomber units, considerably eased the development of tactics and gave their crews every chance to train on and then operate one well-known type.

R.A.F. men will often compare the 6,000-lb maximum

bomb-load of the B-17 with the load of up to 14,000 lb that the Lancaster could carry in 1943. But the whole purpose of the Americans was to bomb accurately by day. Area Bombing, which depended upon a great weight of bombs, was not their business. The R.A.F. bomber relied for its safety on concealment in the dark of night, with never more than three gun positions and carrying only light 0·303 machine-guns; it could be loaded almost to its limits with bombs. The American bomber was in sight of its enemies from the moment it entered German air space and it needed that extra 6,000 feet and its ten-man crew, of whom no less than eight could be manning gun positions when under fighter attack. The lighter bombload was the price the Americans paid in order to survive by daylight. The prize was a bombing accuracy that the R.A.F. could never achieve by night.

When the R.A.F. formed a new bomber squadron, it did so by detaching parts of existing squadrons; the new squadron formed in this way always contained a proportion of experienced crews. The Americans had no time for this method and the speed at which they created their bomber force was astonishing. Not one of the groups that bombed Hamburg in July 1943 had existed before the United States entered the war in December 1941. Two-thirds of the July 1943 groups had not even existed on paper a year before they bombed Hamburg. Within this short period, they had been formed in the United States, trained, moved to England, settled into their airfields and commenced wartime operations in the strange environment of European weather conditions. Disparaging remarks were often made about the inexperience of the American units. The wonder was that they were even raiding Germany at all.

A bomb group commenced its life by being 'constituted', then 'activated', these being mostly paper exercises before the group received its planes and flying crews at one of the pre-war American airfields. Individual crew members – almost all men who had joined in wartime – had received basic training at specialist schools. Much of the pilots' training was carried out at private flying schools or clubs. 'They often brought in airline mail pilots or barnstormers. Quite a few of them were grey-haired old men to us – but could they fly! They really were dedicated instructors. They were like fathers to us.'

On reaching their new groups, the individual aircrew members were formed into the basic, ten-man B-17 crew. I asked one navigator how this selection of crews was carried out, after telling him of the R.A.F. method of leaving a hundred or so men to sort themselves into crews.

We were formed into crews by written order. The R.A.F. method would never have worked with us Americans. We would have formed about five crews fairly quickly but the rest would have milled around for evermore and never settled down. If I had been a unit commander, I would have grabbed them by the throat, stuck them together, and told them to get on with it. It worked better for us that way. (Lieutenant Carl B. Stackhouse, 351st Bomb Group)

There is some interest in a comparison between the R.A.F. and U.S.A.A.F. attitude to rank in their aircrews. An R.A.F. crew could be a completely random mixture of officers and non-commissioned ranks, with the pilot being the aircraft captain irrespective of rank. A sergeant-pilot, who might once have been a butcher's boy but who had the aptitude and intelligence to become a bomber pilot, could quite easily have one or more officers under his command in the air. The Americans, however, had a rigid system whereby only officers could become pilots, navigators or bombardiers, leaving 'enlisted men', who had little chance of ever becoming officers, to fill all the other crew positions. To become an officer in the United States Army Air Force, a man had to have an educational background of at least two years in college (university). The U.S.A.A.F. thus cut itself off from a useful source of pilot, navigator and bombardier supply by refusing applicants who had not been to college.

There were two exceptions to these rules. One was the temporary introduction of the rank of 'flight officer' which was equivalent to a British warrant officer and was the last leftover from the now abandoned system of having pilots of staff-sergeant rank. A few flight officers were eventually commissioned in order to eliminate that rank, a move that brought great pride to the families of these non-college men.

Many American bombers later flew without a commissioned bombardier. His place was taken by an enlisted-man gunner who had become a 'togglier'; he manned the bombardier's old position on the bombing run and simply released the bombs when he saw bombs leaving the lead plane in his group formation.

This contrast, between the flexibility in using men of different ranks shown by the supposedly class-ridden British and the rigidity of the supposedly classless Americans, is an interesting one.

When its crews had all been formed, the new bomb group then commenced crew training, mostly from the clear-weather airfields of the sunny south and west of the United States. 'Boy, we flew night and day. It was really intense.' After approximately four months of this training, the group was deemed ready for service in England. The ground personnel crossed the Atlantic, mostly in the *Queen Elizabeth* or the *Queen Mary* liners. The aircrews, after receiving brand-new B-17s, flew these planes across the Atlantic using the Newfoundland–Prestwick route in summer and a more southerly and longer route, but with a shorter ocean crossing between Brazil and West Africa, in the winter. The newly arrived group then settled into its new airfield. The standard B-17s of the 1st Bombardment Wing were mostly well inland, in the counties of Bedfordshire, Northamptonshire and Huntingdonshire, and the Tokyo-tank-equipped groups of the 4th Wing were nearer the coast, astride the Norfolk–Suffolk border and sixty miles closer to their German targets.

It was a strange new life for the Americans, hardly any of whom had ever been outside their own country before. They discovered the changeable and often miserable English weather, quaint old villages near their airfields with thatched cottages and cosy pubs which served warm beer, beautiful English countryside, towns with ancient churches, cathedrals and other buildings centuries older than anything in the United States, friendly girls – but mostly from what the English called the working class – and London, an amazing centre in which to spend leave. Some of the Americans felt that they were returning to the homeland of their ancestors but, if one examines B-17 crew lists, a high proportion of mid-European and Italian names will be found. At least as many B-17 men were bombing the homeland of their ancestors as were flying from it.

Although it could be a thrill for the Americans to be in Europe, the picture of the happy American in England was not always a correct one. Not only was there all the strain and danger of operations for the aircrews but the 'Yank' was not always popular with the English. The pay of the Americans was high compared to the wages received by local civilians or British servicemen and the effect of American money spent in the pursuit of local girls caused much jealousy. Many of the younger Americans, particularly those who had never before left close-knit families or small communities in the United States, were also intensely homesick.

Approximately one month was spent on settling down in England, most of this time being utilized by intensive formation flying practice. Lieutenant Stackhouse says that it was 'all a brand new experience. It was kind of fun, flying with British navigational aids. Mind you, it had its weak-kneed moments, particularly when you were flying in the soupy British weather. That was an experience never to be forgotten!'

When the new group had finished its final training period, it was ready to take its place in the growing bomber strength of the Eighth Air Force. The Americans flew only by day, operations depending entirely on the weather. Enemy targets could not be bombed if cloud was forecast over them but an equally important factor was the state of the weather expected over home airfields for the bombers' return. To forecast this accurately in the changeable English climate was the greatest single problem facing the American commanders and changing forecasts caused many raids to be cancelled right up to the time of take-off. The records show that the weather allowed the B-17 groups to carry out an average of exactly twelve raids per month in 1943, roughly the same number as the R.A.F. night squadrons. The men of both bomber forces became well used to the nature of their own method of operations and both U.S.A.A.F. and R.A.F. survivors are emphatic that neither would have changed with the other.

Like their British counterparts, the Americans had their tour of operations. Their basic heavy-bomber tour in Europe consisted of twenty-five flights crossing the coast of enemy-occupied territory. After completing the first five of these, every aircrew member received the Air Medal. Flying his missions over Germany may have been frightening but one thought was uppermost in the mind of the American airman in England. He could only get back to his home by completing his tour of operations.

Casualties were heavy. German Flak liked targets that could be seen, particularly close-packed formations of bombers. When the German fighters appeared, the self-defending bomber formations did not always defend themselves adequately and no long-range fighter escort had yet been developed. As has been mentioned, the B-24s had to be taken off operations from England but the B-17s persisted. Their casualty rate grew steadily as they were sent to targets deeper and deeper into territory defended by the Luftwaffe. As soon as a group commenced combat flying, the band of brothers of original members who had brought the group over to England started to fade away and replacements were brought in. The groups which flew to Hamburg in July 1943 were mostly at a transitional stage, with part of their original complement of crews still flying.

There was a natural feeling of superiority by the old hands over the replacements. Lieutenant Stackhouse remembers that 'once you had five or six missions under your belt, you lorded it over the other kids on the block. Over a few drinks at the bar, you made the Flak heavier than it was and the German fighters tougher than they were. But it was only in fun and, apart from that, we tried to help them get settled in as well as possible.'

Another man, the captain of a replacement crew, asks that his group be not identified but his is a typical comment:

We were the first replacements and I think they were pleased to see us. They weren't that much ahead of us but now, at the reunions, the originals who trained together in the States and went overseas together are the core of the group reunions. They had started from nothing and formed that group, so I suppose it is understandable.

A proportion of the American airmen could not stand the strain of combat flying.

Strains, if they occurred – and they did – were indicated by increased abortion rates, heavier sick calls and, on occasion, a declaration by the individual and the flight surgeon of a condition of battle fatigue. In my opinion, the instances were quite rare. Usually a period at a 'Flak House' – a rest home – for a week would straighten a man out.* On these cases, the Squadron Flight Surgeon would make the determination. I personally never heard of an outright case of refusal to fly. Those men who did not believe they would survive the next mission usually contrived an earache, bellyache, sore toe, etc. and checked in on sick call. (Major Clinton F. Ball, 351st Bomb Group)

Lieutenant Stackhouse again:

We had had a couple of hot-shot pilots in the States, excellent pilots with good discipline in their crews and anxious to get to combat but they were no good on operations. They didn't have the guts for it. One aborted on his first five missions and the other quit after five missions and refused to fly again. The names of those two pilots were often mentioned as people who couldn't hack it but they were the only ones in the thirty-six or so pilots in the original group.

The Americans had a more sympathetic attitude to men unwilling to continue flying than had the R.A.F. Major Ball goes on to make the following comparison: 'Lacking in Moral Fibre was not a term we hung on a scared, sick kid.'

How many Americans survived to complete their tour satisfactorily and return home? The Eighth Air Force flew 144 operations in 1943, sometimes bombing several targets in one day. From 22,779 sorties, 967 planes did not return.[1] This loss rate of 4·24 per cent was significantly higher than the 3·6 per cent loss rate of R.A.F. Bomber Command for the same period but, while 33 per cent of the R.A.F. men would complete their first tour of thirty bomber operations, 34 per cent of the U.S.A.A.F. men could expect to survive their shorter tour. The R.A.F. men then had to fly a second tour.

The fortunate Americans who survived their tour in the dangerous days of 1943 and early 1944 were usually awarded the Distinguished Flying Cross. If lucky, they 'rotated back to the States' at once; if unlucky, they could be kept back on a non-operational duty. A few men volunteered to stay on and fly anything from an extra five missions to a full second tour of twenty operations but the number of men asking to do this was minute. The lure of home pulled them back to the United States and, afterwards, there was the prospect of flying on the Pacific bombing operations that the U.S.A.A.F. was starting

* The officers' rest home was in a country mansion near Southport in Lancashire, that for the enlisted men was somewhere on the River Thames at a building known as 'Gremlin Gables-on-the-Thames'.

to develop. The Pacific was considered to be 'much more relaxing and informal, much less dangerous. We thought we would try a different enemy.'

There was much pride, however, in having completed a tour of combat flying in the tough, prestigious European Theater of Operations.

NOTE

1. These figures come from W. F. Craven and J. L. Cate, *The Army Air Forces in World War II*, Vol. II, pp. 843–52. Aircraft dispatched and then recalled and those engaged on 'diversionary sweeps' which did not cross an enemy-defended coast are not included. Separate figures are not available for men whose planes were lost at sea but who were rescued and returned to their units nor for men whose planes returned to their airfields but who were killed and wounded in those planes. These two factors may approximately cancel each other out.

4

The Defenders

The defence of the German cities was in many hands. The outermost limits were the radio monitoring stations of the Luftwaffe's Signal Service which could detect the test transmissions of the Allied bombers' radio operators several hours before they took off for a raid. The innermost limit of the defence was the German city householder who was ordered to keep buckets of sand and water always ready to extinguish any incendiary bomb that might come through the roof of his house. If all the elements between these limits functioned well, the efforts of the Allied bombers could be partly frustrated, but no more than partly. If any major section of the German defence failed, extensive areas of the city chosen as the next target were likely to be reduced to rubble and ashes.

It is important, for any proper understanding of what was about to befall Hamburg, that the main elements making up the German defence on the eve of the Battle of Hamburg be identified and described. It has been said before that the main emphasis in this book is not on technical matters, but there are some technical aspects which are important because what happened in Hamburg was partly the result of a new device that the British bombers used to break wide open the outer ring of the German defences. I will try to present the technical part of this chapter in as simple terms as possible.[1]

As has been said, the outermost defence of the Reich was the radio listening watch kept by the Luftwaffe's Nachrichtentruppe, the Signal Service. It was the Luftwaffe that controlled and manned almost every part of the armed-service element of the German defence against air attack, unlike in Britain where the anti-aircraft artillery and searchlight units were part of the British Army. The Luftwaffe radio listening service could do little more than give warning that a raid was possible in the coming period of day or night, but it could give no advice about which part of Europe might be raided. The first sure information that bombers had actually taken off and were setting course for Germany came from the long-range radar stations – mainly equipped with *Freya* radars – positioned along the extreme edge of the coast of Occupied Europe. The heavily laden Allied bombers always had to gain some height before setting course and this allowed the German early warning radars to 'see' them over the curve of the earth, often before the bombers had even crossed the coast of England! Because of their forward position, the radar stations at Ostend, in Belgium, and on the Dutch island of Texel often made the first contact. It was then a simple matter to track the bombing force over the North Sea and forecast its approximate entry point into German-defended air space.

When the R.A.F. had been forced to give up daylight bombing early in the war, the British had purchased one inestimable advantage – the cover of darkness. Although a German radar set could perform as well by night as by day, the German fighter pilots were virtually blind and what can only be described as a vast amount of technical effort and manpower was being devoted by the Germans to penetrate the R.A.F.'s cloak of darkness. The story of the German defence against the night bomber had two distinct phases during the war. When Bomber Command flew to Hamburg on the night of 24 July 1943, the first phase was just three years old and had reached a peak of technical refinement. It was also to be the last night of its useful life.

This defence system had grown up largely under the leadership of one man, General der Flieger Josef Kammhuber, who had been appointed General of Night Fighters in October 1940. Kammhuber was a brilliant technical expert and organizer and he had built up both the night-fighter force and the technical devices on which the night-fighter crews relied. His greatest creation was a system of closely controlled fighter-defended areas covering every approach to Germany from Denmark and France. In the early days, this belt of defences had consisted of searchlights and night fighters, working together, but the searchlights had been moved back to the German cities in 1941 and replaced with a chain of small radar stations for the close control of individual night fighters. Each radar station controlled an area of sky which the Germans called a *Raum*, for which, instead of the direct translation of 'room', the term 'box' was usually used in

English. The boxes were mainly in a double line along the coast with a further group of boxes inland around Berlin. Most were given zoological or marine code names: *Auster, Kiebitz, Hummel, Wachtel, Natter, Wal, Languste, Kröte, Eisbär, Hase* – Oyster, Peewit, Bee, Quail, Viper, Whale, Lobster, Toad, Polar Bear, Hare – and many more. Such innocuous names!

The main belt of boxes along the coast was called by the Germans the *Himmelbett* Line. The direct translation of *Himmelbett* is 'four-poster bed' but the two separate words, *Himmel* and *Bett*, can be taken to mean 'a bed in the sky' and this may have contributed to its choice. The British knew all about General Kammhuber and his creation; they called it the Kammhuber Line.

Let us take a look inside one of General Kammhuber's boxes. The most important thing was that nothing could be achieved in the air unless all went well on the ground. Three ground radar sets were the heart of the box system. One radar was a *Freya* which could scan in all directions to a distance of up to a hundred miles. The *Freya* detected an approaching bomber-stream and directed two narrow-beam *Würzburg* radars on to it. The high-definition *Würzburgs* could pick up the bombers at a range of thirty miles and then begin a process that could lead to the destruction of a bomber.

In charge of the whole operation was a *Jägerleitoffizier*, known as a '*J.L.O.*' for short; this book will call him the 'fighter control officer'. These men were just as important as the pilots whose efforts they directed. A few were former pilots; others had once been the commanders of searchlight units that had since been withdrawn to the cities, but most were signals officers. They became well known to the pilots they controlled and, in the night-fighting world, some of them became aces but their exploits were never made public for security reasons.

The fighter control officer's post was usually near the *Freya* radar so that he could study its cathode-ray display which could show thirty or forty bombers flying across his box. He also knew the position of the night fighter in his box and he selected the 'blip' of the best placed bomber. One of his *Würzburg* radars then concentrated only on that bomber until the interception attempt about to commence was concluded. The second *Würzburg* followed only the night fighter. The two *Würzburg* radars were connected by telephone to two assistants who sat under a glass table, called the *Seeburg* table, and shone two coloured markers upwards on to it. A red marker showed the chosen bomber, a blue one the fighter. No other aircraft symbols appeared on the *Seeburg* table. The fighter control officer stood at this table, broadcasting frequent directions to the night fighter in an attempt to bring it into contact with the bomber, either visually or on the fighter's short-range *Lichtenstein* radar set, before the bomber flew out of the box. Short, standardized phrases were the only words used:

Antreten 170 – Kirchturm 43 – Fahren Sie express – 2 Lisa – Marie 9 – Kirchturm 42 – Marie 8 – 1 Lisa – Marie 5·5 – 1 Lisa – Marie 4 – Marie 2 – Halten – 2 Rolf – Noch mehr halten – Salto Lisa – Antreten 150 – Marie 4 – Marie 3 – Antreten 110 – Marie 1 – Genau vor Ihnen – Sie sind dicht bei Kurier.

Translating the German and interpreting the code words used, this means:

Fly 170 degrees – Height 4,300 (metres) – Top speed – Turn 20 degrees port – Range 9,000 (metres) – Height 4,200 – Range 8,000 – 10 degrees port – Range 5,500 – 10 degrees port – Range 4,000 – Range 2,000 – Slower – 20 degrees starboard – Slower still – Make complete circle to port (the fighter had overtaken the contact) – New course 150 – Range 4,000 – Range 3,000 – Course 110 – Range 1,000 – Right in front of you – You're close to the contact.

And all the time the radar operator in the fighter was replying, mostly '*Viktor*' in acknowledgement of each new order, then, '*Wir berühren. Bitte warten*' (' We are in contact. Stand by').

These details are extracts from the record of an actual interception controlled by Oberleutnant Walter Knickmeier in Raum 5B at Venray in Holland in the early hours of 3 June 1942. This was a busy box on the approaches to the Ruhr. The night fighter was a Messerschmitt 110 piloted by one of the German aces, Hauptmann Werner Streib. Just one minute after Knickmeier was told to 'stand by', he heard the victory message, '*Sieg Heil!*' The bomber had been shot down. In this case it was a Wellington, one of thirteen R.A.F. bombers shot down in a raid on Essen on that night. The entire interception had taken fourteen minutes and had covered a distance of approximately thirty-seven miles. The Wellington was Hauptmann Streib's thirtieth success and, for Oberleutnant Knickmeier, the twenty-seventh in a run of eighty-eight successful interceptions controlled by him in his box between March 1941 and July 1943.

Constant development and much experience had brought this form of night fighting – *Raumnachtjagd* – to perfection but, in truth, it was already outdated. Only one night fighter could be used in one box at any time and, while that fighter was attempting one interception, up to forty other bombers could fly through the box unharmed. Night fighters in neighbouring boxes might pick up one or two bombers well off course but the whole of the remainder of the *Himmelbett* system was ineffective – all the boxes manned with fighters but with no bombers to hunt. A tightly flown bomber-stream could pass through as few as four boxes on its inward flight, although the stream tended to spread out and pass through more boxes on its return. The *Experten* – the aces – were happy building up huge scores in the best boxes but many other Luftwaffe men felt that better ways could be found to utilize the growing strength of night fighters. The box system was too rigid. It depended too much on radar which the R.A.F. might one day jam. A more flexible form of night fighting was slowly being introduced by local initiative. Fighters not required to man boxes or stand by as reserves were occasionally allowed to go hunting independently outside the box system. But such fighters had few aids: their *Lichtenstein* radars were only useful if the fighter found itself in that narrow cone of space behind a bomber in which its radar was effective or if its crew happened to spot a bomber visually. But the night sky was a vast, dark, three-dimensional space and this did not happen often. There was talk of producing a '*laufende Reportage*', a 'running commentary' on the whereabouts of the bomber-stream, broadcast for the use of such freelancing fighters. But little had been done on such advances in technique.

General Kammhuber had worked wonders and the *Himmelbett* system had caused grievous losses to Bomber Command, but he was making few plans for future developments. Kammhuber's creations stood in perfect working order – some called it his 'Maginot Line' – but with little in hand if the British should somehow produce anything that could disrupt box night fighting.

The Luftwaffe had made no serious plans before the war for a night defence of the Reich and the first night raids of 1940 had caught it unawares. The German night-fighter force of July 1943 was still based almost entirely on improvisation and conversion from the Luftwaffe's day units. The main aircraft in use at this time was the Messerschmitt 110, a converted heavy day fighter, and the Junkers 88 and Dornier 217, both converted bombers. The Messerschmitt 110 was the best of the early night fighters because it was faster and more manoeuvrable than the other types but the progressive addition of exhaust covers, more armament and radar had slowed it down and its limited fuel capacity curtailed its flight time. But this plane was popular with its crews, had served the German night-fighter force exceedingly well and still had much life in it. The two converted bombers, the Junkers 88 and Dornier 217, were much heavier aircraft. They were capable of carrying all the extra equipment needed for night fighting and they also proved to be very steady gun platforms and good performers in bad weather conditions. The Dornier 217 was really too slow, however, and was being phased out. 'It was only a worn-out old bomber but was better than nothing.' The Junkers 88 was the best of the three converted day aircraft, faster and with two hours more flying time than the Messerschmitt 110, smaller and more manoeuvrable than the Dornier 217. One pilot said that his Junkers 88 flew so easily that 'you felt as comfortable as though you were at home by the fireplace'.

German aircraft designers spent much effort in producing purpose-built night fighters based on the experience gained by front-line units. The Heinkel 219 was the first of these to arrive and had only recently been tested operationally. New Messerschmitts and Junkers were also on the way but, because of frequent changes of policy by senior officers of the Luftwaffe or by Hitler, not one of these excellent aircraft ever reached mass production. These advanced night-fighter types were known to R.A.F. Intelligence and the British bomber crews were given details of them. It is often interesting to read the reports of bomber crews that had returned after surviving a combat with a German night fighter. A high proportion claimed that they had been attacked by a Junkers 188 or a Messerschmitt 210, rather than by the humbler types with which they had actually fought. The Dornier 217 was hardly ever mentioned by the British bomber men and it was probably this unsuspected type that was the basis of many of the more exotic sightings.

The basic night-fighter unit was the *Geschwader*, which contained three or four *Gruppen*, normally of thirty fighters each; the *Gruppe* contained three *Staffeln*, normally of nine aircraft each. There were five *Geschwader* attempting to protect Germany from night raids in 1943 but only three of these were fully operational.* When the British launched the Battle of Hamburg, it would be the less experienced units of NJG 3 – mostly equipped with old Dornier 217s – that would have to face the main impact of the Bomber Command raids and the new device it was about to introduce into the night-bombing war. In particular, it would be on the German airmen flying from Westerland, Schleswig, Nordholz, Stade, Lüneburg, Wunstorf, Vechta and Wittmundhafen that the safety of the citizens of Hamburg would have to depend, although other units would provide some assistance, particularly the skilled crews of NJG 1, the 'mother unit of the German night-fighter force', flying from airfields in Holland.

The order of battle of the German night fighters may have looked fine on paper but it had many weaknesses. The original force had been improvised in 1940 and that of July 1943 showed many signs of a continuing improvisation. New crews arrived at operational airfields with only a basic training on their particular type of aircraft. There were no operational training units in which a new crew could be taught the tactics

---

* Because the *Geschwader* and its sub-units, *Gruppe* and *Staffel*, do not readily equate with equivalent R.A.F. or U.S.A.A.F. units, no attempt has been made to translate these terms. The basic night-fighter unit, *Nachtjagdgeschwader*, is usually abbreviated to 'NJG' with the *Geschwader* number after it. An ordinary numeral before the NJG denotes the *Staffel* or a roman numeral the *Gruppe*. Thus, 5/NJG 3 is the 5th *Staffel* in the 3rd Night-Fighter *Geschwader*; II/NJG 3 is the 2nd *Gruppe* in the same *Geschwader*. This system is widely recognized and has been adopted in this book.

Appendix 3 sets out the Luftwaffe night-fighter order of battle on 24 July 1943. Luftwaffe records show that the night-fighter units contained 371 serviceable aircraft at the end of June 1943 with 307 trained crews.

of night fighting. These they had to learn on their operational unit, if there was time and if their commander took the trouble to see that this was done. The first ten or so operational flights were often a nightmare, with the novice pilot having to devote all his efforts simply to survive in this pitch-black environment and then return to his airfield and land with the crude navigational aids of that period. Any contact made with a bomber during these flights was usually more the result of chance than good flying and any success against that bomber was considered almost a miracle.

If the new crew survived this period without crashing and killing themselves, then they started to operate more effectively. Many of the German survivors say that their first '*Abschuss*' ('shot down' – German pilots did not use the word 'kill' as did some Allied pilots) was a major turning point which gave them so much confidence on which to build, but it could take as many as fifty operational flights before that first success came. The rigid nature of Kammhuber's box system condemned most German night-fighter crews to long periods of operational inactivity. While the crack units in Holland had been flying and scoring night after night, those in other places saw little action other than against the occasional bomber sneaking in to lay mines off the coast or to drop agents and supplies to Resistance groups in the Occupied Countries. During the season of short summer nights when the R.A.F. were unlikely to attack northern Germany, some of the experienced crews in units stationed there were detached to the more active units in Holland and Belgium, leaving the remainder of their units to do little more than carry out practice interception flights to exercise themselves and the radar personnel of the local boxes.

Even in the busier units, the best boxes were manned by the most experienced crews. If a raid developed quickly or there was an unexpected change in course by the bomber-stream, a crew finding itself in a good box might find itself ordered out of it and see one of the *Experten* take its place and pile up more successes. The German public heard plenty about these aces but nothing about the poor fellows who did little more than fly the patrols in unpopular boxes or stand by in reserve. These bore no ill will towards the aces. They realized that the best results were gained by getting experienced crews into the most favourable boxes. But many were becoming critical of Kammhuber's system, which made so little use of their own efforts. They knew all about the growing strength of the R.A.F. and were anxious to do more to protect the German cities. The defence of Hamburg would largely be in the hands of crews who had had so little opportunity to practise their craft.

The *Himmelbett* box system and the German night fighters had only concerned themselves with British bombers flying to and from the target; the system did not allow the ordinary night fighter to fight near the city being bombed. The close defence of the German cities was in the hands of the local Flak and searchlight units. All Bomber Command aircrews were familiar with the dazzling displays put up by the defences of an important German city and very few raids took place without some of the bombers being claimed as their victims.

The core of this defence was the 88-mm Flak gun of which the Germans had large numbers. There were also heavier guns, the 105-mm and the 128-mm guns, but it was the famous 'eighty-eight' that provided the main strength. In the early years, the Flak had either used barrage fire blindly or had relied on the searchlights to illuminate their targets, but the Flak and some of the searchlights were now guided by radar. The radar set used by both was the *Würzburg*, the same type as that on which the fighter box control system relied. Every British bomber man was aware of the blue-tinged 'master searchlight', the single, 2-metre, radar-controlled light in each German searchlight battery. Its blue appearance had no special significance; it only appeared to be that colour when seen from above. Its duty was to find a bomber and then pass it on to the weaker 1·5-metre searchlights. To be caught and held in a cone of such searchlights was the greatest fear of the British bomber crews. But much of the display of Flak seen over German cities was quite harmless to a bomber flying at its normal operational height. This was the 20- and 37-mm light Flak which sprayed its vivid tracer all over the sky. This tracer, called 'flaming onions' by the R.A.F., might just reach the operational height of a Stirling in the case of the 37-mm Flak but the more numerous 20-mm was useless unless a bomber was damaged and had lost considerable height. But local Flak commanders and civil leaders were most reluctant to part with any of their defences. The morale of the local civilians was kept up by the large number of guns which created so much noise and spectacle during a raid; it should be remembered that the German city dwellers rarely saw a night fighter. They placed their trust very much in the local defences which became an everyday part of their city scene. The gun crews were equally happy; the alternative could be a posting to the Russian front.

The static Flak defences of a city could be reinforced quickly if needed. The fine German railway Flak units which lived a completely self-contained life on the railway could be moved from one location to another at will. It was quite normal that, if a city had suffered a particularly heavy raid, several railway batteries would be sent there immediately, partly to strengthen the defences against any follow-up raids, but mainly to bolster the morale of the bombed civilians. There was much competition between cities for this mobile Flak, the donor city always being anxious to get back what it considered to be 'its Flak'. Bomber Command, of course, deliberately spread the scope of its attacks to keep this Flak on the run and was partly successful in doing so. There was a popular German saying: *'Die Flak läuft den Bomben nach'* – 'The Flak runs around after the bombs'.

The general rule, that the German night fighters left the Flak and searchlights to provide the close defence of the city, was about to be broken. The Germans were once more being driven by Bomber Command's relentless pressure into improvisation and a new element was about to be brought into the defence of Germany. The latest innovation was the use of single-engined fighters, with no radar equipment, operating directly over the city that was being bombed.

This unusual method of night fighting was being pioneered and introduced on the initiative of one man – a Luftwaffe officer who had never flown a fighter in action. Major Hajo (Hans-Joachim) Herrmann did, however, know all about night bombing. He had carried out 320 operational flights as a bomber pilot, many of them in the night Blitz of English cities. Hajo Herrmann survived the war and then ten years in Russian prison camps. He was one of the most interesting ex-Luftwaffe men who helped with this book, but unfortunately, there is no room here for a full inclusion of his description of the development of his new type of night fighting. Briefly, Herrmann was concerned that the growing British and American bomber production would overwhelm the German day- and night-fighter forces. Night fighters were already being used in a limited way against American day bombers. Herrmann wanted to use day fighters in night action, thus providing massive reinforcement to the night defence at little cost. Herrmann was convinced that single-engined fighters could operate successfully directly above a city that was under bomber attack at night. The local Flak would be ordered to fire only up to a certain altitude and the fighters should be free to hunt for bombers above that height. They could attack bombers seen to be caught in searchlights or those spotted from above, silhouetted against the general illumination provided by a big target – flares, Target Indicators, searchlights, fires on the ground.

After surmounting much opposition, Major Herrmann was allowed to try out his theory against an R.A.F. raid on the night of 3 July 1943, in the closing stages of the Battle of the Ruhr. The commander of the Ruhr Flak defences was ordered not to fire above 20,000 feet but the British attack turned out to be on Cologne, whose Flak commander had not been warned that German fighters would be operating. Herrmann and nine other pilots went into action. They claimed twelve bombers shot down but so too did the Cologne Flak and only twelve wrecks were found in the vicinity. Herrmann says that these bomber victims were later *'mit der Flak kameradschaftlich geteilt'* – 'shared in friendly manner with the Flak'. The R.A.F. Bomber Command report of this raid contains no reference to this new development but there must have been some confusion over the target because there were four reports of Lancasters firing on other Lancasters and three returning bombers were reported as having been damaged 'by British aircraft'.[2]

After his success over Cologne, Major Herrmann was given permission to raise a *Geschwader* of these new day-turned-night fighters. He established himself at Hangelar airfield near Bonn with one *Gruppe* of specially modified Messerschmitt 109s. Two further *Gruppen* were formed at Rheine and Oldenburg but, for the time being, these would have to use the aircraft of the day-fighter units at these airfields. The new unit was at first called *Geschwader Herrmann*, a title that its commander did not like, 'Luftwaffe units were usually named after dead heroes.' It soon became J G (*Jagdgeschwader*) 300 and was eventually joined by J G 301 and J G 302. The first pilots were mostly bomber or transport pilots with much experience of night and instrument flying and this unit was certainly one of the more colourful in the Luftwaffe, with Herrmann being able to attract many bold characters for this new work.

The new tactic was given the slightly disparaging name of *Wilde Sau* – Wild Boar. 'It was a good choice', says Herrmann. 'We were like wild pigs charging about over the target, mixed up with Flak, searchlights and the bombers.' The formation of this new unit did not remain a secret in the Luftwaffe and the '*Herrmann Knaben*' – the 'Herrmann lads' – and their new ideas soon became well known. There was much speculation, particularly in the conventional night-fighter units, about what they might achieve. Many thought that it would not be much. The main advantage of the Wild Boar tactic was that it required nothing from the existing night-fighter force nor any sophisticated radar equipment, either on the ground or in the fighters.

Major Herrmann's new third arm of the German night defence was still in its training period when the Battle of Hamburg opened.

The reader cannot have failed to notice how the German defence against night bombing was so heavily dependent on the use of radar – *Freya* radars to give early warning of the bombers' approach from England, *Freya* again and the two *Würzburgs* in the box-interception technique, the *Lichtenstein* inside the night fighter for the final stage of the interception unless the bomber was seen by eye first, then, over the city target, more *Würzburgs* to guide the master-searchlight beams and the gun-laying equipment of the Flak. A mere three *Gruppen* of single-engined Wild Boar fighters, still not operational, was the only part of the German armed defence against night raids that was not dependent on radar. Yet the British had made no attempt to jam this mass of radar except for some mild interference of the *Freya* early-warning radars.

This state of affairs was about to be challenged in dramatic fashion.

By 20 July 1943 there were stored on every R.A.F. bomber airfield, under strict security guard, stacks of brown paper parcels of the most innocent appearance. Each parcel contained a number of bundles of paper strips. There were 2,200 strips in each bundle. Each strip measured 27 centimetres long by 2 centimetres wide. The strips were made of coarse black paper with thin aluminium foil stuck to one side of it. It had been proved that, if sufficient of these metallized strips could be released by a force of bombers flying over Germany, most of the German radar sets, particularly the *Würzburgs* and the *Lichtensteins*, would be swamped with false echoes and become useless. All the experiments had been successfully completed, the operational trials done. The device was code-named Window.

The history of the development of Window and of the long delay before it was brought into use by Bomber Command has been described in detail many times. An early form of the device had been ready for operational use as early as April 1942. It had been produced in quantity, delivered to bomber airfields and, according to one version of the story, actually loaded into bombers for use in a raid before an order was received forbidding its use. It was feared that, once Window was used, the Germans would also make use of the device in their bomber raids against England and there were also strong objections by the Royal Navy, which used several types of radar. Bomber Command had to continue operating for the remainder of 1942 and throughout the Battle of the Ruhr in early 1943 without this valuable device.

Sir Arthur Harris was very critical of the delay:

> I was always fighting hard to get Window from the moment I knew of its existence. The biggest mistake anybody can make, militarily, is to credit themselves with being so damn clever that, between two evenly balanced industrially developed nations, you dare not afford to disclose a particular weapon or device to an enemy for fear of giving him something he doesn't already have. Given that there was a slight see-saw position, the enemy could usually be counted on to be discovering the same weapons as you were. I think it was a tremendous error to withhold Window. The Germans never really found the complete answer to it.

It is now commonly accepted that the Luftwaffe's strength of bombers was so small at this time that the Germans could have made little use of the device even if they had possessed it.

A favourable decision to use Window was not reached until 15 July 1943. It was taken at the very highest level – at a meeting of the Combined Chiefs of Staffs attended by the Prime Minister and by Herbert Morrison, the minister responsible for the safety of Britain's civilian population. The Royal Navy agreed that Window should be used as soon as the first phase of the invasion of Sicily – then five days old – was completed. Fighter Command agreed that the new radar sets with which its night fighters were now equipped would not be much troubled by the use of a German version of Window. Mr Morrison was still worried about a renewed bombing of England but Winston Churchill refused to side with him and the doughty little Labour politician was forced to agree. Bomber Command was authorized to use Window from 23 July.

It is most ironic that the technical principles of Window had been known to the enemy all the time. Japanese naval aircraft had actually used a device almost identical to Window in night-bombing attacks against the Americans at Guadalcanal that summer. The Japanese device was called *Giman-shi* – 'deceiving paper' – and it did disrupt the radar sets that the Americans were using with their anti-aircraft guns. Reports of this development were slow to pass through the American Intelligence network and they did not reach the British until after Bomber Command started to use its Window. The Germans, too, had had their version of Window for some time. This was called *Düppel*, from the location near Berlin where the first experimental work was done. *Düppel* had been tested by the Luftwaffe over the Baltic and its implications horrified the Germans. If the R.A.F. should ever discover the use that could be made of these metallized strips, the German defence against night raids would be in ruins. Fearful that the British should hear of this device and knowing how valuable it would be in British hands, Goering ordered that no one, under pain of death, should talk of the existence of *Düppel* and he even ordered that all research, *even on a counter to the device*, should stop. In this way, the Luftwaffe was robbed of six months of valuable time in which it could have been preparing to meet Window.

On 17 July 1943, a Bomber Command order was sent out to the headquarters of each bomber group.[3] Everything was to be made ready to introduce Window on the night of 23/24 July. No target was mentioned for the first use of the device; that decision would be taken later by Sir Arthur Harris. The detailed use of Window will be described in a later chapter but the general intention was that, as soon as the bomber-stream came within range of the *Würzburg* radars in the German night-fighter boxes, every bomber should start releasing Window and continue to do so, right through to the target and on the return flight until the bombers passed out of the *Würzburgs'* range. The bomber-stream would thus be flying above a dense cloud of the slowly descending metallized strips for the whole time of its passage through the *Himmelbett* box system and whenever it was in range of any German search-lights or Flak gun. Also, any German night fighter flying in the Window area would find that its *Lichtenstein* radar set was seriously disturbed by the device.

The only German radars not to be touched were the early-warning *Freya* sets, which operated on a frequency too short to be affected by Window. *Freya* had been the target for an earlier jamming effort by a device called Mandrel, which was carried in a proportion of the British bombers. This device had been used only intermittently in recent months because it had been feared that German night fighters were homing in to the Mandrel impulses. On the day after the Window operation order went out, all the bomber groups were told that it was of 'the utmost importance to use Mandrel to the maximum degree' so that, with Window, 'the complete paralysis of the German defence system could be achieved'.[4]

The German night defences were, indeed, to be tested to the limit. There could be no question about Window not working. It had passed all its trials and sufficient stocks had been manufactured; no special aircraft, sophisticated new tactics or skilled personnel were required. Any spare member in the crew of an ordinary bomber simply pushed out the packets of Window to disperse in the air. The only unknown factors were the depth of the failure into which the German-fighter and Flak defences would be plunged and the length of time before the Germans could produce an answer.

The R.A.F. had been attacking Germany's industrial cities for more than three years and it has been shown how the German defence to this had steadily developed during those years. By contrast, the day attack on Germany by the U.S.A.A.F. had been in progress for less than six months. Even in this period, only twelve raids had actually been carried out against German targets and half of these had been on coastal towns not involving any penetration of the mainland. The daylight battle over Germany was still in its infancy and the force of German day fighters facing the Americans had little more than just started out on what was to prove a long and hard road. Because that day-fighter force was only of modest size and because the manner in which it flew was so free from technical complexity compared to night-fighter operations, this final part of the chapter covering the German defences relevant to the Battle of Hamburg will be short and straight-forward.

Ever since the Germans had invaded Russia in 1941, the Luftwaffe day-fighter force remaining in the West had been a small one. Just two *Geschwader*, J G 1 and J G 26, had covered the coastline from Denmark to France. But the gradual stepping-up of the American offensive had changed this situation. In the north, J G 1 had been split into two parts and expanded to produce a new *Geschwader*, J G 11. These two units were now mainly responsible for the area in which the American bombers would fly to reach Hamburg but they had not yet had much experience in this task. For further reinforcement, the Luftwaffe was being forced to bring back further units from the fighting fronts. It was like the return of the Roman legions, with *Gruppen* returning home after having fought in Russia or the Mediterranean for the past two years.*
All these Luftwaffe units in the West were equipped with the two basic German day fighters of this period. The older Messerschmitt 109G – the beloved *Gustav* of the German pilots – was the more lightly armed but was more manoeuvrable in the thin upper air in which the American bombers flew. The heavier and more modern Focke-Wulf 190 was a sturdier plane but less handy at high altitudes.

The Americans had often met those German fighters that

* Appendix 3 includes the order of battle of the Luftwaffe day-fighter units in the West.

were stationed in France and the Low Countries, giving them the collective name of 'the Abbeville Boys' – 'those yellow-nosed 109s; they were supposed to be Goering's favourite squadron'. The 'Abbeville Boys' had made easy meat of the B-24 Liberator, until that type of bomber had been temporarily pulled out of the battle, but they had great respect for the B-17. They knew of its name, 'the Flying Fortress', but usually called it *'die Boeing'*. The German fighter pilots had serious problems over which method to use when attacking the American defensive formations. The Germans called such formations *'Pulks'* – 'herds'. The standard day-fighter diving attack from above and behind, the classic 'curve of pursuit', turned out to be very expensive. The tough B-17s were hard to shoot down and the massed defensive fire of an American formation to its rear was exceedingly dangerous to fly through. The eighteen bombers in an American bomb group, properly stacked in combat formation, could bring up to 162 heavy calibre machine-guns to bear on any German fighter diving across the rear of that formation.

The Germans then discovered that the early B-17s had no gun capable of firing directly ahead and the German pilots took to making head-on attacks in groups of four fighters – a frightening, high-speed few seconds for both attacker and attacked. To carry out such an attack successfully needed both skill and courage. The closing speed of bomber and fighter was over 500 m.p.h. If the fighter pilot broke away too early, his fire was ineffective, if too late, he risked ramming the bomber he was firing at or having to fly right on through the American formation. The Americans were taken by surprise by this tactic and, at first, suffered heavily. In particular, those planes on the outer edge of the low squadron in a group formation were particularly vulnerable. This position became known as 'Purple Heart Corner'. The Americans immediately started fitting single hand-held guns into the noses of the B-17s already in England and new planes being made in the United States were provided with a power-operated turret, fitted underneath the nose and firing directly forward. No B-17s with the new forward turrets had yet reached the bomb groups in England but even the temporarily fitted forward guns gave valuable protection from the frontal attack and the German losses increased. The Germans sometimes used such unconven-

tional weapons as bombs dropped into the American formations or rockets fired from a safe distance but such methods
did not achieve great success. The most effective German
method of dealing with the American bombers would be the
introduction of specially armoured Focke-Wulf 190s making
massed attacks from ahead but these '*Sturmgruppen*' did not
appear until early 1944.

There were other elements in the German daylight defence.
Twin-engined night fighters were sometimes called out and
ordered to attack American bombers although their poor
daylight performance was a major handicap. They were more
useful in picking off American stragglers than attacking
formations – but everyone was happy to attack stragglers. The
German Flak, too, was a major part of the German defence,
perhaps the only part that could be used equally efficiently by
day or by night. The American airmen hated Flak. They
could at least fire back at the German fighters but they could
only fly steadily on through the miles of Flak barrages that
protected the German targets.

Such were the various hazards that the Americans had to
face. Nearly every one of their raids developed into a pitched
battle. The Americans lost steadily but were easily able to
replace their losses. The American gunners claimed enormous
numbers of German fighters destroyed. Most of these claims
were accepted and published as being genuine. Everyone,
except a few sceptics, believed that the Eighth Air Force was
slaughtering the German day-fighter force. But the German
fighters kept appearing.

The prospect for the German pilots was not a happy one.
They could see that the American strength was increasing
remorselessly. They were engaged in a battle that could have
only one end, although many refused to believe that Hitler
could not yet pull some wonder weapon out of the hat. The
Luftwaffe day-fighter pilots can be compared to the R.A.F.
fighter pilots in the Battle of Britain. Unlike a bomber man,
who was unlikely to be shot down more than once in his
career, the fighter pilot who parachuted to safety when his
plane was hit over friendly territory was simply provided with
a new plane and sent up again. But the Battle of Britain had
lasted for only two months and there were enough R.A.F.
fighter squadrons to allow periods of rest in the quieter areas

of Britain. The daylight Battle of Germany that was just beginning would last for nearly two years. There were no 'tours of operations' or rest areas for the German fighter pilots. They could only fight on until death or serious wounds removed them from action. Many grim things that should never be forgotten were done in Nazi Germany but the courage of the German fighter pilots, battling to defend their homes, deserves some acknowledgement whether they flew by day or in the dark.

NOTES

1. For those readers who would like to study these such matters in greater detail, I particularly recommend Alfred Price, *Instruments of Darkness*, 1977.
2. Bomber Command Operational Research Section Night Raid Report, Public Record Office AIR 14/3410.
3. Bomber Command Instruction No. 70, Public Record Office AIR 24/257.
4. ibid.

5

Hamburg—The City Target

In descriptions of the bombing war, one important point is often missed. It is commonly regarded, perhaps understandably so, that the strategic-bombing offensive was mainly a contest between the Allied bomber forces and the Luftwaffe's fighter units and Flak, with the German cities merely playing the role of the unfortunate recipients of the bombs dropped by those bombers which had evaded the German defence. In fact, the Luftwaffe, or what might be called 'the armed defence', was not the most important adversary of the Allied bombers. Although the armed defence – with a little help from the weather – destroyed no less than 3,222 Allied bombers in 1943, the flights of more than 85,000 other bombers – ninety-six out of every hundred that had taken off – passed safely through the German armed defence and most of these delivered their bomb loads to their targets! The harsh truth is that the Luftwaffe never had a chance of providing complete protection for the German cities. As long as the training camps of the Allies could produce fresh aircrews and their factories fresh bombers, as long as the morale of those aircrews and the will of their commanders did not break, the Luftwaffe could never do more than harry the bombers. I have tried to show in earlier chapters that none of these factors on the British and American side were failing; in fact, they were all in a strong ascendant. It was absolutely inevitable that the bomber forces would cause widespread damage, casualties and dislocation in the German cities.

The real contest was between the Allied air forces and the German cities themselves. The bombers had so to crush the spirit of the German city dwellers and so to smash up the industries in the cities that, either by breakdown of morale or by industrial collapse, the nation of Germany could fight no longer. What happened *in the cities* was the heart of the whole contest. The most important commanders on the German side were not Luftwaffe generals; the chief adversaries of Air Chief Marshal Harris and Brigadier-General Anderson were Josef

Goebbels, the German minister in charge of morale, Heinrich Himmler, whose Gestapo was in charge of what may loosely be termed 'discipline', and Albert Speer, who organized Germany's industry for military purposes. It was these men and their subordinates in the major German cities and the degree to which they could persuade the city dwellers and factory workers to stick it out that would decide the outcome of the bombing war.

Present-day Hamburg is full of cars whose registration plates start with the letters 'HH'. Most large German cities have only a single letter, the first letter of the city's name. Hamburg's 'HH' stands for 'Hansestadt Hamburg'. This much prized Hanse prefix is shared with only two other German cities – Bremen and Lübeck. The Hanseatic League, which existed for four centuries in the Middle Ages, dominated the trade of northern Europe. It was dissolved in the middle of the seventeenth century but four members – Hamburg, Bremen, Lübeck and Frankfurt – remained as *Freistädte*, independent cities, until 1866 when Prussia incorporated Frankfurt. The independence of the other three cities lasted only five more years and Bismarck brought them into his modern German federation in 1871. Hamburg, Bremen and Lübeck each became one of the fifteen states within the new Germany but were allowed to retain their privilege of being Customs-free ports and to retain their 'Hanse' titles by courtesy of the commercial world. In this way, Hamburg emerged with the proud title of 'The Free and Hanseatic State and City of Hamburg'.

Modern Hamburg really dates back to the year 1842. On 5 May of that year, the centre of the city was destroyed in a great fire which started in a typical small Hamburg merchant's property used partly as a house and partly as a grain store in the Deichstrasse near the waterfront on the River Elbe. The fire spread quickly and burnt for three days. A fine new city emerged from the ashes. It is typical of the international character of Hamburg that the three men most responsible for the planning of its reconstruction were a German and a French architect and an English engineer: Gottfried Semper, Alexis de Châteauneuf and William Lindley, the last being a Yorkshireman living in the suburb of Wandsbek.

Hamburg continued to grow in the great years of Germany's prosperity before the First World War and many typically Germanic public buildings were erected around the turn of the century. Most of these massive but often beautiful structures even survived the Second World War bombing and they still stand today. Hamburg became a modern city, the second largest in Germany with a population of one and three-quarter million people, and the largest port in Europe. The city proper is situated almost entirely north of the quarter-mile-wide River Elbe. A visitor to pre-war Hamburg would come away with the impression that he had been in a wealthy city, designed and built on a substantial scale – wide roads, large yet elegant public and commercial buildings, extensive public parks and gardens, a wide river. It was a city that had grown very rich on its centuries of privileged trading, a city that was, in parts, refined and cultured. Pre-war Hamburg was the equal of many a European capital. It had the normal industrial and residential areas of a modern city and also its seamy side. The district of Sankt Pauli, with its famous Reeperbahn, was possibly the most famous entertainment area in Europe.

Through the middle of the city runs the small River Alster which has been dammed up near its mouth to create an extensive lake and also to keep full the numerous *Flets*, or canals, that are to be found in so many parts of Hamburg. One is never far from water in Hamburg. The original port of old Hamburg had been along the north bank of the Elbe but the modern port of 1939 was situated among the miles of quays and basins carved out of a previously empty, low-lying island to the south of the main part of the River Elbe. Many of the harbour workers had to cross the Elbe from Hamburg city each day, either by ferry or by the one tunnel and one road bridge that so limited north–south communications. Hamburg's trade was truly international. Not only was it a major outlet for German goods but the Elbe was navigable inland as far as Czechoslovakia and the newly built Kiel Canal linked the Elbe with the Baltic. Part of the harbour was still a *Freihafen* where goods could be landed and stored without Customs payment until transhipped to destinations outside Germany. Czechoslovakia even had its own administration and police force in part of the *Freihafen*. Most of the modern industrial expansion had also taken place in this area, over the Elbe from Hamburg city.

With the city's long history of independence, the inhabitants of Hamburg had developed a character all of their own. Like all Germans, they had a strong sense of discipline and patriotism but the Hamburger had a greater sense of tradition than most other citizens of modern Germany. He is also considered a harder worker than the average German. He has the reputation of being a sensible man, slow to anger and slow to show other emotions. 'He is a man with both feet firmly on the ground, not easily impressed. He will say exactly what he thinks.' Hamburg people like their fun but are more restrained in their enjoyment of it than many of their more boisterous fellow countrymen. The Hamburg sense of humour is quiet but sharp. There were – and still are – many jokes about *'klein* Erna', the daughter in a mythical Hamburg family. The *klein* Erna jokes are told in a typical Hamburg mixture of *Hoch* and *Plattdeutsch* and contain many subtle shades of humour that would certainly not be understood by a foreigner. Erna's mother pretended to be 'posh' and the jokes are usually connected with the earthy things of life. 'They are not really rude. You can tell them in the best society.'

One will be told many times that the pre-war Hamburger was similar in temperament and character to the Englishman. The two certainly had much in common, both probably having ancestors in the Saxon race, and the trading links between Hamburg and England were centuries-old.

Hamburg was a city that had a special affinity with England. On the one hand, there has been for centuries much trade between merchants. This feeling was not only confined to the owners of the firms but everyone who was employed there identified himself with this link. Then, it was also the done thing for schoolchildren and young people of better families who had just left school, to go to England for at least half a year. Because of that, there were a lot of personal friendships between citizens of Hamburg and English people and, when the war came, many parents were just as worried about the safety of the son of an English friend as about their own. (Helga Rutenick)*

* Quotations by Hamburg women use the surnames that these women had in 1943. The Acknowledgements show both maiden and married names, where applicable.

It must be said, however, that these family links with England did not extend much beyond Hamburg's trading community.

Then, in the early 1930s, the Nazis came, hard on the heels of the terrible inflation and unemployment that racked Germany.† Hamburg had its fair share of Nazi supporters and opponents and also of the street fights and political disturbances of that period. There seems little doubt that the earliest support for the Nazis came from parts of the previously liberal middle classes who had seen their savings and businesses disappear and were convinced by Nazi propaganda that Communism and the Jews were responsible for their troubles. The richer people, at first, showed disdain for the sometimes vulgar Nazis but few dared stand up against them. The bitterest opposition came from the Communists and the Social Democrats who had always been strong among Hamburg's working population. The worst of the disturbances was a vicious street battle between Communists and Nazis in Altona on 17 July 1932 in which seventeen people died. *Blutsonntag* – Bloody Sunday – this day became.

It became almost a joke after the war, for visitors to Germany who tried to discover the degree of support any German community had given to the Nazis, when every community claimed that its support had been less than that of others. Hamburg, when I asked my questions more recently, was no exception. But, in the case of Hamburg, the claim was partly justified. In the series of elections leading up to Hitler's accession to power, the electoral district of which Hamburg was the centre consistently produced pro-Nazi voting figures 5 per cent lower than the rest of Germany. The Nazi vote in Hamburg never exceeded 40 per cent of votes cast and, in the forced referendum of August 1934, called to put a seal of respectability on Hitler's dictatorship, Hamburg gave the highest 'No' vote in Germany. Those Hamburgers who had voted for Hitler were not all convinced Nazis; many did not approve of the viciousness already shown by the Nazis and

† German readers of the English version of this book should not take offence at the frequent use of the word 'Nazi'. This word, although one of enmity and hatred during the war, is still the only word that an average English reader knows when the National Socialist Party needs to be mentioned.

they were certainly not giving that party a mandate for the even worse cruelties that were to follow. But the voters were desperate. Hitler promised work for the unemployed, stability for Germany's currency and a place of pride and prestige again in the world. I venture the possibly unpopular opinion that many who were soon to become Germany's enemies would have been equally taken in by Hitler's promises had they been living in Germany during those desperate economic conditions of the early 1930s.

Hitler split Germany into forty-two administrative areas called *Gaue* and Hamburg and a small area around the city became one of these – possibly the smallest *Gau* in Germany. Hitler sent Karl Otto Kaufmann to be Gauleiter of Hamburg. The office of Gauleiter was a powerful one and the holders were all old friends and early supporters of Hitler. Karl Kaufmann was a Rhinelander, a native of Krefeld, and he had been in the Nazi Party since 1921. The leader of Hamburg's city administration was Bürgermeister Carl Vincent Krogmann, a handsome member of a wealthy Hamburg family who had actually been in office before the Nazis came to power. Krogmann joined the Party. These two, Gauleiter Kaufmann and Bürgermeister Krogmann, looked after the affairs of Hamburg under the Nazi régime from beginning to end. Kaufmann set up his headquarters in a beautiful mansion on the Magdalenenstrasse, a fashionable and exclusive street overlooking the gardens on the west bank of the Alster. His new home and office had previously been the property of an American timber merchant, a Mr Budge. Bürgermeister Krogmann continued to rule from Hamburg's beautiful Rathaus in the Altstadt. The large square in front of the Rathaus soon changed its name and became the Adolf Hitler Platz.

In one respect Hamburg was fortunate. Nazi rule in the city was never as savage as in other parts of Germany. It is true that many Jews and Communists were persecuted and sent to the local concentration camp or executed; indeed, anyone who showed open opposition to the Nazis received no mercy. But Hamburg was not like the rest of Germany. It was the gateway of Germany. The city had a sophisticated population with an outward-looking attitude and many links with the outside world. The Nazis decided to tread warily in

Hamburg. Karl Kaufmann was not like the run-of-the-mill bully boys who often became Germany's Gauleiters. There is no doubt that he was one of the most intelligent and less extreme, handpicked by Hitler for this sensitive part of Germany. Many inhabitants of Hamburg would later stress how fortunate the city had been to have men like Gauleiter Kaufmann and Bürgermeister Krogmann in charge during the war. This Jewish doctor, who escaped from Hamburg just before the war, has no cause to be charitable in this matter:

The whole mentality of Hamburg was different from the rest of Germany. There was an enormous difference between Hamburg and Berlin, for instance. It was the contact with the outside world that made all the difference. Of course, Gauleiter Kaufmann was a very strong Nazi because he would not, otherwise, have become a Gauleiter but, among the different Gauleiters in Germany, he was possibly the best. I have no need to say anything good about him because I had a bad experience under him but, speaking objectively, I can say that he was a relatively decent man. Bürgermeister Krogmann was also a decent man. (Hans Enoch)

These eminent people were, of course, only the pinnacle of a large pyramid of power. Supporters of the National Socialist Party took over every important official position and many minor ones; there were many sudden political conversions. Henceforth, nothing happened in Hamburg except by the authority of a Nazi official.

So, Hamburg settled down to eleven years of Nazi rule. There were many benefits. Business recovered. Trade flourished. There was work for all. Currency once more became stable. Hitler visited the city at least three times and received rapturous welcomes. He promised a new bridge across the Elbe and a new railway station – both would be the biggest and finest in the world but they were not to be built during his time. Hamburg could be a good place to live in for the next five years – as long as one said not one word in opposition to the form of government that had descended upon the city.

Then came the war. The young men were called up and disappeared to serve on Germany's fighting fronts and Hamburg, like all other German cities, became a community of mainly old people, women and children. Because the Wehrmacht was fighting a continental war on interior lines, the whole homeland acted as the base for Germany's fighting forces and Hamburg soon had its share of military establishments. But Hamburg was far more important as an industrial target than as a military one for the Allied bombers. The city was famous throughout wartime Germany for one important product: submarines. The shipyards of the city produced more than 400 U-boats during the war, of which at least half had been launched, fitted out and delivered to the Kriegsmarine before the Battle of Hamburg commenced. The firm Blohm & Voss was the most famous of the Hamburg ship-builders. It had built most of Germany's submarines in the First World War and among its more recent achievements were the 50,000-ton Blue Riband liner *Europa*, the heavy cruiser *Admiral Hipper* and, then, the shipyard's greatest achievement, the super battleship *Bismarck* of 41,700 tons, launched by Hitler just before the war. But in 1943 this fine ship was already at the bottom of the Atlantic.

After fitting out the *Bismarck*, Blohm & Voss had been ordered to concentrate on U-boat production and, in July 1943, these yards had been producing slightly more than one new U-boat every week for nearly two years. Blohm & Voss built more than half Hamburg's U-boats, the remaining production being shared by Howaldtswerke, Deutsche Werft and Stülcken & Son. These firms all carried out other work for the Kriegsmarine but U-boat production had absolute priority and one cannot stress too much the importance of this work to Germany's war effort.

(It is difficult to be completely accurate about the number of U-boats built in Hamburg because some were damaged by bombing and completed elsewhere and others were incomplete at the end of the war. Figures from reference books would suggest that Hamburg shipyards built, launched and completed 408 U-boats before the war ended out of the 1,131 U-boats completed by all German shipyards.)

There were other important industries: factories producing aircraft or aircraft parts, engineering works of many kinds, oil refineries. There is no need to go into detail about these; suffice it to say that they were all important to Germany's war effort but none were so vital as the submarine yards. By the time of the Battle of Hamburg, all of Hamburg's industry was centrally controlled by Albert Speer's Ministry of Armaments.

The local office of the ministry was the Rüstungsinspektion X and the official in charge here in July 1943 was Doktor Otto Wolff, whose office was near Gauleiter Kaufmann's.

There is one comment that should be made about the industrial empire that Doktor Wolff administered in Hamburg. All the U-boat yards, aircraft works, oil refineries and most of the engineering works, together with the harbour warehouses which were often used to store the raw materials of war, were situated on the south side of the River Elbe. The great city of Hamburg proper, with its shops and offices, its cultural and residential areas, lay on the northern bank, separated from the industrial areas by that wide river.

Of course the British bombers had been to Hamburg – no less than 137 times before the Battle of Hamburg, according to the records of Hamburg's Chief of Police. Bomber Command records say that there had been ninety-eight raids during this period. The difference is accounted for by small numbers of bombers mistaking Hamburg for other targets or deliberately using Hamburg as an alternative target when they could not reach other cities. Hamburg did not know how fortunate it had been in May 1942. Sir Arthur Harris had intended that Hamburg would be the target for his first Thousand-Bomber Raid, which was carried out at the end of that month. Detailed plans had been prepared for Hamburg to be the primary target, with Cologne as a reserve, and it was only some heavy, thundery clouds, forecast for the Hamburg area, that caused Cologne to be promoted to first place. That year, 1942, was just a century after the great fire that had destroyed medieval Hamburg. What Sir Arthur Harris called 'the centenary conflagration' had to be postponed.

Harris patiently kept Hamburg high on his list of German city targets. He selected it for the first use of his new navigational radar device, H2S, on the night of 30 January 1943. The city, on the broad River Elbe, should have been a good radar prospect when fourteen H2S-equipped Pathfinders led 134 four-engined bombers in a carefully prepared attack. The reports of returning crews were optimistic but photographic reconnaissance revealed disappointing results. Two follow-up raids were no more successful. In the third raid in this series, on the night of 3 March, the Pathfinders dropped most of their Target Indicators well to the west of the city. The Elbe at low tide had left a number of mudbanks exposed in this area and it is believed that the radar picture of the small town of Wedel, on the north bank of the river and twelve miles downstream from the centre of Hamburg, was assumed by the Pathfinders to be Hamburg and the exposed mudbanks to be Hamburg's dock area on the south side of the Elbe. It was a typical error of the early days of H2S, and Hamburg gained another reprieve when most of the Main Force dropped their bombs in the wrong place. After this raid there came a lull with no major raid for nearly five months, although a few Mosquitoes were sent to carry out nuisance raids. Hamburg carried a few bombing scars but life was able to carry on as normal in most parts of the city.

Hamburg had gained an evil reputation among Bomber Command aircrew for the strength of its defences. These were situated in a wide circle up to twenty miles from the city centre and it took a bomber fifteen minutes to fly through the full spread of the city's guns and searchlights. On the eve of the July 1943 raids, Hamburg had fifty-four batteries of heavy Flak, twenty-four batteries of searchlights and three smoke-generating units. The heavy Flak batteries contained 166 88-mm guns, ninety-six 105-mm guns and sixteen 128-mm guns, the last being mounted on the huge *Flaktürme* of which there were three, two near the centre of Hamburg on the Heiligengeistfeld and the other in Wilhelmsburg, south of the Elbe. There may have been some mobile railway Flak in Hamburg when the first of the July 1943 raids came, but this is unlikely. Goebbels, in his diary, says that some of Hamburg's Flak had even been removed to other parts of Germany two days before the first raid, although no other document that I have seen confirms such an untimely move. Most of the regular Luftwaffe men in the Flak and searchlight batteries were in the higher military-age groups. They were the men of the *Heimatfront* – the Home Front. Their numbers were made up with Russian prisoners of war, local schoolboys and female auxiliaries. It is reputed that one German Flak commander addressed his unit in the following terms, 'Ladies and gentlemen, fellow workers, schoolboys, *tovarishtchi!*'[1] The schoolboys had to serve with the Flak for up to a year before they were eligible for full-time military service. They went to live with one of the local Flak units and their days were a mixture of gun drill and school lessons conducted by Hamburg teachers visiting the Flak sites.

The gradual increase in the scale of R.A.F. raids during the past three years had enabled Hamburg's civil defence forces to gain much valuable experience without ever having to face an overwhelming attack. It is often stated that, at this time, Hamburg had one of the most advanced and strongest civil-defence organizations in Germany. As with everything else in wartime Germany, this organization was completely under party control. The overall commander was S.S. Gruppenführer Count von Bassewitz-Behr, operating from his headquarters at Feldbrunnenstrasse 16. The core of the civil defence was the police and fire departments, which came under Chief of Police (Polizeipräsident) Hans Kehrl, a career policeman who had risen in the pre-war police service because of his ability in the legal departments of various forces outside Hamburg; it was because of this ability that he had been appointed to his present position although it was necessary for him to be a member of the Nazi Party to rise to this height and he now held the rank of major-general in the S.S. Kehrl had a particularly elegant residence and office in the Milchstrasse, again close to the home of Gauleiter Kaufmann, but his operational headquarters were at the Main Police Station in Neuer Wall, not far from the Rathaus. The senior fire officer was Oberstleutnant Otto Zaps, whose headquarters were at the Main Fire Station at Berliner Tor. The inhabitants of Hamburg were to depend for their lives on the ability of these men and their departments in the great test to come.

I do not intend to give a complete breakdown of every element in Hamburg's civil-defence organization. It was identical to that in every other German city and similar to that in English cities during the war. The backbone was provided by the pre-war professional police and fire departments, which had been reinforced by reservists called up in 1939 and 1940, men usually too old for military service. These full-time men were supplemented by a large number of auxiliaries, prominent among whom were the fanatical but brave members of the Hitler Youth. Every industrial firm was also obliged to provide workers to man mobile pumps either for service in their own factory or at any other place where needed. There were at least 309 of these mobile factory pumps in Hamburg and another ninety-three provided by local Nazi Party headquarters and manned by party members.

The ordinary people of Hamburg were also prepared. Every office, factory or shop had its group of fire-watchers who took it in turns to ensure that the premises were occupied every night of the year. Every apartment building – most of Hamburg's residential dwellings were flats – had its *Blockwart*, who made sure that there was a supply of sand and water on every floor. If a raid came, he would call upon the men in his block to fight any incendiary bombs that fell. It was constantly stressed that the best time to tackle a fire was the moment the incendiary bomb dropped, even if high-explosive bombs were also falling.

British civil-defence experts who visited Germany after the war came to the conclusion that German civilians were provided with better air-raid shelters than those in their own country had been. Every single civilian in Hamburg had an excellent shelter. Those whose homes were on dry ground – 60 per cent of the population – could go down to the *Keller* of their apartment blocks. (The word '*Keller*' gives the wrong impression when translated as 'cellar'. The German *Keller* was a normal-sized room and the English term 'basement' is preferred.) Public shelters were provided for those whose homes had no basements or for people who were away from home when a raid occurred. These ranged from the picturesque round *Winkel* tower shelters, of which there were fifteen in Hamburg, to the ugly large multi-storey *Bunker* shelters, of which there were sixty-nine above ground and thirty underground ones, in the basements of large city-centre shops or office blocks. The public were also allowed to take shelter in the lower storeys of the large, fortress-like Flak towers.

If the Allied bomber offensive had done nothing else, it had succeeded in tying down a vast amount of German manpower in the civil defence and Flak defences, to say nothing of the labour required to produce anti-aircraft guns, searchlights, radar equipment, fire-fighting equipment, and the steel-and-concrete structures now so prominent a part of the Hamburg landscape.

The war had brought many changes in the population of Hamburg. With the young men gone to the front and the war industries working flat out, Germany made use of her conquered territories to fill the manpower gap. A report from the local armaments industry office shows that no less than 66,000 foreigners – 51,000 men and 15,000 women – were among Hamburg's 634,000 working population at the end of June 1943.[2] There were four groups of foreign workers: *Fremdarbeiter, Ostarbeiter*, prisoners of war and the concentration camp *Aussenkommandos*.

I must admit that I have no details about the numbers or life-style of the prisoner-of-war working parties in Hamburg. It is probable that there were no British or Americans among them at this period of the war and the majority were probably Russians. The *Fremdarbeiter* had been 'guest workers,' men from the German-occupied countries of western Europe who had been recruited on a voluntary basis to work in German industry. They lived in special camps but were paid normal wages, were free to spend their leisure time in the city and to travel home for limited holidays. But the German effort to secure voluntary labour from these countries had proved a failure and the majority of foreigners from Western Europe now working in Hamburg had been conscripted in their home countries and sent to work in Germany. They were the 'forced workers' on which so much of German industry now depended. Most of those in Hamburg were Dutch, French, and Belgians. Blohm & Voss certainly had 800 Dutch and French mechanics; they were described as good workers by their works' director. As the war progressed, the Germans would find it less easy to get volunteer workers from these countries and more drastic measures would have to be used.

Another type of foreign worker had never had any choice in the matter. There was no restraint to the East. The *Ostarbeiter* – Eastern workers – were little more than slaves and Poland, the Ukraine and Russia had always lost large numbers of their young people, forced to work in Germany. Irena Chmiel, a schoolgirl from Lublin, was one of the Polish workers:

We came to Hamburg in cattle trucks and forty-nine of us were sent to work in this lemonade factory. The German woman who looked after us in the old house where we lived was very hard on us. She wore a party badge and was a blooming sod. We went looking for her after the war. But Frau Niemeyer, our forewoman at work, was very nice; she gave me clothes and brought me bits of food, leaving them for me to find. Mind you, she 'Heil Hitlered' every time the boss came in. We saw him every now and again; he wasn't a bad boss. There were only three men in the factory; one had three fingers missing; one was an old man who called us '*Polen Schwein*' and spat at us; and one was a mentally deficient who carried dirty pictures to show us.

The food was very bad, fit for pigs. I got sick of strong *Sauerkraut* but we had to eat it. We got one slice of bread a day; it was so thin that we used to say we could see Warsaw through it. It was a good job we worked in a lemonade factory. There was plenty of fruit juice to drink and there was a barrel of black molasses for mixing with the tomato juice. We used to eat that until we saw some dead rats in it one day.

In our off-duty time we were allowed out as long as we wore our 'P' badge but some of the children spat at us and threw stones when they saw the badge and we had to be back by eight in the evening. The older girls started courting the Polish boys in a camp near by but they weren't allowed to marry. We were taken to the doctors every month and, if any girl was pregnant, she had to have an abortion. We were treated like animals.

By contrast, Zygmunt Skowronski, a Polish boy, was more happy to leave home.

I was not all that sorry to find myself in Germany. I wanted to travel and the further I went by train the better I liked it. I had never seen a big city like Hamburg in all my life and it made a big impression on me. It was a very beautiful city but I didn't like the people much. I preferred the people in the village outside the city where I worked. I was lucky. The farmer I was with – Heinrich Riege of Kirchwerder-Hove – treated me like a son but there were a lot of bastards as well, particularly the Hitler Youth.

There were many other forced workers besides the Poles. There were Ukrainians, who had more privileges than the Poles; they were allowed to marry and they could join the civil-defence forces, thus attaining equal status with German civilians according to a special section of the German law. One Hamburg Red Cross woman comments that the Ukrainian firemen at her post were 'the most daring, the most energetic and the most steadfast of men when it came to fighting fires', but they got drunk on anti-freeze at Christmas 1943 and two of them died. Some of the ordinary Hamburg people showed kindness to the foreigners but one Hamburg woman says that she always felt isolated by language barriers from the Russians with whom she worked. 'To us, every Russian man was called Ivan; every woman was Olga.'

Concentration camps were another feature of German life that provided a supply of cheap labour. Originally built for Germans who had fallen foul of the Nazis' many regulations, they were now packed with men and women of the many countries that Germany had occupied. The concentration camps were places of cruel punishment, poor food and back-breaking work. They were administered by the S.S., who hired out the inmates in the form of *Aussenkommandos* to local industry. The original Hamburg concentration camp had been in a disused section of the Fuhlsbüttel prison (near Hamburg's civil airport) but this was full by 1938 and a new camp had been built at an isolated spot in the country at Neuengamme. Neuengamme never achieved the notoriety of the worst of the German concentration camps. It was not an extermination camp, just an ordinary, run-of-the-mill concentration camp. People in Hamburg knew vaguely of it – it was only twelve miles from the city centre – but such places were not the subject of casual conversation in wartime Hamburg.

Another subject that decent Hamburg people tried to shut their minds to was what had happened to the Jews in their city. Pre-Nazi Hamburg had contained approximately 15,000 Jewish people. There was no ghetto and the Jews were well integrated into the life of this liberal, outward-looking German city. But the Nazis had soon started to harass and persecute Hamburg's Jews and many fled the country before the war. It was in 1941 that the fullest horrors of the Nazi extermination policy fell upon Hamburg as on every other part of German-occupied Europe. On 26 October 1941, 1,034 Jews were loaded into cattle trucks at a disused passenger station, the Hannoversche Bahnhof. This first 'transport' had finished up in the ghetto at Lodz, in Poland, and most were dead within the year, the able-bodied worked to death, the rest shot or gassed.

The remainder of Hamburg's Jews followed to various places in eastern Europe. So many Hamburg people will say that they never knew what was happening and certainly none was able to do anything about it. It was the Hamburg civil police who were forced to do the rounding up and escorting of the Jews to the trains. Hamburger had to round up Hamburger and the poor Jews were sent to a fate only known to God and the S.S. A total of 5,343 Jews had left the Hannoversche Bahnhof before the time in which we are interested. Transport Number 14 had just departed, on 23 June 1943, with ninety-four Jews, most of them very old or very young. They were almost the last remnants of Hamburg's Jewish community. Frau Gretchen Meyer, ninety-three years, was the oldest; Berl Blumenthal, not yet two years, was the youngest. Their destination was Theresienstadt (now Terezín) in Czechoslovakian Bohemia, a well-known death camp.[3] A few hundred Hamburg Jews, of mixed marriage or of privileged position, were allowed to remain. A few hundred more returned as survivors from the East after the war.

German readers may not like my resurrecting these subjects – the forced labour brought to Hamburg, the concentration camps, the Jews – but they were all part of the local scene in the Hamburg that I am trying to describe before the July 1943 bombing. I recognize that the ordinary German could do little to prevent these excesses and I do not believe in collective guilt. But it is not fair to those who suffered and died that these events should be deliberately omitted and they are also relevant to the moral issues surrounding the bombing of Hamburg.

The war dragged on for all the people of Hamburg. There could be no doubt now that it was *totaler Krieg* – total war. On 18 February 1943, just after the national catastrophe of Stalingrad, Propaganda Minister Goebbels had made a famous speech at a massed assembly of faithful party members in the Sportpalast in Berlin. In this carefully prepared 'show', Goebbels had gradually roused his audience to a fever of excitement and they had answered enthusiastically to his final questions: 'The English say that Germany is nearly finished. Are we?' 'Shall we fight to the end?' It was then that Goebbels had promised his audience 'total war'. The event had been broadcast throughout Germany.

The ordinary, mostly decent, folk of Hamburg went about their everyday business, some getting tired of this war they had got themselves into and which was now going wrong. It was beginning to seem a long time since the heady years of victory. Nothing but bad news now came from the fighting fronts. Other cities in Germany had been badly bombed. People were becoming nervous, frightened. In a few, there was the fear of eventual defeat, in most the fear of the Gestapo – 'Be careful! Keep quiet and say nothing! Keep working!' And every single night there was the fear that the bombers would come again to Hamburg.

As summer nights always meant a threat of raids, there was constant fear – especially after the bad raids in 1942 which had given us some idea what a heavy raid could mean. But it was a fear that we had learned to live with, a case of what can't be cured must be endured. And I must admit that there seemed to be a certain pride in showing the country what the citizens of Hamburg were made of. Being a Free and Hanse city, Hamburg had – and still has, I believe – a tendency to feel separate and rather superior. It wasn't so much a case of showing the Allies we could take it; it was a case of showing the rest of Germany. (Louise Schäfer)

Hamburg had been fortunate thus far. It had missed being the target for the Thousand-Bomber Raid in 1942 and the first H2S radar raids in early 1943 had proved failures. The Americans had not been able to raid the city at all. But, by mid-July 1943, the Americans were ready to tackle this heavily defended target and the British had the new device, Window. The commander-in-chief of Bomber Command had already decided that, as soon as weather conditions permitted, he would use Window in a new attempt to gain an elusive prize, the destruction of that 'Free and Hanseatic City' on the River Elbe.

A large proportion of the bombers would inevitably reach Hamburg. Then, if the weather conditions over the target were suitable, the city would face the supreme test. The outcome of the battle for Hamburg would depend upon the skill of the forces deployed by Gauleiter Kaufmann, Bürgermeister Krogmann, S.S. Gruppenführer Count von Bassewitz-Behr, Polizeipräsident Kehrl, Oberstleutnant Zaps and armaments ministry representative Doktor Wolff. But the outcome would be decided, above all, by the behaviour of the citizens of Hamburg – in their loyalty to their country and government, in the sturdiness of character and resolution they could summon in the face of such an assault on their morale and will-power.

NOTES

1. Hans Rumpf, *The Bombing of Germany*, p. 197.
2. Bundesarchiv document RW20–10/20.
3. These details are from *Die jüdischen Opfer des Nationalsozialismus in Hamburg* (1965), which lists the name and age of every Jew transported from Hamburg.

6

Plans for Battle

The decision to launch the Battle of Hamburg was taken at approximately 9.15 a.m. on Thursday, 22 July 1943, just before Air Chief Marshal Harris ended the routine morning planning conference at Bomber Command Headquarters.

The end of July 1943 was not a dramatic period of the war, except in the case of the position of Italy which was about to drop out of the war as Germany's partner. There were no other major turning points at this time. The great offensives of aggression – the German ones in Europe and Russia and that of the Japanese in the Pacific – had all run their course and been blunted. The most active theatre of war for British and American troops was the Mediterranean. The German and Italian forces in North Africa had been defeated two months earlier and Sicily had been successfully invaded on 10 July. The great bloodletting in Russia continued. The German summer offensive here had been launched seventeen days earlier but, this time, it had run out of steam after only ten days and powerful Russian armies were now on the counter-offensive and would soon capture the city of Orel. The newer war in the Pacific had only just turned in favour of the Allies. The island of Guadalcanal had been recaptured in February but, since then, the mainly American forces in this theatre had been able to do little more than regroup and prepare for further invasions of Japanese-held islands.

It was true that the Allies were everywhere on the offensive but they still had a massive task before them in defeating their various enemies. It was true that Italy would drop out of the war within a few weeks but, at Orel, the Russians were still nearly a thousand miles from Berlin and not one British or American soldier had yet set foot on the mainland of western Europe. In Washington, an American admiral had just announced his opinion that it would take a further six years of hard fighting to defeat Japan.

The bombers had not been busy recently. The last raid by the full strength of Bomber Command had been that on

Cologne, eighteen nights earlier. There had then followed five raids, using much smaller forces, to a variety of targets during the next two weeks – Cologne again, Gelsenkirchen, Turin, Aachen and, finally, an interesting low-level moonlight attack by 165 Halifaxes on the virtually undefended Peugeot factory at Montbéliard in eastern France. The Cologne, Gelsenkirchen and Aachen raids marked the end of the period known as the Battle of the Ruhr. A full moon had then prevented any major bombing operations for the next week, although there had been a few mining and leaflet flights to France and a small raid by eighteen Lancasters on an undefended power station in northern Italy. But this was all small stuff. Bomber Command now had 800 operational bombers and its commander was anxious to resume the main offensive against the German cities.

The American bombers had also been grounded but for completely different reasons. The Americans were not bothered with the state of the moon; their main problem was cloud-covered targets. The month of July – midsummer as it was – had been a great disappointment so far. Only four times in three weeks had the American bombers taken off, mostly bound for targets in France and Holland. It has been stated earlier that the American commanders had decided to wait until their B-17 force reached a strength of 300 aircraft before commencing their full-scale offensive on German targets. That figure had been reached in the middle of July, when the recently arrived 385th and 388th Bomb Groups became operational, but continued cloud cover of Germany had meant that a mere thirty-four B-17s had managed to drop bombs on Germany so far in that month. There were signs that this situation was about to change. A large area of high pressure was moving slowly south from the Iceland area, bringing with it the promise of a period of fine, clear weather over northern Europe. Both R.A.F. Bomber Command and the Eighth Air Force were watching this anxiously – the British to use their new device, Window, and the Americans to attempt, at long last, their ambition to launch daylight raids deep into Germany.

The morning conference at Bomber Command Headquarters at High Wycombe commenced at 9.0 a.m. on

Thursday, 22 July. Sir Arthur Harris came down into the underground Operations Room and seated himself. No minutes were ever kept of these conferences but it can be assumed that Brigadier-General Fred Anderson had come over from his headquarters near by and was now seated next to Harris.

There can be no doubt that there was only one main target in Harris's mind that morning: Hamburg. An important document has fortunately survived the war. This is a letter, dated as early as 27 May 1943, and written by Harris to his six group commanders, setting out his future intentions.[1] The first part can usefully be included here.

MOST SECRET

BOMBER COMMAND
OPERATION ORDER NO. 173

Copy No: 23   Date: *27th May, 1943*

INFORMATION

The importance of HAMBURG, the second largest city in Germany with a population of one and a half millions, is well known and needs no further emphasis. The total destruction of this city would achieve immeasurable results in reducing the industrial capacity of the enemy's war machine. This, together with the effect on German morale, which would be felt throughout the country, would play a very important part in shortening and in winning the war.

2. The 'Battle of Hamburg' cannot be won in a single night. It is estimated that at least 10,000 tons of bombs will have to be dropped to complete the process of elimination. To achieve the maximum effect of air bombardment, this city should be subjected to sustained attack.

Forces to be Employed

3. Bomber Command forces will consist of all available heavies in operational squadrons until sufficient hours of darkness enable the medium bombers to take part. It is hoped that the night attacks will be preceded and/or followed by heavy daylight attacks by the United States VIIIth Bomber Command.

INTENTION

4. To destroy HAMBURG.

So, here, six weeks before the end of the Battle of the Ruhr, Harris's intentions for the next stage were clear, even the title of 'The Battle of Hamburg' being used. The letter to the group commanders had gone on to give details of bomb-loads and possible routes and tactics, and it is obvious that Harris had been thinking of starting this battle in June, using only his four-engined bombers and approaching Hamburg by an indirect route far to the north of the city. But he had obviously thought better of this plan, which would have been risky in the short nights of midsummer, and had decided to wait for the slightly longer nights after the next full moon period so that his routes could be more direct, giving him heavier bomb-loads, and also allowing the Wellingtons to join in. It was another small reprieve for Hamburg.

Sir Arthur Harris had often been criticized for ignoring the directives he so frequently received from the Air Ministry about the future operations of Bomber Command. In particular, Harris believed more in the general bombing of German industrial cities than in the particular bombing of those cities associated with specific industries. This attitude was partly the result of the limitations in target-finding and bombing accuracy that Harris knew existed in Bomber Command and partly the result of a deep-seated conviction that the general Area Bombing offensive would bring a swifter result than any attempt to knock out particular industries. On this occasion, however, the wishes of the Air Ministry and the personal policies of Harris did not clash. The famous 'Pointblank' directive of 10 June 1943 had reiterated that the general destruction of German industry remained the ultimate objective of the British and American bomber forces but took account of the increasing toll that the German fighters had been taking on both the British and American bombers. It was feared that, if the growth of the German fighter force could not be checked, the complete air supremacy that was deemed essential to a successful invasion of Europe would not be achieved. The two bomber-force commanders received orders to attack German cities involved in producing aircraft and, particularly, those associated with the ball-bearing industry which was believed to be essential to the production of aircraft. But it was also stated that cities involved in U-boat construction were to be attacked 'when tactical and weather conditions preclude attacks upon objectives associated with the German fighter force'.[2] Hamburg was the most important U-boat production city in Germany and also a minor aircraft-industry target. Its name appeared in the list of twenty-two cities and towns that Bomber Command was ordered to attack.

Sir Arthur Harris would not dispute, however, that he was mounting the Battle of Hamburg more because it fitted in with what he thought Bomber Command should be doing than because it appeared in the Pointblank directive. 'I had always wanted to have a real dead set at Hamburg. It was the second biggest city in Germany and I wanted to make a tremendous show.' Although the targets in the Pointblank list feature frequently in the American operations of the next nine months, not many were attacked by Bomber Command. After the Battle of Hamburg, Harris was to set his eyes on the third of his great 'battles', the Battle of Berlin, which would occupy Bomber Command for most of the coming winter. He had to be given a direct order by the Air Ministry before he would attack the ball-bearing town of Schweinfurt in February 1944. All this has been recorded here because it is important that the basis on which Hamburg was selected as a target should be established. The Bomber Command code-name for the Battle of Hamburg was 'Operation Gomorrah'.

At the conference on that Thursday morning, Harris heard his meteorological officer forecast that there was a chance that the high-pressure area would have pushed the cloud away from north-west Germany by the coming night and that the Hamburg area might be clear. The weather over England would also be good and the bomber airfields would be clear for both take-off and landing. That was enough for the commander-in-chief. The Battle of Hamburg could commence that night, subject to the flights of two meteorological reconnaissance Mosquito aircraft establishing that the forecast was accurate. In the slight event of Hamburg being found to be still covered by cloud but areas near by being clear, Bremen was selected as an alternative target. The full force of Bomber Command's operational squadrons – the famous 'maximum effort' – was to be employed against Hamburg but a slightly smaller force would be used if Bremen became the target.

A few more minutes were spent discussing the Aiming Points of the proposed targets and rough outlines of the tactics to be used, so that the Bomber Command operational staff would know their chief's mind when they prepared the detailed plans during the next few hours. There was one final point. Bomber Command had been given authority to use Window from 23 July. With a slightly dramatic touch, the plans for the coming night's operations included the instruction that Window was to be dropped from one minute past midnight.

Brigadier-General Fred Anderson had listened to the decision being made. The R.A.F. and the Americans had never planned to coordinate their operations as closely as on a day-to-day basis but Harris, as early as his May letter to the group commanders, had expressed the hope that the American bombers would bomb Hamburg either on the days before or the days after Bomber Command's night attacks. Anderson had every intention of doing this. It would be the first real application of the long-heralded Combined Bomber Offensive, or what newspapers would call 'round-the-clock bombing'.

About ten officers remained in the Operations Room when the conference broke up. The senior of these was Air Marshal Sir Robert Saundby, the deputy commander-in-chief of Bomber Command. Saundby and his planning team set to work to produce the detailed plan for the coming night's operation. It has sometimes been suggested that the raids of the Battle of Hamburg were special ones. It is true that the introduction of Window was a novelty, but the use of this device would have little effect upon the tactics employed. It cannot be stressed too strongly that the methods to be used in the raids about to be carried out against Hamburg were routine ones, no different from dozens of raids that these staff officers had planned in recent months. The plan being prepared did contain some slight advances but these were merely part of the general development in tactics that was taking place all the time.

The core of every raid plan was the selection of the Aiming Point in the city and the route that the bomber-stream would take during its final run in to that Aiming Point. These two decisions would, in turn, depend upon which area of the target city had been selected for bombing. Hamburg was too large a city for the whole of it to be seriously damaged in one night and the intention was to bomb it area by area over several nights. Hamburg was not an easy target for Area Bombing. The presence of the wide River Elbe and the two extensive Alster lakes would dominate the tactics of the Battle of Hamburg. Aiming Points and bombing runs had to be so chosen that as few bombs as possible would be wasted by falling into these areas of water. The area to be bombed in this first night of the battle had already been chosen. The western districts of the main city, north of the River Elbe and west of the Alster lakes, were to be the night's target.

It is necessary now to explain an important point about the nature of R.A.F. night bombing. The Pathfinders always placed their Target Indicator markers as near as possible to the chosen Aiming Point. The Main Force bombers then aimed their bombs as near as possible to the Pathfinder markers. It sounds simple and one would expect that the bombs would fall in a circle about the Aiming Point – but they never did. For years, the planners of Bomber Command had had to cope with a phenomenon known as 'creep-back'. Imagine a bomb aimer lying in the nose of his aircraft 20,000 feet above a German city, with searchlights trying to trap him in a cone and with Flak shells bursting all around. His pilot had to keep the bomber flying straight and level. It was a terrible and dangerous time, this bombing run. The bomb aimer's orders were to bomb the *centre* of any group of Target Indicators he could see in his bomb sight. The temptation to release the bombs before reaching the exact centre of those markers was enormous. Some of the less stout-hearted bombed the first markers they came to or even just a fraction short of the first markers. Such men were known in Bomber Command as 'fringe merchants'. It was often only a question of seconds or even fractions of a second but, inevitably, bombs tended to be released shorter and shorter of the Aiming Point – they 'crept back'. There was also the factor of the smoke and dust of early bombs obscuring the early markers and of later Target Indicators dropped by Pathfinder Backer-Up crews also tending to fall short of the Aiming Point. So, the bombing inevitably crept back along the line of the bomb run.

Because no method had been found to stop this sequence of events, a virtue was made out of necessity and the creep-back was brought into the planning of raids. An Aiming Point was selected *beyond* the area of the city chosen for destruction and the Main Force bombing was allowed to spread back over that area. Civilian survivors of the Hamburg bombing so often refer to *'ein Bombenteppich'* – 'a carpet of bombs'. That was the creep-back steadily progressing across the city during a raid. An understanding of this point is all-important to any description of the Hamburg raids.

The Aiming Point for this first raid of the Battle of Hamburg was chosen exactly half-way between the southern end of the Binnen Alster (the smaller of the two Alster lakes) and the wide River Elbe. Both features should show up clearly both visually and on the H2S radar screens of the Pathfinders. This Aiming Point actually lay very close to the Rathaus and the Nikolaikirche but these buildings had no significance in the bombing plan. They just happened to be situated at the convenient point of aim for the early markers.

The direction of the bombing run followed from the choice of the Aiming Point. The bombing run for this night was selected to come in from the north-north-west, actually on a course of 160 degrees, it being angled slightly north to avoid the large open area of the Volkspark on the western outskirts of the city. If all went according to plan, the bombing would spread back from the area near the Aiming Point, across the districts of Neustadt, Rotherbaum, Harvestehude, Eimsbüttel, Eppendorf and Lokstedt. The creep-back of the bombing could travel more than four miles before becoming completely wasted in open country but the last part of those four miles consisted of sparsely populated suburban areas where bombing would not be very profitable. Every one of the districts named above was mainly residential. There were no sizeable industrial establishments anywhere in the area that it was hoped to bomb. No part of the attack was planned to fall south of the river where the U-boat yards and other major war industries were located. It was pure Area Bombing.

Other parts of the Hamburg plan can be described more quickly. The method of target marking would be chosen later by Pathfinder Headquarters in the light of a further weather forecast, and this can be dealt with later. Zero Hour for the opening of the main attack was fixed for 1.40 a.m. and the attack was planned to last for fifty minutes from that time.

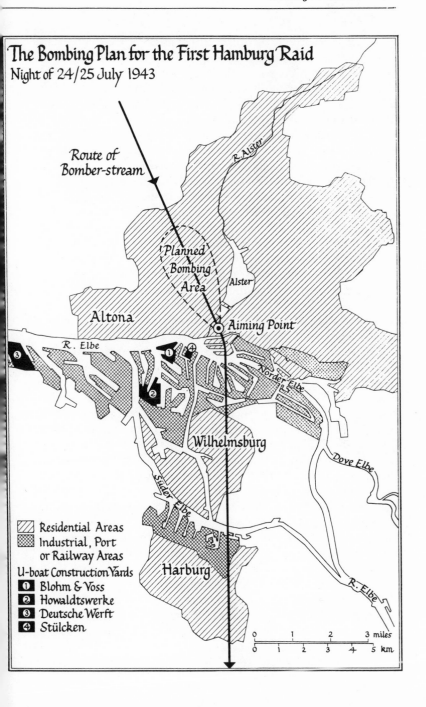

The Bombing Plan for the First Hamburg Raid
Night of 24/25 July 1943

Route of
Bomber-stream

R. Alster

'Planned
Bombing
Area'

Alster

Altona

Aiming Point

R. Elbe

Norder Elbe

Wilhelmsburg

Dove Elbe

Süder Elbe

R. Elbe

Residential Areas
Industrial, Port
or Railway Areas
U-boat Construction Yards
① Blohm & Voss
② Howaldtswerke
③ Deutsche Werft
④ Stülcken

Harburg

0   1   2   3 miles
0   1   2   3   4   5 km

(This Zero Hour was later changed, but the details given here about the duration of the attack are all valid.) This was ten minutes shorter than on the last occasion that a similar number of bombers had been used. The bombing of the Main Force was to be split into six phases or 'waves'. It is often believed that the raids of the Battle of Hamburg contained a specially high proportion of incendiary bombs but this is not true. It is also believed that Hamburg was a good fire target. This also is a misconception. Because of Hamburg's great fire of 1842, the city contained few really old timbered buildings; most were of fairly modern brick or concrete construction. There was also the presence in Hamburg of so many waterways which might act as firebreaks and which provided convenient sources of water for the city's fire-fighters. Hamburg would not be an easy city to set alight and a study of Bomber Command records shows that the bomb-loads of the first raid of the Battle of Hamburg contained a lower proportion of incendiary bombs than other city raids of this period. The increased number of high explosives were needed to blow apart the strongly built buildings of the city.

The routes to and from the target area were the next items to be settled. It was here that Window was going to be of some help. Bomber Command sometimes made use of evasive routeing to fox the German defences but, on this occasion, a relatively simple route was chosen. The bombers would fly out over the North Sea, diverting slightly north to keep well away from the night-fighter boxes along the Dutch coast, then turn into the Heligoland Bight and make a landfall at a distinctive peninsula before turning to make the final bomb run into Hamburg. After bombing, another simple route out, south of the River Elbe and back over the North Sea, would bring the bombers home. Navigation should be simple and would be aided by 'route-markers' – Target Indicators dropped by radar-equipped Pathfinder aircraft at the German coast on both the outward and return flights to help keep the Main Force on track. The absence of major diversions would keep the fuel requirements down, with a corresponding increase in bomb-loads and only 140 miles of the route – a mere forty-two minutes flying time – lay over German territory.

It took Air Marshal Saundby and his assistants about an hour to produce these plans and similar ones in case the target

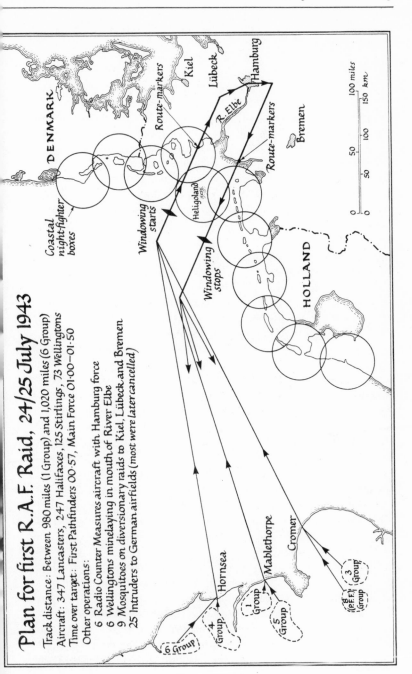

Plan for first R.A.F. Raid, 24/25 July 1943

Track distance: Between 980 miles (1 Group) and 1,020 miles (6 Group)
Aircraft: 347 Lancasters, 247 Halifaxes, 125 Stirlings, 73 Wellingtons
Time over target: First Pathfinders 00·57, Main Force 01·00–01·50
Other operations:
  6 Radio Counter Measures aircraft with Hamburg force
  6 Wellingtons minelaying in mouth of River Elbe
  9 Mosquitoes on diversionary raids to Kiel, Lübeck and Bremen
  25 Intruders to German airfields (most were later cancelled)

was changed to Bremen. There were a few minor details to decide upon but the main plan was now ready.

A little earlier, it was stated that the proposed Zero Hour of 1.40 a.m. for the coming raid on Hamburg would later be altered. The reader should now be told that the alteration would actually be one of just under forty-eight hours. The opening of the Battle of Hamburg, proposed for the early hours of Friday, 23 July, had to be delayed until the early hours of Sunday, 25 July.

On the R.A.F. airfield at Oakington, near Cambridge, was stationed a small unit, No. 1409 (Meteorological) Flight, equipped with unarmed Mosquitoes. The 'Met Flight' was responsible for all the long-range weather reconnaissance flights (code-named Pampas) both for Bomber Command and the American Eighth Air Force. The Met Flight was no sinecure. It had been formed with nine crews on 1 April 1943 and had lost one crew in each of its first four months of life. Now, on 22 July, Flight Lieutenant C. L. H. Dennis and his navigator, Flight Sergeant J. Boyle, took off in late morning for a Pampa flight right up the centre of the North Sea to a position midway between Scotland and Norway. A few minutes later, Flying Officer A. F. Pethick and Sergeant J. Burgess took off but headed in a more easterly and more dangerous direction to fly across Denmark as far as Copenhagen. None of these airmen had been told the purpose of their flights and the routes had been deliberately chosen so as not to disclose an undue interest in Hamburg. There was not, in fact, any need to go to Hamburg. With the high-pressure system known to be moving south into the North Sea, an examination of the areas to the north of the proposed Bomber Command route to Hamburg and of the target area should reveal the weather likely to be experienced by the bombers twelve hours later.

The Copenhagen flight was back first, at 3.15 p.m. The navigator hurried to a telephone and spoke to the Meteorological Office at Dunstable. Sergeant Burgess reported that heavy cumulus cloud up to 15,000 feet had been found over Denmark with some cumulo-nimbus 'anvils' up to 22,000 feet. The second Mosquito landed safely soon afterwards. It had found continuous low cloud over the North Sea but no high cloud. All this information was digested at Dunstable and a new forecast for the routes to Hamburg and the city itself was passed to Bomber Command Headquarters. The high-pressure area was moving southwards too slowly. The more distant parts of the routes to Hamburg would be too difficult, with many of the poorer-performance aircraft unable to climb above the cloud, and the city of Hamburg was likely to be cloud-covered with no prospect of any visual marking. There was another and, possibly, more important factor. If Window was used on a night which gave little prospect of accurate bombing, that new device would be revealed to the Germans for little reward.

The decision whether or not to continue with a raid was one of the heavy responsibilities borne by the commander-in-chief. Sir Arthur Harris cancelled this one, both the attack on Hamburg and on the secondary target of Bremen. Such cancellations were a regular feature of Bomber Command life. A vast amount of preparatory work by the ground staffs was wasted and much attrition waged on the nerves of aircrews. The Operational Record Book of 83 Pathfinder Squadron contains this entry:

Crews assembled for briefing at 18.00 hours and waited impatiently until 18.45 when the 'Scrub' came through. An air of gloom spread rapidly; it's so long since we went to war. The C.O. instructed all crews on the importance of security as this target (███████) would no doubt be on again. Gunners had aircraft recco. Lecture and test.[3]

The night passed with no R.A.F. operations of any kind. There are no records to show whether the U.S.A.A.F. had prepared a raid to Hamburg for the next day to follow up the R.A.F. attack. If such a raid had been prepared, then it, too, was cancelled.

There was another planning conference at Bomber Command Headquarters on the following morning, Friday, 23 July. Keeping his eye on the main aim, Sir Arthur Harris again chose Hamburg as the primary target for the coming night but, this time, with Mönchen-Gladbach, the industrial city just west of the Ruhr, as the alternative. Two more Met Flight Mosquitoes took off in mid-morning, again one flying up the North Sea and the second to Copenhagen. Conditions over the North Sea were found to be the same as on the previous day with no high cloud. The Denmark flight also found an absence of high cloud but it made this ominous report about the conditions seen on either side of its route – 'large masses of cumulus and cumulo-nimbus were observed over N.W. Germany and to the south of Norway'.[4]

These conditions were still not good enough for the first use of Window and the grand opening of the Battle of Hamburg that Sir Arthur Harris was so patiently awaiting. The proposed Hamburg raid was cancelled again. Harris also cancelled the Mönchen-Gladbach raid which could have been carried out using Oboe blind marking, possibly because the new forecast came too late to switch to this target, possibly also because Window was being saved for something more important. If the Mönchen-Gladbach raid had gone ahead, the written history of the bombing war would have been different with the Battle of the Ruhr being recorded as having lasted until 24 July instead of the generally recognized closing date of 14 July. But the Mönchen-Gladbach raid was cancelled and the German cities, the Luftwaffe night-fighter force and Bomber Command were all to have another quiet night except for the crews of seven Whitleys from training units who would fly to various towns around Paris to drop propaganda leaflets. All returned safely although two of the Whitleys were damaged by Flak.

Brigadier-General Anderson had also held his planning conference that morning (Friday the 23rd) and he had decided to prepare a major raid by all of his B-17 groups the following day. The meteorologists now believed that the high-pressure area was moving south-east rather than south and that there was a good chance of clear weather over southern Norway the following day. There were several Norwegian targets on the American priority list and General Anderson had decided that he would send his bombers to three of these: the U-boat bases at Bergen and Trondheim and a new metal and chemical factory at Heroya, south-west of Oslo. The necessary orders went out to the two American bombardment wings. It would be the first American operation for a week.

The next morning (Saturday the 24th), approximately one

hour before the American bombers took off for Norway, Sir Arthur Harris selected Hamburg as the primary target for Bomber Command in the coming night yet again, hoping that the clearance over the North Sea would at last reach that city. An alternative target was again chosen but no documents have survived to show what that alternative target would have been. The final touches were put to the night's plans. Zero Hour for Hamburg was fixed for 1.0 a.m. Three small diversionary raids by Mosquitoes were planned on Kiel, Lübeck and Bremen; six Wellingtons were to take advantage of the Hamburg raid and lay mines in the mouth of the River Elbe; some radio-counter-measures aircraft would fly with the Hamburg force; Fighter Command Mosquitoes were to carry out Intruder flights. Further afield, a few Mosquito bombers would carry out nuisance raids to the Ruhr; training-unit Wellingtons would drop more leaflets over France; fourteen Halifaxes would drop supplies to Resistance groups in France and a force of thirty-three Lancasters which needed to fly home from North Africa would do so, bombing a target in Italy on the way.

Flight Lieutenant George Hatton, the commander of the Met Flight, with navigator Pilot Officer W. F. John, carried out the only Pampa of the day, taking off an hour earlier than normal. They flew a course parallel with the one planned for the bombers flying to Hamburg but 100 miles to the north. It was a thorough flight, reaching as far as the Danish town of Vordingbord, seventy miles beyond the level of Hamburg. The Mosquito encountered no trouble, the only unusual incident being the sighting of a floating mine during their low-level return across the North Sea; its position was later reported to Intelligence. The Mosquito landed at 2.20 p.m. and Pilot Officer John was able to report that, although there was continuous low cloud over the North Sea, there were completely clear conditions north of Hamburg, apart from one large but isolated cumulus cloud.

The long-awaited conditions for the opening of the Battle of Hamburg and the first use of Window were at hand. There was no cancellation.

NOTES

1. The letter is now Public Record Office AIR 24/257.
2. The directive is in Public Record Office AIR 14/779.
3. Public Record Office AIR 27/687.
4. Operational Record Book 1409 Flight, Public Record Office AIR 29/867.

7

Preparations for Battle

The 24th of July, 1943, began as a summer day should, warm and bright; a day to live and taste and enjoy, a day to spend on the river at St Neots with a girl and a drifting boat. I was in no mood for war as I walked to the Mess that morning. I had not been at close quarters with an aeroplane since the 11th of July, just before I had gone on leave. More than that, I had not been on 'ops' since the 21st of June over Krefeld and, with 39 'ops' behind me – statistically equivalent to three 'lives' – the break had felt like a reprieve.

35 Squadron 'A' Flight crewroom united us again as a crew. We swapped yarns about the merits of our leave before I reported to my Flight Commander. Not long afterwards, the news came through from Group Headquarters that we would be operating that night and my gut began its familiar crawl. (Flight Lieutenant A. J. F. Davidson, 35 Squadron)

The squadrons of Bomber Command had prepared for a major raid many, many times. We can pass quickly over the next few hours; a few statistics will give some idea of the work that had to be done although, with the cancellations of the two previous days, the work was not all done on that hot, midsummer Saturday.

Bomber Command Headquarters had ordered a 'maximum effort'. Its 'Aircraft State' board had shown that the command had 871 operational bombers and 957 fully effective crews not on leave at 6.0 p.m. the previous evening. Of these aircraft, 792 bombers and crews would take off for the main Hamburg raid. A further eighty-seven aircraft – not all from Bomber Command – would fly on the various subsidiary operations. The only operational squadrons of Bomber Command excused from the coming night's work were 105 and 109 Squadrons, whose Oboe-equipped Mosquitoes would not be needed. The table that follows shows the total R.A.F. air effort that would fly to German-defended Europe that night. Of the Hamburg force, 4 Group, with 158 Halifaxes and seventeen Wellingtons, would supply the greatest number of aircraft but 1 Group, with its strong Lancaster squadrons, would carry the greatest weight of bombs (5 Group would have done so if some of its Lancasters had not been absent in North Africa). The largest single squadron effort would be from 1 Group, whose 103 Squadron would send twenty-seven Lancasters on the raid.

	Lancasters	Halifaxes	Stirlings	Wellingtons	Mosquitoes	Totals
Bombing Hamburg	347	247	125	73	—	792
Bombing Italy	33	—	—	—	—	33
Diversions and nuisance	—	—	—	—	13	13
Mining R. Elbe	—	—	—	6	—	6
R.C.M.	—	2	—	2	2	6
Intruder	—	—	—	—	4	4
Resistance supplies	—	18	—	—	—	18
Leaflets	—	—	—	7	—	7
Total	380	267	125	88	19	879

The operational strength of Bomber Command had increased remarkably in recent months. Not only had it replaced the 872 bombers lost in the Battle of the Ruhr but it had added a further 300 aircraft – all four-engined – to its strength. The British official historians make this comment on the strength of Bomber Command at the opening of the Battle of Hamburg: 'Such a force as was now disposed in Bomber Command would, in the days of crystal gazing before the war, undoubtedly have given rise to optimistic expectations of an immediate and complete knock-out blow.'[1] The reality of 'knocking-out' Germany was proving more difficult than the pre-war strategic-bomber men had imagined.

The various aircraft that would take off that night would contain 5,959 aircrew members: 5,475 on the main Hamburg raid and 484 on other endeavours. A study of squadron crew lists shows that the first use of Window caused more than half the commanders of the operational bomber squadrons – twenty-three out of forty-five – to put themselves on the battle order for what promised to be an interesting raid. Three station commanders also decided to fly: Group Captains Cozens from Hemswell, Crummy from Wickenby and Mason from Faldingworth.* Another effect of Window was the decision by many squadron commanders to send a maximum number of pilots from the new crews on their squadrons to get in their 'second pilot' trips with experienced crews before flying with their own crews. At least seventy-six such pilots flew that night. One squadron commander and three of the new pilots would fail to return. A naval liaison officer attached to 78 Squadron and an Australian ground-crew flight sergeant of 460 Squadron both returned safely from the flights they managed to organize for themselves.

The coming raid would consume a vast quantity of war material. Bombs had to be hauled from dumps and loaded into bomb bays – 2,460 tons for the Hamburg raid, consisting of 1,454 tons of high explosives and 1,006 tons of incendiaries. It would be a record tonnage for a Bomber Command raid. Approximately 1,300,000 gallons of high-octane petrol were pumped into the bombers' fuel tanks. The following are typical examples of bomb- and fuel-loads:

	Bombs	*Fuel*
Lancaster I and III	9,840–13,280 lb	1,600 gallons
Lancaster II	7,600–9,200 lb	1,700 gallons
Halifax II and V	5,960–7,960 lb	1,775 gallons
Stirling I and III	4,788–5,136 lb	1,875 gallons
Wellington X	2,640–4,000 lb	900 gallons

These figures show why the Lancaster was considered so desirable an aircraft. It is not known how many high-explosive bombs, which varied in size between 500 and 8,000 lb, were loaded but the incendiary loads for the first raid totalled 26,858 of the 30-lb bomb, which contained some phosphorus and which will be the subject of later comment, and no less than 327,250 of the magnesium or thermite 4-lb 'stick' incendiaries.

The Pathfinders had their own special devices: 489 of their 250-lb Target Indicator bombs were loaded and a variety of flares. Although all Pathfinder aircraft also carried a load of

* An observation that can be made on the squadron crew lists is that the bombers that flew to Hamburg were manned by a predominantly non-commissioned force of aircrew. An examination of one squadron from each of the six bomber groups shows that of their 807 men who flew to Hamburg, 173 were officers, twelve were warrant officers and 622 were flight sergeants or sergeants.[2]

normal bombs, some of them had an unusual addition to their load on this night. The Pathfinder aircraft, except the early markers, were given a number of small 40-lb anti-personnel bombs, some aircraft carrying as many as fifty-six such bombs. Their bomb aimers were ordered to scatter these bombs on Flak or searchlight positions seen beneath them while either entering or leaving the target area. As far as is known, this type of bombing had not taken place before. I asked three senior Pathfinder officers whose idea this was. None remembered these small bombs being used, although the squadron records show quite clearly that they were. All three poured scorn on the idea that they would have been of any value. Air Vice-Marshal Bennett said that it was one of the many 'gimmicks' that were tried and his Senior Air Staff Officer, Group Captain Boyce, thought that it was 'a lunatic idea. If I had been in the Ops Room when this came through, I would have got on to Bomber Command and asked who'd gone balmy'. Wing Commander John Searby, whose aircraft actually carried some of these bombs, said, 'Such bombs may have been excellent against tribesmen in Waziristan, between the wars, or against troops on the march but they formed no part of our bomber armament in the period under question.'

The loads of Window being stacked inside the fuselages of the bombers were a more widespread novelty. It was forbidden for anyone to open the paper-wrapped bundles before take-off; the ground crews believed that a massive dropping of propaganda leaflets was to be incorporated into the raid. More than 90 million of these metallized strips were loaded on to the bombers. In this first Window operation, it was planned that the strips should be dropped by being forced down the flare chute in each bomber, but some squadron commanders who were in the know about the new device had ordered that a special chute be made, usually near the bomb aimer's position in the aircraft. The two-day postponement of the raid had allowed time for several bombers to be modified in this way. There are many claimants for the honour of inventing these first 'Window chutes'. All bombers would later have them as a standard fitting.

The Americans flew to Norway during that day, the first time they had raided targets in that country. The groups of the

1st Bombardment Wing attacked a new factory at Heroya, near Oslo, which was about to come into production to supply the Germans with aluminium, magnesium and nitrates. The raid was a cleanly executed success. The damage caused was never repaired and the factory never did produce anything useful for the German war effort. The longer-range B-17s of the 4th Bombardment Wing flew to the U-boat bases at Trondheim and Bergen. Two groups bombed at Trondheim with what later Norwegian reports said was 'impressive accuracy' but Bergen was found to be covered by cloud, so the groups that had flown there made no attempt to bomb because friendly civilians might be hit by blind bombing.

The Luftwaffe had been caught unprepared and no fighters appeared. One Fortress of the 381st Bomb Group was badly damaged by Flak at Heroya and had to fly to Sweden but, before the day was out, Swedish radio announced that its crew was safely interned. All other aircraft returned safely to England. These raids were a good example of the versatility of air power. If, after taking off, these B-17s had flown south instead of north, they could have raided the U-boat base at Bordeaux, 1,300 miles from Trondheim; it was in this manner that the Luftwaffe was kept at full stretch. Much damage had been caused and the easy flights had lifted the morale of over 3,000 American bomber-crew members on the eve of a round of operations that would be far more testing.

The records of the 384th Bomb Group tell the story of Lieutenant Edwin Halseth, co-pilot of one of their planes, whose parents had been born at Moss, a town at the edge of Oslo Fjord over which his group had flown on the bomb run into Heroya. Halseth stated that 'it was painful for me to see it for the first time in my life and to know that the people down there, many of them my relatives, were suffering humiliation under Nazi rule. It was beautiful and I intend to go back there again some day under different conditions.' Lieutenant Halseth was destined to be a prisoner of war in Germany the next day.

The Americans flying to Norway had caused the sirens to sound in Hamburg – but only the preliminary *Luftwarnung*, not a real *Alarm* – although the American bombers had never been nearer than 300 miles to the city. No Allied bomber had flown over Hamburg since three Mosquitoes had carried out a nuisance raid nearly three weeks earlier. To guard against any complacency that the city would continue to be free from serious attack, local newspapers were publishing a constant stream of notices signed by Chief of Police Kehrl, urging the people of Hamburg not to become lax in their attitude to air-raid precautions:

The recent terror raids by the British-American murderers have shown again how important it is to keep houses and apartments prepared for air raids at all times.

Hamburg has lately enjoyed a long respite from enemy air raids. Despite this, all citizens are warned: 'Remain vigilant!' The most important thing is to check all civil defence equipment regularly and keep it in good condition.

STILL MORE WATER AND SAND NEEDED!

It is preferable to resign oneself to an apartment made 'unsightly' by boxes of sand and buckets of water than to watch helplessly when, during an attack, all one's possessions go up in flames.

Your primary duty is still to fight home fires.[3]

The month of July had so far been very hot in Hamburg. Daytime temperatures during the first fortnight had reached 21° Centigrade (nearly 70° Fahrenheit) but, then, a real heat wave had arrived and temperatures had touched 27° Centigrade (over 80° Fahrenheit). It had been mostly dry and, although there had been a heavy thundery downpour just two days earlier, most of the rain had soon evaporated in the heat. Many people in Hamburg later assumed that the Allies had waited for this heat wave before commencing their onslaught on the city. I was told many times during my Hamburg research that the R.A.F. had actually dropped leaflets, warning the population of Hamburg to leave the city because it was about to be bombed. People who told me this leaflet story were quite certain that they had been dropped but no one could say that they had actually seen such a leaflet themselves. It was not the R.A.F.'s policy to warn the inhabitants of a German city that it was about to be attacked, although this was frequently done when targets in the friendly countries occupied by the Germans were to be bombed. The R.A.F.'s 'warning leaflets' over Hamburg were only a rumour. Rumour was rife in every wartime country and false ones often formed the basis of beliefs and prejudices strongly held for many years afterwards.

The people of Hamburg were enjoying themselves on this sunny Saturday after their week of hard work. Many were strolling with their families or sitting in the cafés by the Alster or the Elbe or in Hamburg's beautiful public parks and gardens. Carl Hagenbeck's famous zoo was open to its usual crowd of weekend visitors. When evening came, the queues formed at the cinemas. Films were the backbone of wartime Hamburg's entertainment. After the weekly *Wochenschau* of propaganda newsreels came the 'big picture' – the great escape from reality for the cinemagoers. The largest cinema in Hamburg – indeed the largest in all Germany – was the Ufa-Palast, which could seat 3,000 people and even had a complete orchestra platform that could descend silently out of sight when the main film began. 'The little man in the street put on collar and tie to go to the Ufa-Palast; it was always the highlight of his cultural life.'

The drinking halls were mostly full, although there were more female patrons than men. Beer and schnapps were in short supply but wine was plentiful, although not really thirst-quenching on this hot evening. The restaurant beneath the Rathaus, the Ratskeller, was a favourite rendezvous. 'It was a good place for us middle-class girls. The food was good and we could order a bottle of wine and sit round a table, talking. Our reputation was safe there.' All dancing and private parties were forbidden by direct order of Hitler; the civilians at home were not to enjoy such pleasures while the men at the front were having such a hard time. But a few dances and parties did take place just the same. Suites at the best hotels – the Atlantic, the Esplanade and the Reichshof – could be hired by private parties of the privileged class and discreet dances were taking place there. There could even be parties in homes – perhaps to celebrate an engagement or a soldier's return for leave – provided one's neighbours could be trusted not to report the celebration. In some of these parties, the forbidden English and American dance records so loved by the bright young things of Hamburg could be brought out and played. One such girl remembers her favourite: 'Boo Hoo. You've Got Me Crying for You.'

The weekend entertainment was planned to continue on

the following day. The Hamburger was a great horse-racing enthusiast and Sunday races were to be held at the local Farmsen course. The most important race at Farmsen was to be the *Preis von Deutschland* with 50,000 Reichsmarks prize money. In central Hamburg, the local Hitler Youth were busy preparing for a canoe-race rally to be held on the Alster. Sixty-five teams were planning to travel to Hamburg on the Sunday morning to compete in a series of races in the afternoon.

All these plans were to be sadly disrupted. Goodbye, old Hamburg!

NOTES

1. Official History, Vol. II, p. 138.
2. The squadrons were 7 (Pathfinder), 61, 76, 218, 419 (Canadian) and 460 (Australian) whose records are in Public Record Office AIR 27/100, 258, 651, 1351, 1822 and 1908.
3. Extracts from the *Hamburger Tageblatt* and *Hamburger Fremdenblatt* of 10 June to 20 July 1943, reproduced in the Chief of Police Report, Appendix 7.

8

The First Blow

The first bomber to take off was an old Stirling of 75 (New Zealand) Squadron from Mepal airfield on the edge of the Cambridgeshire Fens. The pilot was an Englishman, Sergeant P. Moseley, on his fourth operation. His take-off time was 9.45 p.m. The weather was calm and clear and it was not yet dark; it was a perfect evening for flying. Sergeant Moseley was off first because his squadron was sending twenty-three of the slowest-climbing aircraft in Bomber Command to Hamburg. Nearly 300 faster bombers would overtake him before he reached the target. The first of the Pathfinders took off very soon after Sergeant Moseley; they would be opening the raid over Hamburg in three hours time.* Most of the Main Force squadrons were taking off by 10.00 p.m. This New Zealand navigator was on his first operation.

With 'Have a good trip' from our ground crew, we climbed in and took our places. Soon, our engines were ticking over and soon the first aircraft was racing down the runway, then another, and another, while we taxied slowly behind the one in front of us. Now it was our turn. The engines roared louder and louder and, with a 'hisss' of escaping air as the brakes were released, we started slowly to move forward – then faster and faster. We bumped and rocked but, when my Air Speed Indicator showed 115 miles per hour, the bumping stopped and I knew we were airborne. I made the first entry in my first operational Log Sheet: '22.40 hours – Airborne'. We climbed slowly in a wide circle, Tony and 'Boost', the flight engineer, indulging in long cross-talks about temperatures, pressures, revs and boost. At 5,000 feet the Skipper told us to don our oxygen masks. With two minutes to go before 'Set Course' time, I called Tony and gave him the course. He began to turn slowly and passed over our airfield at 7,000 feet as he called, 'On course, zero six zero'. My next log entry reads: '22.52 hours. Base, set course Cromer'. We were on our way

---

* Stirling BF443 was retired from operational service in mid-August 1943 after carrying out thirty-seven operational flights. Sergeant Moseley and his crew survived their operational tour, being released after twenty-five operations in mid-December 1943, and he followed the Stirling to the same training unit.

to Hamburg, still climbing in gathering darkness. (Flight Sergeant
E. J. Insull, 218 Squadron)

There was only one take-off accident. The first attempt by
Flight Sergeant Nicholas Matich, another New Zealander, to
take off in his Halifax at the airfield of 35 (Pathfinder)
Squadron at Graveley had not been successful. One engine
had cut but Matich had been able to brake before reaching
the end of the runway. The faulty engine had then picked up
again and, after a quick crew conference, Matich had taxied
round to the beginning of the runway to try again. On this
second take-off attempt, both outer engines suffered petrol
failure just as the Halifax was leaving the ground. Matich
managed to avoid the control caravan at the end of the runway and, after crashing through the boundary fence, the
bomber slithered to a halt in the next field. It was carrying
two Target Indicators and four 1,000-lb high-explosive bombs.
The pilot and flight engineer cut the magnetos and petrol
supply and switched on the engine fire extinguishers but 'the
general crew dispersal still anticipated Roger Bannister's
record by some years'. When it became clear that the Halifax
was not going to burst into flames, the crew stopped running and
burst into laughter with nervous relief. No one had been hurt.

The last bombers took off soon after 11.00 p.m. A total of
791 bombers had taken off successfully from forty-two airfields. It was an excellent start. The bombers flew out over
the coast, climbing steadily, the aircraft of each group making
their departure from a coastal town: 4 and 6 Groups leaving
from Hornsea, 1 and 5 Groups from Mablethorpe and 3 and 8
Groups from Cromer. There is no doubt that the men in the
bombers were happier on this night than they would normally
be during this stage of a flight. They had become weary of
going back to the Ruhr over and over again, simply 'turning
over the rubble'. Many were also pleased to be off after so
many cancelled operations. Few had been to Hamburg before
and the change to a longer flight over the sea and to a target
in a completely different part of Germany was a welcome one.
But there was also the feeling that this raid was really important. At their briefings a few hours earlier, a message from
Sir Arthur Harris had been read out to all aircrew saying
that the intention was to destroy this important target com-

pletely and that this was only the first of a series of raids that would concentrate on Hamburg until the city was destroyed. And then there was Window, the purpose of which had been revealed at the briefings, although some of the more experienced aircrew had been doubtful about the new device. 'After it had been explained in glowing terms by a non-flying type, it was discussed with some scepticism by the old sods and bods who had flown on previous trips when briefed in similar rosy terms about a raid being a piece of cake.'

The usual crop of mechanical difficulties became apparent when the heavily laden bombers were pushed hard in the long climb for height over the North Sea. Forty-five aircraft would turn back before reaching the German coast; this figure, representing 5·7 per cent of the bomber force, was about average for a raid of this kind. Lancasters, with twelve returns (3·5 per cent), suffered the fewest failures, Halifaxes the most, with twenty returns (8·1 per cent). Hamburg was spared the 129 tons of bombs that these aircraft were carrying, most of them being dumped in the North Sea. One Halifax, returning early with a failed engine, crash-landed when it returned to its airfield at Holme on Spalding Moor, but, again, no one was hurt.

Flying conditions continued to be perfect. Although low cloud covered the North Sea, it was clear at the height at which the bombers were flying. Gee continued to give the navigators a series of reliable fixes until the pulses started to weaken 300 miles from England. The normal German interference was late and not very effective; on this night they had chosen to jam the wrong Gee chain of the several chains available and some of the bomber navigators were able to obtain limited help from Gee throughout the whole flight. The Gee fixes being obtained now showed that there was only a light wind from the north. There were no serious navigational problems. The bombers were flying at varying heights between 15,000 and 18,000 feet, still climbing steadily; they would not reach their full operational height until after crossing the German coast. They pressed on with a steady 160 m.p.h. indicated on their instruments but their actual speed in the thinner upper air was more than 200 m.p.h. It became quite dark; what little moon there would be had not yet risen. Most of the bomber crews saw nothing of the many other aircraft in the sky although one Lancaster navigator has 'a lasting impression of the exhausts of the poor old Stirlings below us which were visible for miles'.

The first warning that the R.A.F. were coming had probably reached the German night-fighter airfields earlier in the evening when the codeword *Fasan* (Pheasant) had passed down through the chain of command from the headquarters of General Kammhuber's XII Fliegerkorps at Zeist in Holland. Kammhuber himself was not at Zeist; he was at Berlin and would watch the disintegration of his defence system from the elaborate operations room of the Luftwaffe's central head-quarters at the old Olympic Sports Field at Wannsee, just outside Berlin. Kammhuber's staff had carried out the routine task of assessing the volume and nature of R.A.F. signal traffic during the day, had studied the weather and, particularly, the moon conditions, and had probably decided that the R.A.F. would strike somewhere at night.

It was a long-range *Wassermann* radar station near Ostend that picked up the bombers first, just before 11.00 p.m. These first radar contacts were probably the Pathfinder aircraft of 8 Group climbing for height over the English coast 125 miles to the north. The well-placed radar station on the Dutch island of Texel had probably taken over the plotting soon afterwards and the bombers flying across the North Sea had then been steadily followed by the long-range German radars positioned all along the Dutch and German Frisian Islands.

This information had been passed to the underground control rooms of all the German fighter divisions. During these early stages of the raid, it was of most interest to the 1st Fighter Division at Deelen in Holland. The British bombers could have turned south at any point during their flight across the North Sea and struck down towards the Ruhr as they had done so often during recent months. The *Gruppen* of the famous NJG 1 had been alerted and ordered to send up fighters to man the coastal boxes. But, as the bombers continued to fly eastwards, parallel with the Frisians, the *Gruppen* of the 2nd Fighter Division at Stade, not far from Hamburg, were also alerted and their fighters too started to take off. All this happened before the British bombers started to drop Window.

But at first combat did not involve a bomber. Approximately twenty-five Mosquitoes of Fighter Command had been ordered to carry out Intruder operations – some to France but more to the airfields of northern Germany – but the possibility of fog coming down over their airfields in southern England had led to all but two of the Intruder squadrons cancelling their flights. Only four Mosquitoes had taken off. Someone had then decided that even these should be recalled – possibly to allow Window a clear run against the German night fighters on its first night. The crews of three of the Mosquitoes received the recall signal and returned but the fourth, a 25 Squadron aircraft crewed by Flight Lieutenant E. R. F. Cooke and Flight Sergeant F. M. Ellacott, carried on. Only that afternoon, these airmen had taken part in the station sports at Church Fenton airfield. It is recorded that 'it was a most enjoyable afternoon; bright sun and summer dresses combined to make a social occasion reminiscent of peacetime. The presence of an ice-cream vendor would have completed the illusion. After dinner, sterner thoughts prevailed.'[1]

Now this Mosquito was over the German night-fighter airfield at Westerland on the German island of Sylt, its crew watching a German plane, with navigation lights on, taking off. The German climbed towards some low cloud and Flight Lieutenant Cooke hurried to make an attack, opening fire at the comparatively long range of 600 yards just before his quarry entered the cloud. The German plane reappeared immediately, with its port engine burning, and Cooke closed in to 200 yards to deliver a final attack. The German plane spun into the sea. It was a Junkers 88 night fighter of the 4th Staffel of NJG 3. Lieutenant Wilhelm Töpfer and Obergefreiter Reinhold Hostmann were the first fatal casualties of the Battle of Hamburg. The Mosquito flew back towards England. This incident took place just before midnight, while the leading bombers were still some distance from the German coast and it was the only Intruder activity of the night.

The British bombers were soon in action, in the German night-fighter boxes on the north coast of Holland which had been manned in case the bombers turned south towards the Ruhr. Although this possibility soon faded, the bombers' routes had sometimes been only sixty miles from the Frisian Islands. The German coastal boxes were open-ended on their seaward side and night fighters could be sent as far out to sea as their fighter control officers could 'see' by radar. Although the *Würzburg* radars had a maximum range of forty-five miles, the *Freyas* were capable of following the general course of the bombers at much greater ranges. Window was not being dropped in this area.

There appear to have been four combats, all involving Messerschmitt 110s of NJG 1 and Lancaster bombers. The first two combats were brief and inconclusive. In both cases it was alert air gunners in the bombers who saw the fighter first. Pilot Officer Bill Benton, of 207 Squadron, was one of the pilots:

One of the gunners saw a night fighter making an attack from the rear. We corkscrewed violently and both gunners opened fire. As we were on our first trip, I expect they hosepiped all over the place; at that stage in our career, I expect we were in a state of utter panic. I think we claimed it as damaged but the Intelligence bloke probably said that it was a phoney claim and we never got any credit for it.

The second combat, in which a 61 Squadron Lancaster was involved, had the same outcome. It is probable that no hits had been scored by the bombers and neither night fighter had even opened fire.

It is important that a note on sources and on the methods used in matching combats be included here. Much effort has been expended by myself and by valuable helpers in Germany in analysing the many combats that took place during the Battle of Hamburg. The sources of information are numerous but none is completely comprehensive. On the R.A.F. side, there are the reports of returned British aircraft, of men who were shot down and became prisoners of war, and of the R.A.F.'s Missing Research Teams which worked so hard in Europe after the war. But there are gaps in such information, particularly in those parts of the Battle of Hamburg which were fought over the sea and resulted in aircraft disappearing without trace. The German side is less well covered, with an almost complete absence of the unit reports which could have provided so much valuable information. The only semi-comprehensive German document available is the daily return of the Luftwaffe Quartermaster General, which supposedly records all German aircraft casualties in which damage of more than 10 per cent was sustained. Unfortunately this document does not seem to be complete and it is possible that up to 15 per cent of the Luftwaffe losses are not recorded.

There are ways of filling some of the gaps. Some bodies later drifted ashore from R.A.F. aircraft that had crashed into the sea; the dates and localities at which these bodies were recovered, with a study of prevailing currents and winds, gives some indication of the location of crashes – an unfortunate method to use but of valuable historical interest. The lack of German unit records can be partly overcome by the availability of such documents as private log-books and diaries and of official Luftwaffe victory-confirmation certificates. Partial records of the former Luftgaukommando Holland also exist. Such documents often contain valuable details of times and locations of combats. They are in private hands but it is hoped that the results of many years of study of them will one day be published; the relevant parts for the Battle of Hamburg have kindly been made available to me. There are other useful German documents in the Bundesarchiv, including certain Flak unit records and the interesting documents of the Luftwaffe aircraft-recovery transport units of Luftgaukommando XI which covered much of the area of the Battle of Hamburg.

The R.A.F. 'Y' Service, which listened to the German communications between ground controllers and their night fighters, produced reports of each night's and day's operations. These were not released to the Public Record Office with the documents of the Second World War in 1972 but copies of many of the 'Y' Service reports that had been passed to the U.S.A.A.F. did turn up in the American VIII Bomber Command Mission Reports. Regrettably, the report for this most interesting first night of the Battle of Hamburg was not filed by the Americans but those for all the remaining night and day raids of the battle are available.

The result of these diverse sources is that a partial, though sometimes conflicting, picture can be presented of the aerial encounters of the Hamburg raids. If a combat is presented here as completely factual, the reader can depend upon it being fully supported by reliable evidence. If the words 'probably' or 'possibly' are used, then these terms represent just those degrees of reliability. I am satisfied that the general picture of the aerial combats of the Battle of Hamburg can be presented accurately, but some of the finer details will never be known.

More positive results came from the other two early combats. Both were so close to the Dutch coast that they were within the range of the *Würzburg* radars and were, thus, fully controlled box interceptions. Oberleutnant Ernst-Georg Drünkler caught his Lancaster in Box *Tiger* and shot it straight into the sea with one burst of fire. Another German pilot, probably Hauptmann Rudolf Sigmund, caught another Lancaster and shot it down in Box *Salzhering*. The locations of these British losses are known with reasonable accuracy. The two bombers had been sixty and 100 miles off course (in strict aviation parlance the bombers were 'off track') respectively and should have been many miles further west at the time they were shot down. It can only be assumed that they had both suffered mechanical defects when approaching the German coast and were returning to the nearest point on the English coast. It is recorded that Drünkler's victim was only flying at 1,600 metres (5,000 feet) at the time he shot it down. These combats show how efficient the German box system was in snapping up any bomber that strayed far from the bomber-stream. By coincidence, both Lancasters were from 103 Squadron, which had flown off the highest number of bombers of the night from its airfield at Elsham Wolds.* Twelve Englishmen and two Canadians died.

On the chart of every bomber navigator was marked 'Position A', at 54.45°N, 07.00°E, the point eighty miles from the landfall on the German coast at which the various routes of the bombers from England converged, the place where the vital bomber-stream finally assembled. Position A was 290 miles from England and was reached by the leading aircraft at about twenty minutes after midnight. In theory the stream would be 203 miles long when formed, a distance based on the 53-minute duration planned for the raid on Hamburg and the estimated speed of the bombers when they reached the city.

* Appendixes 4, 5 and 6 contain details of all British, American and German aircraft destroyed in the Battle of Hamburg.

R.A.F. bombers of the Battle of Hamburg period

△ 1. A Halifax Mark II of 405 Squadron, the Canadian Pathfinder squadron based at Gransden Lodge. The semicylindrical object on the ground is probably an extra fuel tank that could be fitted when needed. This Halifax, HR723, flew three times in the Battle of Hamburg and survived operations with two other squadrons before being involved in an accident in a training unit in October 1944.

▽ 2. Aircrews of 75 (New Zealand) Squadron wait for take-off near their Stirlings at Mepal.

(The main R.A.F. bomber of this period, the Lancaster, appears in later photographs.)

The American B-17 – the Flying Fortress

△ 3. The 381st Bomb Group prepares to take off from Ridgewell.

▽ 4. A B-17 of the same group over Germany. Puffs of dark smoke are the bursts of Flak shells, probably fired by radar through the cloud cover.

German night fighters

△ 5. The Messerschmitt 110, the converted day fighter that was so useful as a night fighter. These are early night-fighter examples, not yet fitted with bulky radar aerials on their noses.

▷ 6. A Dornier 217, the converted bomber with which many of the night-fighter units around Hamburg were equipped. This plane, of the 4th Staffel, II/NJG 3, was caught by an Intruder Mosquito while taking off from Westerland, Sylt, on the night of the last R.A.F. raid of the Battle of Hamburg and its pilot, Hauptmann Bahr, had to crash-land in the nearby sand dunes.

▽ 7. A Wild Boar Messerschmitt 109, the day fighter pressed into service for night fighting.

German Flak

△ 8. A battery of 88-mm guns. The photograph shows this standard German gun to advantage but it is probably taken at a training camp. In action, the guns would be dispersed to protected gun pits.

▽ 9. The reflector dish of a *Würzburg* radar set, the standard radar set of both the night-fighter ground control stations and the Flak batteries. The *Würzburgs* were the target for Window, the new device introduced by the R.A.F. in the Battle of Hamburg. These Luftwaffe men are from 3rd Battery, 122nd Railway Flak Regiment, brought to Hamburg as reinforcements after the first raid. The painted bomber symbols are battery successes.

◁ 10. Air Marshal Sir Arthur Harris, Commander-in-Chief of R.A.F. Bomber Command.

▷ 11. Brigadier-General Fred L. Anderson, Commanding General, VIII Bomber Command U.S.A.A.F.

▽ 12. Hitler visits Hamburg in 1935. He is talking with Bürgermeister Karl Krogmann, with a merchant training ship in the background.

Pre-war Hamburg

△ 13. One of Hamburg's many waterways. This is the Nikolaifleet in the Altstadt with the tower of the Nikolaikirche in the centre background and that of the Rathaus further away. This is the area which became the Aiming Point for three of the R.A.F. raids in the Battle of Hamburg.

▽ 14. The public buildings of central Hamburg, seen from the tower of the Nikolaikirche. The Rathaus, with its copper roof, fills the centre of the picture. In the background are the Binnen Alster and the Aussen Alster with the high-class residential area of Rotherbaum on its left bank. The Binnen Alster was completely covered by camouflage during the war.

The weapons of Area Bombing

15. Four-thousand-pound High Capacity blast bombs being delivered to 83 Squadron Lancasters. One of these bombs formed the core of each Lancaster's Area Bombing load.

16. Four-pound 'stick' incendiaries being unpacked and loaded into the 'small-bomb containers' which will then be loaded into bomb bays. It is believed that this scene was photographed at Syerston, home of 61 and 106 Squadrons, during the day before the opening raid of the Battle of Hamburg. The average Syerston Lancaster carried one 4,000-lb bomb and either 1,200 of these 4-lb incendiaries or 960 of the 4-lb and sixty-four of the larger 30-lb incendiaries.

The bomber crews

△ 17. R.A.F., Empire and a few Norwegian aircrew of 76 Squadron relax at Holme on Spalding Moor before going out to their Halifax bombers for one of the raids in the Battle of Hamburg.

▽ 18. Men of the 381st Bomb Group are interrogated after a raid in June 1943. In the centre of the picture is the group commander, Col. Joseph J. Nazzaro, later to become a four-star general.

In theory, also, the bombers in the stream were all flying at exactly the same speed and along the same track from Position A onwards, although at the various heights that their types of aircraft could achieve. But the bomber-stream achieved this neat and compact shape only on paper. In practice, it was an irregular gaggle of aircraft, flying roughly the same course and speed but with increasing extremes of error depending upon the varying degrees of success shown by crews in coping with the problems of dead-reckoning navigation.

Five minutes after flying through the assembly point, the leading aircraft in the bomber-stream started dropping the first Window to be used operationally by the R.A.F. These aircraft had reached that point, thirty-five miles from the first German territory – the islands of Heligoland and Sylt in this case – at which the scientists believed the *Würzburg* radars in the German coastal night-fighter boxes became fully effective. It is not known which aircraft dropped the first bundle of Window; it was almost certainly a Pathfinder. Within twenty seconds, the 2,200 metallized strips in the bundle had dispersed to form a twisting, fluttering little cloud which would descend at 300/400 feet per minute. This one little cloud would appear on a German radar set as the echo of one bomber and would remain effective for at least fifteen minutes. Every bomber would drop one such bundle of Window every minute until it reached the same distance from the German coast on the return flight in two hours time.

When the use of Window became established, it was the bomb aimer in each crew, using a specially fitted chute near his normal position in the nose of the bomber, who became the regular Window dropper. On this first night, however, the squadrons had been told to designate whichever member was thought most suitable for this duty. Most squadrons had decided that the flight engineer was the best man, although wireless operators and bomb aimers were sometimes used and, on one squadron at least, the mid-upper gunners had been given the job, a decision that most of the crews concerned thought a bad one, leaving as it did one of the bomber's gun turrets unoccupied throughout the duration of the flight over enemy territory. Whichever crew member was chosen went down to the flare chute in the cold, dark and empty fuselage or used one of the various traps, sliding windows or small hatches in his aircraft. He settled himself down with a torch and a stop-watch to push out the bundles of strips; it was an uncomfortable and much disliked duty.

I had told my skipper that, as flight engineer, my place was in the cockpit, helping him in operating the aircraft, especially in any emergency. He talked me into it with the famous words, 'They also serve who shove tinfoil strips down the flare chutes.' (Sergeant F. G. Miller, 467 Squadron)

There are a host of stories about minor mishaps that occurred. One man found that the bundles were too bulky to slip easily through the chute so he took off one of his flying boots and pushed the Window out with a foot which became 'rather cold'. Another man pushed his hat out by mistake and another held on to a bundle of Window with one hand and dropped his stop-watch out with the other, 'which took a bit of explaining when we got back'. The records of one squadron show that two of their aircraft had radio aerials carried away after being hit by unopened bundles. An inexperienced flight engineer lost his oxygen connection and switched on the fuselage lights to find it again, resulting in his unhappy mid-upper gunner sitting in a turret which was 'lit up like a large electric bulb'. The black coating of one side of the strips rubbed off easily. Several mid-upper turrets became blackened over and most of the men who had been handling the Window looked like 'nigger minstrels' on their return to England.

Our bomb aimer dropped the Window out of a trap in the underside of the nose. When this was opened, we had an almighty draught straight back down the fuselage and most of the Window seemed to be blowing back into the aeroplane, instead of dropping clear. I have a vivid mental picture of sitting in the wireless position with just the glow of a tiny lamp on the set and watching a steady stream of these little strips streaming past me and disappearing into darkness over the main spar – a bit like watching a shoal of river fish darting along in murky water. (Pilot Officer R. Clarke, 12 Squadron)

It is my claim that I am the only gunner to be wounded by Window. The engineer forgot to remove the elastic from one bundle and, suddenly, there was a tremendous crash and rush of air into the turret and I was hit on the side of the head and eye with a solid bundle of Window, which drew blood. I thought the turret canopy was about to blow off and I grabbed the first thing to hand, the gun triggers. Pandemonium reigned for a few seconds as I loosed off a couple of hundred rounds. Fortunately, apart from my slight scratch, no one else was hurt. Had I been with the U.S.A.A.F., I might have been awarded a Purple Heart. (Sergeant O. Roberts, 49 Squadron)

I was given instructions from the captain to count sixty 'Lancasters' and at the end of each such count to drop a bundle of something in the parcel down the flare chute. One almost strangled as the oxygen cord caught round the chute and, because of the temperature, one could not squat on the floor. So, crouch over the flare chute, count your sixty 'Lancasters' and drop a bundle. Evasive action and bloody bundles scattered all over the place. Banged shins, breathing difficulty, cramps, but oh boy, was it worth it! (Flight Sergeant A. J. O'Brien, 460 Squadron)

It should be stressed that these mishaps did not prevent the majority of the British bombers dropping their Window properly and, as Flight Sergeant O'Brien says, it was to be worth all the trouble.

The first outposts of the *Himmelbett* system protecting Hamburg from the bomber's approach were the boxes of *Auster* and *Hummer*, whose radar stations were on the islands of Sylt and Heligoland respectively. Their *Freya* radars had been plotting the head of the approaching bomber-stream for some time and without difficulty. It is not known who the fighter-control officers were at *Auster* and *Hummer* but it can be assumed that reliable men were in charge of these important boxes. Neither is it known which German night fighters were patrolling the north-western edges of these boxes but it can also be assumed that their crews were the most experienced available. It was always the policy of the night-fighter boxes on the coast to reach out as far as possible and attempt to strike as early as possible at the head of a bomber-stream.

Window was an instant success for the British. Within twenty minutes of the first dropping of the metallized strips, the bomber-stream was flying through three of the main chain of night-fighter boxes on the coast – *Hummer*, *Auster* and *Pelikan* – and, also, through four smaller inland boxes – *1C*, *2A* and the *Hummel A* and *C* boxes. There were further boxes on the fringe of the bombers' route that would normally have been picking up targets on the flanks of the stream. Because of Window, not one of these boxes was able to perform normally.

There is no need for a long description of what the Germans

later called '*der Düppelschock*'. The *Freya* radars of the ground stations were not affected but the *Würzburgs*, which were essential for the close control of the German fighters, were. It can be calculated that the echoes produced by 7,000 bundles of Window were effective at any one time. So, for every genuine echo on the *Würzburg* radars, there were ten false ones. The German fighters were sent chasing all over the sky for bombers that did not exist. During some periods, the slowly descending strips became so intermingled that the German radars were completely flooded with false returns and the control officers had to give up attempting to guide the fighters at all. Ober-leutnant Joachim Wendtland was an experienced fighter control officer who was absent from his own box at that time but was at the headquarters of the 2nd Fighter Division at Stade, training other control officers. 'It was just like trying to find a ball of glass in a barrel of peas, but you had to find it at once; there was no time for looking because the screen was constantly changing.'

It was just as frustrating in the air, where Window was equally effective against the *Lichtenstein* radar sets fitted to the night fighters.

My radar operator suddenly had more targets than could have been possible. I know that I got some directions from him to head on but these were impossible to maintain because we couldn't possibly have overtaken the bombers so fast if they had been real targets. I was picking up targets that didn't exist everywhere. We kept finishing up behind a target but there was never the slipstream of the bomber. In addition to all these troubles, it was my first operational flight. I had no success. (Unteroffizier Otto Kutzner, 5./NJG 3)

Otto Kutzner's experience was typical of many. This next man was the radar operator in a fighter originally detailed to patrol a box just south of Hamburg.

When we reached our box, we were immediately told by the fighter control officer that everything was jammed and that we were simply to fly in the direction of Hamburg. This was unusual; I had never heard this order before. I was surprised. We flew towards Hamburg and soon had many contacts on my radar screen. We thought that we were right in the centre of the bomber-stream. The first impression was that the bombers were heading straight for us. Therefore, we turned, in order to get in behind one of these but, after the turn, they were still coming too fast. I said, 'slow down, slower still, you're too fast'. The pilot said there must be something wrong because he had already let down the flaps and was flying as slowly as possible. We got contact after contact but not one of them was a firm one. We could hear on the radio that the officer on the ground was having trouble too.

This went on for a good hour. We saw firing here and there but I couldn't tell whether any aircraft were being shot down. We landed at Stade, instead of our own airfield at Vechta. I seem to remember that we were ordered to land there so that the *Gruppe* staff could ask us all about the flight. My pilot went into the headquarters and had a conversation with Major Lent, whom he knew very well. He came back and said something like, 'they seem to be all helpless and bewildered'. (Unteroffizier Rolf Angersbach, 3./NJG 3)

Every British bomber wireless operator was normally given a radio frequency known to be used between the German ground controllers and their night fighters. The wireless operators would normally listen to this frequency and, whenever they heard German voices, would turn on a small radio transmitter that would broadcast the sound of one of the bomber's engines in an attempt to drown the German voices. On this night, however, the wireless operators were ordered not to carry out this jamming so that the effects of Window on the German defences could be more clearly heard. The German voices were also being listened to at the three stations of the R.A.F.'s 'Y' Listening Service in England. The reaction of the German controllers was a source of great satisfaction to those R.A.F. personnel who heard the German voices. 'We gained an impression of panic and confusion from the German controllers. They were highly agitated.' 'Stress, fear, anger and bewilderment were evident in their voices.'

In Germany, the bad news of the dislocation caused by Window travelled fast through the Luftwaffe chain of command. General Kammhuber in Berlin heard it within the hour. He says, *'Die ganze Abwehr war mit einem Schlag blind'* – 'The whole defence was blinded at one stroke.' Walter Knickmeier, an ace fighter-control officer in Holland says *'Düppel war das Todesurteil für die geführte Raumnachtjagd'* – 'Window was the death sentence for controlled night fighting in boxes.'

Sixty miles and fifteen minutes flying time after the first

Window had been dropped, the navigators and bomb aimers of six Pathfinder aircraft at the front of the bomber-stream peered intently into the flickering screens of their H2S radar sets. At the moment that the outline of the German coast passed through the centre of the screen, each of these aircraft released one Target Indicator bomb. Target Indicators were manufactured in three standard colours: red, green and yellow. The ones released over the German coast were yellow. Their tails were blown off by a barometric fuse at a height of 3,000 feet and sixty brilliant pyrotechnic candles cascaded out of each bomb and fell slowly to the ground. The beautiful firework display of golden colour was visible for miles. These were 'route-markers' and were dropped by these skilled Pathfinder crews so that the bombers behind them could pack themselves into the tightest possible stream after their long crossing over the featureless North Sea. The time was forty minutes after midnight and thirty of the Pathfinder Backer-Up crews would renew the markers until the tail of the bomber-stream crossed the coast.

The yellow route-markers were dropped over a small but prominent peninsula on the coast of Schleswig, just north of the little seaside resort of Büsum and west of the larger town of Heide. This point was some fifty miles south of the Danish border and the bomber routes would not pass much nearer to that friendly country during the Battle of Hamburg. Despite this, the letters and diaries of former Bomber Command men contain frequent references to incidents taking place 'over Denmark' or 'at the Danish coast'. One man even refers to 'Heide, Denmark' in his dairy. The error is repeated in the records of several R.A.F. squadrons. It appears that, to many men, anything north of Hamburg was in Denmark, although the navigators in every crew had maps showing the actual border quite clearly. It would be interesting to know why this error became so widespread. Two bombers with mechanical trouble took the opportunity to unload their bombs as soon as they crossed the coast; the dropping of the bombs on German soil would allow their crews to count this as an operational flight. One person was killed in Heide.

The route-markers were of some help to the Germans. An observer post ten miles away, at Meldorf, reported what it had seen to the Headquarters of the 2nd Fighter Division at Stade and the report would have been repeated to all other interested units. The German night fighters in the area also saw the markers and some came looking around that point for bomber targets. Once again, there are gaps in our knowledge but a fairly reliable picture can be given. Incredibly, nothing happened for thirty minutes, during which time the route-markers were steadily renewed and more than 500 bombers flew safely over them. Then, a night fighter, scouting around on the seaward side of the markers, finally picked up a bomber. One long burst of cannon fire was enough. There was no return fire and the bomber was seen by many other crews to fall in flames and then break up or explode above the sea. The bomber involved was probably a 76 Squadron Halifax which was flying in the fifth wave of the attack. The identity of the German night fighter is not known. It was the only German success at the coast.

The next combat occurred just five minutes later. The crew of Sergeant A. Fletcher, flying a Halifax of 51 Squadron, were on their first operation. A German fighter spotted the Halifax and attacked from dead astern but the bombers' tail gunner was alert and returned the fire at once. The German fire missed; the bombers' fire did not and the fighter, the type of which was not identified by the bomber's crew, went down in a steep dive and with a red glow indicating a fire. This combat probably ties in with a German report of a Dornier 217 of 5./NJG 3 which crashed near Flensburg after being damaged in action. Oberfeldwebel Wilhelm Ziegler was probably trying to find his home airfield at Schleswig when he crashed. He and his flight engineer were killed but his radar operator was unhurt. It is possible that Ziegler had just shot down the 76 Squadron Halifax; the two combats took place in the same area. The success of Sergeant Fletcher's crew had a sad aftermath. They flew three more operations in the next five nights but, on the last of these, were shot down by a German night fighter into the sea only a few miles from the scene of this first nights' success. There were no survivors.

The bomber-stream flew on towards its next turning point, twenty-seven miles north-north-west of Hamburg. Some air-craft released leaflets near the German towns along the route and more would be dropped over Hamburg and on the return route. This leaflet effort was part of the Allied propa-

ganda warfare. Bomber Command had agreed to drop leaflets
on Germany but only along the routes its aircraft would be
flying on bomber operations. American bombers performed
the same service by day. Flak and searchlights were encountered, the greatest concentration being along the banks of the
Kiel Canal over which the bomber-stream passed. This was
a very unpopular area and crews disliked being routed over it.
The Flak and searchlight defences here led to the destruction
of another bomber. A Stirling of 75 Squadron, struggling along
at a lower height than the better types, was coned in searchlights and heavily engaged by Flak. The pilot dived and turned
to get out of the searchlights but, in doing so, left the bomber-
stream and the protection of Window. The radar operator of
Feldwebel Meissner, whose fighter had been patrolling Box
Kiebitz C a little to the north, picked up the Stirling on his
radar and the bomber was soon finished off. Three of the
bomber's crew managed to get out and parachute to safety,
becoming the first prisoners of the Battle of Hamburg.

Only one more combat was recorded by a bomber during
this part of the flight; it was an inconclusive brush between
another Stirling and a fighter reported as a Messerschmitt 109.
The entire bomber-stream – over 200 miles long and containing over 700 aircraft – had passed through all the boxes
guarding the northern approaches to Hamburg with the loss
of only two bombers on or near the designated route. It is
probable that not one combat had been the result of a standard
ground-controlled interception. Window had already saved
many R.A.F. lives. But Window could never save the lives of
the men in those bombers which strayed too far from the
bomber-stream and two more of these had also been detected
and swiftly dispatched. Both were Halifaxes and both were
badly off course to the north. In Box *Kiebitz A*, near Schleswig,
Leutnant Böttinger gained the first success of his night-fighting
career when he shot down a 158 Squadron aircraft which was
thirty miles off course and, over the Danish border, a 51
Squadron aircraft was caught in Box *Ameise* flying the correct
heading but sixty miles from the bomber-stream. The losses
of these two bombers were typical examples of the inexperience
of new crews; these were on their first and second operations
respectively.*

* Two contributors give further details of what happened to the 51

Some space has been devoted to descriptions of these early combats because they demonstrate the effect of Window in protecting those aircraft able to keep in the bomber-stream and the dangers to those that could not. The vast majority of the bombers had flown safely on to reach the last turning point before the target. The head of the bomber-stream reached this spot, above the village of Kellinghausen and only seven minutes flying time from the centre of Hamburg. They were the forerunners of a force of 740 bombers preparing to attack the city.

Two airmen, both on their first operational flight, have recorded those moments as they approached Hamburg:

I remember, on the outward journey, how forlorn I felt, wondering what lay ahead and feeling distinctly queasy in the stomach but at the same time determined to put on a brave front with these hardened veterans I was flying with. It was when we were flying south over the Kiel Canal that certain changes came over the crew. The breathing over the intercom, which before had been fairly measured, now became quickened and loudened quite considerably; the speech became very clipped and, at odd moments, tempers were obviously rather frayed with more than a spot of bad language as the target area approached. However, the thing that impressed me about Warrant Officer Haywood and his crew, and still does, was that at no time was discipline or efficiency ever lost and, afterwards, I was very thankful indeed that I cut my teeth with such a crew. (Flight Sergeant F. H. Tritton, 100 Squadron)

Squadron Halifax, which was captained by Sergeant W. J. Murray. A letter from the Danish town of Aabenraa tells how the Halifax crashed in an orchard on the north bank of the Flensburg Fjord near Sønderborg. Local police and German soldiers found five dead airmen and two more who were still alive but badly hurt. One of these asked for a Catholic priest and the other, in German, asked where he was. 'When he heard that he was in Denmark he said, "With friends!" When it was rumoured that two English sergeants were in the Sønderborg hospital, the population sent heaps of flowers but, when the German authorities learnt of this, they demanded that the flowers be removed.' The two men died soon afterwards.

The second postscript comes in a letter from the radar operator of the night fighter. He tells how a party of German sailors arrived the following morning to examine the wrecked bomber. A curious naval rating was advised not to go too near because of the possibility of unexploded bombs. The Halifax had been carrying a 1,000-lb bomb with a twelve-hour delay. The orderly was blown to pieces when this exploded.

I made final calculations to alter course so that we would run over the centre of Hamburg. After a double check, I called the Skipper. 'In four minutes time, we turn on to the target, course one six zero. I'll call you again.' I timed the four minutes and called, 'O.K. Turn one six zero.' Tony acknowledged and the plane banked. I called the bomb aimer, 'It will be all yours in three and a half minutes, Dennie.' Bill took over the releasing of the Window bundles and I could hear Dennie's heavy breathing as he made himself comfortable on his belly over the bomb-sight. (Flight Sergeant E. J. Insull, 218 Squadron)

Bomber Command raids on German cities so often proved to be disappointing. Bad weather could delay or split up the bombers; Pathfinder markers could go astray; strong German defences could deter even the bravest bomb aimers. Some raids might appear successful, with apparently accurate marking and concentrated bombing, but photographic reconnaissance later showed that the raid had missed the main part of the target city, perhaps falling in open country or on decoy fire targets. But, on this night, Window had enabled the bomber force to arrive almost intact just to the north of an important German city which, with its position on the wide River Elbe, should be clearly seen on the H2S sets of the Pathfinders. There was no cloud and only a gentle wind. Bomber Command was not often presented with such a favourable set of conditions for bombing.

At the head of the bomber-stream flew the leading elements of the Pathfinders. There should have been fifty-eight of these – twenty-eight marker aircraft and thirty 'non-markers'. These last were Pathfinder training crews which had not yet graduated to marking duties; they carried only bombs and flares and were present here to 'thicken up' the front of the bomber-stream so that the early marker aircraft should not be exposed alone to the German defences. None of the aircraft from this opening force had been shot down but four had been forced to turn back and sixteen more were either late reaching Hamburg or unsure of their position and they did not mark and bomb on time. In theory, the opening Pathfinder aircraft all turned at exactly the same position, twenty-seven miles north-north-west of the centre of Hamburg, but it can be assumed from later events that a moderate amount of scattering had taken place since the German coast had been crossed.

Bomb doors were opened soon after the turn and the bombing runs commenced.

The German defences were quiet. The Flak commanders of German cities sometimes ordered their searchlights and Flak batteries to remain silent in the hope that the bombers would fail to find the city and there was a considerable lull on this occasion. This was of great benefit to the leading bombers. They were able to cross the entire outer ring of Hamburg's defences without being fired at and the delay enabled the Window that was being dropped to start becoming effective.

The Pathfinder method chosen for this attack was 'Newhaven Groundmarking' and the timetable for the opening of the raid was as follows:

00.57 — Twenty Blind Marker-Illuminators each drop two yellow markers and sixteen flares.
Thirty Non-Markers drop H.E. bombs and flares.
00.58–01.00   Eight Visual Markers each drop five red markers.
01.00   Zero Hour.
01.02   Lancasters of 1st Wave start bombing.

The twenty Blind Markers were to attempt to identify the Aiming Point by H2S radar and drop their yellow Target Indicators there, at the same time releasing white illuminating flares. With these yellow Target Indicators as a guide and the flares providing illumination, the bomb aimers of the Visual Marker aircraft were then to find the Aiming Point by eye and place their red Target Indicators on it. These red markers – forty if the plan worked properly – would then take priority over the yellows when the Main Force started bombing. All these Pathfinder aircraft – markers and non-markers – also dropped bombs but only high explosives. No incendiaries were allowed before Zero Hour so that early fires should not be confused with markers.

Fifty-four aircraft had arrived and should have bombed in the first three minutes of the raid; forty-one actually bombed in the first *five* minutes. The honour of opening the raid – dead on time at 00.57 – was shared by three aircraft: Lancasters of 83 and 97 Squadrons and a Halifax of 405 Squadron. The greater credit should perhaps go to the 83 Squadron aircraft, captained by Pilot Officer A. C. Shipway. This aircraft had developed faults in most of the pilot's instruments soon after take-off; only the artificial horizon had remained reliable.

Instead of turning back, Shipway had pressed on, guessing his speed and height. He had reached Hamburg six minutes early and had flown around the city, his navigator and bomb aimer studying its layout on their H2S set. Shipway had then said, 'It's about time someone started this party' and released his two yellow Target Indicators and bomb-load. The other two aircraft that bombed at this time did not release markers.

The German searchlights and Flak had come into action just as Pilot Officer Shipway bombed. His aircraft collected a small Flak hole but he returned safely to receive a Distinguished Flying Cross for his night's work. Several of the other leading Pathfinder aircraft were also hit. Flak could be very effective and dangerous at the opening of a raid. The Halifaxes, flying slightly lower than the Lancasters, seem to have been the worst affected. Pilot Officer Harry Gowan was the Canadian pilot of a 405 Squadron Halifax.

As a Pathfinder, I was very conscious of my responsibility to mark the target accurately and a straight and level bombing run was essential. As we approached the target we were caught in searchlights; the feeling of nakedness in the glare of searchlights was most unnerving and the light was blinding in intensity. The Flak was extremely accurate. Shells were bursting all around us and we received several hits. One piece came through the windscreen in front of me and passed between me and the engineer so close that I could almost feel the displacement of air. It passed through the bulkhead and narrowly missed the navigator who was bent over his charts. My face was peppered with glass fragments but, fortunately, I received no major cuts and my eyes escaped injury.

Suddenly, I heard a cry of pain on the intercom. By the process of elimination I found it was the mid-upper gunner. I sent the wireless operator to look after the wounded man while we continued our run-up. The bomb aimer found that the electrical system was out of order so he had to release the bombs manually. The relief when they went was immeasurable and I immediately took evasive action and finally got clear of the searchlights.

The wireless operator had gotten the wounded man out of the turret and laid him on the floor of the fuselage. He told me that he had been badly hit and was in extreme pain. I told him to give him a shot of morphine but Mac – the gunner – would not hear of it so I told the wireless operator to make him as comfortable and as warm as possible and to stay with him. We headed for base as fast as our damaged aircraft would take us.

The mid-upper gunner survived the flight to England but died eight days later.

The Pathfinders completed their first task but many of their markers had not been dropped accurately. At least two Blind Markers and one Visual Marker had placed their Target Indicators short of the city and the remaining markers had fallen in four groups, marking out the corners of a rough rectangle measuring four miles by three miles, with only a few markers forming a fifth group in the middle of this rectangle. Thirty-nine yellow and red Target Indicators cascaded prettily over Hamburg. The Pathfinder crews who had opened the raid flew away to the south. None had been shot down.

The first wave of the Main Force, all Lancasters, came in hard on the heels of the Pathfinders and, without a moment's delay, their large 4,000-pounder blast bombs and thousands and thousands of incendiaries rained down on to the areas marked by the Pathfinders. It was at this time that Window became fully effective and Hamburg's Flak and searchlight defences – both controlled by *Würzburg* radars – were rendered almost useless. Any doubts that the bomber crews may have had about the effectiveness of the bundles of strips they had been dropping so laboriously, vanished. The most vivid memories of these men about this first Hamburg raid were of the effect of Window on the defences of this target.

The sight approaching Hamburg was quite fantastic. It was as if a black swath had been cut through a sea of light and flashes. The few lights and flashes from guns within the black area, such as there still were, were completely out of control, the searchlight beams quickly traversing the area at random. The searchlights and guns at either side of the swath were under control but at too far a distance to cause any problems. My navigator told me I was slightly off course but I was happy to fly the aircraft down the centre of this dark corridor. It was obviously safer to keep to the middle of the road. (Flight Lieutenant V. Wood, 12 Squadron)

Until that moment, we had treated this Window – all these bundles in the aircraft – with some levity. But it was a magic effect, still very vivid in my mind. The Flak and searchlights were all over the place from that moment. (Flight Lieutenant S. Baker, 7 Squadron)

Our 'sprog' crew had been thrown in at the deep end during the

Battle of the Ruhr; our grand total of five ops had all been on targets in 'Happy Valley'. We had returned from the target on no less than four out of these occasions with damage to the aircraft caused by Flak. This high standard of accuracy by the German defences was my only criterion until July 24/25th.

It was with much relief that I observed the disorganized defences of Hamburg from my mid-upper turret. Over the very well lit-up target, I could see dozens of our aircraft proceeding on their bombing runs in what I can only describe as 'a most orderly and peaceful manner'. This was a new experience for me and I felt reasonably safe over a target for the first time in my short operational career. (Sergeant S. Bethell, 467 Squadron)

The master searchlights and all the others were waving aimlessly about in the sky like a man trying to swat a flying ant in a swarm. All the crew were delighted. My bomb aimer said that his bloody hands were frozen with dropping Window but it was well worth it and could we try to do as many trips in the next few weeks as possible so as to finish our tour before the enemy found a solution. (Flight Lieutenant G. F. Pentony, 429 Squadron)

It was amazing.... It was the most interesting trip of my whole tour. (Flight Sergeant M. M. Cole, 50 Squadron)

The attack of the Main Force was timed to last for fifty minutes and, for once, it was carried out faster than planned. The good flying conditions and the effect of Window on the German defences allowed many crews to reach Hamburg before the time allotted for their bombing wave and these crews took advantage of this to bomb early and get away on their return flight. The table opposite gives both the planned and the actual progress of the Main Force bombing.

Unharried by the German defences and flying under perfect conditions, the majority of the Main Force aircraft could carry out their bombing runs in the approved manner, the light from Hamburg's erratic searchlights and from the spreading fires in the city turning night into partial day. Men remember the sight of many other aircraft running into the target together. There were the usual stories of men looking up in horror to see another bomber just above them, bomb doors open, but there were no accidents. There were, also, the usual examples of crews failing to bomb on a first run and coming back, in one case against the stream, to try again. The naval officer who was flying as bomb aimer in a 78 Squadron

Halifax surprised his crew when he treated his first run as a dummy one and asked his pilot to go round again. 'Normally, I was known as "the Admiral" but, after Hamburg, I was known as "Round-again Robertson"' One Halifax flew right over the city but could not release its bomb-load because the bomb doors would not open. The bombs were eventually dropped on a ship seen off the German coast. One crew deserves particular mention for its steadfastness. Pilot Officer Clinton's Halifax, of 405 Squadron, was an early Pathfinder which had flown fifty miles of its return flight before the crew discovered that three 1,000-pounders had 'hung up' in the bomb bay. Clinton's crew took the bombs back to Hamburg.

Wave	Planned Bombing	Actual Bombing
1st Wave 01.02–01.10	118 Lancasters of 1 and 5 Groups 10 Pathfinder Backers-Up	151 Main Force 14 Pathfinders
2nd Wave 01.10–01.18	43 Lancasters of 3 and 5 Groups 70 Halifaxes of 4 Group 9 Pathfinder Backers-Up	131 Main Force 13 Pathfinders
3rd Wave 01.18–01.26	117 Stirlings of 3 and 8 Groups 9 Pathfinder Backers-Up	116 Main Force 10 Pathfinders
4th Wave 01.26–01.34	73 Wellingtons of 1, 4 and 6 Groups 34 Halifaxes of 4 Group 9 Pathfinder Backers-Up	79 Main Force 11 Pathfinders
5th Wave 01.34–01.42	105 Halifaxes of 4 and 6 Groups 9 Pathfinder Backers-Up	119 Main Force 7 Pathfinders
6th Wave 01.42–01.50	121 Lancasters of 1 and 5 Groups 7 Pathfinder Backers-Up	13 Main Force 3 Pathfinders

One Main Force Halifax bombed late, at 01.55.

A successful Bomber Command raid, seen from above the target, was like a gigantic firework display. The yellow and red Target Indicators of the early Pathfinders were replaced by the green ones of the Backers-Up; over 200 of these beautiful 'greens' were dropped over Hamburg during the Main Force attack. Among and around the markers could be seen the bright, quick flashes of the ordinary high-explosive bombs or the larger, slower explosions of the 4,000-pounders, described as being 'like giant sunflowers opening out as they burst', 'exploding as white circles of concussion spread out on their impact and then slowly resuming their original flame colour', 'not a sudden flash, as one might expect, but like a flare brightening and then disappearing, rather like a light from a lighthouse'. And, all the time, there were the twinkling little white lights of thousands of incendiaries igniting all over the bombing area. Fires, some of them large, started to burn on the ground, glowing red but soon becoming obscured by the dense columns of smoke they produced.

In the air, most of the German searchlights continued to wave aimlessly about; other searchlights stood rigidly upright, 'like a forest of American redwood trees', one man says. The Hamburg Flak continued to fire vast quantities of shells into the sky but the bomber men soon realized that this was now wild 'barrage' fire, not the radar-predicted Flak that could be so dangerous. Many diaries and squadron records contain references to new kinds of Flak shell seen bursting over the city that night. The most spectacular of these were shells seen bursting 'like a Catherine-wheel in a circle, with points of white light shooting out' or like 'flaming daisies or Prince of Wales feathers'. Some crews thought that these were heavy shells fired by warships in Hamburg's docks.

The German night fighters could do little more than the Flak to protect Hamburg from the battering the city was so obviously receiving. A few fighters were seen but these did little more than hang around the northern and southern edges of the city's defences, hoping for a lucky contact with a bomber. There are several reports of single-engined German fighters seen. It is known that the Wild Boar unit, JG 300, was not sent into action in its entirety on this night but it is possible that some aircraft of the Wild Boar *Gruppe* at Oldenburg, only seventy-five miles from Hamburg, had been sent off by local initiative. Although this cannot be confirmed, the Catherine-wheel shell bursts seen over Hamburg were undoubtedly a special type of shell fired in various combinations over German cities as aerial 'signposts' for the Wild Boar fighters.

The Main Force lost only three bombers over this, one of the most heavily defended cities in Germany. A Halifax of the second wave and a squadron commander's Stirling of the third wave fell on the southern and northern edges of the target area respectively; the only man in each crew to survive later reported that a German fighter was responsible in each case. Another Stirling was manoeuvring to avoid searchlights when it struck another aircraft, believed to be a Junkers 88, head on. A four-foot section of the Stirling's starboard wing disappeared but its Canadian pilot, Flying Officer Geoff Turner, brought his plane safely back to England.* The other aircraft was seen to dive steeply towards the ground and was claimed as a German fighter destroyed but the Luftwaffe Quartermaster General's documents do not contain an entry that can confirm this. The only success for the Flak was the complete destruction of a 166 Squadron Wellington which was seen by many crews to be caught in one searchlight beam and then coned by many others. The Wellington did not escape from the hail of Flak fired into the cone and there were no survivors when it crashed into countryside south of Hamburg.

* Flying Officer Turner's crew and the new second pilot they were carrying were all killed when their Stirling was shot down on a raid to Mannheim on 23 September 1943.

NOTE

1. Public Record Office AIR 27/306.

9

Under the Bombs

It had been a beautiful summer's evening in Hamburg. One lady, in the suburbs, remembers that her family had sat up late in their garden, debating whether to go to bed or whether to wait up to see if there would be an alarm. The sirens had sounded at 9.20 p.m. but the All Clear had followed only ten minutes later. It is not known what had caused this false alarm. When the bombers did approach, the warning system of the Hamburg defence authorities worked smoothly and the several degrees of alert were all given in very generous time. *Luftgefahr 30*, a thirty-minute warning by telephone to all Flak, searchlight and civil-defence units and also to railways and factories, warning them to douse the outside lights that they were allowed to use until the danger of air raid became imminent, was issued at nineteen minutes past midnight when the head of the bomber-stream had been thirty-eight minutes away.

This preliminary warning brought many people out of their beds. Traugott Bauer-Schlichtegroll, a schoolboy Flak helper at a battery at Schnelsen, on the northern outskirts of Hamburg, was one of them.

We staggered from our beds when the loudspeakers awoke us with the order. One of my friends said, 'What nonsense! Always these alerts and nothing ever happens. It's stupid to lose so much sleep.' But the second degree of readiness soon came and then the report that the enemy were assembling at Brunsbüttel for an attack on Hamburg. Everyone was looking over to the west where the first Flak fire would be seen and we waited for information from the radar post.

Some of us had only been there for a few days and our excitement was feverish. Some boys behaved very dramatically and said that our eardrums would burst when we opened fire but the old hands calmed them down. 'It won't be too bad.' We soon heard the humming of engines, like a thousand bees.

The control rooms of the various authorities in Hamburg were soon fully manned. The party hierarchy took up their positions in the concrete bunker dug into the garden of

Gauleiter Kaufmann's residence. The police, fire and other civil-defence leaders sat round a large table in their bomb-proof operations room under the Police Headquarters at Neuer Wall in the old city; this was only 400 yards from the Pathfinders' Aiming Point. Chief of Police Kehrl presided here. The Flak and searchlight defences were controlled by the Luftwaffe officers of Luftgau XI inside one of the Flak towers on the Heiligengeistfeld. Gauleiter Kaufmann was in theoretical overall charge but most of his subordinates and colleagues knew their jobs and no big decisions would need to be taken yet.

There is some evidence that the bombers were initially thought to be flying on further east, towards Lübeck, instead of towards Hamburg. This mistake was partly the result of the disturbance of the German radars caused by Window and partly because no previous raid had ever approached Hamburg from the north. However, this confusion did not prevent further timely warnings being issued. *Luftgefahr 15* was given thirty-three minutes before the first bombs fell and the main public alarm, the *Fliegeralarm*, was sounded at 12.33 a.m. before the leading bombers had even crossed the German coast.

One of the greatest problems for the authorities was that of persuading the city's one and a half million civilians to go to their shelters. The majority of air-raid alarms turned out to be false ones and those alarms that did develop into raids were rarely serious. A great many people preferred to stand at their windows or in doorways with their neighbours watching developments. Air raids could be highly spectacular events provided bombs did not fall in one's immediate neighbourhood.

The people of Hamburg listened carefully to their radios for information. The first sign that their city might be threatened had come when all regular stations in the Hamburg area went off the air. The silence that followed was broken by an announcement that *Reichssender Hamburg* had taken over and, then, a voice familiar to all Hamburgers had spoken. 'Many aircraft approaching Hamburg. The first bombs will fall in a few minutes. Everyone must go to their shelters.' The voice was that of Staatssekretär Georg Ahrens who was sitting in Gauleiter Kaufmann's bunker with a direct line to Hamburg's radio station. Ahrens always performed this duty and many people still remember him. He was trusted because the information he broadcast was always reliable and was popular because the tone of his voice was so reassuring. Everyone in Hamburg called him 'Onkel Baldrian'.*

The first bombers were heard over the city at 12.51 a.m. – Pathfinders which had arrived early and were flying around, trying to establish their position before their marking time six minutes later. The aircraft noises were duly reported to the control room at Police Headquarters and logged:

Air Raid Alarm No. 319

12.51 a.m.   Enemy planes arriving from Hensmoore Heide.

12.53 a.m.   Three or four planes over Altona, flying north-west to outskirts of city.[1]

A short-lived hope that the bombers were not intending to mount a major raid on Hamburg soon died when the first reports of bombs dropped in the city were received.

I must now declare to the reader that it is impossible to provide a fully comprehensive description of what happened in Hamburg during this series of raids. In dealing with a city of nearly two million persons which had nearly 10,000 tons of bombs dropped upon it during a short period, the scale of events was too vast to allow a full coverage in any one book. Different authors will use different methods to deal with this problem. This book will use a combination of general description and résumé – both based on reliable sources – and personal accounts from survivors. Journalistic-type descriptions of events will not be employed; I was not there and I prefer eyewitnesses who were there to provide their own first-hand images. The reader is asked to do two things that will help to a better understanding of these events. Please remember that these raids were not a corporate event; they were a mass of highly individual incidents experienced by ordinary people. If you read a description by one person, you must try to imagine a whole host of similar experiences by many other persons. Second, please remember that it is only the survivors who speak to you. The dead suffered even greater horrors. Those readers who have lived through a heavy air raid will

---

* *Baldrian* is German for valerian, an old herbal medicine taken to soothe indigestion. 'Staatssekretär' means 'Clerk to the State Council', the 'right-hand man' of the Gauleiter.

have some idea of what happened in Hamburg. For those fortunate ones who never had that experience, this book will never be more than a partial substitute.

The Target Indicators were beautiful but frightening. The official observers were the policemen who had been sent to the tops of the various water towers in the city. Oberfeldwebel Kretschmer was on the Rothenburgsort tower.

The whole of Rothenburgsort glowed in a bright white light from flares. After the enemy had set up this illumination, the first 'Christmas trees' began to fall. Immediately afterwards, in rapid succession, the fire, the high-explosive, and the phosphorus bombs were dropped. I also observed that phosphorus appeared to be raining down. At first, a large fireball was visible in the sky; after some time it dissolved into flowing strips that spilled over the houses, most of which were already aflame. Now fires were visible everywhere, even on the water, where boats and ships were aflame. The latter fact constituted my last message to Sector IV before our communications were interrupted.

Shortly after my last message, the water tower was hit by a high-explosive bomb to the right of the entrance. The entrance door was thrown into the tower and a terrific blast of air went up through the building. In the meantime, the storm of fire had reached such proportions that I had to take cover on my knees behind the parapet.[2]

Leutnant Walter Luth was a naval doctor whose patrol boat was in Hamburg for refitting after a long tour of duty in the Gulf of Finland. He also observed the opening of the attack.

There were only odd bursts of Flak in the distance and the ghostly arms of the searchlights in the clear, starlit sky. Then, suddenly, there were yellow torches in the sky and the murmuring of engines coming ever nearer. Red and green marker bombs followed. They floated slowly towards the ground – boundary markers of death! The engine noise above us became louder and every gun of the Flak from Hamburg and of the ships fired. But still no bombs! It was so bright that one could have read the *Hamburger Tageblatt* without difficulty. And then it all started!

Frau Alma Zeiher was a housewife in Winterhude.

We didn't go down to the shelter; we wanted to see the opening of the raid. There were four of us on the flat roof of our block. We could see these things burning in the sky – like burning gold – not actually burning but glowing in many strips. It was the first time we had seen this type of thing and we asked each other what it was. No one knew. After ten minutes, we went down to the basement. The bombs started to fall, not near us yet, but we were frightened.

Next day, people in the street were talking about the golden colours we had seen. They said it was *Phosphorregen* – phosphor-rain.

Target Indicators had been used in the Hamburg area before but the multitude dropped on this night provided the first sight of them for many local people. Most Germans called them *Christbäume* – Christmas trees – but the local dialect word – *Tannenbaum* – was the expression more often used in Hamburg. Two people in the quotations above – the Rothenburgsort tower observer and the Winterhude housewife – refer to a 'rain of phosphorus'. The first reference is understandable because it is in a report written soon after the event but the second occurred in a conversation with the lady concerned, while this book was being prepared. Frau Zeiher's belief, that the Target Indicators 'rained' phosphorus down over the city, is still a strongly held one among many Hamburg people. Even after a long conversation, she was most reluctant to accept the true explanation. It is true that the R.A.F. was using large 30-lb incendiaries to reach the bottom floors of German buildings. This was the infamous 'phosphorus bomb' part of whose filling consisted of eleven pounds of phosphorus, usually in solid form but sometimes, because of production difficulties, in liquid form. Phosphorus is a chemical which burns brightly on being exposed to air and is most difficult to extinguish, often flaring up again as soon as a stream of water is turned off it. The Germans hated these bombs and any type of burn was, and often still is, attributed to phosphorus although the number of true phosphorus burns was minute. It is commonly believed in Hamburg that the city was subjected to particularly large numbers of this type of bomb. No attempt has been made to correct the misconceptions about phosphorus contained in the personal accounts of survivors – so as to preserve their freshness and originality – but it must be stated categorically that the R.A.F. did not subject Hamburg to 'a rain of phosphorus' from Target Indicators and a study of Bomber Command documents even shows that the number of 30-lb incendiaries dropped during the Battle of Hamburg was slightly less than on other German targets during this period of the war. On the other hand, it has to be stated that the 'anti-morale' aspect of the 30-lb 'phosphorus' incendiary was fully appreciated by Bomber Command Headquarters.

The sight of the Target Indicators and the sound of the bombs that followed persuaded those people who had been reluctant to take shelter to do so now. People rushed down the stairs to their basements or through the streets to public shelters, some scantily dressed, most carrying the suitcases stuffed with valuables that every family kept packed for just this eventuality. They could not be sure that the rest of their belongings would exist in an hour's time.

Frau Otti Schwarze lived in Harvestehude.

When my husband and I came out of the house, we could already see the Christmas trees nearly overhead; they were whitish yellow. They lit up the street so brightly that we could have read a book. We knew what these meant and we were frightened. We ran to the public shelter, not down the middle of the street but along the side. A young boy was running down the centre of the street and it was so bright that we could recognize him. We could hear the loud noise of the bombers' engines and we didn't want the men in the planes to see us. It was darker against the side, under the balconies. There were no bombs just yet – at least not near us. We reached the shelter safely and showed the shelter warden our place card which gave each person's room and seat number. I still have my card for Room Number 229.

Frau Rosa Todt was in Neustadt, only half a mile from the Aiming Point.

I had sat on my own in the shelter at the 'Michel', near the Michaeliskirche, for quite a while, seeing to my son. Around me, everything was as it always was when an alarm had sounded but there was suddenly a loud crash; I had never heard such an explosion. All at once, crowds of people who had been standing talking on the street and in front of the entrance to the air-raid shelter wanted to come into it. A lot of planes had suddenly appeared in the sky above and were dropping bombs, canisters of phosphorus, incendiary bombs and blast bombs. People who got phosphorus on them presented a fearful sight. Their skin was bright red, water dripping out of the pores of their skin; their ears and nose, their whole face, was a nauseating mask. People drummed with their fists against the entrance to the air-raid shelter but it was closed because it was full. People were running around outside, frantically trying to save their lives.

After the raid had got well started, there were very few
people in Hamburg who could actually see what was happening. All civilians had taken shelter and many of the civil-
defence workers were also under cover until called out to
bombing incidents. The streets were mostly deserted. The
people of Hamburg sat in their shelters, listening to the
bombing – sometimes far away, sometimes with loud detona-
tions rocking their shelters. The public *Bunker* shelters were
often hit but they usually survived, shaken but intact. Emergency lighting and ventilation was available if the normal
electricity supply was disrupted. Those sheltering in the
basements of housing blocks were more vulnerable. Some such
shelters were buried under rubble when the houses above
were destroyed by high explosives but many people broke down
the thin walls into neighbouring basements or were dug out
after the raid. Fire was the more common danger but there
was usually some notice that a house above had started to
burn and the shelter inhabitants usually had time to get out,
housewives and children running off through the streets,
clutching their suitcases of valuables, looking for another
shelter. Here are further examples of individual experiences
during this part of the raid. Once again, the reader must
realize that such incidents could be multiplied many times.

Frau Schwarze again:

Soon after we got into the shelter a blast bomb dropped in a nearby
street. This cut out the electric light and blew dust and dirt through
the ventilators. Then, I think a little bomb fell on top of the bunker
because it shook badly. There was a small diesel generator and
someone soon got the lights going again.

During the attack, more people came into the bunker and it
became overcrowded. The newcomers were filthy and some were
bloodstained. The shelter warden knew that my husband was a
policeman and he was allowed out. Between two waves of the raid,
he went out to look at our house and saw that the first and third
storeys were on fire. He felt that, by a miracle, our flat on the second
storey would be saved but, even as he looked at the house, he saw a
piece of blackout material in our window burst into flames. He could
see, then, that burning pieces of the house were coming through the
ceiling of our flat and falling on our furniture and this had started to
burn. He was terrified because we were losing everything we had.
He came back to tell the families in the shelter that the whole street

was in flames. His face was all black and his whole body was trembling. He said, '*Es ist alles aus*' – 'It's all gone'.

The raid continued – you had no sensation of time.

Hanni Paulsen was a schoolgirl in Altona whose family had been packed ready to leave for a holiday the next morning, the first holiday her parents would ever have had. When the raid started, the family had gone down to their basement shelter, taking their holiday luggage with them, hanging the holiday clothes on coat-hangers from the steel girder supporting the basement roof.

The people from some burning houses near by came into our basement and soon there were forty to fifty people inside it. These newcomers were very upset. They had seen their houses burning down and their belongings lost. Some could speak; some were crying; others were shocked. We tried to calm them down because there were a lot of children.

When we saw that these people had lost their possessions, we decided to save ours. So, even though the bombs were still falling, we went upstairs to gather our most valuable belongings from cupboards into a sheet to bring down to the basement. My mother was terrified and stayed in the shelter but Papa and I went up and down several times. We really did not realize that we were risking our lives in this old house, full of inflammable timber. We found the glass in the windows all broken, with the curtains streaming out. My room was full of smoke from the burning buildings near by. We wetted our handkerchiefs but could not hold them over our mouths because we needed both hands to gather up our possessions. We had no idea of time; I don't know how long all this took.

While we were doing this, some incendiary bombs fell into the attic. Some old men went up to try to put them out but they couldn't extinguish them all and they came down and told us they could do no more. We all had to leave the basement. The exit had become blocked and we had to break down the wall into the basement next door and clamber through. The basement warden of this house was waiting and told us to run to the nearby public shelter at the police station but that we had to leave all our belongings because 'lives were more important than belongings'.

I thought, 'I have lost nearly everything. Why should I leave what little I have got left? It is my luggage after all!' I squeezed past the warden and ran with my bags. I think some others did the same. We all reached the new shelter safely but, then, I found that the bags I was carrying were not mine. I was very disappointed but the owners of the two bags were delighted; one of them was my sister. The people who had got into this new shelter before us had brought in all their pets – chickens, brought in baskets but now running round the shelter, cats, dogs and rabbits. All that one woman had saved was her canary in its cage.

I found out later that the warden had saved all his belongings; he must have made several journeys from the old shelter to the new one. When my mother saw him with all his luggage at the evacuation collecting place later, she and the other women who had left all their bags when he had told them to, were furious. The only reason why they didn't beat him up was that he was a party member.

When I went back to our basement after the raids I found that all our bags had burned to ashes and, of the holiday clothes that I had hung from the girder, all I found were the metal hooks of the coathangers.

Irena Chmiel was the fifteen-year-old Polish girl worker in Eppendorf.

The German woman in charge of us had left us without saying anything; she locked the door behind her and disappeared. We assumed that she had gone to the shelter and left us girls locked in. You could almost 'feel' the planes; they sounded really heavy with loads of bombs.

They started falling straight away. The house shook and we started screaming because we were locked in. We were banging the door and shouting for someone to let us out. Then, a policeman and some other man came along and knocked our door down. They started taking us, one by one, into the air-raid shelter in the next building. It was only when we got outside that we found the upper storey of our building was on fire. As I crossed to the shelter, a hot brick came down and just caught my leg. It really frightened me and, when I got to the shelter, I fainted. This policeman saved our lives really because, when we came out next morning, the house had burnt down and we had lost all our clothes. We never knew whether he knew we were Poles or not.

Hamburg's civil-defence forces were facing their greatest test. This was heavier than any previous raid because of the great increase in Bomber Command's bomb-carrying capacity since the last visits of the R.A.F. in the spring. It is beyond doubt that the Hamburg civil-defence workers came out into the dangerous open and worked most valiantly while the raid was still in progress but it is also certain that the number of incidents to which they were called were too numerous to enable all to be dealt with at once. Quite simply, the R.A.F.'s tactics did succeed and the civil-defence forces were overwhelmed. Just two or three small incendiary bombs would hit the roof of an apartment block or one larger incendiary bomb would penetrate deeper into the building. Block wardens called men from shelters and tried to extinguish these bombs before larger fires were caused but the continued dropping of high explosives often killed these brave men and further incendiaries started even more fires. The first public firefighters on the scene were usually the *Schnellkommandos*, motorized teams consisting of a reserve policeman and four Hitler Youth boys. Again, their task was to quell small fires before they took too great a hold, but they too suffered casualties while travelling or found roads blocked and there were always too many fires for their attention. Finally, the fully equipped regular fire units were similarly exposed to the dangers of the bombing and outnumbered by the sheer multitude of fires. There were soon hundreds of apartment blocks, shops and offices on fire, usually burning first in the upper storeys with the fires slowly descending through the rest of the buildings. It was later estimated that, in the western part of Hamburg alone, there were burning buildings equivalent to a combined street frontage of fifty-four miles that night. After reinforcements from outside the city had arrived, there were as many as eighty-six fire-brigade units working in Hamburg and these eventually deployed no less than 692 individual fire-fighting teams in the city, but it would take these units many hours finally to control the fires started during this raid.

Gauleiter Kaufmann's party *Bunker* was not affected by the bombing although it was on the edge of the area that the R.A.F. had intended to destroy. Kaufmann's staff were receiving reports from two sources: from the police and from subsidiary party headquarters; one person who was present says that the police reports arrived more quickly and were more accurate. It was not long before everyone present realized that their city was experiencing an exceptionally heavy raid. Gauleiter Kaufmann was observed to deal with everything in a very calm and meticulous way. It was not long before a messenger came in with a metallized strip that he had found out in the open. When other examples arrived, it was soon realized that these were of some importance and that they probably had something to do with the widespread radar failure that had been reported.

While the raid was actually in progress, the most important place in Hamburg was the Control Room in the bomb-proof shelter under the main Police Headquarters, which was near the Aiming Point and right on the line of the intended creep-back of the bombing. Two witnesses are available to describe the scene here.*

In previous attacks, pins for representing every single incident had been carefully stuck into the large table map around which all the departmental heads were sitting. But the pin system soon broke down on this night when the first flood of reports came in from the tower watchers. There were so many reports that it was at first thought that the watchers were drunk, 'it was known that they always kept a bottle of alcohol with them at night to keep out the cold'. It was not long before the reports from most of the watch-towers stopped arriving, the observers being killed, driven into shelter by bombs, or their telephone lines cut. It was then that Otto Müller's motor-cyclists had to be turned out of their safe quarters and sent into the city to get reports. Official records show that these men were the main source of information in the following hours and several were killed while carrying out this hazardous duty.

A major breakdown in the city's carefully prepared fire-control system also occurred. For control purposes, the main city north of the Elbe was split into two main areas: Group West and Group East. Fifteen minutes after the first bombs landed, the telephone line connecting the headquarters of Group West to the Police Control Room was broken. Group West was the area of the city which was the R.A.F.'s main target for the night but no messages came in from it until well after the raid was over. A stream of reports continued to come in from Group East and from Group Harbour, south of the

* The two men present in the Police Control Room were Heinz Bumann, adjutant to Chief of Police Kehrl, and Otto Müller, an ex-speedway motor-cycle champion who had often raced in England and was now a Haupt-sturmführer in charge of most of the city's motor-cycle emergency messenger service. The witness in the Party Control Room was Hermann Matthies, director of the Hamburg Public Welfare Service.

Elbe, in both of which only scattered bombing was being experienced. Because of this telephone failure, fire units from unaffected parts of the city and the reinforcements that soon started arriving from outside were all sent to the East and Harbour areas. It was only two hours later that it was realized that the major part of the attack had fallen in the area covered by Group West – in the districts of Sankt Pauli, Altona, Eimsbüttel and Hoheluft. Many fires raged unattended in these districts. In one of Group West's areas, District XI (West Altona), only seven out of 320 fires were reported.

Another vital communications link was severed when the top storeys of the Long-Distance Telephone Exchange in Rotherbaum caught fire and all lines to the rest of Germany were cut. The only communications out of the city remaining were a private telephone line belonging to the railway and a Nazi Party line to a small 'Hamburg office' in Berlin. These slender means of communication would be heavily used in the hours to come.

These effects of the bombing – breakdowns in communication, blocked streets, the confusion and overwhelming of the fire forces – were all part of Bomber Command's Area Bombing technique and it is known that they caused much depression in the Control Room at Police Headquarters. Fire Chief Otto Zaps decided to leave the underground shelter in order to find out what was happening outside. He returned, tired and dirty, reporting that he had not been able to reach the control point in the worst-affected area. It was not long before this Control Room itself had to be evacuated. Heavy fires were burning in the surrounding streets and in the Police Headquarters above. All the civil-defence department heads had to move to a standby location in the Gestapo Headquarters in the Feldbrunnenstrasse. More dislocation!

The staff of Luftgau XI were quite safe in their control room inside the Heiligengeistfeld Flak tower but their Flak and searchlight units in and around the city were completely disorganized by the breakdown of their *Würzburg* radar equipment. Two young Flak helpers have recorded their memories of that night.

There was so much tension over the next ninety minutes that I have hardly any conscious memory of that period. The constant dropping of Target Indicators gave us an idea of the severity of the raid on Hamburg. We soon fired off the 160 rounds of ammunition in the gun position and had to go and fetch fresh supplies from the reserve bunker some distance away. We seventeen-year-old '*Spiddel-finken*'* were very happy to find that we could carry one round over each shoulder. In the excitement of the battle, we did not notice that the command post was ordering the guns to fire in a completely wrong direction. The radar, on whose green screen an aeroplane normally appeared as a small spike, had gone completely crazy. The whole screen was sown over with spikes and it was impossible to pick out a target. What was happening? The enemy had put this modern radar equipment out of action with one stroke. After an hour, the blood-red sky over Hamburg told us that the city must have been hit hard. (Traugott Bauer-Schlichtegroll, 267th Heavy Flak Battalion)

We were up on a hill at Neu-Wulmstorf, south of the city, and we had a panoramic view of the bombing. I know it sounds a bit silly now but it was a lovely view. We couldn't hear the bombs falling because there was a Flak battery firing near by. We didn't see the effects of the bombs, only this marvellous firework display. I changed my mind when I saw the destruction a few days later.

Our radar was hopelessly confused, chaotic. The master searchlight with radar was useless and the ordinary searchlights had to try on their own. It was like going around with a torch in a dark room, trying to find a fly. We found the strips of aluminium all over when the raid was finished. At first, we thought they were poisonous. These Hamburg raids were over before we realized the connection between these strips and the interference of the radar. There never was an official announcement. (Albert Hartung, 608th Searchlight Battalion)

The Hamburg Flak defences could do no more than fire blindly into the area of sky through which the bombers were believed to be flying. But the sky is an immense place. There is a German report which gives the number of shells that needed to be replaced at the Hamburg Flak batteries during the Battle of Hamburg.[3] From this report it can be calculated that approximately 50,000 rounds of heavy Flak were fired during that first night. The average 88-mm gun probably fired just over 200 rounds, the 105-mm guns 150 rounds and the 128-mm Flak-tower guns 110 rounds each. The only certain victims of the Flak were one Wellington which was

* *Spiddelfinken* is Hamburg dialect and a difficult word to translate: 'skinny kids' might be the most appropriate phrase.

shot down by Flak after being coned by searchlights and a Canadian Pathfinder Halifax which was seriously damaged and had one of its crew members killed.

Because it was a clear night, Bomber Command's Operational Research Section was later able to reconstruct the progress of this raid from a careful study of the flashlit bombing photographs taken by each bomber. A total of 647 such photographs produced enough detail to enable them to be plotted. Of these, 114 showed ground features that could be identified and the remainder were plotted by means of their relation to known fires on the ground. The time of each photograph was also known so that it was possible to reconstruct the progress of the various phases of the raid.[4] An attempt by a Pathfinder aircraft to bring back a colour film of the raid proved a disappointment. Sergeant K. Miller of 83 Squadron flew across the target throughout the raid but, when the film was later developed, it was ruined because it was placed in the wrong solution.

It is clear that the Pathfinders marked five separate areas of the city at the opening of the raid and that the early waves of the Main Force bombed all these. This spread in the marking illustrates the difficulty experienced by the Pathfinders in finding an Aiming Point in a large city, even though this city was on a broad river and had a large lake – both being features that should have shown up on the H2S sets of the Blind Markers and might have been visible to the eye for Visual Markers. The Pathfinder post-mortem on this early spread in marking blames the use by the Germans of smoke-screens and on the fact that the flare-dropping Pathfinders were too spread out in time, with their flares being insufficiently concentrated for the Visual Markers.

Two of the early marking areas were in the Hamburg dock area, south of the Elbe, and there is some evidence that two shipyards were hit here. At the Blohm & Voss yard, one U-boat commissioned three days earlier was hit and so badly damaged that it was never repaired and two more U-boats still on the slipway were hit and their completion delayed. At the Deutsche Werft yard in Reiherstieg, a small floating dock and a small steamer were sunk and another small ship was burned out. Several warehouses containing food and raw

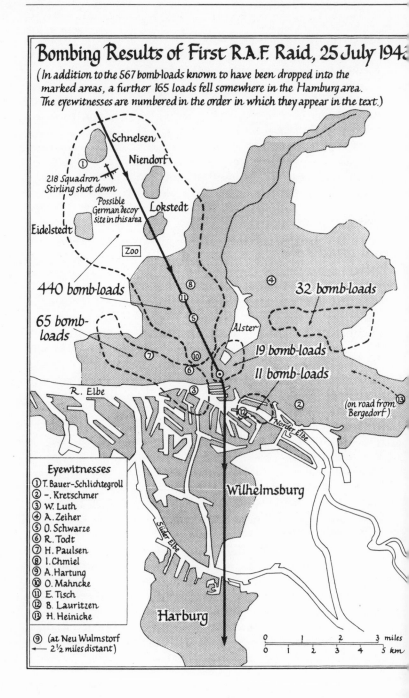

Bombing Results of First R.A.F. Raid, 25 July 194...

(In addition to the 567 bomb-loads known to have been dropped into the marked areas, a further 165 loads fell somewhere in the Hamburg area. The eyewitnesses are numbered in the order in which they appear in the text.)

Schnelsen

Niendorf

① 218 Squadron Stirling shot down

Possible German decoy site in this area

Lokstedt

Eidelstedt

Zoo

440 bomb-loads

65 bomb-loads

⑧

⑪

⑤

⑦

⑩

⑥

④

32 bomb-loads

Alster

19 bomb-loads

11 bomb-loads

R. Elbe

③

②

⑬ (on road from Bergedorf)

⑫

Norder Elbe

Wilhelmsburg

Suder Elbe

Harburg

Eyewitnesses

① T. Bauer-Schlichtegroll
② -. Kretschmer
③ W. Luth
④ A. Zeiher
⑤ O. Schwarze
⑥ R. Todt
⑦ H. Paulsen
⑧ I. Chmiel
⑨ A. Hartung
⑩ O. Mahncke
⑪ E. Tisch
⑫ B. Lauritzen
⑬ H. Heinicke

⑨ (at Neu Wulmstorf ← 2½ miles distant)

0   1   2   3 miles
0 1 2 3 4 5 km

materials in the nearby docks were also set alight and it is believed that an oil-storage tank in the Peute group of docks blew up. But the bombing in these industrial areas was never heavy and it did not last for long. A widely quoted report that a tunnel under the Elbe, in which several thousand civilians were sheltering, collapsed after being hit by heavy bombs is without foundation.

The three bombing areas north of the river attracted a greater number of bombs. The more easterly of these was centred on the residential area of Wandsbek, three miles north-east of the Aiming Point. Many Lancaster crews of 1 and 5 Groups, which provided the aircraft for the first wave of the Main Force attack, produced bombing photographs here. So, too, did three Pathfinder marker crews. There was some accurate marking and some bombing around the Aiming Point, where the Nikolaikirche was partially destroyed, the roof of the Rathaus set afire and other buildings hit. But the final first-phase bombing area, in the Eimsbüttel district, two miles north-west of the Aiming Point, was the most heavily bombed area in the first phase of the raid. This was in the planned bombing area, but bombs were not intended to drop here until the final phases of the creep-back reached that area. These scattered marking and bombing areas had hardly been a promising beginning for what was intended to be one concentrated knock-out blow against the western districts of the city.

The raid ran its planned course, with Pathfinder Backers-Up attempting to keep the bombing in the planned area, with wave after wave of Main Force bombers coming in to choose a group of markers and bomb. The evidence of bombing photographs shows that the bombing soon subsided in all but one of the early bombing areas and the Pathfinder Backers-Up were able to concentrate the bombing into the western half of the main city. The north-eastern bombing area, in the district of Wandsbek, persisted a little longer and many fires were started, but most of the bombing here stopped well before the half-way point in the raid. This improved concentration may have owed something to a remarkably accurate group of five red Target Indicators which were plotted as having dropped just 300 yards beyond the Aiming Point. This was the work of Sergeant D. W. Burt, the bomb aimer in Flight Lieutenant

S. Wareing's 97 Squadron Lancaster. So, approximately one-third of the way through the planned course of the main attack, the bombing at last became concentrated in the main built-up area of Hamburg west of the Alster, particularly in the districts of Neustadt, Sankt Pauli, Altona, Ottensen, Eimsbüttel and Hoheluft. It was in this area that the telephone link between the local civil-defence centre and the city's main control room was broken, resulting in no fire-fighting reinforcements being sent to the growing number of fires here. With more than half of the Main Force still to bomb, it had seemed that the R.A.F. were on the verge of dealing a crushing blow to this half of Hamburg.

It did not happen. The examination of bombing photographs showed that the marking and the bombing rapidly drifted back for seven miles instead of being restricted to the three-mile area that contained the built-up part of western Hamburg. A great number of bombs fell in and around Niendorf, Schnelsen, Lokstedt and Eidelstedt. Today, these places are built-up suburbs of Hamburg but in 1943 they were much smaller communities, surrounded by open land and woods. A total of 617 bombing photographs were eventually plotted by Bomber Command's Operational Research Section; only 275 of these showed that aircraft had bombed within three miles of the Aiming Point with 342 being outside that distance. Such a result, though disappointing, was not unusual. As has been said before, it was very difficult to keep a night raid concentrated. Bomber Command's Operational Research Section traces the breakdown in concentration to the scattered early marking. The Visual Backers-Up had been given too many choices of markers to re-mark and had tended to place their Target Indicators on the earliest of these, thus accelerating the creep-back. Eleven 'Recenterer' Pathfinders, which were being used for the first time, might have corrected this but their Target Indicators – aimed by H2S radar – were of the same colour as the Visual Backers-Up and only four of them had found their H2S sets to be working properly. Their limited number of more accurate markers were ignored.

There were other factors. Experienced Pathfinders reported that some of the red markers seen had not been as good as genuine Pathfinder ones. They were German decoys. Ninety-three bombers of the Main Force claimed to have aimed their bombs at red Target Indicators after the time at which the last genuine Pathfinder markers had been dropped. These 'markers' were almost certainly German imitation ones lit at a decoy fire site in open country. Many German cities had several such sites to lead bombers astray. This one must have saved many lives and much property damage in Hamburg.

There was a final factor in the extended creep-back. In 1943, Hamburg city measured about six miles from end to end, whichever way one approached, but the city's searchlight and Flak defences extended for approximately twenty-five miles. Once a bomber had entered this area, its crew considered themselves to be 'over the target'. It seemed reasonable to bomb any marker of the right colour in this area and crews were pleased to bomb and get away from the target area quickly. One basic weakness – the inability of both Pathfinders and Main Force bomb aimers to see the ground – was the price that Bomber Command had to pay for operating by night instead of by day.

In his listing of the damage caused during the Battle of Hamburg, the Chief of Police unfortunately treated the whole series of raids as one event and little detail is attributed to individual raids. However, it can reliably be stated that, in this first night, the districts of Altona, Eimsbüttel and Hoheluft suffered heavy damage, which was most severe in the more densely built-up residential areas. Surrounding districts had also suffered serious damage and no district of Hamburg north of the river escaped completely, with Wandsbek having the worst damage, in the eastern part of the city. Also, as has already been stated, some damage was caused in the dock area south of the river, although this had not been the target for the bombing.

A great variety of buildings were hit, ranging from the public buildings, hotels, department stores, offices, cinemas and hospitals in the central part of the city to the multitude of private dwellings in the residential areas. I can only suggest that the reader takes a look at the type of property to be seen today in the inner areas of any city that has not been modernized; the type of property to be seen in the streets of such cities was the type to be blown up or burnt out in large numbers during this raid. Some famous Hamburg landmarks had been hit. The Rathaus, the Nikolaikirche, the Central Police Station and the Long-Distance Telephone Exchange have already been mentioned. The Ufa-Palast cinema, where 'the little man in the street put on collar and tie' for the 'highlight of his cultural life', was burnt out, the fire-engines here being hampered by lack of water. A favourite old church in Wandsbek caught fire and its blazing roof and tower fell into the body of the church. The old house in the Speckstrasse in which Johannes Brahms had been born 110 years earlier was destroyed. It was here that he had composed his famous lullaby: '*Guten Abend, gute Nacht, mit Rosen bedacht . . .*'.

The famous Hagenbeck Zoo was hit by four 'blockbuster' blast bombs, sixteen other high-explosive bombs and many incendiaries. This had been in the area in which telephone communications had broken down and the zoo employees who were on fire-watching duty had to cope without outside help. Four of them were killed as well as five of the zoo's restaurant staff who were sheltering in the Zebra House. Many valuable animals were killed by the bombing and others had to be shot afterwards. Approximately 140 animals died in all. It was noticed that few of the supposedly 'wild' animals tried to escape when their cages were blown away and that many badly injured animals stood patiently waiting for attention. A notoriously lively stallion lost an eye but used his new freedom to play with a circus mare that he met. The most difficult animals to catch proved to be the monkeys, which swept through the surrounding streets. On 8 September the *Hamburger Anzeiger* printed an article about the bombing of the Hagenbeck Zoo, ending with these words:

> What made this place of research, education and entertainment, well known all over the world and an example for numerous zoos in foreign countries, an attractive target for the enemy? This is a question for which the British-Americans will owe us an answer.

No exact figure exists for the human casualties. The best estimate that the Chief of Police was able to make was that 1,500 people had died with many more injured and many, many thousands made homeless. At least seventeen people were killed by stray bombs outside Hamburg. To achieve the damage and casualties caused, Bomber Command had dropped 184 flares, 263 Target Indicators, approximately

1,346 tons of high-explosive bombs and 938 tons of incendiaries. It is obvious that a high proportion of these bombs had not hit Hamburg, but the raid had still been a very heavy one by all preceding standards for that city and it was no more than the opening engagement in the Battle of Hamburg.

The last bomber to fly over Hamburg that night was a Halifax of 102 Squadron piloted by Flight Sergeant E. M. Cartwright whose crew were on their first operational flight. This aircraft dropped its bombs at 01.55, a clear five minutes after the last previous aircraft had bombed. The Halifax was caught by searchlights and coned but the entire Flak defences of Hamburg could not hit it and Cartwright dived away to safety. He left behind a burning, smoking city that the returning R.A.F. men would see glowing behind them for a considerable part of their flight to England.

The first part of the bombers' return-flight plan called for a short leg of twenty-two miles due south out of the target area, then a sharp turn to starboard to cross the German coast south of the Elbe and fly out into the Heligoland Bight. When the bomber-stream reached a point 125 miles out from the German coast, it would break up and individual bombers would be free to fly back to make landfalls near their home airfields. The whole flight from Hamburg to the English coast was a theoretical 454 miles, to be carried out in two hours and eleven minutes of flying time. The weather remained clear and calm; a half moon rose as the bombers were leaving Hamburg. Various crew members continued their uncomfortable task of dropping Window; they would keep up this important work until reaching a point sixty miles out over the sea.

The German night fighters continued to be in disarray because of Window. The bomber-stream had to fly through five more night-fighter boxes before reaching their final turning point out over the Heligoland Bight. It can be assumed that experienced night-fighter crews had been sent to patrol every one of these boxes, but only one combat is recorded as having taken place between Hamburg and the coast. A 214 Squadron Stirling was cruising steadily along, on its correct course and with two other Stirlings in sight. These Stirlings, being the lowest-flying aircraft of all, should have been receiving the most protection from Window, but the 214 Squadron aircraft was suddenly attacked by an unseen fighter. Two bursts of cannon fire caused severe damage to the Stirling and it was soon ablaze and going down. Only two men escaped by parachute. The identity of the German pilot and the circumstances of his interception are not known; it may have been a chance visual sighting.

The bomber-stream crossed the German coast at a point midway between Bremerhaven and Cuxhaven. (Bremerhaven was known as Wesermünde at that time.) The Pathfinders dropped more route-markers at the coast to keep the bomber-stream from straying over the strong Flak defences of the cities on either side. The bombers managed to avoid the Bremerhaven defences but there was trouble over Cuxhaven, a notorious Flak area, it being sometimes said that 'there was a little man at the end of Cuxhaven pier who regularly shot up Bomber Command aircraft'. A 460 Squadron Lancaster strayed over Cuxhaven and was immediately coned in searchlights. Many crews flying past to the south watched the bomber struggle for some time to get out of the searchlights but it was eventually hit by Flak and was seen to go down. It crashed on the small sandy island of Neuwerk, just off the coast, and there were no survivors. Two other bombers reported brushes with a single-engined German night fighter near Cuxhaven. This may have been a Wild Boar aircraft from Oldenburg airfield, freelancing in the neighbourhood of the Cuxhaven searchlights.

With the loss of only two aircraft since leaving the target, the bombers departed from Germany, flew out to the last turning point and then pulled round to port for the final flight across the North Sea to England. For all but one more bomber crew, this turned out to be the peaceful flight for which they hoped. Oberleutnant Hermann Greiner was patrolling well out to sea in Box *Tiger*, whose radar station was on the Dutch Frisian Island of Terschelling.

I was controlled from the ground on to this bomber which was crossing *Tiger* in a north-westerly direction. It was going so slowly that I overshot it on my first run. I soon saw the reason for this was that it had two engines failed, both on one side! It took me – for a combat situation – rather a long time to make up my mind what to do next. I realized that he had probably been damaged over Ham-

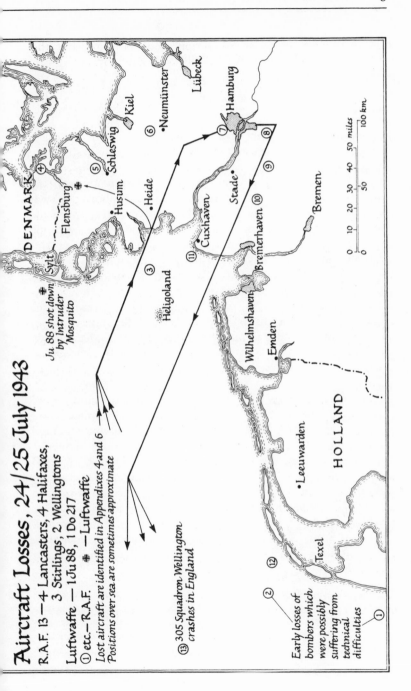

Aircraft Losses, 24/25 July 1943

R.A.F. 13 — 4 Lancasters, 4 Halifaxes,
3 Stirlings, 2 Wellingtons

Luftwaffe — 1 Ju 88, 1 Do 217

① etc. — R.A.F.   ✠ — Luftwaffe

Lost aircraft are identified in Appendices 4 and 6
Positions over sea are sometimes approximate

Ju 88 shot down
by Intruder
Mosquito

⑬ 305 Squadron Wellington
crashes in England

Early losses of
bombers which
were possibly
suffering from
technical
difficulties

DENMARK

Sylt

Flensburg

Husum

Heide

Schleswig

Kiel

•Neumünster

Lübeck

Hamburg

Heligoland

Cuxhaven

Stade•

Bremerhaven

Bremen

Wilhelmshaven

Emden

Leeuwarden

HOLLAND

Texel

0   10   20   30   40   50 miles

0   50   100 km

burg and that he had been lucky to get so far towards England. I thought about letting him succeed in this exploit but I had to consider other factors and decided that I had to force a result. I didn't feel too happy about shooting him down though. However, I aimed, as in most other cases, very carefully at the wing tanks to give the crew a chance.

Oberleutnant Greiner was convinced that his victim was a Halifax and he appears to have had plenty of time to study the bomber. His letter expressed surprise that the bomber was not protected by Window but this lone bomber, probably damaged, as Greiner suggests, and taking a short cut, was forty miles south of the bomber-stream's route. Because the bomber crashed into the sea and because there were no survivors, there are the usual difficulties over identifying this aircraft but it must have been a Lancaster, almost certainly the third aircraft lost by 103 Squadron during the raid. All three had fallen into the North Sea.

These descriptions of the circumstances in which three bombers were lost during the homeward flight may be of interest but it is more important to record that, thanks mainly to Window, more than 700 bombers flew back through the German defensive system without difficulty.

The first bombers were home and starting to land before 3.30 a.m. The first down was probably the Lancaster of Warrant Officer G. Denwood of 156 Squadron which landed at Warboys at 3.19 a.m. There were three landing accidents. The first involved the Lancaster of Wing Commander J. H. Searby, commander of 83 (Pathfinder) Squadron, when he was orbiting his home airfield at Wyton, waiting his turn to land. The Wyton circuit was very close to that of neighbouring Warboys and Searby had ordered his crew to keep a careful look-out. Squadron Leader Norman Scrivener, the navigator, was standing just behind his pilot and he describes the accident.

Then the impossible happened. I was probably the first to see the dark shape approaching dead ahead at 500 m.p.h. closing speed. I shouted and pointed ahead but whether my speaking mike was switched on or not I cannot tell. However, there was a brief ejaculation from Wing Commander Searby – unusual, as he was always calm and never panicked.

I can remember being lifted off my feet as Searby thrust the stick forward and we began to lose height. But it all happened too quickly for thought or action. The terrifying shape of another Lancaster flashed overhead and we heard some dull thumps like Flak bursting too near. There was a rush of cold air and we waited apprehensively for a second or two but we did not crash. The captain called for reports but Jerry Coley, who had been in the mid-upper turret, had a job to speak. The propeller of the other aircraft had taken part of the mid-upper perspex cleanly away and had shaved a piece of Jerry's helmet off without touching his head. I doubt he or we will ever have a nearer miss.

Searby was quite calm but Jerry Coley lived on the story for years.

The Lancaster landed safely, as did the aircraft it had collided with, although this had two engines damaged. John Searby, this veteran bomber pilot, had narrowly escaped death to survive and carry out what was possibly the most important single bomber-pilot operation of the war, the role of Master Bomber during the raid on the German V-weapon establishment at Peenemünde three weeks later. Searby survived the war.

The other two landing accidents both involved Wellingtons of the Polish 305 Squadron. The aircraft of Sergeant Stefan Grzeskowiak was in trouble when it crossed the Lincolnshire coast and the pilot was forced to crash-land in a field near Skegness. He was only on his first flight as aircraft captain but, although he wrote off the Wellington, not one member of his crew was seriously hurt. Sergeant Grzeskowiak was to be killed on his second operation, later in the Battle of Hamburg.

The mishap suffered by the other 305 Squadron Wellington had a more humorous side. Near the Poles' home airfield there was a complete decoy airfield lighting system set among open agricultural land. Flight Sergeant K. Ignatowski made a careful approach on the decoy lighting but did not receive the red signal flare that a duty airman should have fired to warn him off.

After landing and switching off the engines, the front hatch was opened and the wireless operator, who was first out, exclaimed, to the amusement of the whole crew, that he was standing in a cornfield and that the corn was up to his neck. When I got out of the aircraft I confirmed this and, to my amazement, noticed that the flarepath lights were well above my head – the electric lights were glowing on seven-foot-high poles instead of on the ground. I and the crew were at a loss to understand this and we did not have a clue where we were. We realized that we had more luck than brains and we did not know whether to laugh or cry. A breathless airman soon appeared on the scene. He was very apologetic and informed us that we had landed on the decoy site and he was sorry that he did not warn us due to the fact that he was being entertained in a local farmhouse by a lonely widow.

At 5.15 a.m., seven and a half hours exactly after the first aircraft had taken off to open the Battle of Hamburg, the last landing took place. This was the Halifax of a Canadian pilot, Sergeant R. L. Henry of 427 Squadron, which landed safely at Leeming airfield. These successful landings, with only one aircraft lost through a crash and with no casualties to aircrew, completed a highly successful operation for Bomber Command. Men went to the debriefings, maybe stiff and tired, but with morale uplifted by the beneficial effects of Window. 'Debriefing after the first raid could nearly be called hilarious – everybody happy and excited at the effectiveness of Window.' 'The effect of Window was an eerie sensation but a tremendous boost for morale. We were sure that life would be easier from then on.' 'Most crews realized that there had been a breakthrough in the constant battle against the German defences.' 'On the night of Hamburg One, our morale took a leap upwards. We were all tickled pink with the crazy confusion caused to the defences. I do not believe, however, that anyone was deluded into believing that this jolly situation would last.'

Of the 792 bombers that had taken off, 732 – or 92·4 per cent – had bombed somewhere in the Hamburg area and only twelve – 1·5 per cent – were missing; one more had been written off after its crash landing and thirty-one aircraft had returned with varying degrees of damage. These were excellent results. A German report says that seventy-eight German night fighters from five *Gruppen* had manned the boxes on the bomber routes to and from Hamburg. The best estimate of the achievement of this night-fighter effort is that they had probably shot down ten bombers, five of which had been well off course and without the protection of Window, two were on the fringes of the target area and one after the bomber concerned had been coned by searchlights. This left only two bombers shot down in the bomber-stream by normal means of interception. The German fighters had suffered two certain losses, with a possible third for which there is no documentary evidence. German Flak, similarly disrupted by Window, had claimed only two victims – one over Hamburg and one at Cuxhaven.

There are no particular lessons to be learned from a listing of the types of British bombers lost: four Lancasters (all from 1 Group), four Halifaxes (all from 4 Group), three Stirlings (all from 3 Group) and a 1 Group Wellington. Numbers 5, 6 (Canadian) and 8 (Pathfinder) Groups had operated 328 aircraft without a single loss! What was unusual was the great experience of many of the lost crews. Six of them had at least ten completed operations to their credit and a seventh was on the ninth operation of a second tour. This was the Stirling crew of Wing Commander D. T. Saville, D.S.O., D.F.C., the thirty-nine-year-old Australian commander of 218 Squadron. Again, there are no lessons to be drawn from this; these veteran crews had just been unfortunate. Eighty R.A.F. and Empire airmen had been killed and seven became prisoners of war.

The other R.A.F. operations of the night had all been concluded successfully and without any loss – six Wellingtons minelaying in the mouth of the River Elbe, six Radio-Counter-Measures aircraft plotting the radar and radio signals of the German night-fighter boxes around Hamburg, diversionary Mosquitoes that had bombed Lübeck, Kiel and Bremen, and the ones that had made nuisances of themselves over the Ruhr, thirty-three Lancasters of 5 Group that had flown back from North Africa, bombing the Italian port of Leghorn on the way, and aircraft carrying leaflets and Resistance supplies to France. The only German offensive action had been a flight to the mouth of the River Humber by an estimated ten minelaying aircraft.

Thus ended the first night of the Battle of Hamburg.

NOTES

1. From the Log of Events kept by a Fire Department Officer, later translated for the United States Defense Civil Preparedness Agency and published by the National Technical Information Service. These and later extracts of the log are from Appendix 5, p. 302 onwards.

2. ibid., Appendix 4, p. 224.
3. The report is in the History of Luftgaukommando XI by General der Flieger Wolff, Bundesarchiv document R L 19/424.
4. The results of this study are in Public Record Office A I R 14/3012 and 3410.

10

After the Bombs

We could hear this terrible humming, just like a swarm of bees, but it eventually faded away and the All Clear sounded at 3.01 a.m. We assembled on the afterdeck and had a rum issue. We sat and talked through the early hours while Hamburg burned around us like daylight and, in the docks, fuel tanks and delayed action bombs still blew up with loud explosions.

We were particularly happy when the wind came and blew the screen of smoke away so that the old 'Michel' – the Michaeliskirche, the landmark of our old Hanse city – appeared again. Like us, it had survived the bombardment. (Leutnant Walter Luth)

The civilians left their shelters, anxious to discover how the bombing had affected their homes. In the streets, the first examples of Window were found, objects of great curiosity and suspicion which most people came to call '*Aluminiumstreifen*' – 'aluminium strips'. They excitedly warned each other not to touch them; a rumour spread that the strips were treated with bacteria to spread infection in the bombed city. Another rumour soon circulating was that the Germans had themselves released the strips from their own barrage balloons to disorganize, by some secret, unrevealed means, the R.A.F. bombing. The lady who told me this story did not know the real purpose of Window until I explained it to her in 1978. Back on that early Sunday morning in 1943, however, it was quickly discovered that the strips were harmless and children were soon collecting bunches of Window as playthings and souvenirs.

But, in the worst-bombed areas, people had little thought for the new shiny strips. Otto Mahncke describes his journey, with a neighbour, through the bombed streets near the city centre. They were searching for relatives and other neighbours who had gone to a public shelter during the raid.

The streets were full of soot and tears kept streaming from our eyes. We cleaned them with handkerchiefs dipped in buckets of water which people had put out on the street. On the corner of the Elbstrasse and Marienstrasse, a woman who had come back from a birthday party was screaming, 'My child! My child! Up there!'

None of the men or women dared to go into the house to save the baby.

I ran with Fräulein Köppen, who was now clinging to me like a leech, towards the shelter at the 'Michel' where I thought I would find my mother and my sister but we just couldn't get through. All the overhead tram cables in the Mühlenstrasse and Michaelisstrasse were down and were lying in the street, still live.

In the Martin-Luther-Strasse there was a small dairy shop where a woman – the only one with her wits about her in all this confusion – was handing out free milk, butter and sausage, as long as stocks lasted.

On the Schaarmarkt we saw sailors rescuing people out of a burning house, passing them from balcony to balcony. Some people were saved. Then, suddenly, the house collapsed like a pack of cards. Everybody standing on the balconies fell into the ruins. It was a dreadful sight.

On our arrival at the 'Michel', we shouted out the names of my sister, mother and aunt as loud as we could. There was no reply. Even the 'Michel' shelter, secure as it was, afforded a fearful sight of human misery – people who were wounded and dying, people who had lost everything and were seeking refuge here after escaping from their burning homes.

We went back to the Grossneumarkt and there we saw another terrible sight. An old woman of seventy was calling for help from the third-floor window of a half-timbered house. The room was ablaze. I ran with some other men to fetch a ladder. We found a long one and a number of men climbed up to save the woman. But they all came back after the second floor; it was too hot. I tried, too, but had to retreat only a few steps under the window. The heat was too great. When I got to the ground, I saw the woman looking down with wild eyes and then fall back to her death among the flames. The men at the police station, which was less than thirty yards away, were not doing anything to help. I suppose they had more important things to do.

Elsbeth Tisch was in a burning part of Eimsbüttel:

When the planes had gone, we ran down the steps into the open. Our throats were parched from the heat, the dust, the smoke and the phosphorus fumes. Our street runs along the Isebek Canal and the trees and bushes on the banks were burning. People had tried to save some belongings and had placed them on the other side of the street. Suddenly, because of the enormous heat that had built up, an incredible firestorm* started up. Our hair was standing on end,

* The word 'firestorm', '*Feuersturm*' in German, was one that this lady

blackened, and we tried to clean it with pieces of cloth dipped in the water of the canal but the heat was so great that the cloth dissolved! After that, the fire brigade arrived. A large hosepipe was led from the canal into our house, which had been burnt down to the third storey, and we spent the night till six o'clock in the morning trying to save what we could.

Then, suddenly, S.S. men were standing in front of us. They were in full uniform and jackboots, as if on parade, and they wanted to load us on to lorries which were just arriving to take us somewhere or other. But we refused to go and only the fact that the raid had just finished stopped the S.S. from arresting us when we cursed and shouted at them. There they stood, in full uniform, and I can still hear my mother saying to them, 'Go on. Get out! This isn't the time or the place for your S.S. parades!'

When dawn came, daylight did not. A thick pall of smoke was drifting across the city from the fires still burning, specially from those many fires still unattended in the western areas. A schoolgirl remembers waking up. 'It was dark but I didn't feel tired. I couldn't understand it but I must have had enough sleep. When I went out, I realized that the darkness was caused by smoke – it was a big, black, greyish cloud, very low, just like when a thunderstorm comes up in the middle of the summer.' Another person remembers that 'it all looked very spooky'. The streets were busy with people clambering over the ruins, some searching out relatives to see if they had survived, others on their way back to their own homes if they had been away. Bruno Lauritzen had been on fire-watching duty at a warehouse in the dock area:

All of us had only one thought in mind – to leave the Freihafen and go to our families. I only reached home after a three-hour walk through the burning areas but, at last, I was able to take my wife, safe and sound, into my arms.

Many of the people tramping through the streets were the bombed-out, the unfortunate who had been robbed of the security of their homes by the bombing. Herbert Heinicke was a Hamburg businessman, now serving in the Wehrmacht

---

would not have known at that time. The sudden flare-up of fire that she experienced on this night was not the phenomenon later known as a firestorm.

and normally stationed in his native city. He had travelled to East Prussia on duty and was returning to Hamburg that Sunday morning.

The train only ran as far as Bergedorf, the last stop before Hamburg. I was given a lift into the city in a Luftwaffe lorry. It was from *Jagdgeschwader 'Udet'* which was coming from the Russian front to an airfield near Hamburg because of the recent Boeing raids.

Between Bergedorf and Hamburg we met many fleeing people. There were some strange scenes, people carrying all they could save, some were quite dazed. I remember a little boy, about twelve years old, with a head sticking out of the rucksack on his back. We stopped and talked to him; we saw that the head was that of a dead brother. I remember, also, a girl with a burn right down an arm but no bandages on. Nevertheless, she had met her soldier boy-friend and they had put their arms round each other and were kissing. I got the impression that the whole crowd were suffering from shock. My first thought was that this was the highest degree of barbarism.

We came into Hamburg along the Hammer Landstrasse. There were debris and dead bodies in the streets. A cinema was burning fiercely, the flames seemed to be a hundred metres long, coming right across the road. Our lorry nipped underneath these. The Luftwaffe men driving the lorries into the city told me that they had never seen anything like this, even in Russia.

Herr Heinicke found that his own family were safe.

The efficient German civil-defence system was in full swing and help was soon on the way to Hamburg from many parts of northern Germany, ranging from the village fire brigades that only had to travel a few kilometres to the powerful mobile Luftwaffe fire-fighting regiments that came roaring down the Autobahns from distant locations. Every military unit in and around Hamburg was mobilized and at least 35,000 men were soon hard at work in the bombed city. The Hamburg Fire Department's master log gives an indication of the demands made upon it that early Sunday morning.

3.02 a.m.   All Clear. In An der Alster, all houses reported on fire. Hospital at corner of Richardstrasse and Eilbeker Weg, 200 people trapped. Fire-fighting forces too weak to combat fires.

3.22 a.m.   Fire Department Division III to Dresdner Bank, Jung-fernsteig.

3.29 a.m. Large fires at Schenkendorfstrasse, Schillerstrasse, Kanal-strasse, Zimmerstrasse and the Reeperbahn. Request for five more fire units.

3.45 a.m. The following units promised to Group West: one Emergency Unit from Kiel, one from Neumünster, five from Bremen, one from Lübeck, two from Oldenburg. Oberstleutnant Westphal to Group Harbour. Conflagration in warehouse district threatens to spread to Pickhuben. Asks that two brigades from the Second Unit be assigned. Granted.

4.00 a.m. Ukrainian Training Corps VIII Unit assigned to Harbour. All industrial civil-defence units ordered to Harbour.

4.05 a.m. Fires at Dresdner Bank, Command Post of Division III. Fire Station III moved to Hapag Travel Bureau.

4.10 a.m. Situation of Major Catastrophe declared.

4.45 a.m. Two out-of-town units to arrive within half an hour.

5.45 a.m. Leutnant Müssfeld to Rathaus; send two brigades to Rathaus immediately.

6.15 a.m. Army barracks at Bundesstrasse in danger of explosion from burning ammunition.

6.20 a.m. Fire Station IX received a direct hit.

6.45 a.m. One unit from Kiel arrives at Fire Station III. Assigned to the inner city.

7.00 a.m. Three units arrived from Eidelstedt. Three units arrived from Bremen. Two units assigned to Group East, one to Party H.Q.

8.50 a.m. Eight large areas of fires are still without fire-fighting forces.[1]

The declaration of a Situation of Major Catastrophe at 4.10 a.m. signified the putting into effect, by Gauleiter Kaufmann's order, of a comprehensive plan prepared earlier that year.[2] There is no need to go into the details of the plan for dealing with the catastrophe. It simply meant that every man and woman working in the bombed city and all matters affecting civilian existence in it were now brought more closely under party control. This is not to suggest that widespread repressive measures were used. The main result was intended to be a firm central guidance to the work that needed carrying out in the city and, for some time at least, this was achieved. As has already been seen, the S.S. were soon out on the streets and there is an interesting note in the Hamburg Fire Department documents stating that, in the fighting of fires, the S.S. insisted 'with great vigour' that all fire forces should remain on duty so that every fire could be extinguished by midnight in case the R.A.F. came again the following night. The document goes on to say, however, that the fires were so numerous that these orders could not be carried out and many fires continued to blaze for more than twenty-four hours.[3]

It was nothing new. Hapless civilians had been trapped in bombed and burning buildings, had stood in streets watching the possessions of a lifetime burn away, had fled their cities in fear and misery in many places before.

NOTES

1. From the American translation of the Hamburg Chief of Police Report, Fire Department Documents, Appendix 5, pp. 305–6.
2. The Hamburg Major Catastrophe Plan runs to forty-two pages in Appendix 7 of the American translation of the Chief of Police Report and is dated 20 April 1943. There is an interesting note, added on 9 December 1943, stating that, by order of Doktor Goebbels's Ministry of Propaganda, the word 'catastrophe' was no longer to be used and was to be replaced by 'extreme emergency'.
3. Appendix 1 of the Fire Department documents, page 66 of the translation.

11

The American Way

This story must now go backwards in time one day and also change its scene. The time in which we are interested was approximately 9.30 a.m. on Saturday, 24 July — the last day of the twenty-one-year reign of power in Italy of Benito Mussolini. He was dismissed by his king the next day but escaped to Germany to survive until 1945. The place is a former girls' boarding school in Buckinghamshire, England, now the headquarters of the United States VIII Bomber Command. Brigadier-General Fred Anderson had just left the morning conference at the headquarters of R.A.F. Bomber Command at which the final British decision to start the Battle of Hamburg had been taken. Anderson had been driven back to his own headquarters at Wycombe Abbey Girls' School, only three miles away. It was time for Anderson's own daily planning conference, held in an operations room dug deep into a hillside on the top of which stood the home of an English aristocrat.* The officers of his staff were waiting. They were a mixed group. Most were wartime-commissioned, chosen by Major-General Eaker when that officer had been assembling a new staff to take to England to form the Eighth Air Force a year earlier. Before Pearl Harbor they had been academics, businessmen, lawyers, publishers, architects. As long as they had brains, they were good enough for General Eaker. Now, they were captains, majors and lieutenant-colonels in the U.S.A.A.F., helping to plan and prepare heavy-bomber operations over German-occupied Europe.

It must be stressed here that the American operations being planned at Wycombe Abbey that morning would not be flown until the following day, Sunday, 25 July. While an R.A.F. night raid was decided upon, prepared and carried out in less than twenty-four hours, an American raid, because of its daylight nature, contained an extra half day in its

* At the top of the hill was Dawes Hill House, home of Lord Carrington. At the time of writing this book, the U.S.A.F. still has an active operational headquarters there.

lifespan. So, while the B-17s were flying the raids to Norway on that Saturday, Brigadier-General Anderson and his staff were already making plans for the Sunday.

The major factor in the American decision was the weather position and Anderson's meteorological officer no doubt agreed with the R.A.F. forecast that a high-pressure system was steadily pushing away the clouds and uncovering targets in northern Germany; the R.A.F. and U.S.A.A.F. weather men drew their information from the same source. Another factor, not as important to the American decision but still very useful, was the knowledge that Fred Anderson had brought back from High Wycombe – that any American operation the following day would follow hard on the heels of a major R.A.F. night raid to Hamburg which would have used an important new device that was certain to have caused disorganization to the Luftwaffe's ground and air defences. The main decision – whether to mount major operations or not – was soon taken; in fact, given the promise of fine weather, it was almost automatic. The American heavy-bomber force was to be dispatched the following day to targets in Northern Germany.

The next decision, the selection of the actual targets, illustrates a major difference between the methods used by the two Allied air forces. While R.A.F. Bomber Command would concentrate its 800 bombers on a single target, the Eighth Air Force was about to split its force of slightly over 300 bombers into attacks on four different targets at three different locations. The Americans had long lists of targets that they wanted to bomb, stretching from Norway to France. After all the delays of the slow build-up of their forces and then poor flying conditions over Europe during the early part of that summer, there is no doubt that they were very anxious to start reducing the length of that list as quickly as possible. First, decided Fred Anderson, he would certainly follow up the R.A.F. attack on Hamburg with a raid on targets in that city and, from the target lists, he chose the Blohm & Voss U-boat construction yard and the Klöckner aero-engine factory. It seemed to make good sense for the Americans to tackle these heavily defended targets in Hamburg only a few hours after the R.A.F. had raided the city and this decision also complied with Sir Arthur Harris's request that the Americans should join in the Battle of Hamburg. But it was also decided that the Deutsche Werke U-boat yard at Kiel and the Focke-Wulf fighter factory at Warnemünde, outside Rostock on the Baltic coast, were to be attacked. The selection of these targets was in strict accordance with the recent Pointblank Directive – German fighter factories and U-boat yards were top of the Pointblank list – but there is no doubt that the Americans were unduly optimistic in attempting to knock out four targets in one day with the modest forces available at that time. One of the American staff officers present says, 'we were rather starry-eyed at that stage of the game'.

As for the tactical plan, the targets selected were all within 100 miles of each other and the American formations sent to each target could be routed and timed in such ways as to split the German fighter defence. The American heavy bombers could have no fighter support to these targets but arrangements were made for small formations of R.A.F. and U.S.A.A.F. light bombers, with huge escorts of R.A.F. fighters, to operate over Holland, Belgium and France and draw some of the German fighters to the south. It was also decided that the raids should not take place until as late in the day as possible, partly to give the improving weather conditions a chance to clear away more cloud but also to allow any smoke over Hamburg from the R.A.F. bombing to clear. It is ironic that the strenuous efforts of the Hamburg fire-fighters, under S.S. direction, to put out all the fires would also benefit the American bombardiers.

The targets chosen for the American heavy bombers were ambitious ones. It was the first time that a target as strongly defended as Hamburg had been attacked, although a previous raid had been attempted, a month earlier, only to be turned back by bad weather. It was the first time that a target as distant as Warnemünde had been attacked. But it was the first time that the Americans had sent 300 heavy bombers to Germany.

The information that there was to be a raid the next day was immediately passed to the headquarters of the two bombardment wings and, from there, to the operational airfields. But, while the operational units were preparing for the raid, there still remained much detailed planning to be carried out. VIII Bomber Command Headquarters had to allocate forces to each of the targets to be attacked. The unit of currency for this exercise was the 'combat wing', a minimum of fifty-four B-17s provided by three bomb groups flying in high, lead and low positions. This combat wing was the maximum number of bombers that it had so far been found practical to use in one defensive formation. It was convenient that Brigadier-General Frank Armstrong's 1st Bombardment Wing contained nine bomb groups and that Colonel Curtis LeMay's 4th Wing six groups. The 1st Wing was ordered to provide two combat wings for the two Hamburg targets and a third for Kiel. The 4th Wing, having the longer-range version of the B-17, was to provide two combat wings for the more distant Warnemünde raid. The B-24 Liberator groups of the 2nd Bombardment Wing were still absent in North Africa.

The routes and timings for the various raids were decided by the planning staff at Wycombe Abbey. It was hoped that the efforts of the German fighters could be partly frustrated by the clever use of timing and feints and much thought was put into producing a tactical plan to achieve this. The plan called for the two Warnemünde-bound combat wings to fly out over the North Sea forty minutes ahead of the Hamburg and Kiel wings. On reaching a point fifty miles from the German coast, the leading wings would turn north and fly a feint, hoping that the German fighters in that area would have been forced to take off too early. Then, when the three remaining wings arrived forty minutes later, all five wings would fly straight to their targets. These moves might protect the American bombers from the worst of German fighter attack during the approach flights to their targets but, with German fighters able to refuel quickly, little could be done to save the American formations from facing fighter attack on their return flights. The German fighter controllers were skilful men, gradually getting used to the American tactics, but not only was this force of American bombers the largest so far used over Germany, the deception plan was also the most advanced yet attempted by the Americans. The outcome of these operations would be most interesting.

Secondary targets were allocated for all the combat wings in case their primaries were unreachable for any reason or found to be covered by cloud. The secondary for the Hamburg and Warnemünde wings was Kiel; that for the Kiel wing is not

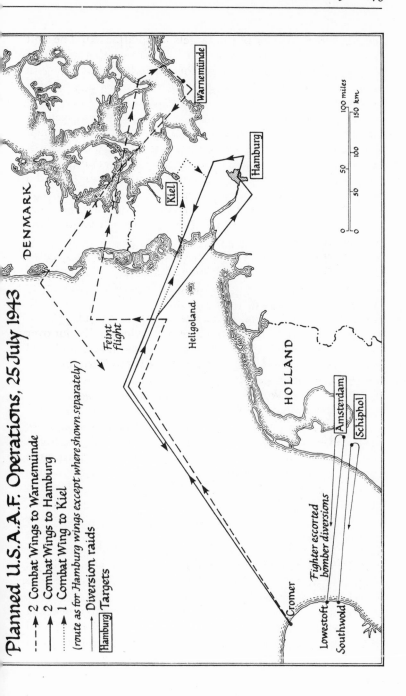

Planned U.S.A.A.F. Operations, 25 July 1943

- - - ▶ 2 Combat Wings to Warnemünde
———▶ 2 Combat Wings to Hamburg
· · · · · ▶ 1 Combat Wing to Kiel
(route as for Hamburg wings except where shown separately)
- - -▶ Diversion raids
Hamburg Targets

DENMARK

Warnemünde

Hamburg

Kiel

Feint
flight

Heligoland

HOLLAND

Amsterdam

Schiphol

Fighter escorted
bomber diversions

Cromer

Lowestoft

Southwold

0   50   100   150 km
0   50   100 miles

known. If the secondary targets were also found to be impossible to bomb, then the 'last resort target' for this day was given as 'any industrial target of opportunity'.

By late afternoon, all the planning details had been incorporated into formal orders and, as Field Order No. 171, sent by teleprinter to the two bombardment wings. The operations being planned would not be cancelled and they would eventually appear in VIII Bomber Command's records as Mission No. 76, the difference in numbering showing that ninety-five other operations had been planned but then cancelled since the beginning of the operational life of that command.

It is essential that this narrative now starts to concentrate in detail on the activities of those American units chosen to fly to Hamburg. The operations of the other units due to fly on Sunday, 25 July, however important or interesting, are not the subject of this book. The following six of the nine bomb groups in the 1st Bombardment Wing were selected for the raid on Hamburg:

Combat Wing Target: BLOHM & VOSS U-BOAT YARD

> High Box: 303rd Bomb Group
> Lead Box: 379th Bomb Group
> Low Box: 384th Bomb Group

Combat Wing Leader: Lieutenant-Colonel Maurice A. Preston, commander of the 379th Bomb Group.

Combat Wing Target: KLÖCKNER AERO-ENGINE FACTORY

> High Box: 381st Bomb Group
> Lead Box: 91st Bomb Group
> Low Box: 351st Bomb Group

Combat Wing Leader: Major David G. Alford, operations officer of the 91st Bomb Group

It will be convenient, in this narrative, to refer to these two formations as the 'Blohm & Voss wing' and the 'Klöckner wing', although they were not so named at the time. The allocation of groups to combat wings was automatic; the same three groups always flew in company with each other in these wings. The positioning of groups within the wings was a routine procedure; the high, lead and low positions were rotated between groups in strict sequence. It was generally accepted that the low box was the most dangerous, the lead box the safest, and the high box the most difficult in which to keep formation because the planes there were flying near their maximum ceiling.

The average American raid was far less demanding than that of R.A.F. Bomber Command. Nearly every R.A.F. raid was a 'maximum effort' one, with every available aircraft having to fly. The Americans rarely used the maximum effort. The standard group box required only three of a group's four squadrons to fly. In this way, one quarter of the planes and their crews could be rested on each raid so that the Eighth Air Force could continue operating for several consecutive days when one of the rare periods of prolonged clear weather became available. The best period of such weather in 1943 was just commencing.

There was much work to be done at the American airfields – work in offices, in workshops, at bomb dumps and out at the hardstandings on which the B-17s were parked. Much of this work was done during the night but, because the take-off time was not to be until early afternoon of the Sunday, the pressure on the ground crews and office personnel was not so intense on this occasion. There is no need to go into too much detail but some details are essential. Each Fortress was loaded with ten 500-lb high-explosive bombs if its group was flying in the high or lead position or sixteen 250-lb incendiaries if in the low position. It is probable that the planes carrying these lighter incendiary loads should have been in the high position and that there was a mix-up in the orders on this day. Approximately 1,850 U.S. gallons of fuel were pumped into the tanks of each of the Hamburg-bound planes.

A total of 323 B-17s were fuelled and armed ready for the operations of Sunday, 25 July. The names of 3,230 airmen appeared on the 'loading lists' – the U.S.A.A.F. equivalent to the R.A.F. 'battle order' – to fly these planes. Of these planes and their crews 123 were to fly to Hamburg and drop the first American bombs on that city.

The alert that we would be flying next day would, in most cases, have the effect of cancelling any plans one might have for romancing or pub-crawling, or just plain 'living-it-up' at the Officers' Club mess. But there were many 'last flings' the night before a mission, with participants suffering the consequences the following day, followed by great gulps of oxygen to help chase away the effects of the 'morning-after' feeling. (Lieutenant Carl B. Stackhouse, 351st Bomb Group)

At 7.55 a.m. on that Sunday, another Mosquito of the R.A.F.'s Meteorological Flight took off from Oakington and flew out over the North Sea. It had become a regular duty for the R.A.F. to carry out weather reconnaissance flights for the Americans, the code word for the Eighth Air Force in the Met. Flight's record book being 'Pinetrees'. The Mosquito made a landfall at the island of Sylt, near the Danish border, then turned south and flew across the Heligoland Bight as far as Heligoland itself before turning for home. Its crew's orders were to observe both the high and low cloud in this area and to report details by wireless to their base. The flight was carried out successfully and, by approximately 9.30 a.m., the Americans knew that their proposed flights to Kiel and Hamburg could expect to find comparatively cloud-free conditions. The more distant flight to Warnemünde could not be so accurately forecast. This R.A.F. report set in motion the final preparations for the American raids.

There was much apprehension at the crew briefings. Raids were known as 'milk runs' or 'toughies'; today's targets were definitely the latter. These are some of the memories of the men in the groups ordered to fly to Hamburg.

When the cover was pulled off the mission board, I wanted to crawl under my chair. Good God, the flight tape was all over the goddamm place – and into Germany, mostly, to boot. As the cover was taken off the board, revealing our mission, there was the sound of everyone drawing in their breath. Then dead silence for four or five seconds. Our engineer, sitting next to me, gave out a drawn out 'Goddamm', while Captain Joe just said a quiet 'Sheeiitt!' I never heard much of the briefing statistics because I had to keep swallowing my heart down and fight to keep my stomach from bouncing around out of place. I was really scared! (Staff Sergeant George H. Orin, 381st Bomb Group)

When Pop Dolan, the briefing officer, rolled back the curtain he didn't say anything to start with. It was self-explanatory. There was an air of apprehension – dismay would be a better word – because this was our deepest penetration into Germany. When we saw the lines on the map, after the successful mission to Norway the day before, we didn't look forward to this deep one. We expected terrific opposition. There was a sound went up from all of us. You could hear such as, 'Boy! That's going to be a tough one', 'It's going to be a long one.' It was all quietly done, each man saying something to the next man. (Second Lieutenant Paul H. Gordy, 384th Bomb Group)

There was definitely an air of apprehension about this briefing. It's always stuck in my mind that, after the target had been revealed, every navigator in the group prepared a course for the nearest friendly country. Sweden, I think it was, on this day. (Lieutenant Howard L. Cromwell, 384th Bomb Group)

The Americans had lunch after the briefings, one radio man remembering 'a very fine roast beef meal that I ate many times in my memory in the following months when I was a prisoner'. The crews were taken out to their planes and stood around, waiting for the signal to board and start engines. The scene was exactly the same as on the R.A.F. heavy-bomber airfields before a raid, except that the action now was all in the middle of a beautiful summer day. The graceful B-17s rumbled round the perimeter tracks to the main runways, the eighteen or so bombers preparing to take off creating a most impressive picture of strength. This scene was being repeated on fifteen airfields.

After the Hamburg groups started taking off, soon after 1.0 p.m., came one of the most difficult parts of the mission – the assembly of the combat wings. It was relatively easy to assemble the three squadrons of one group above the home airfield but it was more difficult to get the planes of three groups from three separate airfields together in the correct formation, especially in cloudy weather. On this afternoon, there was only some patchy low cloud but there was much haze at the levels at which the combat wings were assembling. So, while an R.A.F. bomber could take off in the dark and fly straight off to Germany without a thought to other aircraft in the sky, the Americans had to wheel their large formations around the skies over East Anglia looking for each other. The theoretical procedure was to rendezvous over the airfield of the high group in the combat wing and then fly a direct line, firstly away from the coast and then towards the coast, along a series of radio beacons to effect the wing assembly. Groups that were ahead of the combat wing reduced speed slightly –

not easy with fully laden aircraft at low altitudes – or they 'essed' their way in a series of shallow turns. Groups lagging behind had to increase speed, again not an easy thing to do without consuming too much fuel.

On that Sunday afternoon, while thousands of English families were sitting out in their gardens below, the three groups that were to bomb the Blohm & Voss shipyards managed their assembly without too much difficulty and were soon heading out over the North Sea from the same seaside town of Cromer that had been the last sight of land for some of the R.A.F. bombers the previous evening. This combat wing left the English coast exactly on time and in good formation. The Klöckner combat wing had less success. The lead group – the 91st – was one minute early at the rendezvous point and could find neither of its two companion groups for some time. It flew on through its line of radio beacons but, when no other aircraft joined, it circled back, firing red flares to attract attention. This brought in the low group – the 351st – but there was still no sign of the high group. Major David Alford, the wing leader, had now lost several minutes and he decided to set course for Germany. After leaving the coast, the missing group – the 381st – was sighted ahead. This group then circled to get into the wing formation but lost ground on the turn and finished up well to the rear. This combat wing flew out over the North Sea, late, in poor formation and with the three groups due to expend much effort in the next two hours in attempts to come together properly.

While these complicated assembly manoeuvres had been taking place, a number of aircraft had turned back because of mechanical or other difficulties. The question of 'abortives' was a sensitive one and, just as in the R.A.F., every effort was being made to reduce their numbers. Many groups took 'air spares', up to three extra aircraft that would fly as far as the English coast to replace early returns. The two Hamburg formations lost thirteen aircraft returning early, twelve for mechanical reasons and one because its pilot reported that he was ill. This abortive rate of 10·4 per cent was almost twice that for the R.A.F. the previous night but, as in so many matters of an operational nature, the Americans had so much less experience. The Americans would improve. The two combat wings flew on across the North Sea, 112 aircraft strong. The Blohm & Voss wing had fifty-nine planes. This was five more than the standard combat-wing formation; some of its squadrons were flying in formations of seven rather than six.

The afternoon became a brilliantly sunny one once the Fortresses had climbed through the haze. The formations settled down for their flight across the North Sea. Their crossing would take 110 minutes, exactly the same as that of the R.A.F. night bombers. The American knowledge of European geography was often faulty; a large number of American airmen refer to this flight as being 'across the Channel'. This part of the flight was an important one for the navigators in the lead planes of each wing. Upon their skill depended a good landfall on the German coast and the subsequent approach to the target. The navigators had the help of Gee until this useful device was jammed about two-thirds of the way through the sea crossing. All other navigators could only fill in a 'follow-the-pilot' plot. Their skills would not be fully tested unless their plane was forced out of formation. The climb to full operational height was delayed for as long as possible because of the low temperatures and more difficult aircraft handling conditions encountered at altitude. The first part of the sea crossing was flown in a gentle climb to 13,000 feet where the outside temperature was −3° Centigrade, but a steeper climb was later used to reach operational height which, for the high groups, was 28,000 feet. The temperature at this height was a ferocious −35°. The forward part of each B-17 was heated but the four men in the rear – the tail gunner, the ball gunner in the belly of the plane and the two waist gunners – would fight a constant battle against the cold even though they had heated suits. These waist gunners, at their open side windows, had the coldest positions of all. It was a common sight to see them pounding their fingers on their guns or on ammunition boxes, trying to maintain the circulation in their fingers.

The pilots were working hard to keep position in their formations. Formation flying was always difficult and often dangerous. No American pilot will forget the horrible sensation of flying into the invisible 'prop wash' of another bomber. 'You were thrown right off, just like running out of road suddenly with a car.' This pilot was leading a flight of three planes in a high group.

The memory that most bomber pilots have is of the extreme physical exertion required in flying close formation in the turbulent air generated by so many propellers. Normal movement of controls would not suffice to make corrections in flight due to the turbulence. After climbing to high altitudes, where air was thinner, lead times for corrections had to be lengthened due to slow response in this element. Even though the air temperature is twenty to thirty below zero, the pilots were always bathed in sweat. The further back in formation, the more difficult to maintain formation, due to the accordion effect of every pilot's constant changing of power settings et cetera. It was sort of like the end man of crack-the-whip kid's game. (Lieutenant Jack H. Owen, 381st Bomb Group)

After passing through the turning point at 06.00 E, 125 miles out from the German coast, the combat wings turned to the south-easterly course that would take them into the Heligoland Bight and on, past the landfall at Cuxhaven and then straight through to the position south-west of Hamburg at which they would turn to commence their bomb runs. The final preparations for action were taken. The bombardier of each aircraft had to go down into the bomb bay and, walking along the narrow catwalk between the bombs and holding his portable oxygen bottle in one hand, pull out the arming pins of his bombs. Gunners tested their weapons. Captains called up all crew positions to check that every man was ready for whatever was to come. Steel Flak helmets were donned by those crew members who had bothered to bring them; Flak suits had not yet been issued.

A résumé of the state in which the various American formations reached the German coast is important. One of the Hamburg combat wings made a good landfall at the correct time ordered for it by the overall American tactical plan and in good formation. The other Hamburg wing was late and still not properly assembled into combat formation. The two combat wings bound for Warnemünde, which had been flying forty minutes ahead, had carried out their part in the tactical plan efficiently. They had completed their diversionary flight off the German coast between Heligoland and the Danish frontier and, at the time that the leading Hamburg wing was crossing the German coast, these Fortresses

had already crossed the Danish coast 100 miles to the north.
But the combat wing, whose target was to have been Kiel,
was not present. It had never managed to complete its assembly
and, although its groups had flown separately to within sight
of the German coast, the combat-wing leader had ordered the
entire force of fifty-nine aircraft to return to England.

The first part of the American tactical plan had been
partially successful. The approach of the two American and
British light bomber forces with strong fighter escorts had been
detected approaching Holland by the German long-range
radar and had successfully attracted attention. German
fighter controllers had sent up twenty-four Messerschmitt 109s
from Schiphol airfield to attack 'a force of heavy bombers'. It
was only when the German fighters made contact with the
raiders that it was realized that these were not B-17s. There
had been a short but fierce fight in which seven Spitfires and
two German fighters were shot down. Then, 160 miles to the
north, the 4th Bombardment Wing's two combat wings had
been detected approaching the German coast in the Heligoland
Bight. Again the Germans reacted, this time more strongly. A
force of twenty to thirty twin-engined fighters took off from
Leeuwarden, in Holland, and a further force of single-engined
fighters – probably about fifty in number – were dispatched
from the North German airfields of Jever, Heligoland and
Husum. But, when these B-17s did not fly straight into
Germany but turned north and flew parallel with the German
coast for twenty minutes, only one *Staffel* of the five that had
been ordered up found the bombers. The remainder had to
return to their bases and refuel. Those German fighters that
had found the American bombers were only in contact with
them for four minutes, during which time they made two
attacks but the B-17 combat wings were both flying in tight
formation and no bombers were shot down. One Messerschmitt 109 went down to join that host of wrecked aeroplanes
that must litter the floor of the North Sea.

The result of these early actions was that, when the two
Hamburg-bound combat wings approached the German
coast, a large part of the available German fighter effort had
been successfully drawn into wasted flights and were now
flying home to refuel. This major new American force, only
thirty minutes flying time from Hamburg, was now recognized

by the Germans to be a dangerous threat and all or most of those fighters still available were ordered to take off and attempt to intercept it. The initial success of the American plan had given this force an excellent opportunity of getting through to its target without serious opposition. The withdrawal flight would be another matter.

The Hamburg combat wings approached the German coast in perfect flying conditions. There was no cloud, high or low. Visibility to the ground was estimated at ten miles but, at the height at which the bombers were flying, it was that known as CAVU – 'ceiling and visibility unlimited'. The Fortresses were leaving only faint condensation trails on this day and, from the ground, the American bombers would appear only as the tiniest of silver dots. The Blohm & Voss combat wing crossed the German coast dead on time but 1,500 feet below its ordered height. The wing leader, Lieutenant-Colonel Preston, had climbed more slowly during the last stage of the sea crossing in order to give his wing a chance to close up really tight. That final 1,500 feet of height would be achieved before Hamburg was reached. The landfall on the German coast was an important moment. The distinctive port of Cuxhaven on the southern bank of the mouth of the River Elbe had been chosen on this occasion and the lead navigator, Lieutenant Andrew K. Dutch, made a perfect arrival over it. The Klöckner combat wing made a less accurate landfall but it soon adjusted and followed on, approximately seven minutes behind, although its high group, the 381st, had still not closed up with the remainder of the combat wing.

Some German fighters had been seen just before the coast was crossed but no attack had developed. These were probably fighters which had been out looking for the earlier B-17 formation, and were now returning to their airfields. A more immediate danger to the Fortresses was the fierce Flak that greeted them at the German coast. There were many heavy Flak batteries in this area and also there appeared to be Flak ships in Cuxhaven harbour. The two combat wings were soon surrounded by the black puffs of exploding shells.

The American airmen hated Flak; there was so little that any individual man could do about it. The combat wing had to remain on its basic course although lead pilots of squadrons or flights could try a series of very gentle turns, hoping to avoid the radar-predicted shells that took thirty seconds to reach their height. The natural tendency for individual pilots was to fly slightly apart from their neighbours, in order not to present the German gunners with too compact a target. 'When the Flak starts, you shake it out a little. When the fighters come in, you close it up – and pray.' But such 'shaking out' under Flak fire was not approved of. It was the mark of a good group that its planes kept well closed up at all times, ready to meet fighter attack.

The Flak had some success. There were no direct hits but one of the B-17s in the lead group of the Blohm & Voss wing had an engine damaged near Cuxhaven. The bomber fell back out of the formation and its pilot, Lieutenant Ashley, decided to turn back. His bombardier released their ten 500-lb bombs on two merchant ships seen in the mouth of the River Elbe. This aircraft reached England safely. Deeper into Germany, several more planes were hit by fragments of shell and suffered serious damage to engines. Three B-17s, all in the Blohm & Voss wing, started to fall back from their formation – a typical example of the results of Flak fire disabling individual American bombers and forcing them to become lone stragglers.

Among the German fighter units ordered up to attack the Hamburg bombers was II/JG 11 – the second *Gruppe* of *Jagdgeschwader* 11 – whose airfield was at Jever, only forty-five miles south-west of the bombers' route inland from Cuxhaven. It is not known exactly how many of this *Gruppe*'s Messerschmitt 109s took off – probably between thirty and forty – but it is known that the *Gruppenkommandeur*, Hauptmann Günther Specht, led his unit into action. There were many German units in action on that Sunday afternoon but it is possible to highlight part of the action of this one because, for once in a day-fighter unit, a good witness from the German side is available and there is enough documentary evidence to provide a sound basis for the following account.

Flying in '*Schwarms*' of four aircraft, the *Gruppe* started to make a series of head-on attacks against the Blohm & Voss wing. As each *Schwarm* completed its attack, it dived away, bellies uppermost, then came round to the front to attack again. Second Lieutenants James E. Armstrong and Paul H.

Gordy were a pilot and co-pilot respectively in two planes of the 384th Bomb Group which were in the American formation being attacked.

Of course, I was watching the flight leader's plane all the time, to tuck our wing in as close to his as we could, but I did see the fighters going out to the front and then turning in to attack. Most of them were dropping away below after attacking but one of them didn't; he just came right on through our squadron. For the first time I could see an Me 109 up close, not more than a hundred feet away. I could clearly see the cross on the side in black and the pilot at the controls. It was the first real battle we had gotten into and I thought that German was quite a daredevil. I can still see him today, barrelling through. He was firing but I don't know which plane he was firing at. He certainly didn't hit us. I don't think our gunners were firing at him because of the fear of hitting our own planes.

I remember seeing a group of fifteen or so on the right-hand side and some of the gunners were reporting others. I'd never seen that many before and I felt the same kind of fear that I had felt every time since my first mission – the fear of not knowing what was ahead. At this time in the war, the American flyer had the greatest respect for the ability and equipment of the Luftwaffe.

We started to receive fighter passes and you could hear our guns firing. In a ship like ours, there was quite a racket when you had six or eight fifty-calibre guns starting to fire over the normal engine and wind noises that you were used to. You got a quickening of the heart beat because you know they're coming in. The guys had a tendency to become very excitable and, when one of them kept his mike on, no one else could talk. Whichever pilot wasn't flying the plane had to keep monitoring the crew, telling someone to get off so that he could get reports from others.

We had been under attack for about five minutes when there was a loud banging sound and the first pilot, Floyd Edwards, who was flying the ship at that time, turned and hit me on the shoulder with his right hand and simply said, 'Take it.' He immediately grabbed a knife and reached down and ripped his flying suit on his left leg side. He had a bullet through the calf of his leg and he was in a great deal of pain. I was kept pretty busy then, maintaining formation. We said nothing over the intercom; we didn't want to tell the crew that anything was wrong in the cockpit. Everything was under control and we just wanted everyone to keep at his job.

Paul Gordy flew his plane safely home but was to become a prisoner of war four days later.

One of the German pilots taking part in this action was

Leutnant Wolfgang Gloerfeld. Gloerfeld's fighter had been specially fitted with two heavy 30-mm cannons instead of the standard 20-mm cannons of the Messerschmitt 109. Because this heavier armament made his plane less manoeuvrable, he flew alone, just above and behind one of the *Schwarms*. Leutnant Gloerfeld's account will be presented exactly as it was given; the errors in it, understandable in a high-speed, head-on combat, will be corrected later.

I followed the others in on their second attack. I felt sorry for the American pilots having to face this mass of fire. If even one per cent of our shots had hit, we would have shot down the whole *Pulk* but, fortunately for them, we didn't. I felt that the American formation was not as tight as on our first attack and I chose the extreme right-hand Boeing that I could see. It came into my gun sight in copybook fashion but my timing was wrong; I was too near when I opened fire. Although I was only firing for half a second or a second at most, the left wing of that bomber fell right off. I saw it before me, the whole wing with both engines. I don't know what happened to the bomber because I must have touched this falling wing with my own right wing which broke off at once and, when my plane whipped over, the left wing came off too. It was very useful that they both came off because that saved the aircraft from spinning.

I tried to bale out but the cockpit cover was jammed. The whole lot came off normally but, on this occasion, the rear part didn't release and my parachute caught inside it. Naturally, I pushed hard with my feet and I think that I must have jerked the control column, thus shaking the aircraft and throwing me out. I didn't remember anything else but I came down near a Flak position in open country just south of the Elbe. The soldiers told me, later, that they had seen me leaving the aircraft at only one thousand metres and my parachute opened just before I hit the ground. The aircraft was never found; I think it went into a marsh.

Gloerfeld suffered a double fracture of the skull and broken ribs, cheek, jaw and forearm. He was back on combat flying in November 1943 but was shot down again on 11 January 1944 – his third time by B-17s – and so severely injured that he never flew again.

The 'wing' that Leutnant Gloerfeld's fighter had hit was actually one of the stabilizers (sometimes known as 'tailplanes') from the tail of the Fortress of Second Lieutenant Philip A. Mohr, who had been flying as 'tail end Charlie' in the low squadron of the 379th Bomb Group. Gloerfeld's heavy

30-mm cannon shells had shot the stabilizer clean off the Fortress. Mohr's bomber flew on for some time, possibly even remaining in the formation through the target area, but it fell out later, was attacked by fighters again and eventually crashed twenty-five miles west of Hamburg. Four of its crew were killed. Another Fortress in the same squadron, captained by Lieutenant Frank Hildebrandt, was also damaged in the earlier fighter attack. It went down more quickly and crashed into the Wandsbek district of Hamburg but not before all ten men in its crew had baled out. A third plane in this squadron, that of Lieutenant Willis Carlisle, was also hit. A cannon shell exploded in the cockpit and killed Carlisle. His co-pilot, Lieutenant Bigler, took the controls and kept the bomber flying in its formation right back to England despite the fact that its oxygen system had been damaged. Three of his crew were unconscious by the time this plane landed in England.

The Germans also suffered casualties. Besides the loss of Leutnant Gloerfeld's fighter, one more Messerschmitt 109 had been shot down and a third was severely damaged when its pilot crash-landed. When the American formation drew near Hamburg, the *Gruppe* still had fuel remaining and they stayed in contact with the bombers and would resume their attacks after the Americans had flown through the Hamburg Flak barrage.

This fierce engagement highlights several interesting points. More than thirty heavily armed German fighters, each making two attacks, had failed to break up this combat wing. Two B-17s had been damaged so severely that they would be forced out of their formation and would eventually crash but the sturdy construction of these American Fortresses had protected them from the sudden and drastic explosion or fire that destroyed so many R.A.F. bombers when attacked. The second of the two combat wings heading for Hamburg was not attacked at all on its flight to the target. These results show, first, that the American tactical plan had worked well in its opening stages and had helped many bombers to remain free of serious fighter attack and, second, that a well-led, tightly flown B-17 formation was a very difficult target for a force of German fighters to tackle.

Throughout the German fighter attacks, the B-17s had been flying steadily on, true airspeed 215 m.p.h., heights now between 26,000 and 28,500 feet. The lead navigators were working hard, scanning the ground below to ensure they were exactly on course. Lead bombardiers were also busy, calculating the speed and strength of the wind. These vital details were needed to make final adjustments to bomb-sights.

Sixty miles inland from Cuxhaven and just off the Hamburg–Bremen Autobahn lies the small village of Hollenstedt. In 1943, the Buchholz–Bremervörde railway line crossed over the wide Autobahn here – a distinctive junction easily visible to the men in the American bombers. This was the 'Initial Point', an important position in the American bombing plan and the choice of which had been the result of careful thought. It was from this point that the bombers would commence their bombing run. Until now, the two combat wings had been flying south-east, giving every intention of passing south of Hamburg and striking deeper into Germany. But a sharp turn to port over the Initial Point put the bombers on to a direct course for their targets in Hamburg only fifteen miles or four minutes flying time away. It was hoped that Hamburg's Flak defences would be caught unawares by this sudden turn.

The road and railway junction was successfully spotted and identified well before it was reached but the sharp turn here was not an easy manoeuvre. Major Clinton Ball was the lead pilot in the low group – the 351st – of the Klöckner wing.

Running up to the I.P., the lead navigators and bombardiers are looking out of the nose, trying hard to guide the lead pilots. The combat-wing leader would have swung south a little, first, then turned to fly up the Autobahn until he crossed the road–rail junction. He has to be careful to make sure that his turn is neither too tight nor too loose. His group follow him and the high and low groups slide across and get into position above and below, in echelon.

Immediately above the I.P., the bombardier in the lead ship of each group takes over; you could have left the rest of the bombardiers and navigators at home. The lead pilot switches to AFCE – automatic pilot – and it is 'hands off' for him then. The plane's controls are actually moved by the bombardier's manipulation of his bombsight. Lead pilots hated this; we had no control over our own planes. It was against all a pilot's instinct.

On this afternoon, both combat wings found the Initial Point without difficulty, turned correctly, and settled down to commence their separate bombing runs to the targets. The Blohm & Voss wing was still approximately seven minutes flying time ahead of and just out of visual contact with the Klöckner wing.

Lieutenant-Colonel Preston's plane led his 379th Bomb Group on the course heading directly at its target. The two other groups in this wing fell slightly back, behind one another, to become 'column of groups' so that the lead bombardier of each group could pass over the centre of the Blohm & Voss shipyard. The groups would reassemble into their combat-wing formation as soon as they had bombed. The American airmen now saw a fantastic sight – the still burning city of Hamburg, with a huge pall of dark smoke from the R.A.F. bombing of fourteen hours earlier hovering in the sky. None of the Americans had seen a German city burning like this before. One pilot thought, at first, that he was flying towards a thunderstorm and many of the Americans did not realize that the smoke came from fires. The records of one group contain this entry: 'The target area was very heavily covered with an intense smoke-screen. . . . Effective smoke-screens were obscuring target areas for approximately fifty square miles.'[1] This unexpected smoke was to have much influence on the efforts of the American bombardiers.

The full might of Hamburg's formidable Flak defences was now let loose on the American formations. It appears that the Flak was firing a series of successive 'box barrages' through which the B-17s had to fly, fresh boxes of fire being laid down ahead of the groups as they drew nearer to the city. This was a dangerous and frightening experience for the American airmen, who say that this was easily the densest Flak fire they had yet encountered, more severe than that over the U-boat base at St Nazaire in France.

Bomb doors were opened forty seconds before the release point. All the American planes were carrying cameras which took a series of photographs after their bombs had been released. The many photographs available from this source enable a reliable account to be given of the American bombing that afternoon. The three groups of Lieutenant-Colonel Preston's wing all bombed within a four-minute period starting at 4.34 p.m. Unfortunately, the conditions that the bombardiers found were difficult ones.

Between the bombers and the ground, a light wind was blowing from a direction of 330 degrees, approximately from the north-west. The dense clouds of smoke still being produced from the R.A.F. bombing areas north of the Elbe, particularly from the Altona district just across the river from the Blohm & Voss shipyard, were billowing upwards and then being carried away in a direction which just covered the shipyard. As the American planes approached, the bombardiers could see their target clearly but, as the planes came nearer and the angle changed, the shipyard became obscured. The bombardiers could only aim as best they could at the gradually disappearing target. The American photographs show that no artificial smoke-screen was being produced at this time. The bomb-loads of the three American groups went down, each plane's bombardier releasing his load when he saw the bombs of his group leader start to fall. Forty-nine aircraft in the leading wing are believed to have bombed the main target, dropping 340 500-lb high-explosive bombs and 272 250-lb incendiaries. (Some American reports say that 100-lb incendiaries were also dropped but this is believed to be an error.) The bombs were seen to burst, some dimly through the smoke over the Blohm & Voss yard, some in the clear area south of it. As soon as they had bombed, the American planes turned away to the east, to avoid the worst of Hamburg's Flak, but the unwieldy turns of the groups took them over the centre and then the eastern districts of the city.

If bombing conditions had been difficult for the Blohm & Voss wing, they were impossible for the Klöckner wing following behind. This wing should have been immediately behind the Blohm & Voss wing so that the two combat wings could approach Hamburg and fly through the target area during the same period, thus splitting the Hamburg Flak. Being late, this wing had to face the full force of the Flak alone. Worse still, the wing's high group had still not closed up and was lagging one or two minutes behind. This wing used the same Initial Point as the earlier wing but, then, should have flown a slightly more easterly course towards the Klöckner factory. But, as Major Alford's lead plane approached the southern part of Hamburg, his bombardier saw that the area

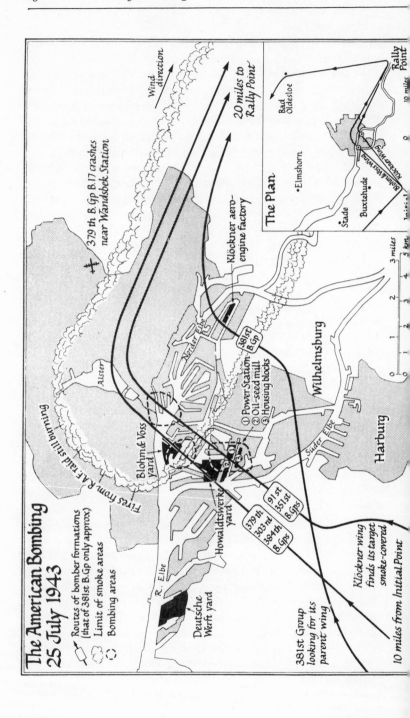

The American Bombing
25 July 1943

Routes of bomber formations
(that of 381st B.Gp only approx.)
Limit of smoke areas
Bombing areas

Wind direction

379th B.Gp B.17 crashes
near Wandsbek Station

Fires from R.A.F. raid still burning

R. Elbe

Alster

Blohm & Voss yard

Howaldtswerke yard

Deutsche Werft yard

Nieder Elbe

① Power Station
② Oil-seed mill
③ Housing blocks

Klöckner aero-
engine factory

20 miles to
Rally Point

381st
B.Gp

91st
351st
B.Gps

379th
303rd
384th
B.Gps

Süder Elbe

Wilhelmsburg

Harburg

Klöckner wing finds its target
smoke-covered

381st Group
looking for its
parent wing

10 miles from Initial Point

0   1   2   3 miles
0 1 2 3 4 5 km

The Plan

Bad
Oldesloe

Elmshorn

Stade

Buxtehude

Blohm & Voss Wing

Klöckner Wing

Rally
Point

10 miles

Initial

in which the Klöckner factory was situated was completely covered by smoke. It was at this time that the aircraft of the wing ahead were seen for the first time during the flight. The bombardier made the swift decision to give up the attempt to bomb the Klöckner factory and to follow the leading wing in, hoping to find a suitable target. The lead plane soon reached the area recently bombed by the preceding bombers but the bombardier had no time to study his maps which would have shown what useful targets there might be here. German smoke-screens were just starting but they had not yet developed and visibility was good over the area not covered by the smoke cloud. The intricate network of quays and basins of part of the Hamburg dock area could be seen below. A prominent group of red-topped buildings, on a strip of land between two waterways, caught the bombardier's eye. The 500-lb bombs of the eighteen planes of the 91st Bomb Group were dropped on these buildings and, after the period of their fall had elapsed, the bombs could be seen bursting in a group around the buildings. Then, among the bomb bursts, could be seen one large white explosion which was duly photographed by one bomber's camera.

The group flying with the 91st was the 351st Bomb Group, led by Major Ball and carrying incendiary bomb-loads. It is probable that, because of the confusion over the last-minute change of target, Major Ball had received no orders from his combat-wing leader or, if he had, he had only been told to find any useful target he could. The photographs taken by Major Ball's group show that his bombardier had followed the 91st Bomb Group's flight path but had flown on further to release his group's bombs into the smoke cloud.

The poor 381st Bomb Group had had a difficult time all through the flight so far. Six of its aircraft had aborted, including the designated group leader and, ever since then, the deputy leader, Captain George Shackley, had been unsuccessfully struggling to join his depleted group up with the two other groups in his wing which he could see ahead. On approaching Hamburg, Captain Shackley decided to catch up by a drastic cutting of the corner at the Initial Point and had, thus, approached the city from the west rather than the south-west. He led his group, alone, right across the southern part of Hamburg to the area where he expected to find the remainder of his wing bombing the Klöckner factory. But the other two groups were not to be found there and no sign of the Klöckner factory could be seen through the dense smoke. Shackley ordered his bombardier to retain his bomb-load and close the bomb doors and he flew on, hoping to catch up with his wing at the reassembly point east of Ham-burg and hoping, too, to find some other target to bomb during the return flight to the German coast. The seventeen aircraft of this group attracted the attention of most of Hamburg's Flak in their lone flight over the city. Sixteen of the seventeen Fortresses were damaged by fragments of Flak shell.

This American bombing of Hamburg had taken twelve minutes. If the second combat wing had been on time, the bombing could have taken no more than six minutes. This compares with the fifty-eight minutes of the R.A.F. raid the previous night. Ninety B-17s had dropped 186 tons of bombs in as accurate a manner as the smoke had permitted, compared with the 2,290 tons dropped by 733 R.A.F. bombers in their Area Bombing attack. Thanks to Window, the R.A.F. bombers had been very little troubled by Flak the previous night but, in the bright sunshine of this afternoon, the B-17s had suffered badly. No less than seventy-eight of the 109 planes that flew in formation over Hamburg suffered some form of Flak damage. There had been no spectacular explo-sions of bombers blowing up but several planes had suffered serious damage to engines or vital controls and were starting to fall back from their formations. The fortunes of these limping casualties will be described later.

The six B-17 groups made for the designated reassembly point – called the 'Rally Point' – twenty-five miles east of Hamburg, where they hoped to regroup their defensive formations ready for the battle with German fighters that was expected to take place during the withdrawal flight round the north of Hamburg and back to the German coast.

Hamburg had never been bombed by the Americans before. There had been many daylight alerts but never any bombs. The city authorities had their hands full on that Sunday, dealing with the aftermath of the R.A.F. night raid and some of them had undoubtedly been taken by surprise by the sudden approach of the American bombers. The Flak had been ready and had given the bombers the warm welcome already described but the customary *Luftgefahr* advance warnings, given by telephone to industry, railways and civil-defence units, were never given at all and the public alarm was not sounded until 4.26 p.m., four minutes before the first bombs fell outside the city and eight minutes before the Blohm & Voss area was bombed.

By using German records and many American bombing photographs, it is possible to provide a reliable account of the effects of the bombing. It was probably early Flak damage that caused several of the American planes to release their bombs short of the target. The Hamburg Chief of Police's report contains photographs of several cows killed in fields south of the city. In Hamburg itself, it was the bombing of the three groups of Lieutenant-Colonel Preston's combat wing – first over the target – that had been the most concentrated but, probably because of the gradual intrusion of the smoke cloud over the Blohm & Voss shipyard, the centre of the bombing concentration had been 350 yards short of the centre of that target. Some bombs had fallen in the eastern corner of the yard but this was not where the great phalanx of U-boat slipways were located. Several important buildings were destroyed and the yard's own casting foundry suffered a bad fire. Blohm & Voss were the only Hamburg shipyard to have its own foundry. No one in the yard was hurt. A lookout on a watch-tower had seen the American bombers approaching and his warning was just timely enough to allow those workers who were in the yard that Sunday afternoon to reach the air-raid shelters. The damage caused must have delayed the building of some U-boats but it is impossible to measure the exact effect because the R.A.F. bombing of the previous night had also hit this yard.

Not all of those American bombs that had fallen short of the Blohm & Voss yard had been wasted. To the south of the yard were the quays and the harbour installations of the Kuhwärder Hafen and Kaiser-Wilhelm Hafen. Although most of the bombs had exploded harmlessly in the water, direct hits were certainly scored on two important ships. The first of these was the 36,000-ton passenger ship *Vaterland*, which had never been completed because of the outbreak of war. The management of Blohm & Voss had known that the firm's stocks of timber would be vulnerable to fire in the event of air raids and had, therefore, loaded all the timber into this ship and towed it round to the Kuhwärder Hafen at the back of the shipyard to act as a permanent timber store. A spectacular 500-lb bomb explosion had ripped open the *Vaterland*'s foredeck and flung it back against the bridge. The timber inside the ship had then caught fire and most of it had been reduced to ashes. A smaller passenger ship near by, the 11,254-ton *General Artigas*, had also been hit and sunk. This ship was being used as an accommodation ship by the German Navy. It is not known whether any German sailors were killed. It is probable that the serious damage known to have been caused to two floating docks in this area was also caused by the American bombs.

Major Alford's 91st Bomb Group had aimed their bombs at a cluster of prominent buildings with red roofs seen short of the smoke area. These were in the Neuhof part of the Wilhelmsburg district; the 'red-roofed buildings' were undoubtedly the important Neuhof electricity generating station – the largest in Hamburg – the Hansa–Mühle vegetable-oil factory and some very large workers' apartment buildings in the Köhlbrandstrasse and the Nippoldstrasse, only 150 yards from the generating station. The bombs dropped here had not achieved such a tight concentration as those of the leading groups, being spread over an area 2,000 yards long, but it should be remembered that this was the bombing of a group that had been forced to abandon its designated target – the Klöckner aero-engine factory – and find this new target under very difficult conditions. Again, many of the bombs had fallen uselessly into waterways but two had hit the workers' apartments, one bomb had blown up an oil-storage tank at the generating station, causing the big explosion seen by the American airmen, and at least one bomb had hit the Hansa-Mühle factory, starting a big oil fire and killing seven of the mixed work-force: four Russians, two Germans and a Dutchman. Several bombs had fallen into the Howaldtswerke shipyard a little further north. Howaldtswerke was also a U-boat yard and much damage was done here, including much destruction in a diesel-engine works of the M.A.N. company that was situated within the Howaldtswerke premises.

In the red-roofed apartment block that had been hit by two bombs, the civilians had heard the air-raid sirens but many had thought that this could only be because of the routine visit of an R.A.F. reconnaissance plane to photograph the results of the previous night's bombing. It was only when the block warden had heard nearby Flak batteries firing, that he had rushed around and made the inhabitants go down to the basement shelters. Frau Maria Stanke, the pregnant wife of a railwayman, was preparing a meal for her husband who had just come in from work. Her mother-in-law told her to take her three children down to the shelter while she looked after the cooking. Herr Stanke and his mother were the only people killed from approximately 1,000 civilians living in these blocks. The block warden was afterwards given the credit for preventing a much greater loss of life.

The last American bombing had been the incendiary bombs dropped by Major Ball's 351st Bomb Group into the smoke cloud. Buried deep in the appendixes of the Hamburg Chief of Police's report is an interesting item about the activities of factory fire-fighters of the Rhenania Ossag firm, which had a small oil refinery at Grasbrook, on the south bank of the Elbe and just opposite the centre of the main city of Hamburg.[2] The incendiary bombs had set fire to two oil-storage tanks and a workshop building here. It can be assumed that other bombs fell in this industrial area but there are no other reports which might give details.

Only a few bombs had fallen in the main city, north of the river. Isolated incidents were reported in the districts of Harvestehude, Hamm and Wandsbek. These may have been caused by some of the 351st Group's incendiaries, although the Wandsbek bombs were high explosives and may have been from Lieutenant Hildebrant's Fortress which crashed near Wandsbek Station after all its crew had baled out. The Chief of Police's report also contains a short reference to the deaths of three railway wagon-loads of animals from the Hagenbeck Zoo which were hit somewhere near the main Hamburg Station while waiting to be evacuated to Vienna Zoo.[3]

Very few people in the main part of the city had been troubled by the American raid; indeed, a few may not have even realized that a raid had taken place. They had probably not seen the tiny silver dots five miles up in the sky. The Flak fire and the explosions of the American bombs south of the river had intermingled with the explosions of R.A.F. delayed-action bombs, which had been bursting all through the day, and with the crashing to the ground of buildings still burning from the previous night.

The All Clear sounded at 5.22 p.m., half an hour after the American bombers had departed. Two of Hamburg's U-boat yards and various minor industrial premises had been damaged, with an effect on production that cannot be measured, but the American method of bombing had resulted in the deaths of possibly no more than twenty people. Several cows and some zoo animals were also killed.

The Americans had really been unlucky. Both of their primary targets had been affected by the smoke cloud of the R.A.F. bombing. If their target planners had selected the Howaldtswerke as a primary target, this could have been properly plastered although its U-boat production was only about one-seventh of the Blohm & Voss output. An even better target lay only four miles to the west. Here the Deutsche Werft U-boat yard at Finkenwerder turned out two of the large type I X C long-range U-boats each month. This target would have been completely clear of smoke and less protected by Flak. But these are academic comments. The Americans had gone boldly for the all-important Blohm & Voss yard, producing nearly five U-boats per month. The Americans would be back.

NOTES

1. S-3 Report on Mission of 25 July 1943, 303rd Bomb Group.
2. The report is on page 417 of Appendix 5 of the American translation.
3. This is from page 112 of Appendix 10 of the American translation.

12

The Withdrawal Battle

The American bombers soon reached the Rally Point, east of Hamburg, then turned north-west to fly well to the north of Hamburg and on to the German coast – a flight of exactly 100 miles that would take the now lighter bombers just twenty-eight minutes. There was every expectation that this next stage of the flight would be hotly contested by the German fighters and the combat boxes of Fortresses tucked themselves in as tightly as they could. The early deceptions of the American tactical plan had now lost their effectiveness. The German controllers had decided that, of the various American formations flying over northern Germany, those bombers that had just bombed Hamburg would be the ones on which they would now concentrate the fighters. The German fighters which had earlier made abortive flights had landed and been refuelled – a process that could take as little as twenty minutes – and were once again in the air. Single-engined fighters from five airfields – Husum, Heligoland, Jever, Nordholz and Oldenburg – were ordered to intercept the Hamburg formations during the flight to the coast and follow as far out to sea as their fuel would allow. A second attack would then be mounted by twin-engined night fighters from Leeuwarden, in Holland; these would attempt to catch the American bombers during their homeward flight across the North Sea.

Initially, however, it was not the Fortresses in the formations that were in danger. No less than eleven bombers were in the process of dropping out of their group formations, ten because of serious Flak damage and one because the supercharger on one of its engines had failed. Those crippled aircraft that were from the high and lead groups could sometimes find shelter by dropping into a lower group, but that shelter was usually only temporary. Once a bomber dropped out of a low group, its crew were completely on their own. It was a desperate position in which to be and which could usually have only one end. There was a school of thought that it was better for a straggler to dive at once and attempt to get home at low level but it was a long, lonely flight down to ground level from 26,000 feet and every instinct led the American pilots to hang on as near to their formations as possible.

The German fighters that had been attacking the Hamburg groups before they reached the target area were still in contact. These immediately started finishing off the American stragglers, a task in which they were soon joined by fresh fighters. Not one of those eleven American stragglers would reach England. One of the American groups was particularly hard hit. This was the 384th Bomb Group, the low group in the combat wing that had bombed the Blohm & Voss yard. Now, five out of its eighteen aircraft – four of them from the 544th Squadron flying in the lowest position of all – were straggling. The following quotations are all from men who were flying in those doomed Fortresses, both from the 384th Bomb Group and from the other Hamburg groups.

The supercharger went, actually while we were banking at the I.P. and we started falling back from the formation. I noticed the manifold pressure gauge falling but there was nothing we could do about it. I hit the button to feather the prop and I cut the switches. I followed training and put the r.p.m.s up, hoping to regain the formation but we couldn't. We were gradually losing altitude and speed. Morale went zip-down. We were just hanging out there in space on our own.

We flew for ten to fifteen minutes on our own. I had thought of going down, to get real low but, being a youngster with not too much training, it was not easy to make split-second decisions. If we had done this, we might have got back to fight another day. But, then, we noticed that the pressure was falling on number two engine. We could see the gauge showing this and, also, actually see the oil coming out of the engine. We feathered the prop and stopped the engine in time to stop it catching fire or having a windmilling prop. By then, we were under heavy fighter attack. The gunners were all firing but I have no idea of how many fighters or what kind of attack. They were certainly hitting us; there was an explosion somewhere behind the co-pilot's head but he wasn't hurt. I heard, later, that the ball-turret gunner and the radio operator were both wounded. I had a conversation with the co-pilot – we had been talking about our problems for the past few minutes – but then I made the decision that there was no chance of escaping and that it was for the welfare of the crew to evacuate the plane.

I gave the orders and put the plane on automatic pilot. The co-pilot later told me that he delayed opening his parachute but I opened mine straight away. I don't mind telling you that I was scared it wouldn't open and I got it open real quick. (Lieutenant Ralph J. Hall, 384th Bomb Group)

The shell burst right between the numbers three and four engines. It tore big holes in the wing and set fire to the big gas tank behind those engines. They were supposed to be self-sealing tanks but a burst like that just knocked great holes in them. The co-pilot and I were working, feathering the two engines, and one of the gunners called out over the intercom that the wing was on fire. I unbuckled my seat belt, in order to stand up and see how serious it was, and I could see that the fire was too big, with the gasoline burning back from the wing and that there was no way I could sideslip and knock out the fire. This one was too big to snuff out. I knew that, as we lost height, the fire would burn even stronger in the lower air which had more oxygen in it. We were falling behind and losing height fast. The rest of the group went away, just like we were standing still, and I thought, 'My God; you're all going back to England and here I am.'

Then the fighters started coming in at us. I saw several on each side, just queuing up to have a go at us. I decided to abandon the aircraft before it exploded. I had previously briefed the crew that, in the event of loss of intercom and a decision being made to abandon, I would dive and zoom the aircraft to alert them. This done, I put the aircraft on auto pilot. Just before leaving my seat, a 20-mm-sized hole appeared with a loud noise in the windshield directly in front of my head. I felt myself all over, to see whether I was hit but, by some miracle, I wasn't.

When it was my turn to go, because I had been manoeuvring around the aircraft without oxygen, I thought it prudent to pull my chute quickly before passing out. Unfortunately, my high speed through the thin air resulted in a terrific slowdown when the chute opened, ripping several panels out of it and it felt as if my groin had been split open. My initial thought when the chute opened, besides the pain, was the tremendous quiet and cold after the noise of the aircraft and the guns firing. Since our heading was from Hamburg northwards, I could see the Baltic Sea some distance ahead from the high altitude. (Lieutenant Jack H. Owen, 381st Bomb Group)

I was stood in my radio room, facing to the rear of the plane with my gun. I didn't see the Flak burst but I heard it. Apparently, it was damn close to the plane, on the left-hand side, because it tore out the side of the radio room – there were several good-sized holes – and cut some of the controls. I remember seeing some of the control wires to the tail stabilizers that had been cut. There were two sets of these, one for the pilot and one for the co-pilot, and they ran right along the top of the radio room. I got a big chunk of Flak in the upper arm and many smaller pieces all along my arm but it didn't hurt at the time. We knew we were in trouble. The ball gunner reported that he was hit and, then, everybody was talking at once, all trying to tell everybody else where we were hit. I don't remember the top gunner saying anything; we found out later that he was seriously wounded and he died.

I think that, with the damaged tail controls, we fell out of the formation straight away although, as far as I know, the engines were running O.K. Then the fighters came straight in at us – Me 109s. We were suffering pretty heavy attack and we were all firing like hell. I don't know how many were attacking us but there were plenty. I remember firing on three or four all round us. I don't remember anyone saying, 'I've got one', so, apparently, we didn't hit any of them. I couldn't see too much from my radio room but I got the impression that they did a pretty thorough job on us. Then, over the intercom, someone said, 'Let's get out of here.' I suppose it must have been the pilot.

I went back through the fuselage. I didn't take the portable oxygen bottle we were supposed to take when we moved about. I just knew that I could make it to the back door. As I passed the waist gunners – they were still at their guns – I tapped them both on the shoulders, one with each hand, and waved them back to the door. I pulled the emergency steel cord which fastened the door and kicked it out. I remember seeing one of the waist gunners right behind me and I assumed the other one was right behind him. I dived out, low to avoid the tail, and, as soon as I got clear of that, I pulled my ripcord. Later, I found that the second waist gunner never made it. (Technical Sergeant Edward R. Keathley, 384th Bomb Group)

We were in the high squadron but could not stay in formation. We gained a little speed by lowering the nose and dropping into the middle squadron but, again, fell behind as we levelled off. The procedure was repeated and we were able to join the low squadron momentarily but, again, we could not maintain enough airspeed to remain in formation. The group was under constant heavy fighter attack at this time and, as we fell behind the low squadron, we were jumped by four or five Me 109s. We descended on course, hoping to reach the coast but, after about fifteen minutes of constant and heavy attack by those fighters, Lieutenant Pilert lowered the landing gear and rang the bale-out bell. When the gear was lowered, the fighters ceased firing and circled our B-17 as we baled out.

My parachute pack was stowed in the nose compartment. We had done violent evasive action during the descent and the compartment was a shambles of ammunition boxes, shell casings, charts and assorted equipment. I had difficulty finding the pack amidst the debris and I estimate that it was sixty to seventy seconds after the bale-out alarm that I located it, snapped on the harness and left the plane.

I heard later that, after setting the plane on autopilot, Lieutenant Pilert went back to the waist where he found the ball-turret gunner still on board. The gunner hadn't worn his parachute harness because of the tight fit in his turret and he couldn't find it in the shambles caused by our evasive action. Lieutenant Pilert, who was wearing a seat-pack, suggested they wrap arms around each other and jump together. He pulled his parachute rip-cord inside the plane and tied the shrouds to the gunner's body. Pilert then jumped from the rear hatch with the opened chute held to his chest. The slipstream immediately pulled the chute from his arms and it caught on the horizontal stabilizer. The gunner was thrown clear and fell with no chute. (Second Lieutenant Lawrence J. Connors, 91st Bomb Group)

A German report shows that the ball-turret gunner was found alive but badly wounded. He died that night.

Ten of the eleven stragglers were shot down by German fighters before the American formations reached the German coast. The stragglers had not succumbed easily and it had usually required several German fighter attacks to finish off each bomber. Because of the great height at which these combats took place and because the American pilots usually set their automatic pilots before baling out, the Fortresses often flew on for some time before crashing. That of Lieutenant Pilert, of the 91st Bomb Group, flew a further eighty miles after its crew baled out near Heide and eventually landed itself in shallow water off Norderney in the Frisian Islands. Another straggler was still flying and managed to reach the German coast. The fate of its crew will be described later.

Meanwhile, the American combat-wing formations had been flying on towards the German coast. Many of the men in the formations had witnessed the shooting down of the cripples by the German fighters but there was nothing they could do. Every American airman knew that, once a bomber left the safety of its group formation, its crew was beyond help. Besides, the formations themselves were also under attack all the way from Hamburg to the coast and beyond. It is not known how many German fighters were active during this period but the American formations sustained attack after attack. The leading combat wing, consisting of the 303rd, 379th and 384th Bomb Groups which had bombed the Blohm

& Voss shipyard, was the target for most of the German fighters.

The combat-wing leaders were in touch by radio with their groups but these officers could do little more than keep urging the groups to keep closed up. Individual pilots were literally sweating it out at their controls, watching their squadron or flight leaders, making constant adjustments to controls in order to keep as tightly tucked in as possible. The pilots saw little of the battle. Eight of the remaining nine men in each bomber were manning guns. The only 'spare' man was the co-pilot, who acted in as best a way as he could as 'fighter-attack co-ordinator', giving a running commentary on the approach of fighters to his gunners, although each gunner chose his own target. The interiors of the American planes were soon littered with empty cartridge cases and ammunition boxes. Experienced gunners fired short bursts; inexperienced ones sprayed bullets all over the place. Twelve B-17s returned home that day with bullet holes inflicted by American gunners and twenty-seven suffered minor damage caused by being struck from above by the thousands of empty cartridge cases that were ejected by the guns of other bombers or thrown out of their windows during lulls in the action. Special devices were later fitted to the B-17s to collect these empty cases and stop this type of damage. The records of one group, the 379th, show that the gunners of its nineteen planes that returned to England fired off a total of 63,544 rounds of ammunition that afternoon, claiming in the process to have destroyed fifteen German fighters with two more 'probables' and four damaged. This type of claim will be discussed later.

The reader may be surprised to learn that these fierce fighter attacks on the American formations during the withdrawal battle did not bring the Germans much success. Although the stragglers had been cut down remorselessly, many American reports say that the Germans were reluctant to press home their attacks on the formations during this stage of the raid. It should be remembered that the German fighters involved were from the North German-based *Gruppen*, which had not had as much experience in tackling the American *Pulks* as had the 'Abbeville Boys' in France. After disposing of the stragglers, the German pilots did little more than hang around the edges of the American formations, making half-hearted attacks – usually from the side or rear – but breaking off early. During the whole of the withdrawal battle, only two B-17s were shot out of their formation and both of these were from the low squadron of the 384th Bomb Group which had already lost four of its seven planes as stragglers.

The German fighters concentrated on this weakened 'Purple Heart Corner'. Lieutenant Howard Cromwell was a Squadron Operations Officer in the 384th and was not often required to fly on combat operations.

They threw up everything that had a propeller. It was the single-engined ones that were making the attacks. They were certainly trying to stop us that day. They kept on coming in through our criss-cross covering fire – they came right on through it; it made no difference to them. They came in from every direction – front, rear, both sides, low and high. I don't know why they didn't run into each other sometimes. I only did three or four raids and this was certainly the worst one for fighters. Why the hell they picked me for this one, I don't know. I would as soon have stopped at home.

One Fortress fell away with four men already dead and the pilot soon to die after a propeller sliced off a leg when he baled out. The bomber glided away to crash into some woods south of the River Elbe. The sixth loss from the squadron was the lead plane, piloted by Lieutenant Thomas Estes. Two of his gun positions ran out of ammunition but the gunners remained at their posts and continued to track their empty guns at the attacking fighters. Eventually, with three engines hit and many other items of damage, this plane also fell away. By then, the German coast had been crossed and Lieutenant Estes was able to make a good landing on the sea. 'I didn't do it; I levelled off about twenty feet above the water and told the Good Lord that he had control and the Good Lord sure made a wonderful landing. It was not a very pleasant feeling but there was a lot of personal satisfaction in the fact that we had ditched and did not lose anyone.' What happened to Estes and his ditched crew will be told later. The last survivor of the low squadron was the plane of Lieutenant Sprague, whose crew were only on their second mission. They returned safely to England and survived a tour of twenty-five operations.

It is unfortunate that it will never be known how many

German fighters were shot down during the withdrawal battle. The files of the American groups contain a host of Combat Forms, giving detailed reports of German fighters seen exploding in the air or crashing to the ground or with pilots baling out, all corroborated by witnesses. The 91st Bomb Group has such a report, giving details of a Messerschmitt 109 credited to a waist gunner, Staff Sergeant Carl Gundersen, who now gives a personal account of the combat.

I looked down and could see the River Elbe, like a silvery snake. I saw this little dot against the silver of the river. I thought I had a spot in my eye and started to rub it. But then the spot started to come up – further and further up – and I realized it was a fighter about ten thousand feet below me. I waited until I was completely sure then I called Niedbalski, the other waist gunner, and pointed it out. He was looking over my shoulder and nodded and gave me a slap on the back. I think you might say we were competitors; he was jealous that it hadn't come up on his side. I called it out then on the intercom, 'Bandit. Nine o'clock low.'

Then I waited till he was level and coming right at us. He came in; he was completely alone. It was an amazing thing. There was nobody else around. He opened fire first; I could see the blinking in his wings of the flashes of his guns firing.

I opened fire and I was angry because my first three bursts missed. He was firing at my aircraft but he wasn't hitting us. He was a lousy shot. Then my next burst, around five to six hundred yards, I watched my tracers going right into him. It must have been in the nose because his engine started to smoke immediately. He went straight down with his smoke, dense smoke, coming out. Then I made a comment, 'The sonofabitch! He's let out a smoke-screen.' I thought he was faking it, like they sometimes did. But then I saw the parachute. I called out, 'Got him. Got him', so that the navigator could make a note of the exact position for the claim. Niedbalski clapped me on the shoulder and said something like, 'Nice shooting. A nice birthday present.' He knew it was my twenty-fourth birthday.

I had a thought at the time that I would shoot at the parachute. You were so keyed up, you know, and you had this hatred of them at the time. But I decided not to; he was probably well out of range anyway. At the time, I had really been determined to get him but, afterwards, I thought he had a hell of a lot of guts. You mellow with time, you know.

It should be stated that Gundersen's engagement with this lone German fighter was not a typical example of the battle around the American formations on that day. The identity of the lone German fighter pilot is not known.

The last of the German single-engined fighters broke off their attacks about sixty miles out over the sea and returned to their bases. More Germans – twin-engined fighters – were to be met later but this is an appropriate point at which to catch up on the activities of the 381st Bomb Group, which had failed to join up with its combat wing before reaching Hamburg and had retained its bombs when it flew over the city. The group was being led by Captain George Shackley who had taken over when the aircraft of the designated group leader had aborted. Two of the group's planes had been shot down and a third was straggling but still in loose contact. The planes of this group were carrying 150 500-lb high-explosive bombs and Captain Shackley was looking for a target for these bombs.

There had been an early, tentative plan to fly to the designated secondary target of Kiel, fifty miles to the north, but this really would have been a bold attempt by this seriously understrength group on its own and this plan was not pursued. The flight plan back to the German coast passed very close to the German town of Heide, just inland from the coast. It was the only sizeable town near the group's route. The bombardier of the lead plane saw Heide coming up before him. He could see a railway junction and a small marshalling yard and Captain Shackley decided that these would be the target for the bombs of his group. A 'straight-in' run was made and the bombs went down to explode in the usual tight cluster of brown bursts 28,000 feet below. The group's cameras brought back their evidence: five bomb bursts seen in the town, five in the railway yards, the remainder just short of the yards and bursting across the main road from Heide to Rendsburg and in open fields. The people of Heide must have taken shelter in good time. Their records show that, although twenty-five houses were destroyed and thirty more damaged, only four people were killed.

The pilot of the damaged Fortress of this group that had managed to keep contact was Captain Joe Alexander, one of the group's characters, a 'playboy' but regarded as one of the 381st's best pilots. Alexander was flying an old B-17, not his regular plane. It had been damaged by Flak near Hamburg and had then developed trouble in two engines. As the group flew away from Heide and out across the North Sea, the other crews watched Alexander trying to keep up but, about thirty miles out over the sea, the engines of the damaged plane were seen to be vibrating badly and Alexander was seen to turn away to the south and head back to Germany. Staff Sergeant George Orin, radio man in Alexander's crew, can take up the story at this point.

The vibration was terrible. Captain Joe somehow got the r.p.m.s reduced and we dropped out, radioing good luck to the formation. A total of five Me 109s soon closed in on us in a circling formation but without firing. We stowed our guns and one German attached himself to each wing-tip of our plane, one followed, one parked himself right over my position – I could have sworn that I could touch his prop – and one pulled ahead of us, motioning us to follow him.

While I was destroying the radio equipment with a spare machine-gun barrel and detonating the rest, the crew were checking parachutes and escape articles. The navigator said that we couldn't reach Sweden or France or England, so what to do? We all voted on whether to ditch, jump, or crash-land. Crash-landing won – the chances of us all remaining uninjured were best in a crash-landing. So, as the crew filed into my radio room to assume their crash positions, I fed them the last of my onion-skin paper radio data along with a lit cigarette and, then, stationed myself at my table so that I could relay information as seen from my side windows.

I was the only crew member in the radio room on intercom. Captain Joe called me and said that he was being directed to land, at an airfield seen coming into view, by motions of a Jerry pilot who had come in over our wing so close to get Captain Joe's attention that I was afraid he might collide with one of our static props. He was smiling and motioning emphatically for us to follow him down. Captain Joe said that he would fake his approach and stretch our glide to an open field seen near a large forest, then land there with wheels up and, as soon as we stopped, everyone except me was to get out fast and run for the woods and keep going south towards France. I was to stay and help with the incendiary charges that we had to set the plane afire if necessary.

It was a soft and easy landing with the ball turret coming up into the plane as we settled. As soon as we stopped skidding along the ground, everyone took off and ran. Captain Joe and I were trying to light our parachutes with the incendiaries but they were damp and wouldn't light. While frantically striking matches to do the job, the whole crew came trotting back to the plane. There was a camouflaged camp in the forest. There was nowhere to run to! Nothing but open fields!

People could be seen running towards us, mostly civilians. They stopped at a distance from us and a German with a dog approached carefully and ordered us to stand still, not to speak, and to remove our Mae West jackets and put them at our feet. This German was the exact twin of the movie actor, Victor McLaglan, and lent a touch of unreality to the whole episode. It seemed like a movie to me, and having this guard seeming to be a movie actor made it all the more unreal.

Captain Alexander had landed near a camp for Polish workers, not far from the Luftwaffe fighter airfield at Aurich, just north of Emden. The virtual surrender of this crew raises the interesting question of what the captain of a bomber that had no hope of reaching England should do. The Americans knew that the Luftwaffe already had an intact and flyable B-17 which was used to help German fighter pilots practise their targets. It is doubtful if any official guidance was ever given but the unofficial attitude was that the survival of the crew was the most important factor and no one would have frowned upon Captain Alexander's action. Unfortunately, Joe Alexander was killed soon after the war in a motor crash in his home state of Alabama.

The next event in the flight of the main American formations demonstrates another aspect of the flexibility of air power, this time by the Luftwaffe. The night-fighter airfield at Leeuwarden in northern Holland was only sixty-five miles from the return route of the American bombers across the North Sea. A few of the Messerschmitt 110s from Leeuwarden had flown earlier in the afternoon but had made no contact with the Americans. Now a stronger force, approximately sixteen aircraft, had been sent off in an attempt to intercept the Americans on their flight home. The German night-fighter crews were not often used in daylight operations but they were required to fly today.

The Messerschmitts had taken off at approximately 4.45 p.m. – when the B-17s were just leaving Hamburg – and were directed, first, to climb to 26,000 feet above the German coast near Wilhelmshaven. It was an unusual experience for the

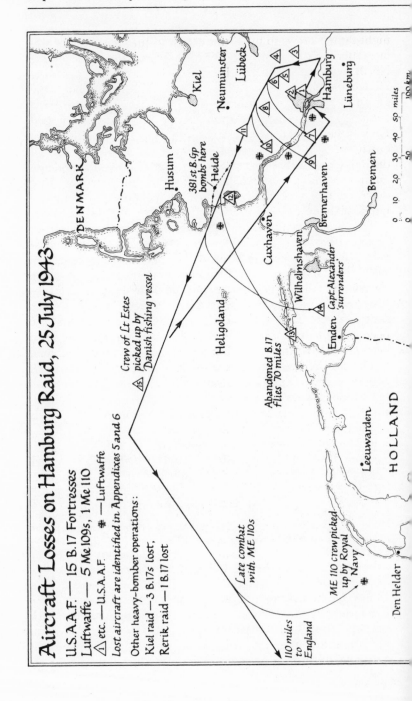

Aircraft Losses on Hamburg Raid, 25 July 1943

U.S.A.A.F. — 15 B.17 Fortresses
Luftwaffe — 5 Me 109s, 1 Me 110
△ etc. — U.S.A.A.F.   ✠ — Luftwaffe
Lost aircraft are identified in Appendices 5 and 6

Other heavy-bomber operations:
Kiel raid — 3 B.17s lost,
Rerik raid — 1 B.17 lost

night-fighter crews to fly at this height in the clear light of this late afternoon of summer. They could see the whole of the North Sea coast from the Ijsselmeer, in Holland, across the Heligoland Bight to the Danish coast. From that point, one group of fighters was ordered to fly north and it soon made contact with an American combat wing that had just bombed Kiel. Oberleutnant Drünkler was credited with shooting down the only B-17 – from the 94th Bomb Group – that fell during the ensuing engagement. Drünkler's success completed an interesting day-and-night double for him; he had shot down an R.A.F. Lancaster bound for Hamburg in the early hours of that day.

The main group of Leeuwarden fighters was directed almost due west from Wilhelmshaven and towards the American formations returning from Hamburg, which were still being plotted by the long-range German coastal radar stations. The German fighters did not make contact until the Americans were two-thirds of the way home across the North Sea, 140 miles from the English coast. If friendly fighters had been sent out to meet the Americans, the B-17s would have been escorted at this point, but there were no friendly fighters.

The use by the Germans of Messerschmitt 110s to attack American formations was almost a last resort. These heavy, twin-engined fighters were not so fast or so handy as the single-engined ones and their crews had little training in the methods needed to tackle the Fortresses.

It was the first time I had seen Boeings from the air. From five or six kilometres away, they looked like a great heap, like a great swarm of birds. You couldn't see individual planes, only those at the front. We had been told that the Americans were very dangerous, that each plane had eighteen guns. We only had these little, slow, night fighters. When we saw a bomber at night, there was a feeling of joy but, in the day, it was a strange feeling because you knew that, instead of shooting at only one bomber, many bombers would now be shooting at us. (Unteroffizier Friedrich Abromeit, IV/NJG1)

The Germans had one advantage – the Americans were flying directly into the low evening sun. The fighters flew well past the American formation, then positioned themselves in the sun and commenced their attacks from ahead. The eight Germans did not make a massed attack but came in one by one, each fighter making its attack, then turning away and coming back round to the front of the American formation to start again. They concentrated their attacks on a B-17 from the high squadron of the 303rd Bomb Group which was lagging slightly. The first series of attacks from the sun caught the American by surprise and there was no return fire but every attack after that was hotly opposed. The combat did not last long; the Messerschmitts received a recall signal because their fuel was running low and all but one turned for home. The last attack was made by Leutnant Eberhard Gardiewski whose radar operator, Friedrich Abromeit, resumes his account.

We completed our attack because the bomber we were firing at was falling back and we were in a good position. We could see the Americans firing back. They were using tracer but, from the front, you could only see the little ring of smoke around the bullet. I think the one that we were after was firing nervously but the others were taking careful aim.

Then we saw that both our engines had been hit and were starting to smoke. I think it was the other Boeings that hit us. We could see our own fighters and tried to follow them, but we became slower and slower and they finally disappeared. They couldn't stay or they would have run out of fuel. Our engines were still running but the temperatures were rising. We wanted to get as near to the coast as possible so we throttled back to get the most out of the engines. Naturally I was signalling on all frequencies, saying that we had been hit and asking them to take bearings on us.

Eventually we had to come down before we could see any land. We hit the water at nearly two hundred kilometres an hour – a rough landing. We stopped in a great spray of water. I was hurt with a cut head. I could see the pilot sitting still and with even more blood on his head; I thought he was dead. That was the worst moment for me. But, then, he opened his cockpit, smiled and jumped out. I did all the wrong things. I didn't think. I still had my parachute on when I got into the water and I hadn't blown up my life vest. We eventually got into our yellow, one-man dinghies and sat down to wait. There were a few jokes. 'Ring up H.Q. to fetch us in a car.' 'How far to land?' 'Fifty metres – straight down!'

The bomber that the Germans had been attacking – piloted by a Lieutenant Baker – was not shot down although it was badly damaged and one of its gunners was severely wounded in the arm by a cannon shell. The gunners of two other B-17s, one in the high and one in the low squadron of the group, both claimed Leutnant Gardiewski's fighter as damaged. This Messerschmitt had not been seen to crash by anyone, friend or foe.

The two Germans sat in their dinghies for four hours, firing their flare pistol occasionally to attract the help they were sure would come. They were only twenty miles from the Dutch coast but it was a British motor torpedo-boat, M.T.B. 621, which picked them up. It was part of a small British force out looking for a German convoy believed to be sailing that night from Den Helder. The two Germans were well treated, survived a gun battle six hours later in which M.T.B. 621 was damaged, and were landed next day at Great Yarmouth. They finished up in a prison camp in Canada.

This combat with the Messerschmitt 110s was the last significant event of the day. The American formations crossed the English coast at about 7 p.m., one man in the 384th Bomb Group, which had lost seven planes, being 'very glad to see land; I felt like getting out and putting my feet on it'. All the B-17s landed safely within the next hour. There were no landing crashes although some planes had to put down hurriedly at strange airfields through fuel shortage, battle damage or casualties needing urgent treatment.

The Eighth Air Force had, on this day, attempted its most ambitious operation to date and had paid the price for that ambition. The groups dispatched to Hamburg had suffered the greatest loss. Fifteen B-17s out of the 127 that had taken off had been shot down. Thirty-six men from these planes had been killed and 104 taken prisoner. The remaining ten men would return safely to England four days later because the crew of Lieutenant Estes, whose plane had come down in the sea, was to have the interesting experience of being picked up by a Danish fishing vessel, the *Ternan* from Frederikshavn, brought to within fifty miles of the English coast and, then, handed over to an R.A.F. rescue launch. A large number of the B-17s that had returned from Hamburg had suffered battle damage. Records of the six bomb groups involved show that more than half of their planes had been damaged, some severely; only one aircraft had returned undamaged from the unfortunate 384th Bomb Group.

In return for this toll of human and material loss, 225 B-17s had found useful targets for their bombs. The experience of the Hamburg groups has already been described. The six groups of the 4th Wing which had been sent to attack the aircraft factory at Warnemünde, near Rostock, had found that target covered by cloud. One group – the 385th – had bombed through this cloud at a dead-reckoning position but German records show that these bombs had been largely wasted. One person was killed on the ground here and no serious damage was caused. The 388th Bomb Group had found a useful 'target of opportunity' at Rerik airfield, further west along the Baltic coast, and its bombs caused much damage to hangars and other buildings on the airfield. Twenty-four people, fifteen of them being servicemen, were killed at Rerik and forty more were wounded. The remaining four groups – the 94th, 95th, 96th and 100th Bomb Groups – had attacked Kiel, their accurate bombing causing much damage in two U-boat yards – Howaldtswerke and Deutsche Werft – and in the German Navy fitting-out yard. An old cruiser, ironically its name was the *Hamburg*, and one newly launched U-boat were sunk and many important buildings destroyed. Nineteen people were killed in Kiel and twenty-seven dwelling houses destroyed by bombs which missed the shipyards. The 4th Bombardment Wing had only lost four planes – three from the groups attacking Kiel and one from that which had attacked Rerik airfield. Total American losses for the day were nineteen planes, the third highest loss suffered so far by the Eighth Air Force.

The American units that had flown over Germany filed claims for forty-one German fighters destroyed, six 'probables' and twenty-seven damaged. All but seven of these claims were by the groups that had bombed Hamburg. According to the Luftwaffe Quartermaster General's records, the actual German losses were six fighters destroyed – five Messerschmitt 109s and one Messerschmitt 110 – and five other fighters damaged. One German pilot, a *Gruppenkommandeur*, Major Karl-Heinz Leesmann of III/JG 1, was killed, four more were wounded and the night-fighter crew were taken prisoner. It is possible that the German records are not quite complete but there still remains a vast gap between American claims and German losses. This was not unusual. Several American gunners often claimed a single fighter seen going down. For example, the interrogation officers of the 303rd Bomb Group allowed claims from four separate gunners, all showing exactly the same time, for the destruction of what was probably one German fighter. But ground intelligence officers were reluctant to tell tired, excited, sometimes wounded gunners that their claims could not be confirmed. It was also good for morale that the American aircrews should believe that they were slaughtering the Luftwaffe. But there is evidence that, although these exaggerated claims were repeated in the British and American press, the Eighth Air Force were, internally, far more realistic. A document later passed to the R.A.F. for inclusion in the R.A.F. Listening Service's report of the day's operations, reduced the estimated German casualties to ten fighters destroyed, four probables and seven damaged. The VIII Bomber Command Mission Report, filed as an official record, used the higher figures sent in by the groups but did no more than record that these were 'claims'.

It had been a tough day for the Americans. Second Lieutenant Paul Gordy describes the atmosphere that evening in the Officers' Club of the 384th Bomb Group at Grafton Underwood:

There was some hilarity that night but it was a false hilarity. Most of us were emotionally and physically whipped. We'd had two long days of flying and seen our group really whipped too. We were just walking round in a daze. They had just flat worn us out that day. While we didn't openly bitch or complain, almost every flying crew member knew, inwardly, that it would be almost statistically impossible to finish the tour of duty without being injured, killed or shot down.

That was the only night in my flying career when the Flight Surgeon came round, asking if we were all right and did we want anything.

13

The Americans Again

While the American bombers had been away attacking
Hamburg and their other targets, the squadrons of R.A.F.
Bomber Command had been preparing for another maximum
effort raid to take place that night, 25–26 July. At his morning
conference, Sir Arthur Harris had decided to keep up the
pressure on Hamburg and had selected that city as the night's
main target again. But there were disadvantages about going
to Hamburg twice in two nights. The Germans might be
expecting another attack on the city and concentrate more of
their night fighters in that area. There was also a serious
danger that Hamburg would still be covered by smoke, either
from fires caused by the R.A.F. the night before or by those of
the more recent American bombing. As a precaution, Harris
selected the Ruhr city of Essen as an alternative target and all
the preparations for the coming night were carried out in
such a way as to allow a late final choice to be made.

A meteorological reconnaissance flight was made in the late
afternoon and a Mosquito crewed by Flight Sergeant F.
Clayton and Pilot Officer W. F. John flew right over four
German cities: Flensburg, Kiel, Lübeck and Hamburg. The
main object was to see how much smoke there was over
Hamburg; the flights over the other cities were to divert
German attention from the interest being shown in Hamburg.
The Mosquito crew found that there was still much smoke over
Hamburg when they flew over the city at about 6.30 p.m.; in
particular, there were dense clouds of smoke billowing up
from some new oil fires burning in the dock area. Pilot Officer
John radioed this important news back to England. The
proposed raid on Hamburg was abandoned immediately and
the R.A.F. bombers were ordered instead to raid the so-often-
bombed city of Essen.

There is no need to devote much space to that night's
operations. More than 600 bombers dropped nearly 2,000
tons of bombs on that part of Essen in which the great Krupps
armament works were situated. The marking was carried out

by Oboe-controlled Mosquitoes and was very accurate, as it usually was when targets were within range of that valuable device. Very heavy damage was caused in the Krupps factories and in the housing areas near by. In all, 486 people died. Twenty-three bombers were lost. This loss, a low one for attacks on the Ruhr, must have owed something to the second use of Window in just over twenty-four hours, but there is evidence that the experienced German night-fighter crews based in Holland were less troubled by Window than their colleagues in northern Germany had been the night before.

This Essen raid was really an extension of the Battle of the Ruhr but official historians do not like overlapping 'battles' so the raid is now regarded as part of the Battle of Hamburg.

But Hamburg was not forgotten on this night and six Mosquitoes of 139 Squadron were detailed to carry out a nuisance raid on the city. All six crews found Hamburg easily, the fires still burning there being visible from seventy miles away. The four and a half tons of bombs dropped by the Mosquitoes probably caused little damage – there are no details in the Hamburg records – but the main purpose of this little operation was to cause the Hamburg sirens to sound, to deprive the population of their sleep, and to spread further fear and confusion in the city.

One of the Mosquito pilots was Sergeant James Marshallsay who, with his navigator Sergeant Nick Ranshaw, was flying the first of his fifty-operation Mosquito tour.

At briefing, a list of war industries in Hamburg was read out, including U-boat yards. My navigator said, with a grin, that this was a chance for me to get even with the U-boats. (I had been torpedoed in the South Atlantic on my way back from pilot training in Rhodesia. After the war, I discovered it was an Italian submarine which sank us!) At dispersal, we looked at the bomb-load in place and Nick took out the safety pins and gave one to me. I still have it.

As we approached Hamburg, we saw an explosion on the ground in the fire area. I remember fire, smoke and cloud but no Flak. We flew across the burning city with the strange feeling that we were the only aircraft there and that we were stationary. We unloaded our bombs into the fires and turned for home.

After landing, we taxied to dispersal and, with the chocks in place, opened the bomb doors. A ground-staff man pointed up into the bomb bay and backed away rapidly. I switched off the engine. Nick climbed down the ladder and I followed him. The 250-lb incendiary was still there. It had hung up. An armourer said, 'You've brought back the incendiary.' Nick replied, 'From what we've seen of Hamburg, they won't miss it.'

While the R.A.F. heavy bombers were still on their return flight from Essen, American airmen were going round the living quarters on the American bomber airfields, shaking sleeping crewmen to get them up for another day's flying. Every one of the fifteen bomb groups had been warned for combat operations. It was early on Monday, 26 July, and this would be the third consecutive day that the B-17s were going to war although, with the American system of resting one squadron in each group on every raid, only a few of the men due to fly on this day would have flown on both of the previous days.

The weather forecast continued to give hope of clear weather over northern Germany, the clearance being expected to extend even further south on this day. Take-off for the B-17s was scheduled for 9.0 a.m. and two R.A.F. Mosquitoes made early flights into the Heligoland Bight to carry out last-minute examinations of the weather as far as the German coast. These two flights duly took place and their wireless messages confirmed that the weather still seemed to be favourable.

As on the previous day, the American bombers were to be split into five combat wings, attacking two targets. Two wings were again ordered to Hamburg, to bomb exactly the same targets as the previous day: the Blohm & Voss U-boat yard and the Klöckner aero-engine factory. The three other combat wings were all to fly to Hannover,* to attack the important Continental Gummiwerke, believed to be the largest motor-tyre factory in Germany. Again, a complicated tactical plan had been prepared with two combat wings of the longer-range B-17s of the 4th Bombardment Wing approaching Germany first and flying a feint off the coast to draw up German fighters prematurely. All five combat wings were then to cross the German coast at roughly the same time, approach and bomb their targets, then withdraw in a series of frequently changing courses that would tax the ability of the cleverest German fighter controller. There would also be the usual diversions by

---

* The German spelling is used in the American Official History and I have retained it here. M.M.

light bombers with strong fighter escort, this time flying to targets in Belgium and northern France, to keep the Luftwaffe in those areas fully occupied.

Impressive as this plan may have appeared on paper, these operations promised another hazardous day for the American airmen. The defences of Hamburg had already shown how lethal they could be and they had not been bombed the previous night in any strength by the R.A.F. Hannover, seventy miles south of Hamburg, was fifty miles deeper into German territory and easily the deepest penetration yet attempted by the Americans. The six bomb groups chosen to attack Hamburg were the same six that had raided that city the previous day. They were also split into the same two combat wings but the target for each combat wing was reversed. What can be called the Blohm & Voss wing was now composed of the 381st Bomb Group, leading – with Lieutenant-Colonel Leland G. Fiegel, deputy commander of that group, in the lead plane – and the 351st and 91st Groups in high and low positions. The Klöckner wing had the 303rd Group in the lead – under command of Major William R. Calhoun, a squadron commander – with the 384th and 379th Groups in low and high positions.

There can be no doubt that the American airmen detailed to fly to Hamburg that day were in an extremely apprehensive mood. These groups had lost fifteen planes the previous day while attacking exactly the same city and nearly every aircraft had come back with some type of damage. Also, nearly half of the men who went into the mission briefing rooms had had no more than five hours sleep.

The Hamburg groups started taking off at 9.0 a.m., into the morning of another perfect English summer's day. Although there was more haze and low cloud than on the previous day, the Fortresses soon broke out into clear conditions. The three groups of the Blohm & Voss wing assembled without much difficulty but the assembly of the Klöckner wing was chaotic. Much paperwork was later devoted to the reasons for the failure. It appears that the trouble started when the lead group, the 303rd, having assembled in good order over Molesworth airfield, departed on its assembly line of flight just one and a half minutes early. There is no need to go into much detail on subsequent events. The other two groups in this wing came along and formed up on a group which they spotted but which turned out to be a stranger. Nine bomb groups eventually turned up over Cromer but not all formed into the correct formations. After a good deal of dispersing, wheeling of formations and firing of different-coloured recognition flares, the Blohm & Voss wing departed in its correct order. One of the Klöckner groups, the 379th, realized that it was now thirty minutes behind time and its leader decided to call off the flight and the entire group returned to its airfield. The 303rd Bomb Group tacked itself on to the Blohm & Voss wing as an extra combat box in the high position. The 384th Bomb Group also added itself to another wing, but one which it never identified. It flew with this wing for more than 200 miles out over the North Sea but the lead pilot in the group, Captain William F. Gilmore, was anxious in case the wing he was accompanying might be equipped with the Tokyo-tank version of the B-17 and that he might be committing the 384th to a flight for which its aircraft did not have enough fuel. Any officer who led his group into a mission which ended in eighteen B-17s having to make forced landings in the North Sea would certainly have made his mark in the history of the United States Army Air Force. Captain Gilmore reluctantly turned back for England. He was not to know that the planes in the combat wing that he had been following were of the same type as his own. They were the 92nd, 305th and 306th Bomb Groups, one of the three combat wings flying to Hannover. Gilmore's group would have had a rough time under German fighter attack if he had proceeded but he would have had enough fuel to reach home.

The four bomb groups that were still pressing on towards Hamburg suffered a further depletion in their strength because a large number of individual planes turned back for various reasons. Of the eighty-two Fortresses that had taken off, no less than twenty-five dropped out of their formations and returned to England. It may be thought that the planes which returned were suffering from mechanical stress after two previous days of operations, but the nine other groups flying to Hannover, which were also on their third consecutive day of flying, suffered only half the proportion of abortive sorties as the Hamburg-bound groups. There is no doubt that some of the reasons given for turning back from this Hamburg raid were marginal ones. The records of the 1st Bombardment Wing list some of them: 'Ball-turret malfunction but ground checked as satisfactory'; 'Pilot became ill'; 'Malfunction of supercharger regulator, investigation disclosed no malfunctions'; 'Ball-turret door lost during flight'; 'Loose fittings on bayonet connection of pilot's oxygen hose.' Many engines were 'running rough'. It seems that the daunting prospect of facing the Flak and fighters around Hamburg was one that some of the Americans could not face.

The 91st Bomb Group, ordered to fly the dangerous low position in its wing, lost nine of its twenty planes returning in this way. Staff Sergeant Carl Gundersen was a gunner in one Fortress which turned back from this group.

I was surprised when we turned back and they told me afterwards that we had an oil leak, but I don't think it was all that bad. My own personal opinion is that the pilot didn't want to face that Flak over Hamburg again. It was our third operation in three days but I was pretty teed off about turning back – I was real angry.

The initial German reaction to the approach of the American bombers was almost identical to that of the previous day. The fighter-escorted medium-bomber raids to Belgium and France drew off some of the German fighters based in Holland and the feint flights off the German coast by the B-17s of the 4th Bombardment Wing lured up some of the North German fighters prematurely. But the German fighter controllers covering the Heligoland Bight area did not commit their main force of fighters too early and, when the combat wings of B-17s bound for both Hamburg and Hannover later approached the German coast, they were met by strong fighter opposition.

There was, however, an interesting difference between the tactics employed by the German fighters against the two main American bomber forces. Those fighters in touch with the Hannover B-17s immediately started a series of fierce attacks, usually from the front and pressed home with great determination. The American airmen of the 388th Bomb Group – a group flying only its fourth operational mission – watched one Focke-Wulf carry out a shallow dive-bombing attack on its formation. One bomb exploded on the left wing of one of the group's planes which promptly caught fire. Only four men baled out before the Fortress blew up. Several other planes fell to more conventional attacks. By contrast, the German fighters in contact with the Hamburg wing contented themselves with flying alongside or above and behind the B-17 formation, almost as though providing an escort. A few half-hearted attacks were made on the fringes of the American groups but these were easily beaten off without any serious damage being suffered on either side. It is probable that these German fighters believed that Hamburg was again to be the target and were waiting for the Hamburg Flak to force the B-17s out of their formations again. The American bombers and the German fighters, keeping their distance and watching each other carefully, flew on in the bright sunshine from the landfall at Cuxhaven to the same Initial Point above the place where the railway line ran over the Autobahn as had been used by the Americans the previous day. The German Flak fire between the coast and this Turning Point was not as serious as on the previous day, possibly because of the presence of the German fighters, and the four American groups turned towards Hamburg in good order and in unscathed condition.

But Hamburg's Flak greeted the Americans again with the full force of its barrage. Major Elzia Ledoux, leading the 351st Bomb Group in the high position, remembers the Flak.

> The box of Flak was put up in front of us before we reached the target area. They weren't tracking any individual aircraft; there was just this volume of sky, possibly a quarter of a mile wide and a quarter of a mile deep, right in front of us on our route into the target. The box of Flak would keep moving on and appear in front of you again. You could see these black balls exploding all through this box. Personally, I was never afraid of Flak; it was fighters that I was more worried about. When I saw the Flak ball I knew the shell had burst and it wasn't going to hit me but I know that some of the fellows hated Flak, particularly the gunners. They could do something about the fighters but not Flak. That was the way they felt psychologically.

On the previous day, the Americans had caught the German smoke-screen units unawares but not on this day. As the bombers approached the city, the bombardiers could see dense streams of smoke spreading from dozens of smoke pots on the ground. The primary target for this American combat wing, the Blohm & Voss U-boat yard, was already covered. There was even some smoke still rising from the thirty-six-hour-old fires caused by the R.A.F. in the main city north of the river but the American bombing photographs show that it was the artificial smoke-screen that was providing most of the concealment of the ground on this day. The lead bombardiers had two choices: they could carry out a timed bomb run from the Initial Point and hope that their bombs would hit the target originally designated or they could alter their plans and try to find a clearer target. It appears that the lead bombardiers of all four groups took the second course. The two leading groups, the 381st and 351st, chose the Howaldtswerke U-boat yard, which was clear of smoke cover, and the 91st and 303rd Bomb Groups aimed at the prominent buildings in the Neuhof Power Station area. These were both targets that had been bombed the day before. The 303rd Bomb Group should have been bombing the Klöckner aero-engine factory, four miles to the east, but being now the only group left from the Klöckner wing, its leader, Major Calhoun, had wisely decided to stay with the other groups. The bombing period of the four groups covered no more than *one minute*, exactly at noon; this shows how well closed-up the four groups had kept. Ninety-one tons of high explosive and twenty-seven tons of incendiaries were aimed at the targets and a further ten 500-lb bombs were dropped over Hamburg by a plane whose bomb doors were damaged by Flak and failed to open on time.

There were several individual incidents during the bomb runs. Lieutenant Thomas J. Hester, the bombardier in Lieutenant-Colonel Fiegel's plane which was leading the entire formation, had taken the glove off his right hand to make sure that he was adjusting his bomb sight properly and he suffered frostbite because freezing air was entering his compartment through a small hole. One of the 351st Bomb Group's planes had an incendiary bomb stick in its bomb rack. The plane's engineer, Technical Sergeant Norman Michel, volunteered to go into the bomb bay to kick it free. The plane's captain was advised by his group leader, Major Ledoux, to tie the man to a rope before he tried this difficult task because, on a previous raid, an officer had fallen to his death attempting the same task. This time, the bomb was kicked free but Michel collapsed through lack of oxygen and was thrown around the interior of the bomb bay before he could be pulled back, injured, into the plane.

The Flak fire followed the B-17s right through the target area but with less effect than on the previous day. One man, Lieutenant Sydney Novell, a navigator on his first mission, was killed by a piece of Flak shell. Only two planes, both in the 91st Bomb Group, suffered serious Flak damage over Hamburg and both of these managed, initially at least, to keep up with their formation. The reason for this lack of success by the Hamburg Flak after the mayhem they had caused the previous day is to be found in an interesting comparison between the composition of the American formations on the two days. On the previous day, the American combat wings had been stacked three groups high with the lowest planes at 26,000 feet and it had been the low groups that had suffered most severely from the Flak fire. On this second day, however, this four-group combat wing had formed itself into two sections, each of which was only two groups high. In addition, the whole wing had climbed as high as possible and no bomber was flying at less than 28,000 feet. This had misled the Flak batteries and a large proportion of the shells had burst harmlessly below the American formation. Another factor was that this well closed-up wing had passed through the target area together. The considerable gap between the two American wings on the previous day had given the Hamburg Flak twice the chance of scoring hits.

After bombing, the Fortresses wheeled away to the east of Hamburg, exactly as they had on the previous day, but, this time, they kept on turning to starboard because their return flight was to be to the south of Hamburg.

This American raid had even less impact on the majority of the ordinary citizens of Hamburg than that of the previous day. The air-raid sirens had sounded in ample time and few people saw the bombers. There had been the firing of Flak batteries and, for a few seconds, the rumble of bombing south of the river but nothing else.

The bombing of the Howaldtswerke caused damage but no casualties. Many workers had not reported for duty that Monday morning; the absentees were still engrossed in the after-effects of the bombing of their homes two nights earlier.

There was also trouble with the yard's electricity supply and not much work had been done that morning. Every worker present had taken shelter when the sirens went. When they emerged after the bombing, they found several buildings in the shipyard hit and some were burning, but nothing vital had been harmed. Many bombs had fallen into the surrounding waterways and at least two small ships were hit and set on fire.

The second bombing area had resulted in far more serious damage. The main *Kesselhaus* – the boiler house – at the Neuhof Power Station had suffered a direct hit by a 500-lb bomb and the station immediately ceased to produce electrical power. This was a major blow to Hamburg. The Neuhof station, producing 130,000 kilowatts of electricity, was one of the two largest generating stations in the city. Now it was completely out of action and would remain so for at least a month, reducing the amount of power available in Hamburg by 40 per cent. This one bomb – dropped by a plane of either the 91st or the 303rd Bomb Group – was the most important American contribution to the Battle of Hamburg.

Further bombs in this area had also hit two nearby industrial concerns. At the Hansa Mühle factory, serious fires were started in a soya-bean oil tank and in storehouses full of soya-bean meal and sunflower seeds. At the second factory, that of Ritz & Company, a lanolin factory in the Brückerstrasse, there was a pitiful loss of life. About forty workers, mainly women, had gone into a shelter under the factory. Direct hits on the building above caused two things to happen – some packing material caught fire and some tanks of oil and fats were blown open. The burning oil ran through the bomb debris into the shelter. The exit was blocked by wreckage. Rescue workers could not gain access. The workers in the shelter were burned to death.

Approximately 150 people died in Hamburg because of this day's bombing. Most of them were workpeople killed at their places of work.

That part of the return flight over German territory of the four groups which had bombed Hamburg was twice as long as that of the previous day. It was a protracted and potentially dangerous withdrawal flight through an area thick with

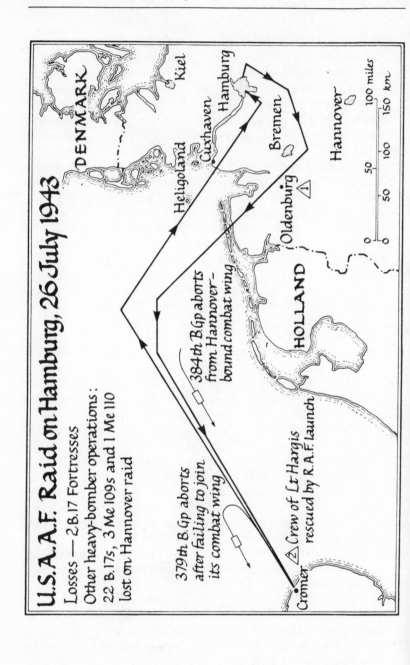

U.S.A.A.F. Raid on Hamburg, 26 July 1943

Losses — 2 B.17 Fortresses
Other heavy-bomber operations:
22 B.17s, 3 Me 109s and 1 Me 110
lost on Hannover raid

379th B.Gp aborts after failing to join its combat wing

384th B.Gp aborts from Hannover-bound combat wing

Crew of Lt Hargis rescued by R.A.F. launch

DENMARK
Kiel
Hamburg
Cuxhaven
Heligoland
Bremen
Oldenburg
HOLLAND
Hannover
Cromer

100 miles
150 km

German fighter airfields. But this flight had been timed to coincide with that of the three combat wings which should have bombed Hannover and these further American formations were also routed back through the same area. It was the Hannover formations that continued to attract the most numerous and the most aggressive of the German fighters and the return flight of the Hamburg formation turned out to be almost the proverbial 'milk run' for which all American bomber men yearned. Although the Hamburg wing was followed by German fighters until well out to sea, the German pilots did little more than continue to nibble away half-heartedly at the edges of the formation and wait to pick off stragglers. In this, the German pilots were destined to be disappointed for they saw only one B-17 drop out of the formation. The Fortress of Lieutenant James W. Rendall, of the 91st Bomb Group, was one of the two that had been damaged by Flak over Hamburg and Rendall gradually fell behind. The inevitable happened and his plane was finished off, probably by Oberleutnant Martin Drewes, a night-fighter pilot who had been ordered up to deal with such stragglers. The Fortress, called 'Local Girl' by its crew, crashed south of Oldenburg with four men dead.

The German fighters eventually left and there were no further casualties until the English coast was almost in sight. The second 91st Bomb Group plane that had been hit by Flak ran out of fuel here and had to land in the sea. Lieutenant Jack Hargis made a perfect 'dead-stick' landing and his crew took to their dinghies safely. Two R.A.F. Walrus seaplanes were soon on the scene and landed but the sea was so rough that they could not take off again. An R.A.F. rescue launch then arrived, picked up Hargis and his crew, and towed the two Walruses into Yarmouth harbour. The remainder of the American planes all landed safely at about 3 p.m. Lieutenant Hargis and his crew were back at their airfield, Bassingbourn, that evening and were sent to rest camps for a week's recuperation (he and another member of his crew were killed on the famous Schweinfurt-Regensburg raid of 17 August 1943).

So the groups that had flown to Hamburg returned with the loss of only two planes and one full crew. The remainder of the American units had not been so fortunate. Two combat wings, of six groups, had pressed on to reach and bomb the motor-tyre factories in Hannover and their accurate bombing had caused severe damage and dense fires. A large part of the Hannover fire brigade was absent, still helping to fight fires in Hamburg, and the fires at the tyre factories burnt on for many hours. Many factory workers were among the 273 civilians killed in Hannover. But sixteen B-17s of the six bomb groups – the 92nd, 95th, 96th, 305th, 306th and 388th – were shot down in a fierce and prolonged air battle. The third of the Hannover combat wings – consisting of the 94th, 100th and 385th Bomb Groups – had had difficulty in assembling and these groups had separately bombed Wilhelmshaven, Bremerhaven and a convoy off the Frisian Islands but none of their bombing caused serious damage to the Germans. German fighters had shot down six of their planes.

The total American losses for the day were twenty-four B-17s. There was some relief in the news that four complete crews were saved from the North Sea by the R.A.F. rescue aircraft and launches which were so highly thought of by the Americans, with some help on this day by Norfolk fishing boats. But, from the other missing planes, ninety-six crewmen had died and 105 became prisoners. The missing rate was 11·5 per cent of those B-17s that had reached the German coast. In addition, six men were dead and several others badly wounded in returned aircraft and one gunner of the 92nd Bomb Group, who had had an arm shot off, had been pushed out of his plane over Germany with his opened parachute under his remaining arm. The gunner, Staff Sergeant Weaver, was found by the Germans and he survived. The co-pilot of the same plane, Flight Officer John C. Morgan, was awarded the Medal of Honor, the highest American award for bravery, for bringing his badly damaged Fortress back to England with a crazed and dying pilot who, for much of the flight, had wrapped himself round the pilot's control column.* Such casualties were the price that the units of the Eighth Air Force had to pay for the American insistence on daylight precision bombing.

Perhaps to encourage their shaken aircrew, the interrogation officers at the American airfields allowed claims to be sub-

---

* A fuller description of this flight can be found in *The Mighty Eighth*, an excellent history of the Eighth Air Force written by Roger A. Freeman.

mitted for the shooting down of sixty German fighters, with ten more probably destroyed and thirty-six damaged. The Luftwaffe Quartermaster General's records contain details for only four German fighters destroyed – with two pilots killed – and three more damaged.

14

Concentrated Bombing

The third night of the Battle of Hamburg was a quiet one. R.A.F. Bomber Command rarely operated on three consecutive nights. Because its raids were usually 'maximum efforts', most of its planes and many of its aircrew had flown in the two previous nights, to Hamburg and Essen. The planes could stand the strain of a third night's operations but not the men. Even though the weather was quite clear over most of Germany, a 'stand down' was ordered early in the day of Monday the 26th and a lot of relaxation and sleeping took place on the British bomber airfields that evening and night. Six Mosquitoes of 139 Squadron were sent to Hamburg, to make sure that the citizens of that city did not get a similar full night's sleep. The Hamburg Chief of Police recorded that these 'sneak raiders' did not cause any significant damage. No other Allied aircraft flew over Germany that night. The following day, Tuesday the 27th, was also quiet. It was the turn of the Americans to have a rest; their units had flown major operations on the last three days and they, too, needed a chance to draw breath. But the Allied airmen and the people of Hamburg were allowed only this twenty-four-hour lull and, at his morning conference on Tuesday the 27th, Sir Arthur Harris decided to resume the Battle of Hamburg. The weather forecast was good; a Mosquito, sent out to confirm this, flew right over Hamburg later in the day and found clear weather. The light smoke haze remaining was not considered sufficient to prevent night bombing. A maximum effort for Hamburg was ordered again. This raid was destined to be the most important of the battle.

In the subsequent planning, the eastern part of the main city was selected as the target. The Aiming Point would remain the same as on the first R.A.F. raid but the approach flight was to be from the east-north-east so that the creep-back would develop across the densely built-up residential areas south-east of the Alster lake and north of the Elbe river. Zero Hour remained the same, at 1.0 a.m., but the bombing time for the Main Force attack was shortened by five minutes, from fifty to forty-five minutes. The number of waves remained the same but their allocated times were condensed. This change was probably incorporated in order to lessen the extent of the creep-back. The routes chosen for the raid were almost identical to those of the previous raid but with one important exception. The bombers were to fly right across the Schleswig–Holstein peninsula north of Hamburg, turn south-east and fly right over Lübeck and, only then, turn west towards Hamburg. (See the map on page 249 for this route.) This roundabout routeing was necessary to bring the bombers into Hamburg from the east for their bombing run but it would also serve the useful purpose of concealing the true identity of the target from the Germans until almost the last minute. In particular, the deliberate flight across Lübeck, although risky because of that city's Flak defences, might mislead the Germans into believing that Lübeck was to be the real target.

A significant change took place in the contents of the bomb-loads for this raid. Although Bomber Command's operational order to groups did not call for any basic change, the incendiary contents in the total bomb-loads rose from the 940 tons carried in the previous raid to Hamburg to over 1,200 tons. The main reason for this change was an operational one. Because of the longer distance to be flown, the Halifax and Stirling squadrons needed to reduce the weight of their bomb-loads. This was done by cutting out the high-explosive part of their loads completely and replacing them by lighter incendiary loads.

There were no other major changes. A full-scale Intruder effort was requested from Fighter Command. Six Wellingtons would take advantage of the bomber activity over Hamburg to lay mines in the River Elbe and the usual Mosquito harassing raids over the Ruhr and the leaflet flights to France by training-unit aircraft were ordered.

That Tuesday was even hotter than preceding days had been and much sweat was expended on the bomber airfields as the squadrons prepared to go to war again. A total of 787 bombers would eventually take off for Hamburg, five less than on the previous raid to that city. A study of the crew lists shows that officers of steadily increasing rank were interested in seeing for themselves the effects of Window. Five station commanders – normally 'rationed' to one operational flight per month – arranged flights for themselves in the coming night.* But Bomber Command would be carrying a much more distinguished passenger that night. Brigadier-General Fred Anderson, commander of the American VIII Bomber Command, would fly to Hamburg, officially listed as second pilot in a Lancaster of 83 Squadron. It would actually be Fred Anderson's second flight with Bomber Command; he had been to Essen two nights earlier. Wing Commander John Searby, commander of 83 Squadron, remembers that 'we took few, if any, generals into battle and my crews were tickled pink'. The crew chosen to take this important passenger, both to Essen and to Hamburg, was that of Flight Lieutenant 'Ricky' Garvey, a Canadian pilot. This experienced crew, who normally flew as Visual Markers in the opening of an attack, were being used as Backers-Up on these flights and could, therefore, be placed in the middle of the attack so that their passenger could see these R.A.F. raids in full swing. General Anderson had returned safely from Essen, declaring that raid 'one of the most impressive sights he had ever seen' and he would be even more impressed with what he was about to see over Hamburg. Ricky Garvey's crew would return safely with their passenger from Hamburg and the American general did not fly with Bomber Command again.†

It is interesting to speculate on the reason for General

* The five station commanders were Group Captains H. I. Edwards, V.C., from Binbrook, making his first flight in heavy bombers, S. C. Elworthy from Waddington, H. L. Patch from Coningsby, A. D. Ross from Middleton St George, and A. H. Willets from Oakington. Two even more senior officers would fly in later raids of the Battle of Hamburg. They were Air Commodore W. A. D. Brooke, of 4 Group, and, from 1 Group, Air Commodore A. M. Wray, a veteran R.A.F. pilot known as 'Hoppin' ' Wray from a First World War leg injury. All would return safely.

† Flight Lieutenant Garvey did not survive the war. After completing his tour with the Pathfinders, he was killed when an Oxford aircraft in which he was a passenger crashed in England. The bomber in which Brigadier-General Anderson carried out his two flights is the famous Lancaster, R5868, now preserved in the R.A.F. Museum at Hendon. This Hamburg raid was the sixty-fifth out of the 137 operational flights that this bomber made while serving with 83 Squadron and, later, 467 (Australian) Squadron.

19. The first R.A.F. raid. The photoflash of a bomber momentarily reveals a plan of the city centre. This bomber is exactly over the Aiming Point in the Altstadt. Visible are: a 4,000-lb bomb at the moment of explosion (bottom right), the streets of St Georg and the dummy streets on the camouflaged Binnen Alster, the dark area of the Aussen Alster (centre right). The left half of the picture shows the many pin-point lights of incendiary bombs and the larger areas of light where fires are becoming established.

Effects of the raid

20–23. These and later photographs of ground scenes were all taken during the Battle of Hamburg but the collection from which they come unfortunately has no individual captions. These four scenes are shown here as being typical of

incidents which could be seen in Hamburg immediately after the first raid. No. 22 is one of the collecting points for people bombed out and awaiting evacuation. No. 23 is a local party headquarters to which people must report, as the board outside states, for emergency accommodation, ration cards, provisions, compensation for damage, urgent repairs, etc.

R.A.F. casualties

△ 24. 'Killed in action.'

▽ 25. 'For you the war is over.'

(These photographs were not taken during the Hamburg raids.)

26. This photograph shows B-17 waist gunners of the 91st Bomb Group at their exposed positions. The official caption for this photograph says that the B-17 is 'winging its way towards the target' but the tree top just visible through the window shows that this is a posed photograph taken while the bomber is still on the ground. Note the sheets of armour plating to protect the gunners.

27. A fine picture of a B-17 combat wing of three bomb groups similar to the
formations used in the Battle of Hamburg. The high and low groups are
keeping in good, compact boxes but at the expense of losing touch with the lead

group. The lead group is not sufficiently compact to prevent German fighters from diving through the formation. One plane from the lead group has fallen back to find temporary shelter between the high and low groups.

U.S.A.A.F. bombing at Hamburg, 25 July 1943

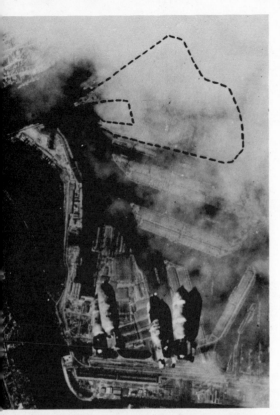

28. The first American bombs of the Battle of Hamburg – 500-lb high explosives from a plane of the 379th Bomb Group – go down. This photograph shows how smoke from R.A.F. bombing of the previous night is rising from the main city and just cover the main target – the Blohm & Voss ya (marked).

29. A few minutes later, the bombs of t' 91st Bomb Group are aimed at the 'grof red-topped buildings'. The large explosion may be an oil-storage tank a' the Neuhof power station. Much too la to be effective, German smoke generators on the left bank of the Elbe' tributary start to operate.

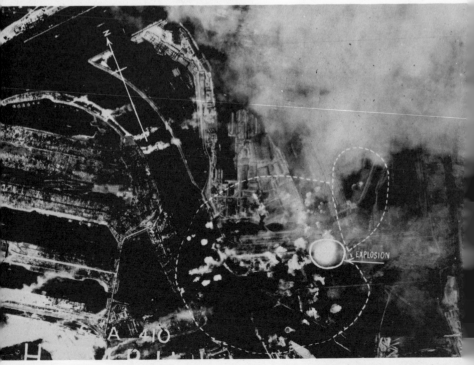

EXPLOSION

A 410

Anderson's wish to fly on these two Bomber Command operations and I have asked many questions about it. Fred Anderson is now dead and he appears to have left no papers on the subject. He had just taken over formal command of all American heavy bombers in England and the British had been urging that the Americans take up night bombing, as being less costly and more effective. It is probable that Anderson wished to have a good look at this night bombing of which the British were so proud. It is possible that he was thinking of turning over to night bombing the B-24 Liberator groups which he was soon expecting to receive under his command. The Liberator had not so far been successful in European bombing operations. But Anderson's superior commander, General Ira Eaker, when asked about this, stated, 'I can assure you that there was no consideration, at any time, on the part of the U.S. political and military leadership to turning the U.S.A.A.F. heavy-bomber forces over to night bombing.' Neither Liberators nor B-17 Fortresses ever were used by the Americans for night-bomber operations.

What is certain is that Fred Anderson kept very quiet about his two flights with the R.A.F. During a week which saw the most hectic operations to date for the bomber units of his own command, Anderson twice quietly took himself off to Wyton to make these flights, leaving his chief of staff to run affairs at VIII Bomber Command Headquarters in his absence and probably bound to secrecy over what Anderson was doing. General Eaker was very surprised when told of these flights, especially as they were not 'milk runs'.

One must admire the courage of Fred Anderson in flying to two of Germany's most strongly defended cities in order to get first-hand experience of another air force's methods.

There is no need to give a detailed account of the opening stages of this second R.A.F. raid. The bombers took off against the beautiful backdrop of cirrus clouds painted pink by the setting sun. There were no crashes on take-off although there were some close shaves. A 305 Squadron Wellington swung violently on take-off at Ingham because one flap had failed to stay down and it nearly hit the top of a hangar. The Polish pilot, Flying Officer Z. Bobinski, was later told, somewhat jokingly, that 'the top brass and others watching what looked like an inevitable crash and the explosion of our 4,000-lb bomb managed to do the sprint of a lifetime – even the portly and elderly; it took them some time to assemble back from faraway fields'. At West Wickham airfield, a Stirling ran off the runway into a field; later examination showed that the Pitot tube – for registering air speed – was blocked by a spider. How many lives in Hamburg did that little spider save?

The bomber crews were not surprised to be going to Hamburg again. They had been told, before the first raid, that a concentrated effort was going to be made on that city and, at the briefings for this raid, a further message from their commander-in-chief had been read out congratulating them on the success of the recent Hamburg and Essen raids. The Operational Record Book of 83 Squadron made this comment:

> We were all given to understand that our last few raids had done more to end this war and save thousands of 'brown types' than anything so far. The aircrew do feel that they are, at last, really achieving something vital towards ending this war and their spirit and press-on attitude is at a peak.[1]

'Brown types' were the soldiers who would one day have to carry out the invasion of German-occupied Europe. 'Press on Regardless' was the unofficial motto of Bomber Command and to have a 'press-on attitude' was the most desirable quality for an R.A.F. bomber man to possess.

On this night, forty-one aircraft – slightly less than average – turned back because of mechanical troubles. No crews went astray to become early victims of the Luftwaffe and 748 bombers arrived at that point, fifty miles off the German coast, where the dropping of Window commenced. Many of the bombers had now been fitted with a Window-dropping chute and most of the difficulties experienced during the first use of that device had been eliminated. Windowing had become a routine operation and would continue so to the end of the war.

It was on this night that the Luftwaffe started its long fight back against Window. There was not yet such a thing as a German night-fighter experimental and trials unit that might have devoted itself to countering Window and most of the first initiatives were taken by front-line operational units.

These were serious days for the German night-fighter force and any scrap of information on how best to deal with this latest British move circulated among these establishments remarkably quickly. Night-fighter radar operators found that, at higher altitudes where Window had not yet dispersed sufficiently to form a single cloud, each bundle of recently released Window still looked like the echo of a single bomber. In such conditions, the many radar 'blips' approaching the fighter at high speed could be recognized as bundles of Window but any more slowly closing blip among this was likely to be a bomber. On the ground, more use was made of the long-range *Freya* radar sets, which were not affected by Window as were the close-control *Würzburg* sets, although skilled *Würzburg* operators soon learned to pick out bombers in marginal conditions, such as on the flanks or at the front and rear of the bomber-stream.

Changes were also taking place in the methods by which the night fighters were controlled. A great many fighters were still confined to their boxes in the hope that their ground-control radars could pick up a bomber in the old way, but more fighters than before were now allowed to go freelancing. They were encouraged to cooperate with searchlights, to use their own eyes, to take advantage, in fact, of anything they saw or heard or felt by intuition that would lead them to a bomber. In addition, there took place on this night the first serious examples of an aid that was later to become famous and, indeed, the main standby of the twin-engined night-fighter force in the months and years to come – the '*laufende Reportage*', the 'running commentary'. This was, quite simply, a continuous broadcast of any information that operations officers on the ground had about the height, course, speed and possible future intentions of the bomber-stream. Such information was collected from many sources – radar sets of all kinds, ground observers, information passed back to the ground by other fighters and, sometimes, by hopeful anticipation. This commentary was available to any freelancing fighter whose crew was able to listen to it.

The R.A.F. Listening Service heard several running commentaries on this night. They probably came from the headquarters operations rooms of the German fighter divisions or night-fighter *Geschwader*, the staffs of which had done little more, before the coming of Window, than allocate crews to boxes and arrange replacements or switches. It must be stressed, however, that it was to take a prolonged period to perfect the running-commentary system and that only a proportion of the night fighters were using it in these early nights of its employment.

A further expedient was employed. The reader will remember that Major Hajo Herrmann's single-engined 'Wild Boar' fighters had had a successful trial against the British bombers over Cologne at the beginning of July and that Herrmann had then been ordered to establish and train a full-strength *Geschwader* of such fighters (see pages 65–7). This new unit was still being created when the Battle of Hamburg started. With Hamburg seriously bombed three nights earlier and with Window creating havoc in the twin-engined night-fighter defence, any available expedient to help stop the bombers was urgently needed. Hajo Herrmann describes how his new unit was brought into action.

Suddenly, while we were still at Bonn, training and expanding, I was called on the phone by Goering. He told me that he wanted us to start operating that night. I said that I couldn't; my unit was not ready. Goering made further calls, telling me that the first Hamburg raid was a catastrophe; he likened it to the earthquake at Lisbon earlier in the century. He asked me to do what I could.

So, we flew on the night of the second Hamburg raid even though our training was not complete. It was very dramatic. I told the pilots what Goering had said about Hamburg. I told them that I would fly and they were to follow me. There were about twenty of us from Bonn and others from Rheine and Oldenburg. Many of them failed and had to return to their airfields. You see, it was the first time that these men faced this task and flew in the night without knowing where and when it would be possible to land.

It should be stated that some of the Wild Boars had been in action during the first Hamburg raid and the recent Essen raid, probably by local initiatives, but this would be the first night that the whole Wild Boar organization was committed to action.

This description of the measures employed by the Luftwaffe to counter Window has anticipated some of the events. At the time that the R.A.F. bombers approached the Schleswig–Holstein coast, in the early minutes of 28 July, many night fighters of NJG3 were still tied to their usual boxes, although a few others were allowed to roam more widely. Neither the running commentaries nor the coming into action of the main Wild Boar contingent would commence until the bombers reached Hamburg. The Germans could not yet be sure that Hamburg was even the target; they were always anxious about Berlin, 150 miles further into Germany, and many night fighters were held back for the defence of the capital.

A Pathfinder Lancaster was the first bomber to be caught by the German fighters. It was a Blind Marker, one of the first to drop a yellow Target Indicator as a route-marker when the head of the bomber-stream crossed the coast at the prominent Sankt Peter peninsula. It is not known what type of fighter shot down the Lancaster but bombers at the front of the stream did not have the full protection of Window. The Lancaster fell blazing, the remainder of its load of yellow Target Indicators flaring up brilliantly before the bomber crashed into the estuary of the River Eider near the small town of Tönning. No survivors!

The yellow route-markers that further Pathfinders put down at the coast continued to attract the attention of German fighters. The markers cascaded and burnt underneath a thin layer of stratus cloud which was lit up 'like ground glass'. This was the sort of thing that would attract freelancing night fighters and another Lancaster which crashed near the route-markers may have been the victim of such a fighter. There were three more combats near the route-markers but the fighter was evaded or driven off in each case and bomber gunners later claimed one fighter destroyed and one damaged. Only three more bombers were lost during the flight across Schleswig–Holstein – a Canadian squadron commander's Wellington, another Canadian squadron Halifax whose crew would have completed their tour on this night if they had reached home and another Halifax with a new crew which ventured into searchlights near Kiel and was promptly shot down by a German fighter. On the first raid of the Battle of Hamburg, six bombers had been lost before the target was reached. In the corresponding parts of the flight in this second raid, only five bombers were lost. Window was still providing valuable protection for Bomber Command.

There were few other incidents before the bombers reached Hamburg. Six bombers suffered various difficulties and were forced to release their bombs on minor targets or over open country. One of these planes, a 15 Squadron Stirling, suffered such serious engine failure, including one engine on fire, that the pilot thought his plane would crash and he ordered his crew to bale out. Five men obeyed this order but the second pilot and the flight engineer delayed sufficiently to take advantage of the pilot's recovery of the aircraft and to help in an adventurous flight back to England.*

The weather continued to be fine, with no navigational difficulties. The deeper flight into Germany, round to the north-east of Hamburg, met no opposition from German fighters and there were no combats in the last eighty miles of the route to Hamburg. The whole of Bomber Command flew right across the port of Lübeck but there was no Flak fire. It is probable that the local Flak commander used the trick of ordering his defences to hold their fire so as not to reveal the location of the city, hoping that the British bombers would fly on elsewhere. They did, and 735 bombers duly arrived at the last turning point, over the town of Ratzeburg thirty miles east of Hamburg, and turned on to a westerly course to commence their bombing runs.

The opening of the raid was similar in many ways to the opening of the first raid of the Battle of Hamburg three nights earlier. Some Pathfinders arrived early and flew around the area but the German Flak and searchlights kept quiet. Flight Lieutenant John Rowland, a pilot of 12 Squadron, was due to bomb in the first wave of the Main Force attack. It was the first time he had flown in the first wave and Rowland describes his crew's doubts over the ability of their navigator.

As Zero Hour approached, we saw absolutely nothing. With one or two minutes to go, we might have been by ourselves in the middle of the Atlantic – perhaps we were – but Eric insisted, vehemently, that we were bang on track and time and that the target would shortly be revealed, or else the Pathfinders had made a mess of it. I opened the

---

* Excellent personal accounts are available from this and several other incidents in the Battle of Hamburg but whose inclusion in the relevant chapters would disturb the balance of those chapters and they will be kept back for inclusion as a separate section at the end of the book.

bomb doors but, if Hamburg was below, the defences were lying absolutely doggo. Ken, the bomb aimer, was reporting from his window, 'Absolutely bugger all; you've made a balls of it, Eric', and the gunners and the rest were all reporting nothing but pitch black.

Suddenly, Ken yelled, 'T.I.s just under the nose, Skip. Left, left, steady. Bombs gone', and, as he spoke, about one thousand searchlights seemed to come on and Flak started bursting in a heavy barrage all about us. I held her steady for the photograph, then closed the bomb doors and put the nose down slightly and, with a few extra revs, we soon realized we had left it all behind us.

We saw the raid carrying on for a long time and there seemed to be a good fire being stoked up behind us.

The first yellow markers and bombs went down at 0.55 a.m. – two minutes early – and the raid was in full swing by 1.00 a.m., the official opening of the main attack. On this occasion, the Main Force bomb aimers found that the Pathfinder markers were well concentrated. Salvo after salvo of yellow Target Indicators went down into one area and the green markers of the Backers-Up followed in the same place. Photographs developed later showed that the exact centre of the area being marked moved slightly but no more than was to be expected during the progress of a good raid and the creep-back was a very slow one. The Main Force took every advantage of this clear and concentrated marking. There were no delays and each wave came in to add its bomb-loads to the heavy assault that was obviously being made on the area of Hamburg marked for them.

It was not long before a large area of fire was seen and a dense column of smoke rose to the height at which the bombers were flying. It was obvious to every R.A.F. man in the middle and later stages of the raid that the fires and the smoke were on a scale none had ever seen before. Violent explosions could be seen on the ground, one appearing as 'a great fountain of burning debris thrown up for what seemed to be thousands of feet'. A Canadian air gunner, in a Stirling, later wrote in his diary of the smoke that penetrated his oxygen mask and the records of an Australian squadron refer to one of its Lancasters that returned with its mid-upper turret covered with particles of soot!

Many of the bomber aircrew have described the sight of Hamburg on fire that night:

I was fascinated by the awesome and amazing spectacle. As far as I could see was one mass of fire. 'A sea of flame' has been the description and that's an understatement. It was so bright that I could read the target maps and adjust the bomb-sight. It was useless even to use the bomb-sight as there was no definite aiming point and I cannot remember giving the pilot any directions. The only aircraft I could see were a Stirling or two, well below, skittering across the flames almost, it seemed, at ground level. (Sergeant W. G. Lamb, 460 Squadron)

As I looked down, it was as if I was looking into what I imagined to be an active volcano. There were great volumes of smoke and, mentally, I could sense the great heat. Our actual bombing was like putting another shovelful of coal into the furnace. (Sergeant W. G. Hart, 51 Squadron)

The burning of Hamburg that night was remarkable in that I saw not many fires but one. Set in the darkness was a turbulent dome of bright red fire, lighted and ignited like the glowing heart of a vast brazier. I saw no streets, no outlines of buildings, only brighter fires which flared like yellow torches against a background of bright red ash. Above the city was a misty red haze. I looked down, fascinated but aghast, satisfied yet horrified. I had never seen a fire like that before and was never to see its like again. (Flight Lieutenant A. Forsdike, 78 Squadron)

Most of the raids we did looked like gigantic firework displays over the target area but this was 'the daddy of them all'. Flak, and fighter and bomber exchanges, the markers going down on the target, multi-coloured sheets of flame from the various explosions, as the bombs found their mark, and, above all, a sea of fire with columns of thick black smoke spiralling upwards. I remember, as we were leaving the target area, the skipper saying over the intercom, 'Those poor bastards!' (Flight Sergeant K. R. Parry, 76 Squadron)

I was amazed at the awe-inspiring sight of the target area. It seemed as though the whole of Hamburg was on fire from one end to the other and a huge column of smoke was towering well above us – and we were on 20,000 feet! It all seemed almost incredible and, when I realized that I was looking at a city with a population of two millions, or about that, it became almost frightening to think of what must be going on down there in Hamburg. This may seem a fairly minor event in the writing of a book on the Battle of Hamburg as a whole but it is a memory which sometimes haunts me, especially when I helped, even if only in a very small way, to cause that cataclysmic event. (Sergeant J. D. Whiteman, 10 Squadron)

The sight of Hamburg burning, apparently from end to end, will be remembered all my life. (Flying Officer W. A. Lennard, 158 Squadron)

The German defences had opened up at full strength when the first bombs fell. Those bomber crews who were over the target early reported that the number of searchlights and the intensity of Flak was heavier than on the previous raid. This was true; the Hamburg defences had been reinforced with mobile batteries from other German cities. For the first half of the raid, these defences continued to operate ferociously although the Window that was being dropped soon became effective. Several bombers were damaged by Flak during this period but there are no cases where the destruction of a bomber can be attributed solely to the Flak. Then, half-way through the attack, two things happened that reduced even further the effectiveness of the ground defences. First, the dense cloud of smoke rising from the burning target area prevented many of the searchlights in the centre of the target area from operating properly, although those further out continued to work unhampered. Second, at 1.21 a.m. precisely, the Hamburg Flak batteries received orders to limit their fire to an altitude of 5,500 metres – approximately 18,000 feet. This order, issued so that the German fighters could operate freely above that height, was imposed during the time allocated to the third wave of the Main Force bombers and it thus came into effect while the low-flying Stirlings were over the target. These aircraft continued to be vulnerable to the Flak and some were damaged but the Stirlings were soon clear of the target and the aircraft of the remaining three waves were all capable of flying above 18,000 feet. It is not surprising that many crews reported that Hamburg's Flak seemed to have given up during this period and these crews were able to bomb and sightsee in what they believed to be safe conditions.

The order restricting the Flak's operations was an important event. For the first time, German night fighters rather than the Flak had priority in the defences of the target city. This was the Wild Boar type of night fighting that Major Herrmann was introducing. His single-engined fighters had arrived on the scene and those twin-engined fighters that had been given permission to freelance were also able to fly safely over the city, their aim being to find and attack bombers caught by the searchlights or silhouetted from above by the blazing city. Few bomber crews had any idea that German fighters were flying with them over Hamburg. Unfortunately for the German cause, the fighters available over Hamburg that night were neither numerous enough nor skilled enough in this new form of night fighting to score a major success against the 350 or so bombers which flew over the city during the second part of the raid.

Several bombers were attacked by fighters during this period, the attackers often being identified as the single-engined fighters of Herrmann's Wild Boar unit, even the pale-blue-colour paintwork of the day fighters borrowed by Herrmann's unit being seen and recorded. Where the bomber crews were alert, the bomber usually escaped, as in this action described by Sergeant Ron Buck, tail gunner of a 207 Squadron Lancaster:

I reported him. 'Fighter port quarter, slightly above. Prepare to corkscrew port.' I held my fire, waiting for him to start his attack. My pilot continued flying a straight course on track, waiting for the signal to corkscrew before starting evasive action. The longer you could delay the dive into the corkscrew, the better the chances of getting away.

I continued to hold my fire and he held his. He held off at approximately 300 yards. He was now at the same height as we were and I knew that he was weighing us up before coming in on his curve of pursuit. The intercom was clear. Suddenly, the fighter dropped his nose and in he came. I screamed, 'Corkscrew port. *Go!*' and, at the same time, opened up with the four Browning machine-guns, backed up by the mid-upper gunner with his two guns. We put up a very lethal wall of bullets between the fighter and ourselves, hosepiping it all around him. From the tracer, I could see we were scoring hits on him. He broke to starboard and shot beneath us into the dark. The pilot got back on course, straight and level, and we didn't see him again.

All this took place in the time it takes to read it.

Major Herrmann caught a bomber that was not so alert.

The clouds of smoke over Hamburg were so dense that it made you shudder. I saw this great column of smoke; I even smelt it. I flew over the target several times and, then, I saw this bomber in the searchlights. He had nearly reached the top of the smoke cloud at the time. I identified the type at the time but I cannot be sure now what it was. I do remember how big it seemed. I think it was a Lancaster.

The attack was very simple. I went into the searchlights. I was not very experienced; another pilot would have kept in the dark. I was almost level with him, probably just above the turbulence of his propellers. It was like daylight in those searchlights. I could see the rear gunner; he was only looking downwards, probably at the inferno below. There was no movement of his guns. You must remember that, at this time, the British were not generally warned to watch out for us over the target. I had seen other bombers over targets with the gunners looking down.

I fired and he burned. He banked to the left and then through 180 degrees to the right. As he fell, he turned and dropped away from the smoke cloud. I followed him a little but, as he got lower and lower, I left him. I watched him burst on the ground. I didn't see anyone bale out but I cannot exclude that. By the light of his explosion, I could see the '*Knicks*' – the small walls with bushes built on them against which the cattle found shelter from the sun and wind. That was my homeland – Schleswig-Holstein – as I knew it.

Of course, I tried to find some more bombers and I think I shot at some more but there were no more shot downs.

It is almost certain that Major Herrmann's victim was a 101 Squadron Lancaster that crashed into Wellingsbüttel, a northern suburb of Hamburg. There were no survivors.

Three other bombers are believed to have been shot down in and around Hamburg. In reply, British crews claimed one Messerschmitt 109 destroyed in the target area and several more fighters damaged. It is also possible that a twin-engined German fighter was shot down by its own Flak, crashing at Niendorf in the north of the city, killing its crew and one civilian. This is based on a 3rd Flakdivision report which recorded the aircraft concerned as being a 'twin-engined enemy plane' but no R.A.F. plane crashed here. Unfortunately, as so often, German records are not complete enough to verify all these German casualties, although one of the Wild Boar pilots was certainly wounded in combat over Hamburg and had to crash-land his Focke-Wulf 190.

It must be stated again that only a proportion of the German fighters operating around Hamburg were allowed to wander freely, using the Wild Boar tactic. Many were still chained uselessly to their boxes. Leutnant Peter Spoden was a pilot of

NJG5, whose planes were patrolling in boxes east of Hamburg in case part of the British bomber force attacked Berlin.

I was in Box *Reiher*, on the Baltic coast east of Lübeck. I was only the new boy in a poor box. I got up to the highest altitude possible – 6,000 to 6,500 metres – and, from there, I could see these four-engined aircraft. There was a layer of stratus cloud over Hamburg, stretching towards Kiel, and I could see these bombers against this layer of cloud. Several times I asked ground control if I could fly to them. 'I can see them. Let me go over there.' But the fighter control officer said that it was not possible. Then, I asked again; I told them to ring up Berlin but I don't think anyone would take the responsibility of leaving Berlin open to a second attack. I even talked to the other pilots in the nearby boxes. They could also see the bombers. We were furious but we couldn't do anything about it. We could see the fire in Hamburg; it was the biggest fire I had ever seen.

After landing, we went to Hauptmann Schoenert in the *Gruppe* Headquarters. We told him that it was crazy. We had had to watch, helplessly, while they were destroying a German city. We were mad. Rudi Schoenert got on the phone to Berlin several times; he even let me and another young fellow who had been flying tell them what was happening. We youngsters were very keen to get our first shot downs.

The raid was planned to end at 1.45 a.m. and the last of the 729 aircraft to bomb released its load two minutes later.* One pilot who bombed late in the raid reported that the target area was 'one mass of fires, smoke and destruction' and another man says that the later bombing was 'like poking the dying embers of a fire'. Of one thing, the R.A.F. men were confident. They had never seen a raid which, from the air, had appeared so devastatingly accurate and concentrated. The Germans appeared to have used decoy markers on an extensive scale again but their choice of colour for these had been unfortunate. All the German decoys on this night were red. The R.A.F. bomb aimers knew that the Pathfinders were only using yellow and green markers on this night.

---

* The last plane to bomb was a 427 Squadron Halifax captained by Sergeant R. L. Henry. The reader may remember that this Canadian pilot had been the last to land back in England from the first raid of the Battle of Hamburg. Sergeant Henry was killed on 29 August 1943 when the Oxford aircraft in which he was taking three groundcrew men to repair a damaged squadron aircraft, in the south of England, crashed in the Pennines.

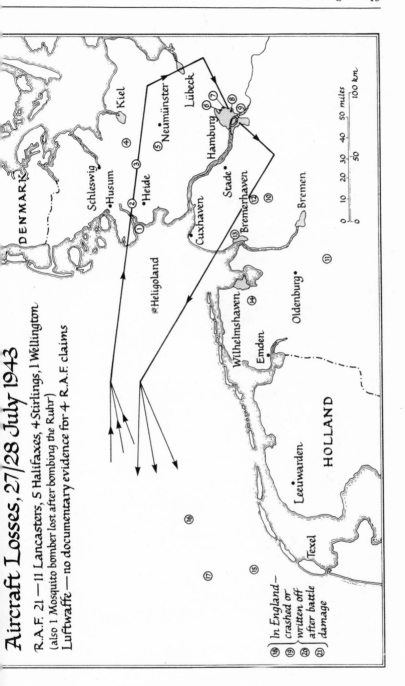

Aircraft Losses, 27/28 July 1943

R.A.F. 21 — 11 Lancasters, 5 Halifaxes, 4 Stirlings, 1 Wellington
(also 1 Mosquito bomber lost after bombing the Ruhr)
Luftwaffe — no documentary evidence for 4 R.A.F. claims

DENMARK

Schleswig
Kiel
Husum
Heide
Neumünster
Lübeck
Hamburg
Stade
Cuxhaven
Bremerhaven
Bremen
Heligoland
Wilhelmshaven
Oldenburg
Emden
Leeuwarden
HOLLAND
Texel

In England —
crashed or
written off
after battle
damage

0 10 20 30 40 50 miles
0   50   100 km

Bomber Command flew home from Hamburg, the gunners in the R.A.F. planes being able to observe the effects of their recent bombing for a considerable time. There were no problems with the weather and it was an easy return flight although eight more bombers, mostly off course, were lost. Six of these casualties were probably victims of German night fighters, one unsuspecting Lancaster being shot down over the sea when Oberfeldwebel Walter Kubisch, a radar operator, was allowed by his pilot, Major Lent, to engage the bomber with his Messerschmitt 110's rarely used rear gun. The other two losses fell to the Flak batteries of Wilhelmshaven and Bremerhaven when the bombers concerned strayed and flew near those strongly defended cities. One Junkers 88 was claimed as destroyed and two more damaged by other bombers. Four more bombers – three Stirlings and a Halifax – were written off after crashing in England, two after suffering battle damage and two in landing accidents. There are many interesting stories of dangers survived, good fortune or death experienced, courage and skill shown in these incidents of the return flight and landings but this narrative cannot cover every phase of the Battle of Hamburg in depth.

Bomber Command had lost seventeen planes and crews on this, the second R.A.F. raid of the Battle of Hamburg. The losses were made up of eleven Lancasters, four Halifaxes, one Stirling and one Wellington. Four other planes had crashed but their crews were mostly unhurt. The missing rate, of 2·2 per cent, was still a very low figure and owed much to the continuing success of Window. The other R.A.F. operations of the night, all minor ones, had been concluded successfully except for the loss of a 139 Squadron Mosquito bomber which was hit by Flak over the Ruhr and crashed in Holland. Its crew, including the station navigation officer from Wyton airfield, were on the run for nearly a month but were eventually captured. Twenty-seven Fighter Command Intruders had drawn a complete blank over the various German airfields they had attempted to patrol. Hazy weather conditions at low altitude were the chief cause of their lack of success.

The most important statistic of the night was that approximately 2,326 tons of bombs had been dropped in the most concentrated manner on part of Hamburg and that nearly 98 per cent of the Bomber Command aircraft involved had returned unharmed and their crews, with even greater confidence, were ready to continue the Battle of Hamburg.

The first two raids on Hamburg were so *obviously* successful to those of us who took part in them. And this was, in itself, unusual. Forgetting the standard line-shooting, one returned from most trips in what I would call a neutral frame of mind. Relief to be back and glad that one more was under your belt – and that was about all. But, with those two to Hamburg, there was an added exhilaration which came from the absolute conviction – actually on the night – that we had pulled off something special. We didn't need to wait for the photographs or the intelligence assessments. We already KNEW, especially after the second trip, that this was a bit more than a run-of-the-mill affair. (Sergeant O. E. Burger, 77 Squadron)

NOTE

1. Public Record Office AIR 27/687.

15

Firestorm

Few people in Hamburg had been surprised when the sirens sounded for this second major R.A.F. raid. During the past three days and nights, the city had already been struck by one heavy R.A.F. raid and two light Mosquito raids by night and by two American daylight raids. Most of the population now realized that they were surely caught up in a major attempt by the Allied bomber forces to destroy their beloved city.

The evacuation of the civilians bombed out in the first R.A.F. raid had continued smoothly. Many other people who had not lost their homes also tried to leave and some succeeded in doing so but the authorities tried to restrain this type of evacuation because of the strain on transport services and because too many workers leaving would affect industrial output. The Flak authorities had made a major attempt to bring help to the city and several railway Flak batteries had clanked their way into Hamburg and taken up position at various railway sidings. It is not known how many such batteries arrived before this second R.A.F. raid but seventeen railway batteries, containing sixty-eight of the heavy 105- and 128-mm guns, are known to have arrived in the city by 31 July, four days later.

The last two nights had been uneasy ones and most people had spent them sleeping in their shelters. The public shelters had been left open and these two warm summer nights had seen many civilians sleeping on the grass outside, ready to go inside the shelter if a raid developed. Then, after all danger of a raid had passed, the civilians had dispersed back to their homes.

On one of these nights my husband was not at home and I went to the public shelter at the railway station. I didn't want to be alone; I wanted company. But, to return home through the city at 3.30 or 4.0 a.m., when foreigners and thousands of sinister people are creeping past you and when you are carrying your last few valued possessions in a suitcase which could be quite easy for someone to snatch – that was something I wouldn't want to experience again. (Anne-Kaete Seiffarth)

The fires started by the R.A.F. three nights earlier had still not all been extinguished. A particular problem was the innumerable stocks of coal and coke which could hardly be seen burning during the day but which glowed brightly at night. Only a few hours before the second big R.A.F. attack, Gauleiter Kaufmann had ordered that an all-out effort be made to put out these fires completely. Thus, nearly every fire appliance in Hamburg was sent to the western part of the city, reeled out their hoses to fight these smouldering coke and coal fires and were still there when the R.A.F. put down their concentrated bombing attack on the other side of Hamburg a few hours later.

The sirens had sounded in Hamburg at twenty minutes to midnight but the longer flight of the bombers round to the east of Hamburg meant that there was a lull of more than an hour before the first aircraft appeared over the city. A lady in the district of Hamm, which was soon to be bombed, remembers standing in front of her house during this period of calm. 'It was completely quiet. No planes. No Flak. It was an enchantingly beautiful summer night.' Then, just before 1.00 a.m., the sound of many aircraft was heard approaching; to everyone's surprise the noise came from the east. The first golden-yellow markers were seen in the sky and the bombs started dropping.

In Chapter 8, on the first R.A.F. night raid of the Battle of Hamburg, the description of where the first markers and bombs dropped and of the subsequent progress of the raid required a long and detailed treatment. The description of the progress of the marking and bombing in this raid can be short and simple.

Fifteen Pathfinder aircraft dropped their loads of markers in the first five minutes of the raid. From the evidence of photographs taken by the bombers at that time, no less than twelve of these loads of markers cascaded over one limited area. These crews were all Blind Markers and they were aiming their loads solely by means of their H2S radar sets. This all-radar primary marking had never before been successful when employed by the Pathfinders. Even now, although the early marking was concentrated, it was not particularly accurate. No markers appear to have been released over the designated Aiming Point in the city centre. The concentration of markers was approximately two miles east of the correct place and was over the Billwärder Ausschlag and Hammerbrook districts, just north of the Elbe. This failure to mark the Aiming Point was due to the difficulties experienced by the radar-set operators in the bombers in establishing their exact position in those early days of radar marking. The Bomber Command interim report on this raid says: 'It is understood that many of the Y [H2S] aircraft did not follow the correct procedure of using Harburg – an isolated built-up area south of Hamburg – to check their positions.'[1] It is probable that an unexpected crosswind had carried the Pathfinders slightly south-east of their planned marking run and that, just before the echo of the wide River Elbe came through the centre of their radar display screens, they released their markers at that point.

The two-mile error was not a serious one; there was plenty of built-up city around the area marked. The Main Force bombers arrived promptly and, finding this one, prominent group of markers, they bombed it with unusual accuracy. There was never more than that one bombing area, starting in Billwärder Ausschlag and Hammerbrook and moving back only slowly north-eastwards into the districts of Borgfelde, Hamm and, finally, into Wandsbek and Horn. Parts of the bombing had even fallen beyond the main area marked, into the Sankt Georg area towards the city centre and south of the Elbe into the dock area. This was an unusual example of Main Force bombing moving *against* the creep-back and the credit for it is due to the doggedness which the Pathfinder Recenterers and Backers-Up applied to their task.

The R.A.F. men had not been mistaken in their belief that they had carried out a raid of unusual concentration and ferocity. The majority of the bombs had not quite fallen into the area of Hamburg chosen by the Bomber Command planners but, because Hamburg was so large, these bombs had hit an equally valid part of the city. That was the nature of Area Bombing.

It is worth taking a closer look at those parts of Hamburg

that were so heavily bombed on this night. The southernmost limits of the bombing area were the districts of Billwärder Ausschlag and Rothenburgsort, both on the north bank of the Elbe. Rothenburgsort did not have a large population, being small in area and semi-industrial in character. It did, however, contain the largest children's hospital in Hamburg. Billwärder Ausschlag was a densely crowded working-class area which could claim the distinction of having produced the lowest pro-Nazi vote – 22·9 per cent – in Hamburg in the 1933 elections. The earliest bombing of the night had fallen in these two districts but the greatest weight of the attack had fallen a little further north. Here was located the old district of Borgfelde, one and a half miles from the city centre, and Hamm, a little further out. Hamm was an extensive area split into Hamm Nord, Hamm Süd and Hammerbrook.

These main bombing areas were 'layered', in that they were split up by a series of prominent roads and two canals, all of which ran from west to east through Borgfelde and Hamm, a main road, the Hammer Landstrasse, being a particularly prominent dividing line. South of this road was a reclaimed area of former marsh, now the home of many thousands of workers and their families. The forbears of these people had been farm-workers who had been drawn into Hamburg when the city's port and industry had been modernized half a century earlier. Now they lived, almost without exception, in that peculiarly German type of property, the low-rental, multi-storey block of flats run by *Wohnungsbaugesellschaften* – non-profit property companies often owned by local authorities, business concerns, trade unions, or any combination of these. Street after narrow street was comprised of these six-storeyed buildings, each block usually housing eighteen families. There were many children. These areas were not slums but they were densely crowded and their streets had certainly seen much poverty during the years of depression. The people who lived in such areas were often called *Proletarier* – 'common workers' – by those who lived only a few streets to the north, across the Hammer Landstrasse. Here, in slightly less crowded conditions, was to be found a more middle-class population: the families of skilled tradesmen, office workers and minor officials. These people paid a higher rent for their flats, which were usually owned by private landlords.

The bombing had also spread into the areas of Sankt Georg, Hohenfelde, Eilbek, Barmbek and Wandsbek. Serious damage and casualties were caused in all of these places but the reader will soon understand why attention must remain in the Borgfelde, Hammerbrook and Hamm districts. It is important to remember that these areas were predominantly residential – although there were a number of small commercial premises of back-street type – and that they were densely populated with families of the middle and lower brackets of Hamburg society. Most of the streets were narrow and there was an almost complete absence of open spaces.

It is sometimes claimed in Hamburg that, on this night, the R.A.F. destroyed those parts of the city that were the least sympathetic to Hitler and his National Socialist cause. The 1933 voting figures do not support this. Although, as has been said, Billwärder Ausschlag had the lowest Nazi vote in Hamburg, Borgfelde and Hamm produced voting figures for that party that were fractionally higher than the Hamburg average. The average Nazi vote in the city was 38·7 per cent. The figures for Borgfelde and Hamm were 39·9 and 42·2 per cent respectively.[2] The truth is that most of the people of Hamm and Borgfelde had never been politically active. They were simple working people, many of whom had voted for Hitler because he had promised them work. 'When you were only getting 8 marks and 50 pfennigs a week, there was no other way.' That sum of money, paid to a workless husband and father in the depression years, had been worth ten English shillings or two American dollars at that time. The hapless people of Hamm and Borgfelde were about to pay dearly for the votes they had cast ten years earlier.

The bombing lasted for no more than an hour. During the first part of that period, the effects on the ground were not greatly different in character from those experienced in the previous raid, three nights earlier, although the bombing was more concentrated and the fires more numerous. Few people in the city were out in the open and had the opportunity to view events during this period but one witness had a good view. Hermann Bock had been a secondary-school teacher in Hamburg until called up for military service. Now, he was back in his native city as commander of a railway Flak battery which had just arrived from Mönchen-Gladbach and taken up position at a railway siding on the Mühlenhagen in Rothenburgsort on the southern edge of the bombing area. On his arrival Bock had been 'not happy to be in Hamburg, as a Hamburger, as everyone knew the seriousness of the possibility of more air raids but, trusting fully in our comradeship and sense of duty, we will protect our home city despite all the danger'. Leutnant Bock goes on to describe the opening of the attack as viewed from his battery position.

Hamburg's night sky became in minutes, even seconds, a sky so absolutely hellish that it is impossible even to try to describe it in words. There were aeroplanes, held in the probing arms of the searchlights, fires breaking out, billowing smoke everywhere, loud, roaring waves of explosions, all broken up by great cathedrals of light as the blast bombs exploded, cascades of marker bombs slowly drifting down, stick incendiary bombs coming down with a rushing noise. No noise made by humans – no outcry – could be heard. It was like the end of the world. One could think, feel, see and speak of nothing more.

The guns of this Flak battery fired for twenty minutes but then bombs bursting in the battery position cut every electrical cable providing power to the guns.

By contrast to the experienced Flak officer, Elli Nawroski was a sixteen-year-old girl worker in a small paint factory in Bankstrasse, Hammerbrook. This night it had been her turn to sleep in the factory air-raid shelter as part of the works' fire-fighting team. When the sirens sounded, the members of this team had gone to various parts of the factory, ready to deal with incendiary bombs.

It wasn't long before we had to go down to the shelter. The houses opposite had no basements and the women and children there ran across into our shelter also. Above this shelter was our paint factory in which there were stored several tons of highly explosive liquid nitrogen.* We were all sitting on the floor, where we thought it would be safer, heads bowed, praying. The civilians who had come thought that we air-raid people, with steel helmets and some sort of uniform, were fully trained and that they would get some protection in the company of such people. This was not true. I didn't even

* The liquid nitrogen would not have exploded but would have evaporated quickly causing skinburns, damage to eyes and suffocation.

know where the water hose was. I was just a sixteen-year-old girl with such a uniform and a steel helmet.

The earth shook, the walls cracked and the plaster came down like flour until the whole basement was one cloud of dust. We thought that it was like an earthquake. No one spoke a word.

Then, the nerves of one of my colleagues snapped. There was complete silence in the shelter when this girl suddenly started to laugh. There were obviously heavy bombs bursting near by and, maybe, this girl thought that her house had been hit. Someone said, 'This is nothing to laugh about,' to which the girl replied, 'This is all I have ever wanted.' She really had no idea what she was saying. Her mother and grandmother were both killed that night.

Hermann Kröger was more experienced. He was a foreman and the leader of the fire-fighting team in a small coffee factory in the Wendenstrasse, also in Hammerbrook but closer to the centre of the main bombing area. After the alarm had sounded, he had ordered all the fire hoses to be rolled out. When this was done, he had posted four men in various parts of the factory, one on each floor, and taken the other five down to the shelter, outside the doors of which stood their mobile fire pump.

Then came this hail of bombs and we all had the impression that our factory was being constantly hit. The building next door certainly got a direct hit and our own building went up and down like a lift but we found out later that we were only hit by incendiary bombs and phosphorus. Five minutes after the opening of the bombing, two men came down from the upper storeys and said that they would be killed if they stayed upstairs any longer. After ten minutes, a third man came back, absolutely frantic. Then the fourth man, Hartmann, came in. We all stayed on the steps of the shelter, ready to leap into action when the bombing stopped and get the motor pump going from the yard.

Suddenly, there came a rain of fire from heaven. We tried to get out to the pump but it was impossible. The air was actually filled with fire. It would have meant certain death to leave the shelter and it would have been impossible under these circumstances to save the factory, even if we could have reached the pump. Also, we couldn't open the doors without endangering the neighbours who had come into the shelter. The fire around us became even more concentrated. Smoke seeped into the shelter through every crack. Every time you opened the steel doors, you could see fire all around.

The joinery works next door had also caught fire. There was not sufficient water in the cellar so we used Minimax hand fire-extinguishers to try to hold back the fire. Then a storm started, a shrill howling in the street. It grew into a hurricane so that we had to abandon all hope of fighting the fire. It was as though we were doing no more than throwing a drop of water on to a hot stone. The whole yard, the canal, in fact as far as we could see, was just a whole, great, massive sea of fire.

'A storm ... a hurricane ... a sea of fire.' Everything experienced in the Battle of Hamburg before this time had been seen in other bombed cities, although not often on the same scale. But what coffee-factory foreman Hermann Kröger saw, in his little corner of Hammerbrook, was a small part of a completely new and most horrific result of aerial bombing. This 'storm of fire' later became the subject of intense scientific study and it was concluded that not even the most severe natural fires, such as forest fires, ever reached the intensity of the occurrence experienced in eastern Hamburg during the early hours of Wednesday, 28 July 1943. The German word *'Feuersturm'* was immediately coined and brought into use to describe this phenomenon; that word was recorded in the main log of events being kept by the Hamburg Fire Department a little over one hour after the storm started. The English word 'firestorm' is a simple and adequate translation.

The firestorm started through a combination of three main factors. Hamburg had an efficient meteorological station and its records show that there had been an unusual combination of very high temperatures and low humidity during the day preceding this raid. At 6 o'clock in the evening, six hours before the R.A.F. bombs fell, the temperature had been 30° Centigrade (86° Fahrenheit) and the humidity only 30 per cent, compared with an average of 40–50 per cent for a normal midsummer's day.

The second factor was the unusually concentrated marking and bombing of the R.A.F., which has already been described. Once this had been achieved, the standard R.A.F. Area Bombing bomb-loads had achieved their purpose. The large 4,000-lb blast bombs had blown in doors and windows. A multitude of small 4-lb incendiaries had started fires in roofs; the larger 30-lb incendiaries had penetrated deeper inside buildings. High-explosive bombs, which were mixed in with the incendiaries all through the attack, had cratered roads, blown debris into streets and discouraged fire-fighting. A great number of fires had thus been started in a relatively small area of a densely built-up district of Hamburg.

The third factor was that Gauleiter Kaufmann's order the previous evening, that the three-day-old fires smouldering in the western part of the city should be extinguished, had resulted in nearly all of Hamburg's fire-fighting appliances being on the wrong side of the city. The prominent position of the Alster lake meant that these fire units had to use the few roads in a bottleneck of the city between the Alster and the Elbe or take the longer route round the north of the Alster to redeploy their fire-engines in the new bombing area in the east. Many of these roads were blocked by recent high-explosive bombs. By the time the fire units reached the east, they were too late to prevent a catastrophe. The block wardens, factory fire teams and other semi-amateur fire-fighters in the east – like Fräulein Nawroski in her paint-works and Herr Kröger in his coffee factory – had had no chance to stop the spread of fire on their own.

Within fifteen minutes of the first bombs being dropped, hardly any of the large number of fires burning were being tackled and they were rapidly becoming out of control. The apartment blocks of Hamburg mostly had good, strong brick walls between each block. The fires did not spread through these walls but, as each individual fire became stronger, it consumed the timber floors and burst through the roof of that block to become a fiercely burning torch. All fires, as a matter of natural course, draw in fresh air in order to consume its oxygen. The strongest of fires in Hammerbrook literally struggled for air and, not only did they draw in fresh air from the narrow streets outside, but they also dragged heated air out of surrounding buildings which had smaller fires. This hot air brought with it sparks and burning brands which, in turn, started fresh fires in those buildings not already alight. Soon, several extensive groups of buildings were on fire, each requiring more and more air. The procedure was repeated again and again, until the whole of that area that had been bombed in the first phase of the raid was one, complete sea of fire, greedily sucking air out of the surrounding areas where the bombing had not been so concentrated. The final part of the process of the joining up of the fires probably took place in a matter of seconds. The area filled with fires became a roaring inferno, the centre of which is estimated to have reached a temperature of 800° Centigrade and into which air was being sucked from all directions at speeds which may have reached hurricane force. That was the firestorm.

It is generally agreed that the firestorm started at 1.20 a.m., twenty-three minutes after the first bombs had fallen. In its first stage, the firestorm area was probably about one square mile (two and a half square kilometres) in extent and was confined to the Borgfelde and Hammerbrook districts. Hans Brunswig, in 1943 a senior fire officer in Hamburg, has written a history of the city's bombing experiences during the war which contains a map showing the estimated centre of the firestorm as being near the junction of two narrow canals: the Mittel Kanal and the Hochwasser Bassin.[3] It may only be a coincidence that on the Normannen Weg, close to this point, there was a large timber-yard and sawmill, owned by a Herr Nienstadt, but it is possible that blazing stacks of timber here may have been the core of the firestorm.

The tremendous updraught from the firestorm and the fierce winds coming into it from all sides at ground level completely overwhelmed the effects of the light natural wind that had been blowing. Because of this, there was none of the normal windborne spread of fire. Left to itself, the early firestorm area would have remained static and would have eventually burned itself out. But the firestorm was not left to itself. The R.A.F. bombing continued for a further half hour after the firestorm became established. This bombing spread slowly back along the line of the bombers' approach, more fires were started and the firestorm was thus extended by the R.A.F. into that new area. This eastward expansion of the firestorm probably measured at least two miles, engulfing the remainder of the extensive Hamm residential district and extending into the less densely populated districts of southern Wandsbek and Horn. It was this extension eastwards of the firestorm that caused the sudden changes of the storm's wind direction mentioned by so many survivors. The original firestorm also spread itself north and west, towards the city centre, partly because of further bombing in these areas and partly through the radiant-heat effect of the firestorm, but this movement was only slight and probably extended the fire area by no more than a few hundred yards in each direction. The large St

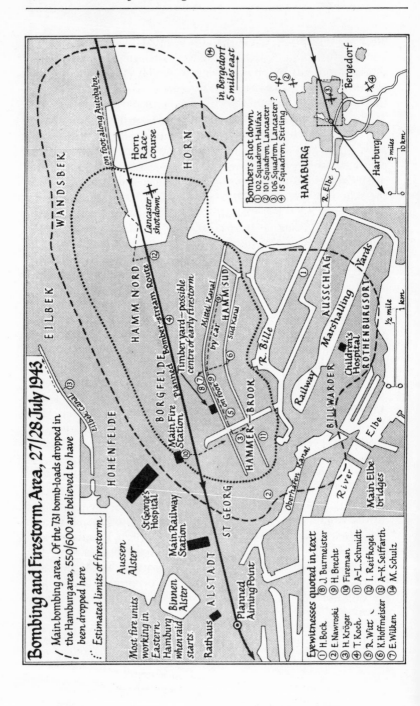

Bombing and Firestorm Area, 27/28 July 1943

Main bombing area. Of the 731 bomb-loads dropped in the Hamburg area, 550/600 are believed to have been dropped here

Estimated limits of firestorm

Bombers shot down:
① 102 Squadron Halifax
② 101 Squadron Lancaster
③ 106 Squadron Lancaster ?
④ 15 Squadron Stirling

Eyewitnesses quoted in text
① H. Bock   ⑧ J. Burmeister
② E. Nawroski   ⑨ H. Brecht
③ H. Kröger   ⑩ Fireman
④ T. Koch   ⑪ A-L. Schmidt
⑤ R. Witt   ⑫ I. Reifvogel
⑥ K. Hoffmeister   ⑬ A-K. Selffarth
⑦ E. Wilken   ⑭ M. Schulz

Most fire units working in Eastern Hamburg when raid starts

Aussen Alster
Binnen Alster

St George's Hospital
Main Railway Station
Rathaus
ALSTADT
Planned Aiming Point

HOHENFELDE
Eilbek Canal

EILBEK
WANDSBEK

on foot along Autobahn

ST GEORG
HAMM NORD
Bomber-stream Route

HAMMERBROOK
Main Fire Station
Timber yard—possible centre of early firestorm
Planned Bomber-stream Route

BORGFELDE
Lancaster shot down

Horn Race-course
HORN
in Bergedorf 5 miles east

by car
on foot
HAMM SUD
Mittel Kanal
Sud Kanal
R. Bille

BILLWARDER
Railway
MARSHALLING
AUSSCHLAG
Oberhafen Kanal
Children's Hospital
ROTHENBURGSORT
Main Elbe bridges
River Elbe
Yards

HAMBURG
R. Elbe
Bergedorf
Harburg
5 miles
10 km

½ mile
1 km

George's Hospital, near the Alster, just escaped both the bombing and the firestorm. There was little southern expansion of the firestorm, the River Bille – a fairly wide tributary of the Elbe – and the extensive railway marshalling yards in that area combining to form a fire-break.

The final extent of the true firestorm area was an irregular rectangle measuring approximately one and a half miles from north to south and nearly three miles from west to east, perhaps making an area of four square miles or nearly ten square kilometres.* For comparison purposes, this is roughly the same area as that part of central London extending from Euston and King's Cross stations down to the River Thames and from Hyde Park Corner across to the Tower of London. A similar area in New York would be almost the whole of Lower Manhattan from Madison Square Park to Battery Park. But neither of these city areas is of the same character as was the Hamburg firestorm area. The tenement buildings of London's old East End or of New York's Harlem were more the type of building in that area of Hamburg subjected to the firestorm. It has been estimated that 16,000 apartment-block buildings on street frontages totalling 133 miles were ablaze during the firestorm.

The height of the firestorm was reached some time between 3.00 and 3.30 a.m., more than an hour after the raid ended, so that no R.A.F. man witnessed its climax. The four men who baled out of crashed bombers near Hamburg that night and survived were all, fortunately for their skins, several miles away, either already locked up or hiding in fields.

Most buildings in these older parts of Hamburg had basement shelters and nearly every member of the civilian population was in one of these when the firestorm started. Even above the crashing noise of high-explosive bombs, the people could hear the howling of the storm in the streets outside, 'like the devil laughing' one survivor says. At the same time, the temperature in the shelters started to rise, smoke or very hot air entered and the houses above their heads caught fire.

---

* The Hamburg Chief of Police's Report says that the firestorm area was twenty-two square kilometres but that figure is probably too high and covers many fringe areas in which there were many fires and strong winds but no true firestorm.

The authorities had always stressed that there was no safer place during a raid than one's air-raid shelter but thousands and thousands of ordinary people, nearly all old folk, house-wives or children, now had to make the most important decision of their lives: stay in their shelters, filling as they were with smoke and burning air and in danger of being buried by the ruins of a burning house above, or venture out into the crazed world of the firestorm streets and try to find safety elsewhere. There are survivors to describe the scene in those streets. They all talk of the tremendous force of the hot, dry wind against which even strong men were sometimes unable to struggle and which forced doors of houses open and broke the glass in windows. Anything light was immediately whipped away, bursting into flames as it went if it was burn-able. Branches were torn off trees; even whole trees were forced over and their roots dragged out of the ground. What appeared to be 'bundles of flames' or 'towers or walls of fire' sometimes shot out of a burning building and along a street. There were 'fiery whirlwinds' which could snatch a person in the street and immediately turn that person into a human torch while other people, only a few yards away, were un-touched. The wind was always accompanied by clouds of sparks which looked like 'a blizzard of red snowflakes' and all survivors remember the shrieking, howling of the storm as it raced through the streets.

That choice – whether to stay or to move – was a terrible one. Most fortunate were the single, able-bodied people. Most agonizing was the state of mind of mothers with babies or young children. We can follow the fortunes of a few of those people who did decide to leave their shelters.

Traute Koch was a fifteen-year-old girl in Hamm.

Mother wrapped me in wet sheets, kissed me, and said, 'Run!' I hesitated at the door. In front of me I could see only fire – everything red, like the door to a furnace. An intense heat struck me. A burning beam fell in front of my feet. I shied back but, then, when I was ready to jump over it, it was whirled away by a ghostly hand. I ran out to the street. The sheets around me acted as sails and I had the feeling that I was being carried away by the storm. I reached the front of a five-storey building in front of which we had arranged to meet again. It had been bombed and burnt out in a previous raid and there was not much left in it for the fire to get hold of. Someone came out, grabbed me in their arms, and pulled me into the doorway. I screamed for my mother and somebody gave me a drink – wine or schnapps – I still screamed and then my mother and my little sister were there.

About twenty people had gathered in the cellar. We sat, holding tightly to each other and waited. My mother wept bitterly and I was terrified.

Rolf Witt was one of the few men of military age still living at home; he had suffered from having a faulty heart valve since childhood. His home – on the Wendenstrasse in Borgfelde – was only 250 yards from the estimated centre of the firestorm.

Word of what was happening in the street must have spread to the people at the back of our shelter because they broke down the wall to the next-door basement. That was a great mistake because, when they did this, they found that they were looking into a furnace. The street door was half open and, with the air being drawn out of our basement, the smoke and fire came pouring through the break in the wall. Everyone became severely affected by smoke. I heard people screaming but this became less and less; I believe they were suffocating.

You must realize that we were within seconds of death. I could not speak to my parents because of the gas mask I was wearing. I tapped father on the shoulder as a sign that I was going. I thought they would follow me. A few seconds before I would have suffocated, I must have had a tremendous burst of strength. At a moment when the door was open and when no burning debris was falling down, I sprang out into the street but against the wind. I think I must have remembered that there was a small park near by and that, in that direction, there might be safety.

The flying sparks of phosphorus were burning my hands. I had an old winter coat and I pulled this over my head. I threw away my briefcases with all my papers in. Everything was done on impulse and I must have had tremendous luck to get out of that steel shelter door and to avoid the falling debris as I crossed the street. I am not a religious man but I believe that God gave me a push just at the right moment.

I ran eighty or a hundred metres to a railway bridge and I lay down under this, behind a steel tube, to protect myself against the sparks. I had a small thermos flask in my jacket. I took off my gas mask and had a little drink of tea. I had a terrific thirst. A second man came and took shelter with me; his clothes were burning. I took off my coat and beat out the fire on the other man. It was then that I looked back at my parents' house and saw that it had already collapsed and was only a heap of ruins. I ran on and managed to reach a football pitch and I found a small ticket kiosk, miraculously saved from the fire. I got inside it and spent the rest of the night there. I saw no one else all night.

I never found my parents and was never sure where or how they died. I have always felt guilty that I abandoned them. Later, when their shelter was cleared, they found fifty-five bodies – at least they found fifty-five skulls. There had only been about twenty-five people there originally. I think the others had maybe come in from the house behind. I never met another survivor from my home or the houses at the back.

The death certificates for Rolf Witt's parents, issued on 20 May 1944, record the time of their death as 1.40 a.m. on 28 July. Witt's own exertions in the firestorm caused no ill effects to his diseased heart and, towards the end of the war, he was declared fit for service with the Volkssturm.

Käte Hoffmeister was a nineteen-year-old milliner whose home was in the Grevenweg in Hammerbrook:

We came to the door which was burning just like a ring in a circus through which a lion has to jump. Someone in front of me hesitated. I pushed her out with my foot; I realized that it was no use staying at that place. The rain of large sparks, blowing down the street, were each as large as a five-mark piece. I struggled to run against the wind in the middle of the street but could only reach a house on the corner of the Sorbenstrasse, the ground floor of which had not yet caught fire and where I was able to rest for a little while in the entrance to regain my breath and to get out of that shower of sparks.

My mother, my Aunt Emma and myself had all left the doorway of our house at about the same time. While I was resting, my aunt came and stood with me. I had a little bag with my papers and jewellery but my hands were already burnt by the sparks and I dropped the bag. My aunt told me to leave it there. I was terrified but she was so calm and determined to get out through the fires to find a safe place. I didn't want to go out into the fire again but she dragged me out and we set off up the street, still against the wind. We knew the area very well and we decided to go to the place known as the Löschplatz – a piece of open ground on the other side of the Mittel Kanal, about 200 yards away. It was an old quay where ships had landed goods years ago. We thought that we could reach there first and then go on to the football pitch on the Eiffestrasse.

We got to the Löschplatz all right but couldn't go on across the Eiffestrasse because the asphalt had melted. There were people on the roadway, some already dead, some still lying alive but stuck in the asphalt. They must have rushed on to the roadway without thinking. Their feet had got stuck and then they had put out their hands to try to get out again. They were on their hands and knees screaming.

Aunt Emma and I stood by a row of four big trees that were on fire and again we discussed what we were going to do. I suggested that we roll down this bank; it was too steep to get down any other way. I took my hand out of my aunt's and went. I think I rolled over some people who were still alive. I lost my aunt at that point. By then, my face and arms and legs had been burnt so that I could only act by touch but my burns had not yet started to hurt. I felt a thick woollen blanket; I knew, by instinct, that it would be safer under that blanket. We had always been told, over and over again, that a woollen blanket would protect us against fire because wool does not burn but only smoulders. I got under it and stayed there.

Next morning, Käte Hoffmeister, although badly burnt, went to look for her relatives. She found the body of Aunt Emma, identifying it by a blue-and-white sapphire ring that she always wore. Her father and two uncles died but she later met her mother, by coincidence, in the same hospital near Kassel, 160 miles from Hamburg.

The Chief of Police's Report contains several eyewitness accounts from civilians who survived the firestorm. Two of these are from people who also reached that little canalside quay where Käte Hoffmeister survived. Frau Erika Wilken and her husband had taken shelter, with a crowd of other people, in some public toilets built under the nearby roadway of the Grevenweg. Herr Wilken had stood on a toilet seat, wetting cloths in the tank above for other people to bathe themselves in the fierce heat.

But the worst was yet to come. To our misfortune, a large phosphorus bomb fell directly outside the toilet. The people nearest the door now gave way to an indescribable panic. The inner toilet doors were torn off and used as shields in front of the bomb. After a few minutes, these doors too were burning brightly.

Terrible scenes took place, since all of us saw certain death in front of us, with the only way out a sea of flames. We were caught like rats in a trap. The doors were thrown on to the canister by screaming people and more smoke and heat poured in. In the meantime, the water in the tank had been used up. My husband was completely worn out and we crouched next to the bowl. The other people here sat down too; some collapsed and never woke up again. Three soldiers committed suicide. I begged my husband to beat back the flames with our blanket but he was no longer able to do so. So I did it. My hair began to singe and my husband extinguished it.

What now? Our hearts were racing, our faces began to puff up and we were close to fainting. Perhaps another five or eight minutes and we will be finished too. On my question, 'Willi, is this the end?', my husband decided to risk everything and try to reach the outside. I took the blanket and he the little suitcase. Quickly, but carefully so that we would not slip on the corpses, we reached the outside. One! Two! Three! We were through the wall of fire. We made it. Both without burns; only our shoes were singed. But our last strength and courage had gone. We lay down on the ground at the side of the canal. People swimming in it kept wetting our blanket for us.[4]

The other account from this place* is by Johann Burmeister, a greengrocer:

Many people started burning and jumped into the canal. Horrible scenes took place at the quay. People burned to death with horrible suffering; some became insane. Many dead bodies were all around us and I became convinced that we, too, would perish here. I crouched with my family behind a large stack of roofing material. Here we lost our daughter. Later on, it transpired that she had jumped into the canal and almost drowned but was saved by an army officer and she returned to us early next morning.

Please spare me from having to describe further details.[5]

Herbert Brecht, a fifteen-year-old boy in a *Schnellkommando* unit, was one of the few people who had to be out on the streets on duty. His small team had been sent from its post at the Osterbrook school, in Hammerbrook, along the Süderstrasse into what became the main firestorm area.

I was in the wooden trailer with two other lads. The heat from the surrounding houses, which were on fire, was unbearable. We whimpered and cried from the pain of it. Our car got stuck behind a burning tramcar but we freed ourselves with a push. After another 300 metres, a man suddenly jumped into the trailer and pressed his hot steel helmet against my face, but not on purpose. We shook him off and he remained lying in the road. Burning people ran and

---

* This canalside area, the Löschplatz, is now the garage and lorry park of a Mercedes-Benz dealer. Only one of the four trees burning that night now remains. The public toilets under the Grevenweg, where so many people died, are now a small lock-up store.

staggered after us. Others were lying on the road, dead or unconscious. At the junction of Süderstrasse and Louisenweg, our trailer got stuck in a bomb crater. We unhitched it and jumped into the car which was still running; there were six of us crammed inside. After another 200 metres we were forced to a halt between the trams standing in front of the tram depot. Our car caught fire immediately. We all managed to get out and we stood there in those fires of hell. The storm pulled me, unwillingly, into an enormous bomb crater in the middle of the road. Those of us who did not get into this crater had no chance of survival. One of my group was never seen again. The noise was like that of an old organ in a church when someone is playing all the notes at once.

There was a smashed water main in the bomb crater. Although there was no pressure left in the pipe, the water still ran into the crater and we had to fight against a flood. Some people drowned or were buried when the sides of the crater caved in. Above, there was this terrible heat but I was lying safely in the water. Because I always wore my goggles on duty, I could see everything very clearly. The burning people who were being driven past our bomb crater by the storm could never have survived. Eventually, there were about forty people lying in the crater. There was a soldier in uniform near me with a lot of medals. He tried to take his life with a knife. He showed me his bleeding breast and said, 'I can't do it.'

About that time, I noticed that a car had driven into our crater and had buried some people beneath it. Because one is only half conscious in such a situation, I hadn't seen this happen. It was only through the crying of a small boy that I noticed it. He was lying with the front bumper of the car on top of him. We managed to pull him out with a lot of effort but I can't say whether he survived.

The screams of the burning and dying people are unforgettable. When a human being dies, he screams and whimpers and, then, there is the death rattle in his throat, not at all bravely and not as beautifully as in a film.

The car which had driven into Herbert Brecht's bomb crater by mistake was that of a Herr Dehler of the Hamburg Water Department. Herr Dehler survived the firestorm and his report of the incident was later filed in the papers of the Chief of Police.

The number of people who were able to save themselves from the firestorm area was surprisingly large. However terrifying and formidable the circumstances, the will in the human spirit to survive drove the brave and resourceful to almost superhuman efforts. Even this was not enough unless

luck also played its part. The successful survivors had to have
avoided the falling timbers and bricks – and even bombs in
the earlier stages of the firestorm; they had to have been
within reach of a place suitable for survival. The people
whose experiences have been quoted above made use of a
house burnt out in a previous raid, a football pitch, a low-
lying piece of ground by the side of a canal and a deep and
partly flooded bomb crater. Many others saved themselves
by jumping into the canals of the area, preferring the risk of
death by drowning to that of death by fire. Exhausted and
often badly burnt, the survivors of the firestorm waited for its
end.

There were many, many thousands who did not have that
combination of will-power, courage and luck necessary for
survival and the firestorm caused death on a scale never seen
before in aerial bombing. Even a high proportion of those bold
enough to quit their shelters and attempt flight through the
streets perished. Many who took to the streets allowed themselves, in their confusion, to be carried along by the storm of
wind towards greater danger. It needed a clear head and
much physical strength to turn and battle against the wind.
Even the taking of the correct path was no guarantee of
survival. The distances to safety were often too great and only
those, similar to the cases already described, who were
fortunate enough to find a place where a little air and temporary salvation from the flames could be found, survived.
People were hit by flying timbers or falling bricks. Babies or
little old people were simply dragged bodily by the storm into
burning buildings. Many others became exhausted; they
staggered and fell. Sometimes they crawled to the gutters,
hoping to find a little air there but, within seconds, their
clothes and very bodies caught fire. Perhaps the worst ends
befell those who ran on to a roadway where the asphalt surface
had melted. All these methods of meeting death in the streets
were observed and later reported by survivors.

The bodies of the victims were later found where they had
died – nearly always face downwards, one arm thrown
around the head. Most of the bodies were blackened and
shrivelled to half their normal size, like mummies, but others
were unburnt, although all their clothes, except their shoes,

had disappeared. This unusual sight was probably the result
of victims attempting to flee while clad in little more than
night clothes, which were torn off by the storm or were
dissolved in the intense heat but without the bodies of their
owners being burnt.

There was a far greater loss of life, however, among those
who had heeded all the advice given about air raids and who
remained in their shelters. The exceptions were those fortunate people who were in the purpose-built public *Bunker*
shelters. These shelters had gas- and smoke-tight doors and,
once these were closed, those inside had a good chance of
survival and there were no examples of any large loss of life
in these shelters. One survivor of them says, 'The people of
Hammerbrook were not often given to praying but they
certainly prayed hard that night.' When she emerged, many
hours later, this person had to step through the fat of the
molten bodies of those who had come to the shelter too late.

But there were few public shelters in the areas where the
firestorm raged. Nearly every block of flats had its basement
shelter. It was to these that the vast majority of the population
had gone when the raid started and it was here that the
citizens of those districts died in their thousands. I have
received no personal contribution nor seen any written record
from any person who remained in a basement shelter and
survived from that area where the firestorm burnt at full
intensity. The manner in which these people died can only be
guessed from the condition in which their bodies were found
when the ruins cooled several days later.

The firestorm had, first, drawn the good air out of these
shelters and replaced it by smoke or, sometimes, by colourless
gases from which the oxygen had all been burnt. Autopsies
established that the overwhelmingly predominant cause of
death was poisoning by carbon monoxide, rarely by burning.
At some stage during this process, the apartment block above
had burnt down and the brickwork of its roof, its internal walls,
and its stairways had collapsed to cover the basement shelters,
rarely crushing the roof of the shelter but usually blocking all
exits. It was in these brick-covered tombs that so many deaths
occurred. The bodies were sometimes found heaped up
around the blocked exits, indicating that the occupants had
realized that they were trapped and in danger of death. But

most of the dead were found sitting at tables or against walls, in the most peaceful of positions, as though they had fallen asleep and, in a way, they had, for they had breathed the invisible and odourless carbon monoxide into their bodies without realization of danger. Such victims were usually fully clothed, although parts of the clothing had scorched away and the intact bodies were always baked a brownish colour. All such bodies were considerably shrunken; the Germans called them '*Bombenbrandschrumpfleischen*' – 'the shrunken bodies of fire bombing'. Some bodies were found lying on the floor of shelters, in the coagulated black mess of their own molten fat tissue.

There was a final category of body. In some shelters, nothing more was found than a thin layer of ash on the floor. In these places, fresh air had penetrated after the firestorm had blown out but while fires were still burning. These bodies had then been incinerated, but only several hours after the deaths of their owners.

Approximately 40,000 people – nearly all civilians and mostly old folk, women and children – died either in the streets of the firestorm area or in their shelters.

The terrible furnace of the firestorm started to subside about three hours after it had started. The first lessening of the wind and fire was observed in the western part of the now two-mile long firestorm area and it started to die down only when nearly all the flammable material had been consumed in that area where the storm had started. Tentative estimates say that this stage was reached at about 4 a.m. The wind gradually dropped and, although there were still some fires where more durable material continued to burn, they burned now in more conventional manner. This process spread steadily eastwards and it has been estimated that the last signs of the firestorm disappeared between 6 and 7 a.m. The five-hour period in which the firestorm had raged would prove to be a turning point in the history of the city of Hamburg, a great divide in the pattern of human life and in the physical appearance and condition of the city.

The great heat in the centre of the firestorm area remained. It would be two days before rescue workers could penetrate to the hottest areas, but there was no hurry; there was no one there to rescue. It would be two weeks before safe and comfortable passage could take place through such areas. But, now, as the new day of Wednesday, 28 July appeared, the air at least became breathable, although the sun did not appear. Smoke from the ruins of Borgfelde, Hamm and Wandsbek would continue to blot out the sun for several days. Rescue workers started to penetrate the edge of the fire area and, there, they met the survivors of the firestorm. It is not overdramatic to describe it as a meeting with those who had come back from the very edges of death.

Hermann Kröger was the leader of the fire-fighting team in the Wendenstrasse coffee factory:

Between six and seven in the morning, we dared to open a few tiny steel windows at the side of the canal. Fresh air streamed in and our breathlessness vanished. Although we could not leave the shelter, we knew one thing – that every soul in there had been saved and would be able to leave that shelter alive. All the people in the surrounding buildings had died. We pulled in some people out of the canal. They had jumped into it from the other side, which was burning fiercely, and they had swum across to us. There were large patches of fire on the water, just like when you pour inflammable spirits on to water and put a match to it. We thought it might have been caused by the liquid phosphorus that the bombers had dropped. These people kept smacking their hands on the water, while they swam, trying to push the flames away. A police patrol appeared on the opposite side of the canal and we called out and told them about our condition. It was decided that those who could not or would not leave the shelter through the yard should go by boat. Unfortunately, this did not happen and everyone had to leave by way of the Wendenstrasse.

After we had convinced ourselves that we could not put out the roaring fire in the factory, the garages and the offices, we left. It was painful that we men, with all our equipment, were quite powerless to fight the fire. It was hell let loose in that night. All the coffee in the factory – about five tons of real coffee for the armed forces and a lot of *Ersatz* – had burnt but there was so much fire that we didn't smell it burning.

At 8.30 a.m., with several other men, we walked along the Wendenstrasse towards our homes, climbing over rubble and bodies as we went – in order to discover whether our families and homes had survived.

Traute Koch was the girl who had taken shelter in a house that had burnt out in a previous raid:

After endless hours, one of the men came and made it clear to us that it was no longer burning in the streets and that we should try to get out of this hell. With great apprehension we stepped out on to the street. There was only one way, in front of us, but what a way! There was a great heat and a leaden gloom over us. Where there had been houses only a few hours before, only some single walls with empty windows towered upwards. In between were large heaps of rubble, still glowing. Torn overhead wires were hanging everywhere.

There was not much rubble on the streets and, after about a hundred metres, we came to the place which, only a few hours earlier, had been our home. The wall between the dining-room and the staircase was still standing. I could still see the radiator and I remember thinking that the Meissen porcelain group that I had loved so much ought to be standing on it – a fleeting thought. We couldn't stay there long; the soles of our feet were too hot. All the time I thought that I would start burning.

We came to the junction of the Hammer Landstrasse and Louisenweg. I carried my little sister and also helped my mother climb over the ruins. Suddenly, I saw tailors' dummies lying around. I said, 'Mummy, no tailors lived here and, yet, so many dummies lying around.' My mother grabbed me by my arm and said, 'Go on. Don't look too closely. On. On. We have to get out of here. Those are dead bodies.'

Herbert Brecht was the *Schnellkommando* boy who had sheltered in the partly flooded bomb crater:

At midday – it never got light – a man came and pulled some of us survivors out of the crater. He was an elderly man who also had a burnt face. When he pulled me out by the hands, my skin stuck to him in shreds. He looked at me – I cannot describe his look – and he could only say, '*Junge! Junge!*' I cannot say how many of us survived in that crater. I had been given a new, brown uniform only three weeks earlier and been told that it was flame-resistant. I feel that this saved my life. My old uniform had been a captured French soldier's uniform with some old First World War boots.

I set off in the direction of Hammerbrook because everything was still burning in the direction of the school where our post was. The air was hardly breathable and my injuries hurt hellishly. Dead lay everywhere. Most were naked because their clothes had been burnt away. All had become shrunken, really small, because of the heat.

I stumbled on as far as Heidenkampsweg but the way was blocked here. I tried to retrace my steps but then I collapsed. I must have been picked up by someone I never saw because I woke up in a *Bunker* shelter with a woman trying to put little pieces of food into my mouth.

The fire brigade had been able to do little fire-fighting,
being overwhelmed by the scale of the fires. Instead, their men
had worked during the raid at saving as much human life as
was possible, but only on the edges of the firestorm area. The
Fire Department Headquarters, at the Berliner Tor Fire
Station, was at the north-west corner of the firestorm area
and had become a major place of refuge where hundreds of
people took shelter. This fireman, who does not wish to be
named, being concerned for some reason over his pension, had
helped look after these people. Now he set out into Hammerbrook to look for his brother – a disabled soldier – and his
family.

I only got to the Heidenkampsweg. In the entrance to the Maizena
Haus (a large office building) I saw a lot of dead, naked people on
the steps. I thought that they had been killed by a blast bomb and
been blown out of the basement air-raid shelter. What surprised
me was that the people were all lying face downwards. Only later
did we find out that these people had died there through lack of
oxygen.
I climbed over the ruins, further into the damaged area. There were
no people alive at all. The houses were all destroyed and still burning.
In the Süderstrasse, I saw a burnt-out tramcar in which naked bodies
were lying on top of each other. The glass of the windows had
melted. Probably these people had sought refuge from the storm in
the tram.
I eventually reached my brother's home on the Grevenweg; it was
just a heap of smoking bricks. I helped to clear their shelter five
weeks later. There was only charred bones and ash. I found a few
objects that belonged to my relatives – their house keys and some
coins that my nephew was always playing with.

The area that had suffered from the firestorm was soon
declared a prohibited zone to ordinary civilians and those
people who tried to enter, seeking to know the fate of relatives,
were turned away by armed guards. Anne-Lies Schmidt had
walked in from the country and, later that day, she tried to
find her parents in Hammerbrook:

My uncle and I went on foot into this terror. No one was allowed
into the devastated district but I believe that one's stubbornness
becomes stronger at the sight of such sacrifice. We fought bodily with
the sentries on duty and we got in. My uncle was arrested.
Four-storey-high blocks of flats were like glowing mounds of stone

right down to the basement. Everything seemed to have melted and pressed the bodies away in front of it. Women and children were so charred as to be unrecognizable; those that had died through lack of oxygen were half charred and recognizable. Their brains tumbled from their burst temples and their insides from the soft parts under the ribs. How terribly must these people have died. The smallest children lay like fried eels on the pavement. Even in death, they showed signs of how they must have suffered – their hands and arms stretched out as if to protect themselves from that pitiless heat.

I found the bodies of my parents but it was forbidden to take them because of the danger of epidemic. Nothing to remember them by. No photographs. Nothing! All their precious little possessions they had taken to the basement were stolen. I had no tears. The eyes became bigger but the mouth remained closed tight.

The first instinct of so many of those civilians who were able to escape from the bombing area without serious injury was to flee, if possible to get clear out of the city. Ingeborg Reifkogel, a young teacher living in Hamm, actually started her flight during the raid when smoke started to pour into the shelter of her home.*

All the houses were on fire in the Sievekingsallee and it was very hot. But I had poured a bucket of water over myself, put on a pair of motoring goggles which protected me from the flying sparks and I held a wet cloth in front of my face. I found this more comfortable than the gas mask which I had hanging round my neck. I also had a head scarf on and, on top of that, a wet old felt hat. Dressed like that, I got through on the tramrails in the middle of the street until I reached the Autobahn. This was full of dense red smoke from the blaze on both sides, but smoke doesn't burn, of course. The main thing was not to panic. If one could keep wet and the sparks didn't start to burn, it would be possible to get through all right.

I kept on walking along the Autobahn, quite calm, in spite of the explosions all around me. In one place the road was covered with water; probably a dud bomb had burst a water main. The embankment was blazing and I couldn't go up and round that way, so I waded through. The water only came up to my knees and my shoes and socks didn't take long to dry in the heat. There was still so much smoke that it was impossible to breathe without the wet cloth.

Shortly before reaching Jenfeld, I met some people by an air-raid shelter built into a bridge over the Autobahn. I dipped my cloth in

* This account and the one following, from Frau Seifarth, are from letters written immediately after the evacuation.

water again there. They asked me to stay with them but I couldn't bear the thought of sitting beside two dead children. The only other people I had met up till then had been a party of prisoners who were running around, unguarded, and who warned me in broken German about the phosphorus that was still smouldering everywhere. I was so calm, almost cheerful, that I grinned as I thought of the picture on the cover of the book, *Gone with the Wind*. At least Scarlett O'Hara had a wagon, whereas I had to walk.

Then I passed through an area where delayed-action bombs were exploding and some friendly people who were living in their garden houses offered me shelter and gave me a piece of bread. I started out again at 5 o'clock in the direction of Rahlstedt. The whole of Jenfeld was on fire; the barracks were badly damaged. In Tonndorf, only windows were broken. Rahlstedt was all in one piece. When I got there, I sat down in the Diffrings' garden so as not to wake them up. At seven o'clock, Frau Diffring looked out of the window and took me upstairs. I was able to wash, have breakfast and go to bed.

Fräulein Reifkogel had walked just four and a half miles, from the edge of the firestorm area to this peaceful village outside Hamburg. She must have been one of the first of what was to become a mass exodus of people fleeing from that part of the city that had been bombed, out along the roads leading to the east. This flight soon received a boost when Gauleiter Kaufmann ordered that an official announcement be made appealing to all those inhabitants of Hamburg who were not needed for essential work to leave the city. (No documentary copy of this appeal seems to exist. It was probably issued in the late morning or early afternoon of that day and was mainly made known to the public by the use of loudspeaker vans.) The news that a massive and horrible catastrophe had occurred in one part of the city had already flashed around the remainder of Hamburg. There could not be the slightest doubt, now, about the R.A.F.'s intention to destroy Hamburg and that other areas could receive the same treatment, perhaps in the next night. The flight now became general and it has been estimated that 1,200,000 people – nearly two-thirds of the total population – left their homes by nightfall of that day.

The early fugitives simply left the city on foot and kept going until they reached open country, but some sort of order was established to the evacuation process as the day progressed. Hermann Matthies, the city's Director of Public Welfare, remembers that his carefully prepared catastrophe plan proved entirely inadequate. 'I threw it into the corner of my office and we improvised everything from then on.' This is where the Nazi Party organization came into its own. Brooking delay, excuse and objection from no one, party officials gradually imposed a limited order out of chaos. It had always been expected that the railways would be used for any mass evacuation but bomb damage to stations or railway lines had rendered fifteen of Hamburg's eighteen stations useless for this purpose. Four huge collecting places were designated: at the Moorweide Park, at the Horn and Farmsen racecourses, and at an open space in Billstedt. It was at the Farmsen racecourse that the important *Preis von Deutschland* race meeting was to have been held only three days earlier. To the dazed and frightened people now resting on the grass with their last few possessions, such innocent pleasures as horse-racing must have seemed a lifetime away.

Herculean efforts produced food and drink. Half a million loaves of bread, 16,000 litres of milk, beer, coffee and tea were all made available during that first day of the big evacuation. Every spare motor vehicle – private and military – was pressed into service to take people to railway stations outside the city. The students of Hamburg University, for example, are credited with transporting 63,000 people in this way. From the country stations, the evacuees spread all over Germany, taking with them news of the recent happenings in Hamburg. Ships on the Elbe were also used, often to carry wounded, and it is reported that Junkers 52 transport planes were taking off from Fuhlsbüttel airport 'ceaselessly'.

It would be many days before the last evacuees could be taken from Hamburg. The accounts of Frau Anne-Kaete Seifarth, who set out on foot with her husband and son from Eilbek, can speak for the thousands who did not wait for official transport.

Father fetched a cart from his workshop and we commenced the most ghastly journey of our lives. We loaded the possessions that we had been able to save on it. Joe got some bread from the Kreffts' house; they happened to be away and their parents had fled. Uncle Waldemar suddenly stood in front of us. His anxiety had driven him to us. His house had fortunately been spared. He brought us his last helping of cold meat. Good old uncle! He cried and cried bitterly as he saw us set off with our cart. Joe was pushing the cart; father pulled it with a rope. I pushed my heavily laden bicycle.

For our flight, we tried to find a safe route, near the canal where the houses were more widely spaced, in the direction of Friedrichsberg. Everything was burning there as well. Prams, bicycles and carts and such like – all heavily laden – were being pulled by some of the fleeing people but most of them didn't take anything; they only wore their night-clothes. Firemen, soldiers, lorries – all mingled together and everyone silent and stunned, their faces almost delirious. Why? Why? What was the reason for all this?

One man has gone mad. He's standing in front of a mound of bricks from a collapsed wall, on top of which he has erected the swastika flag. He is screaming at the fugitives with a steel helmet on his head – his face mad – and he is bombarding the fugitives with bricks. Father screams at him and he is taken aback enough to let us pass. We continue, by large bomb craters, over the ruins of collapsed house fronts. The Tommies have also been here, house after house hit, the fire hoses are everywhere in the road.

Gradually we reach the town boundary of Wandsbek; here we also find bombs everywhere. Slowly the day becomes clearer; the dense clouds of smoke are behind us now. We are in the great stream of fugitives on the Lübecker Chaussee now. Old people, small children – everyone is creeping along under the sun; it is hot now. Every village that we come to is full to bursting point. Compassionate farmers give out some coffee and milk but what can that do for thousands of people. The evening approaches and, completely exhausted, we can go no further. We all have blisters on our feet. We look like stokers. No beds, no barns, no stables to be had. People have settled and are lying down on lawns, in woods. By chance, our tent had been ready to hand in the cellar and father and Joe had wisely brought it along, thinking that it might be needed. We get some water from a farm and, finally, the three of us settled down in the tent. We were at Stapelfeld.

Another quotation describes the exodus as seen through the eyes of an inhabitant of the area outside Hamburg into which these refugees were trudging. Margot Schulz lived in Berge-dorf, the first small town on the broad main road to Berlin.

It was the most pathetic sight I had ever seen. If I think back on it now, I don't think it can have been true. They were in their night dresses – half burned sometimes – and pyjamas, sometimes a coat thrown over their shoulders. They pushed their belongings in a pram, still with the baby in. Sometimes they had a lot of those little carts – '*Handwagen*' we called them – little four-wheeled carts; I don't think you have them in England. You have to imagine the hysteria, with some of the people burnt and crying. It went on for days. It was just endless.

My sister and I got some fruit juice that we had from our garden and a bucket of water. We stood there all day giving drinks to these people. The other people in Bergedorf were doing the same but we ran out in the end and had to give up.

I remember a woman suddenly collapsing on the pavement across the road from where I lived and giving birth to a baby. The baby came after about a quarter of an hour or twenty minutes of moaning and groaning; it must have been a 'shock birth'. Fortunately they took her into a house. There was another woman, sat on the pavement near by, breast-feeding her baby. She was only dressed in a nightdress and all her hair was burnt away. And, all the time, the exodus went on. It was a constant stream of misery.

This great flight by the citizens of Hamburg, given official blessing by the leading official in the city, was, in strictly military terms, the most significant event of the Battle of Hamburg. It was the culmination of Bomber Command's success. The R.A.F. bombing had caused so many problems to Gauleiter Kaufmann and his subordinates that he had been forced to close down all normal life in his city. Death and destruction, although widespread, were not the most serious of Kaufmann's problems. They were simple factors that had to be accepted and dealt with in the course of time. Hamburg was faced with the problems of the living: the rescuing of bomb victims, the putting out of fires, the disarming of hundreds of unexploded bombs, the tending of the injured and homeless, the fear of epidemic, of looting, the restoration of all the public services that had been disrupted. The city of Hamburg, even under the firmest of directions and the most brilliant of organizations, simply could not cope with all these problems and, at the same time, keep going any semblance of normal life. Those people, packed in buses and cars or tramping in their misery out of Hamburg, were the visible evidence that Area Bombing operations had stopped the normal life of a major city.

NOTES

1. Public Record Office AIR 14/3012.
2. The Hamburg *Statistisches Jahrbuch 1932/33*, pp. 240–41.
3. The map is in *Feuersturm über Hamburg*, 1978, pp. 218–19.
4. Appendix 10 of the American translation of the Chief of Police Report, pp. 82–3.
5. ibid., p. 102.

16

A Third Blow

The R.A.F. was now half-way through its involvement in the Battle of Hamburg. The great firestorm raid was not followed up on the next night, that of 28–29 July, almost certainly because Hamburg would still have been covered by smoke. It is interesting to see that, as the Battle of Hamburg progressed, it was the smoke from the R.A.F. bombing that was the major factor dictating the pattern of both R.A.F. and U.S.A.A.F. operations. Although the weather was likely to remain clear over most of Germany on this night, Sir Arthur Harris decided to rest his main bomber force. Among the night's minor operations was the usual nuisance raid against Hamburg by four Mosquitoes, making this the fifth consecutive night that the city had been disturbed by the R.A.F. The report of the Chief of Police does not mention this light raid.

The Americans continued to make maximum use of the fine-weather period. On Wednesday, 28 July, their Fortresses were sent to attack aircraft factories at Kassel and Oschersleben, targets even deeper into Germany than before. It was not a successful day for the Americans. More than two-thirds of their planes failed to reach their targets, mostly because of thick cloud on the outward routes which hindered the assembly of their formations, and twenty-two planes were lost from the groups that did reach the target area. More success came to the 247 Fortresses dispatched on the next day, Thursday the 29th, when the less ambitious targets of Kiel and Warnemünde were raided. Most of the Americans were able to bomb with good results but ten planes were lost.

After a night's rest, R.A.F. Bomber Command prepared for action again. On the morning of Thursday the 29th, Harris decided that a major raid should be carried out that night. Two targets were selected – Hamburg as the primary, with Remscheid, a town in the Ruhr, as reserve. It was a long-range Spitfire of 542 Squadron, making one of that squadron's many photographic reconnaissance runs over Hamburg during the battle, which brought back the news that the weather over

Hamburg was clear and that smoke from the fires still burning in the firestorm area was being carried by the wind well clear of the city. So, Hamburg was soon confirmed as the target for the night. It would be the third major blow by the R.A.F. against Hamburg in six nights.

The usual planning and preparation processes took place; only the main points need be summarized here. The routes to and from the target were almost identical to those of the first two raids; these unvarying routes being a feature of the raids about which some aircrew were becoming unhappy. The routes being used allowed maximum loads of bombs to be carried but the selection of similar landfalls on the German coast and of withdrawal routes from the target must have helped the German defence. Because of this, a small diversion was incorporated into the plan for the coming raid but this can best be described later. The final approach into the target area would be made from a direction only just west of due north. This was to allow the raid to hit the largest part of residential Hamburg not seriously damaged in previous raids. The Aiming Point, in the centre of the Altstadt, would remain the same and it was planned that the bombing would creep back across the districts of Rotherbaum, Harvestehude, Hoheluft and Eppendorf – districts of Hamburg containing a more middle-class population than the area hit by the firestorm raid. Zero Hour was brought forward by fifteen minutes, to forty-five minutes after midnight. The number of bombers available for the raid – 786 – and the contents of their bombloads remained much the same as in the previous raid.

Three aircraft crashed either on take-off or soon afterwards. A 15 Squadron Stirling and a 50 Squadron Lancaster were both completely wrecked. The Lancaster, at Skellingthorpe, caught fire and burnt out, the blaze being clearly visible by crews taking off from the many surrounding airfields. It was a familiar sight in that part of England where the bomber airfields were situated. At Grimsby, the undercarriage of a 100 Squadron Lancaster collapsed and the aircraft came to rest at the intersection of the airfield's runways. Twelve more aircraft, waiting to take off, were prevented from doing so, thus sparing Hamburg their fifty-eight tons of bombs. There were no serious casualties in any of the crashes.

There was an unusual mix-up in the timing of take-offs at Scampton, home of 57 Squadron. The nine Lancasters destined to bomb with the first and second waves of the Main Force took off soon after 10.20 p.m. Nine more Lancasters should have taken off at 11 p.m., to bomb with the sixth and final wave of the attack, but there had been an error, either in the transmission of orders by teleprinter from 5 Group Headquarters or in the translation of those orders into briefing instructions. The nine Lancasters were held back until 11.20 p.m. and given a 'time over target' that was twenty minutes too late. These late take-off and bombing times were queried by some of the crews concerned but they were assured that the times were correct and the nine planes took off and flew to Hamburg twenty minutes behind the remainder of the Main Force. It is said that the error was discovered soon after take-off but this cannot be verified. No recall signal was sent.

The usual crop of mechanical difficulties forced forty-five bombers to return. A more serious mishap befell a Halifax which was seen by another aircraft to spiral down out of control towards the sea. Because the observing plane was itself shot down later that night, no report of that incident reached England but it probably accounts for the loss of a 78 Squadron Halifax whose wireless operator's body was picked up at sea in this area the next day.

As the remainder of the bomber force flew out along their now familiar route across the North Sea, their crews could see a faint glow on the horizon, ahead and slightly to starboard, as though the moon was rising in that direction. The glow gradually became more prominent and the R.A.F. men realized that what they could see was the city of Hamburg, still burning from their raid of two nights earlier. 'I expect we were filled with awe', one Pathfinder pilot says, 'and, as far as I was concerned, I was full of satisfaction. The more we hammered Hamburg, the better we were pleased at that time.'

No bombers went seriously astray while flying over the North Sea and the bomber-stream started Windowing at the usual position, thirty-five miles from the German coast. But, almost at once, it started to suffer casualties. The Germans had made no new major breakthrough in their fight against Window but all the counters tentatively introduced two nights earlier were now being used more confidently. Radar operators, both on the ground and in the air, were becoming more skilled in picking out true bomber targets from the false echoes of Window. German controllers sent their fighters further out to sea than normal in an attempt to pick out bombers at the head of the stream. More night fighters were allowed to fly freely, outside the close confines of the boxes. A running commentary on the height, course and progress of the bomber-stream was heard as early as twenty-three minutes past midnight, when the first bombers were just crossing the German coast near the Sankt Peter peninsula and while the tail of the bomber-stream was still fifty minutes' flying time out to sea. The German fighters took a steady toll. Four bombers went down before the German coast was reached and four more just past the coast, in the vicinity of the route-markers dropped there. This was easily the best defence that the Germans had put up at their coast since Window had been introduced. From these eight lost bombers, three of them Pathfinders, only one man escaped by parachute.

A further bomber, a Lancaster of 100 Squadron, nearly went down the same way as the other lost bombers. Flying Officer L. W. Crum was its navigator.

My first knowledge of the attack was hearing Pick – the Australian skipper, Flight Sergeant Pickles – shouting that we were under attack, 'Strewth! It's a fighter', and he took evasive action and the intercom faded away – a peculiar sensation. After about ten seconds, the intercom came back and I heard the skipper calling the rear and upper gunners. There was no reply. He then told the flight engineer to go back and investigate. He did so and, about ten seconds later, Pick called out that we were being attacked again. The intercom faded as before. I left my table and went to Pick and he signalled me to go aft and investigate.

I found the rear gunner attempting to put on his 'chute, although he was stumbling around blindly. The flight engineer was down on the floor. I grappled with the rear gunner and managed to sit him down. He had been wounded in the arms and face. I found the flight engineer unconscious and tried to revive him. The hydraulic lines to the turrets had been damaged and the floor was very treacherous through the oil which had been spilt. I tried to get up to the mid-upper turret but found it very difficult at first. Eventually, I did so, only to find that the turret had been almost shot away. The gunner was dead. Then, I tried to revive the flight engineer by giving him my oxygen mask, because his had become unclipped and I thought it might have been faulty, causing him to be suffering from oxygen starvation. Unfortunately, it soon became evident that he was dead, having been killed in the second attack, although, apart from a slight wound in his forehead, he seemed unmarked.

During this period, Pick had continued to take evasive action. His evasive technique was to get down as low as possible and it worked. He gave instructions to the bomb aimer to jettison the bomb-load. At the time, I was dismayed by this decision. I felt that our dead comrades would have wished us to press on. I felt that there was a good chance that we wouldn't be attacked again. I felt Pick had arrived at his decision too quickly. Afterwards, I realized that Pick's was the right decision. Mine was an emotional one.

It is probable that the prolonged dropping of route-markers at the German coast proved helpful to those German fighters which were allowed to roam freely. Seven of the eight British bombers lost during this stage of the flight were destroyed within a few miles of those red markers. To counter this danger, a small diversion was created at a position on the German coast south of the River Elbe and sixty miles away from the true landfall. For twenty minutes, four Mosquito light bombers dropped yellow markers, Window and flares similar to those sometimes used by German fighters. This diversion represents a small but interesting development in Bomber Command tactics and it was partially successful. One Mosquito was attacked, briefly, by a night fighter and the records of the Hamburg Chief of Police refer to 'a second strong wave of bombers approaching from the direction of Bremen'.

Further north, the attentions of the German fighters ceased abruptly when the bomber-stream had crossed the coast. Flak was met, particularly in the Kiel Canal area, but the remainder of the short flight to Hamburg was relatively quiet. On approaching Hamburg, there could be little danger of the Pathfinders not finding their target. The glow of Hamburg's fires acted as a vivid beacon above the city. Pilot Officer Dean, navigator in a Pathfinder Blind Marker crew, was studying his H2S display during his final approach to the city when he heard his American pilot, Pilot Officer W. J. Senger, say, 'You can leave that box o' tricks of yours, Dixie. I can see the son-of-a-bitchin' target; it's still lit up from the last trip'.

The first markers and bombs were released at forty minutes past midnight. This will be, for the reader, the third account of an R.A.F. night raid in the Battle of Hamburg. The sequence of primary and backing-up marking and of Main Force bombing and the vigorous reaction of the German defences were, in most respects, similar in this raid to events in the first two raids. This description will concentrate more on the new developments and unusual incidents experienced than on what must now be familiar routine for the reader.

As in the devastating second R.A.F. raid, two nights earlier, all primary marking was carried out by H2S radar, none by visual means. The Main Force attack was soon in full swing and it could be seen that both the marking and the bombing were effective although not quite as concentrated as on the previous raid. An extensive area of the city could be seen burning well and a mushroom-shaped column of smoke rose up to the height at which the later waves of bombers were flying. There could be no doubt that yet another crushing blow was being administered to Hamburg and that few bombs were being wasted by falling outside the city's boundaries. Again, the bomber men have recorded their impressions of the sight. 'The whole crew were awe-stricken and one remarked that it must look like that looking at Hades.' 'Everything was burning and I could see my instruments without a light. Incredible!' 'It seemed to be a crime to put more bombs down into that inferno.' 'Those poor people down there; why didn't they throw it in?' 'I lifted my oxygen mask and smelt a city burning. It must have been terrible for the *Herrenvolk* of Hamburg.' A New Zealander, flying his first operation, remembers that 'the whole area glittered like the sun shining on early morning dew. The whole trip was an unbelievable experience but the sight of my first "flamer" made me realize that there was no guarantee about this living business.'

These 'flamers' – aircraft falling in flames – were the visible sign that the German defences in the target area had also made a considerable recovery from the effects of Window. There is no mystery about the means by which this was achieved. Unusually large reinforcements of searchlights had been sent to the Hamburg area. A Bomber Command report says that these were operating in an area forty miles across and the accounts of many bombers mention this greatly increased searchlight activity. German fighters – both the freelancing twin-engined fighters and Major Herrmann's single-engined fighters – were in action over the burning city and they took full advantage of the increased illumination. The result was a marked success for the German defence. The R.A.F. Listening Service in England heard several expressions of satisfaction from the German pilots involved; for example, the expression 'a great night' was heard twice. Twelve British bombers crashed in and around Hamburg during the course of the main part of the raid, many of them coming down into the open country areas south of the city after passing through the target area. Although many German pilots have individual victories credited to them, it was really a victory for the combined defence. Some of the bombers were shared with the Flak and many of the victories came only after the searchlights had illuminated the bombers. Four German fighters were claimed by the R.A.F. and German records do confirm the loss of three of these.

This account, by Sergeant Joe Weldon, a wireless operator in a 35 Squadron Halifax that was shot down, must suffice as an example of the experiences of the men in those bombers shot down in and around Hamburg that night.

I stood beside the pilot as we approached the target. The bomb aimer and navigator were working hard, to get our position right, because we were Blind Markers. While we were running up, straight and level, we were coned. I'd been in searchlights before but never as bad as this. It felt as though every searchlight in Hamburg was on to us and every gun in Hamburg was firing at us. The pilot started to jink, to avoid the Flak, but with the idea of keeping on to the release point.

We dropped our bombs and markers – as far as I know at the right place – and turned on to our new course, continuing our evasive action all the time. Then, only a few seconds later, I heard a 'clang' as the aircraft was hit, not a heavy hit, just one lump of shrapnel but it hit the navigator. Someone, probably the pilot, asked him if he was all right. The nav said, 'Carry on, lads. Carry on, lads.' It was about then that I got my parachute and the pilot's parachute and put them on; chest-type packs they were. We didn't hear anything more from the navigator and he was either very badly wounded or dead soon after. We seemed to be getting away – the Flak was getting less –

but the searchlights still followed us; we were being passed on by one batch after another.

I think we were over the countryside when the mid-upper shouted, 'Fighter', and he opened up. But we never heard a word from the rear gunner; I am certain that he was unconscious from oxygen failure. He had complained earlier in the flight about oxygen trouble. We were hit by cannon fire straight away. Fortunately for me, when I had come up, earlier, from my own position to stand by the pilot, I had closed the armour-plating door between where I was standing and the rear of the aircraft – something I had rarely done before. The flight engineer would normally have been standing there but, with that recent introduction of Window, he was further back, throwing Window out. I heard the cannon shells exploding against this armour plating. I think they were coming straight along the body of the aircraft. I remember being very thankful that I had shut that door. We never heard another sound from the men in the rear of the aircraft after the cannon shells.

It didn't seem long before we were being hit again and, this time, he got the starboard-outer engine which was set on fire. Ben pressed the fire extinguisher but nothing happened. Then the fighter made another run and the pilot told us to bale out. 'Better go, lads.' Then, almost immediately, I think he was hit because he flopped forward.

All hell broke loose after that. The aircraft went over and must have gone into a spin. I was thrown into a heap and, when I was able to get to my feet, I found the open escape hatch above my head; it was normally in the floor. I can remember what I thought then. 'Bloody hell! The wife's going to get a telegram in the morning, saying I was missing.' But I didn't think I was going to be killed; that was the last thought in my mind. There was someone else in there but I don't know whether it was the bomb aimer or the navigator. I went for that hatch; I didn't hang about, I can assure you.

The crew member behind Weldon had been Flight Sergeant Frank Fenton, the bomb aimer, who had already pushed the dead or dying navigator out with his parachute release pulled and who, now, gave Weldon a push. These two were the only survivors and the Halifax crashed near Moisburg, sixteen miles from the centre of Hamburg.*

* There was a sentimental sequel to the death of the pilot, Flight Lieutenant H. C. 'Ben' Pexton, D.F.C., and the survival of Sergeant Weldon. At his own christening, Pexton had been given a gift of a silver spoon and fork engraved with his initials. Because he had died unmarried, his parents decided to send it as a christening gift to Weldon's daughter,

The main attack was supposed to end at 1.32 a.m. and is believed to have done so at that time. Seven hundred bombers had released approximately 2,323 tons of bombs over Hamburg. A great area of the city was on fire. The Flak barrage died away and many of the searchlights were switched off. But the attack was not yet over. The reader will remember that an error at Scampton airfield had resulted in nine Lancasters of 57 Squadron being allocated late take-off and bombing times. One of the Lancasters had made up time, its crew probably realizing that a mistake had been made, but the remaining eight flew down from the north to attack Hamburg twenty minutes after the rest of the Main Force. The Flak opened up and the searchlights were switched on again. German fighters were still flying in the area. The eight Lancasters made regulation bombing runs, believing that they were in company with 100 other aircraft in the last wave of the attack. Flak destroyed one, which blew up over the northern outskirts of Hamburg. A night fighter shot down a second, which crashed south of the city, and a fighter nearly got a third. Six rather shaken crews flew home where they would later be told of the error in their orders.

Gauleiter Kaufmann's appeal to the civilian population, thirty-six hours earlier, to leave Hamburg saved the lives of a great many people on this night. Some people had, however, refused to leave. Many elderly or infirm had stayed; for them, it was a case of 'here is my home and here I will die if necessary'. Property owners often stayed, prepared to die rather than lose their small investments of a lifetime. The optimistic stayed, convinced that their *Schutzengels* – guardian angels – would save them. It is evident, however, that those who chose to remain in the city made very sure that they had a good shelter to get into if the alarm was given. When the alarm did sound, nearly an hour before the first bombs dropped, the reduced population of the city went to ground with great speed. One report speaks of a *Bunkerkomplex*, in which people

---

Suzette, born in 1946. This has now been passed on to a second Suzette, Weldon's granddaughter.

There is a memorial window to Flight Lieutenant Pexton in the parish church of Watton, near Driffield in Yorkshire.

were only concerned with the quality of shelter and not with its comfort or convenience. The large public *Bunker* shelters, which had shown themselves to be so effective in previous raids, were very popular on this night.

The large area of fire seen by the R.A.F. bomber crews was, indeed, an extensive part of Hamburg ablaze. But, again, the Pathfinders had not managed to mark the designated Aiming Point accurately. On this night, it was the Pathfinders' old enemy, the unexpectedly strong crosswind, that caused them to go astray. This wind, blowing from due west, had steadily pushed the Pathfinder aircraft to the east during the forty-mile flight from the north during their last leg into the target area. The radar operators of three of the early Pathfinder aircraft corrected the drift and were able to place their markers near the true Aiming Point* but the majority of their fellow Pathfinders released their markers three miles downwind. This position was over the districts of Billbrook and Billwärder Ausschlag and was very near to the area marked at the opening of the firestorm raid, two nights earlier. But, on this night, the bombers' approach was from the north rather than from the east and the movement of the resulting bombing, well contained and creeping back only slowly, was to the north. The first part of the raid fell into the still-burning ruins of Hamm and Wandsbek but the bombing soon reached the relatively undamaged districts of Eilbek, Uhlenhorst, Winterhude and Barmbek – all being districts on the eastern side of the Alster when Bomber Command had intended the districts on the western side of the lake to be bombed. Some bombs fell and caused damage in many other parts of Hamburg but the main weight of the attack was always concentrated into one area.

Barmbek was in the centre of this main bombing area. This was an extensive residential district – of suburban rather than working-class character – and it had suffered some damage in the first raid of the Battle of Hamburg.† But, now, in an

---

* These three crews were captained by Squadron Leader C. T. Lofthouse of 7 Squadron, Pilot Officer J. G. Wright of 35 Squadron and Wing Commander K. H. Burns of 97 Squadron.

† The parents of Helmut Schmidt, later Chancellor of West Germany, lived in Barmbek, in the Schellingstrasse. At the time of the Battle of Hamburg, Helmut Schmidt was serving as a junior officer in a light Flak battery at Rerik, on the Baltic coast. Most of his relatives lost their homes and two of his aunts and two uncles were killed in the bombing.

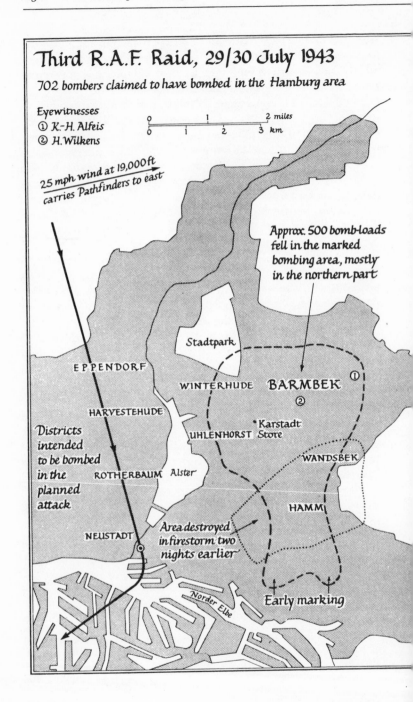

Third R.A.F. Raid, 29/30 July 1943

702 bombers claimed to have bombed in the Hamburg area

Eyewitnesses
① K.-H. Alfeis
② H. Wilkens

0 ___ 1 ___ 2 miles
0 ___ 1 ___ 2 ___ 3 km

25 mph wind at 19,000 ft
carries Pathfinders to east

Approx. 500 bomb-loads
fell in the marked
bombing area, mostly
in the northern part

Stadtpark

EPPENDORF

WINTERHUDE   BARMBEK ①

②

HARVESTEHUDE

Karstadt
Store
UHLENHORST

Districts
intended
to be bombed
in the
planned
attack

ROTHERBAUM Alster

WANDSBEK

HAMM

NEUSTADT

Area destroyed
in firestorm two
nights earlier

Norder Elbe

Early marking

example of bombing almost as concentrated as that of the firestorm raid, Barmbek was almost completely destroyed, mostly by extensive fires which raged unchecked for many hours. Hamburg's exhausted fire units could do little more than concentrate on saving as many lives as possible and on stopping the spread of fire on the edge of the bombing area. No real fire-fighting took place inside the fire area. Reports from Hamburg also make it clear that, with the determination of those few civilians who had remained to find and stay in a good shelter, almost no work was done by the first line of defence against fire – the block wardens and the fire-watchers in commercial premises. The cumulative effects of the recent raids had rendered the city almost incapable of protecting itself.

A long description of this third night raid in the Battle of Hamburg is not needed here but the reader should be left in no doubt that a very heavy blow was struck. Some German reports say that the material effects of this raid were even more serious than those of the firestorm raid and it is certain that severe damage was caused over a greater area. The Chief of Police estimated, incorrectly, that more R.A.F. bombers had taken part and that a greater bomb-load was dropped than two nights earlier. But, in human suffering and loss of life, there was no comparison; there was no repetition of the fearful death toll of the firestorm raid. No German assessment of casualties for the night can be found but an American work suggests that 'about 800' people perished.[1] The worst incident took place at the Karstadt department store, on the Hamburger Strasse in Barmbek. There were two large underground shelters under this building, one mainly for employees of the store, the other for members of the public. Several high-explosive bombs caused this building and the large searchlight positioned on its roof to collapse and the ruins caught fire. As many as 1,200 people were safely rescued from the employees' shelter nine hours after the raid, but the second shelter could not be reached for some time. Passers-by believed they heard noises coming from the ruins, 'like cats fighting'. Another report says that four people escaped from this second shelter, led by a man who knew the building well and who led this small party through a series of narrow passages, the escapers having to remove most of their clothes to squeeze through.

When the shelter was uncovered, 370 people were found to have died from carbon monoxide gas from the nearby coke store which had been burning.

Although the horror of the firestorm was, mercifully for the citizens of Hamburg, not repeated in Barmbek and the other areas bombed, the bombing was still a punishing experience for the people involved. This section can finish with two accounts by young men who describe their experiences during and at the end of the raid. Yet again, the reader is asked to imagine many, many more of these incidents in order to get a true impression. Karl-Heinz Alfeis, fourteen years old, was in a public shelter on the Anemonenweg:

People sat and stood, very close together, in the completely dark air-raid shelter. The air got more foul as the ventilation only let in the hot air from the fires outside. One incident took place which almost caused a panic. A bomb splinter came in with tremendous force and struck a metal air shaft. A flash of flame caught the arm of a woman who was sitting just under it. She was severely burnt as a result. The shelter received three direct hits but it was built in such a way that, when it was hit, it only shook. One corner of the roof was blown off but there were no casualties. We survived.

When the bombing slackened off, the wardens opened the heavy doors – but what a picture was revealed to our eyes! We lads, not knowing the danger, were the first out. There was a sea of flame as far as we could see. Not one house seemed to be spared. A storm of wind howled through the streets. Bicycles, which had been left outside the shelter, looked like crumpled-up balls of wool. It was a desperate sight, all this destruction.

All the young boys and men were called upon to report immediately for rescue work. While most of us carried out these orders, some soldiers who were in the shelter did not want to leave their families. We heard, very clearly, one of them saying that it was more dangerous here than up at the front. It was very shameful for us to see the district party leader having to go from one compartment in the shelter to another, with drawn pistol, hunting down and flushing out these shirkers with a torch. The soldiers went out quietly when he found them.

Helmut Wilkens was seventeen and he lived on the Ahrensburgerstrasse (now the Krausestrasse):

It became very quiet although we had not heard the All Clear. Someone opened the shelter door. Our block of flats, on the other side of the street, had collapsed and the house next door was fully ablaze; even the bricks seemed to be on fire. Someone stood at a second-floor window, calling for help. It was Herr Schwarz, who never went down to the shelter; only his wife did that. People called up to him to jump. We stretched out some blankets for him to jump into but he was afraid. The blankets would not have saved him.

Suddenly, there were two sailors; perhaps they were on leave. They said, 'Shoot him. He won't suffer in agony any more. He's burning already.' They started to fire at him with their pistols. He fell forward, then, and smashed on to the pavement.

Some people tried to get back into their houses to fetch something they had forgotten or to save anything. Everything was in a mess. My father tried to get into our house, even though it had collapsed and nothing could be saved. Bodies were lying on the pavements but we couldn't recognize any of them. They were either shrivelled up or burnt. Perhaps these people had never managed to reach the shelters. I don't know.

As far as I could see, no one was behaving sensibly at that time. Some sat there and cried; others just regarded the scene silently. One spoke to the neighbours about silly little things and wondered what to do next.

The return flight, for most of the R.A.F. bombers that had just caused so much damage, was a quiet one. Weather conditions were good and there were few navigational problems. In various isolated combats, one German fighter was destroyed and another damaged and four bombers were shot down, making a total of twenty-eight bombers lost during the raid. This total was only one less than the combined losses of the first two R.A.F. raids of the Battle of Hamburg and is a measure of the increasing recovery by the Luftwaffe from the introduction of Window. But nearly 700 bombers flew home without encountering any unusual danger. There was only one landing accident; this occurred when there was some confusion over the diversion of a badly damaged Lancaster of 83 Squadron to Wittering, and the Lancaster finished up at the smaller airfield of Sibson, four miles away. Pilot Officer K. A. King received a 'green' to land and, in the words of his squadron record book, 'used the surrounding country to finish his landing'.[2] His plane was written off but no one was hurt.

The earlier landings of the German night fighters had not all been so fortunate. A full Intruder effort had been made by the Mosquitoes and Beaufighters of R.A.F. Fighter Command.

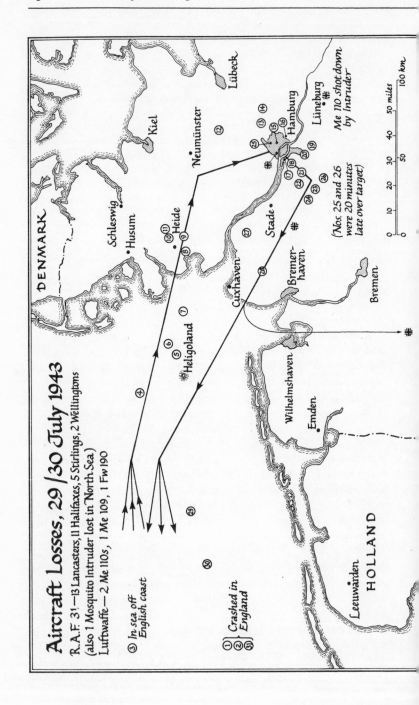

Aircraft Losses, 29/30 July 1943

R.A.F. 31 — 13 Lancasters, 11 Halifaxes, 5 Stirlings, 2 Wellingtons
(also 1 Mosquito Intruder lost in North Sea.)
Luftwaffe — 2 Me 110s, 1 Me 109, 1 Fw 190

③ *In sea off English coast*

①
②   *Crashed in*
⑩   *England*

Me 110 shot down by Intruder

(Nos. 25 and 26 were 20 minutes late over target)

DENMARK

HOLLAND

Kiel

Lübeck

Neumünster

Hamburg

Lüneburg

Schleswig

Husum

Heide

Stade

Cuxhaven

Bremerhaven

Bremen

Heligoland

Wilhelmshaven

Emden

Leeuwarden

100 km
50 miles

Many of these flights had been unsuccessful because of hazy conditions at low level but one Mosquito crew had, in the words of its squadron's records, experienced 'an Intruder's dream come true'.[3] Flying Officer Arthur Woods and Sergeant Wilfred Johnson had arrived over Lüneburg airfield just as many of the German night fighters which had been in action over the Hamburg area were landing. The airfield lighting was on and an estimated ten to fifteen German fighters were circling, with navigation lights burning. During the course of a hectic twenty-three minutes, the Mosquito made six separate attempts to attack German fighters as they tried to land. Four of these attempts were unsuccessful, mainly because of haze – possibly thickened up by smoke from Hamburg, thirty miles away – which distorted distances so badly. But Woods certainly damaged one German on his fifth attempt and, finally, the sixth fighter was seen to burst into flames and crash. German records show that the Intruder's victim was the Messerschmitt 110 of Oberfeldwebel Wilhelm Kurrek, of the 8th *Staffel* of III/NJG 3. Both German crew members were killed. It was a good example of the blow and counterblow of warfare. Oberfeldwebel Kurrek, an experienced night-fighter pilot, had shot down a Lancaster on the firestorm raid two nights earlier.

Flying Officer Woods turned for home.

I was bathed in perspiration but elated with my success; it was the first enemy aircraft I had definitely destroyed. But, at the same time, I was disappointed with myself and the weather conditions. The thoughts still remain in my memory that I had had the best part of an enemy night-fighter squadron in the air with me but, although I flew as best I could to chase and position myself to attack, we kept losing sight of potential targets. However, that's the luck of the game – or, was – and, after all, I felt we had done our job as best we could and survived ourselves.

Flying Officer Woods had nearly achieved a more notable success at Lüneburg. Major Hajo Herrmann had landed just before the Mosquito started its activities among the German fighters landing there and Herrmann had been standing in the control tower when a stray cannon shell came through a window only two or three yards away, nearly ending a career that still had much to achieve.

In return for Flying Officer Woods's success, another

Intruder squadron had suffered a casualty. A 25 Squadron Mosquito had started experiencing engine trouble soon after leaving the English coast and signalled that it was returning to its base at Church Fenton. It never arrived and must have crashed into the sea. The loss of this crew was another example of the way blow and counterblow could come so close on each other's heels. This was the Mosquito crew that had shot down a Junkers 88 near Westerland on the first night of the Battle of Hamburg – 25 Squadron's first Intruder success. The body of Flight Lieutenant E. R. F. Cooke – the son of a judge – was never seen again; that of his navigator, Sergeant F. M. Ellacott, was washed up on the friendly shore of Denmark, 300 miles away, many days later.

NOTES

1. *Fire and the Air War*, edited by Horatio Bond, 1946, p. 86.
2. Public Record Office AIR 27/687.
3. Operations Record Book of 605 Squadron, Public Record Office AIR 27/2090.

17

The Battle Ends

The fine weather continued. The American bombers were up again the next morning, 186 B-17s taking off to attack two targets near Kassel. This was the sixth major operation for the Americans in seven days and it concluded what they would later call their 'Blitz Week', during which eleven major targets in Germany and two in Norway had been attacked at a cost of eighty-eight Fortresses lost. It is not surprising that a lull of nearly a fortnight followed while the American units drew breath and replaced their casualties. It was during this quieter period that a notable page in the history of the U.S.A.A.F. would be written when, on the other side of Europe, 179 B-24 Liberators made their famous low-level attack on the Romanian oil refineries at Ploesti. No less than fifty-four Liberators were lost. More than half of the Ploeşti force was provided by the three B-24 Groups – the 44th, 93rd and 389th – that had been sent from England to operate from North Africa. Their survivors would soon be back to rejoin the Eighth Air Force.

R.A.F. Bomber Command, which had dispatched its maximum effort in four of the past six nights, was ready to go out again on the night of 30–31 July – but not to Hamburg. Bomber Command Headquarters had received an urgent directive from the Air Ministry, ordering raids to be made on three cities in northern Italy – Milan, Turin and Genoa – if weather conditions permitted. But the directive went on to state that 'owing to the possibility of a rapid change in the political situation, these attacks are subject to cancellation at short notice'.[1] Sir Arthur Harris responded at once and, at his conference on the morning of 30 July, he ordered Bomber Command to be split into three forces with two of these to raid Turin and Genoa. The third force, formed around the Stirlings of 3 Group, was not to climb the Alps to raid Italy but was to be sent to attack the Ruhr town of Remscheid. Preparations were carried out for all three raids but, later in the day, the Air Ministry invoked the 'cancellation at short notice' quoted in its directive and the two Italian raids were abandoned, presumably because of the rapidly changing political situation in Italy. Perhaps the raids had formed part of secret pressure – which had borne fruit – on the new Italian government.

The Remscheid raid went ahead. A total of 264 heavy bombers, led by nine Mosquitoes which carried out their usual accurate Oboe marking, inflicted severe damage and 1,063 people were killed in a community which had not had as much practice at taking cover from air raids as the larger Ruhr cities. Fifteen bombers were lost, nine of them being Stirlings which experienced difficulty in keeping up with the flight plan, lost the protection of Window and suffered accordingly, mostly from the accurate Ruhr Flak.

Harris still intended to attack Hamburg once more in the present series of raids and he chose the city for his only target in the next night, that of 31 July/1 August. For once, a maximum effort was not called for, the Stirlings from 3 Group being given a rest after their unhappy experiences over the Ruhr the previous night. The remainder of Bomber Command carried out the usual preparations but a series of heavy thunderstorms struck the bomber airfields, just before the time of take-off. The raid was hurriedly cancelled, several airmen finding out how fast they could run in flying clothes to get away from bomb-laden aircraft that might be struck by lightning. This reprieve for Hamburg was extended on the following night when the stormy weather, passing quickly east across the North Sea to northern Germany, persuaded Harris not to consider any major operation on the first night of August. So, because the Americans had temporarily worked themselves out, because there were political complications with the Italians, and because of a series of thunderstorms, the battered city of Hamburg was allowed a raid-free period lasting four days and three nights. Not even a Mosquito nuisance bomber disturbed this priceless period of rest.

On the morning of Monday, 2 August – Bank Holiday Monday in England – Sir Arthur Harris was still patiently seeking to find the conditions for what he hoped would be a successful conclusion to the Battle of Hamburg. The weather situation was not clear. Two bad-weather fronts had passed through England and were now believed to be giving stormy weather in many parts of Germany. Only a reconnaissance flight could give more precise details. Harris provisionally chose two targets: Hamburg again, with Kiel as an alternative. Kiel was the most northerly substantial target in Germany and probably the one most likely to be clear of cloud.

The alternative target of Kiel was never needed, so the planning for it can be ignored. The plans for the Hamburg raid, however, contained several major changes from those used in the previous three raids of the battle. The first innovation was that a southern approach to the target was to be used. Part of this approach route might mislead the Germans into believing that the bombers were intending to attack Hannover, Brunswick or another target in central Germany. There were to be further major changes at the target. For the first time in the battle, two Aiming Points were to be used. The first of these was to be near the northern end of the Alster lake and was to be used by the first four waves of Main Force bombers. The use of this Aiming Point should produce a bombing pattern that would encompass the wealthy residential areas of Harvestehude and Rotherbaum together with the city centre to the south. The risk that many of the bombs would fall uselessly into the Alster was apparently taken to ensure that the rest fell into districts which had escaped serious damage in earlier raids.

Thirty-one minutes after the opening of the attack, a second force of Pathfinders was to mark a new Aiming Point in the township of Harburg, eight miles to the south of the first Aiming Point. The last two waves of the Main Force were to bomb here. Harburg was officially part of Hamburg but was really a quite different community, being separated from the main part of Hamburg by five miles of docks, waterways and Hamburg's industrial suburb of Wilhelmsburg. The choice of two Aiming Points for this raid was very ambitious, tactically, but a more significant aspect of the target plan was that, even in this fourth raid of the battle, the bombing would continue to be on densely built-up areas of a mainly residential nature.

The weather-reconnaissance flight that was needed before this raid could proceed was delayed as long as possible so that it could bring back the most up-to-date information. Flight

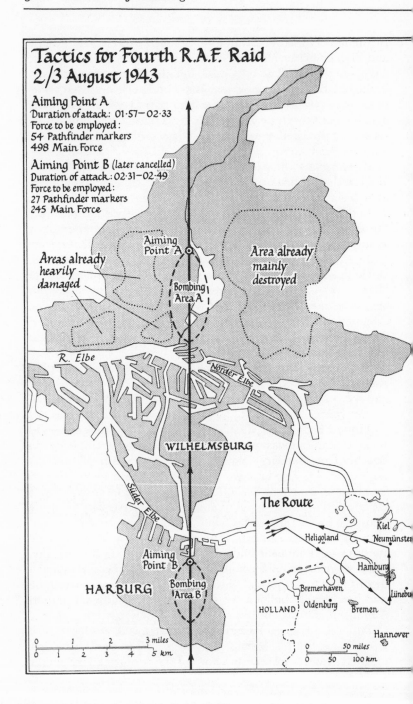

Tactics for Fourth R.A.F. Raid
2/3 August 1943

Aiming Point A
Duration of attack: 01·57 – 02·33
Force to be employed:
54 Pathfinder markers
498 Main Force

Aiming Point B (later cancelled)
Duration of attack: 02·31 – 02·49
Force to be employed:
27 Pathfinder markers
245 Main Force

Areas already
heavily
damaged

Aiming
Point A

Area already
mainly
destroyed

Bombing
Area A

R. Elbe

Norder Elbe

Süder Elbe

WILHELMSBURG

Aiming
Point B

Bombing
Area B

HARBURG

0   1   2   3 miles
0 1 2 3 4 5 km

The Route

Kiel
Heligoland   Neumünster
Hamburg
Bremerhaven   Lüneburg
HOLLAND   Oldenburg   Bremen

Hannover

0   50 miles
0   50   100 km

Lieutenant Geoffrey Hatton, commander of the Met Flight, and Flying Officer Neville Green, one of his most experienced navigators, took off at 6.15 p.m. But they had to land almost immediately when one of the Mosquito's engines was found to be giving trouble. The reserve aircraft was quickly prepared and the crew were away again at 6.45 p.m. The Met Flight's record book, together with personal accounts from both men, ensure that details of this important flight are available.

The Mosquito flew to the Dutch coast – making its landfall at Texel – and then on into Germany, reaching the Oldenburg area before flying out again over Emden to the North Sea. With the weather known to be moving briskly north-eastwards, the conditions encountered in the Oldenburg–Emden area were the ones that the bombers might find in their flight to Hamburg and over the target itself six hours later. Cloud of many kinds and at many levels was met and one particularly large mass of vicious cumulo-nimbus, towering up to 30,000 feet, was seen south-west of Oldenburg. Conditions in the direction of Hamburg, however, appeared to be much clearer. The Mosquito landed at Oakington at 9.45 p.m. and its crew reported what they had seen.

The delayed take-off, caused by the first Mosquito's engine trouble, had squeezed an already tight timetable. Zero Hour over Hamburg could not be later than 2 a.m. because of the early summer dawn. The bombers needed to start taking off within one hour of the weather Mosquito landing. A hurriedly revised forecast was sent by the Meteorological Office to Bomber Command.

Hamburg: Patches of medium cloud between 10,000 and 20,000 feet. Total amount of cloud below 18,000 feet probably less than 5/10ths but slight risk of 10/10ths cumulo-nimbus, tops 30,000 feet.[2]

In other words, fingers were being crossed that the huge storm clouds seen near Oldenburg did not move into that area south of Hamburg through which the bombers' approach flight to the target passed. Sir Arthur Harris did not cancel the raid but he did abandon the ambitious plan to have a second Aiming Point at Harburg. The whole weight of Bomber Command was to go for central Hamburg.

There was barely time to alter the orders for the Pathfinders and for the last two waves of the Main Force before the first bombers started taking off just before 11 p.m. Many of the crews had been surprised to be told at briefing that Hamburg was the target yet again. They had seen the city burning fiercely three times and could scarcely believe that there was anything useful left to bomb. Most briefing officers persuaded the crews that there was just one section of Hamburg left which needed flattening to complete the destruction of the city. At least two squadrons were told that the Aiming Point was in the 'red-light district' near the port installations. Meteorological officers had difficulty in explaining precisely where the area of thunderstorms would be. Some said the storms would be beyond Hamburg; others said well south of the route and the target area. The crews of the Canadian 428 Squadron at Middleton St George were told, bluntly, that they might run into a severe storm and their briefing officer warned them that, if conditions proved too severe, the crews were to drop their bombs anywhere on Germany and come home.

The squadrons took off into an overcast and blustery sky. One man says, 'the clouds were so low that you could almost touch them with your hand'. In many places it was raining steadily. Two Wellingtons from 1 Group made forced landings soon after taking off* and two heavily laden Lancasters in 5 Group suffered collapsed undercarriages. One of these, at Scampton, blocked a runway and prevented six other Lancasters from taking off. The second, at Bardney, caused three other Lancasters to be so late in setting off that they were later recalled by wireless signal. No one was seriously hurt in any of these accidents. In all, 737 bombers headed out over the North Sea to commence an operation that was destined to have little in common with the first three R.A.F. raids of the Battle of Hamburg.

The first unusual incident occurred just off the coast of Lincolnshire. A British coastal convoy, Convoy FS.83, was steaming southwards with twenty-one merchant ships and four naval escorts. Many of the merchant ships had just crossed the North Atlantic in other convoys and were now making their way round to London. The convoy was directly

---

* One of the Wellingtons was actually part of the force of six aircraft detailed to drop mines into the mouth of the River Elbe.

under the flight path of the 280 aircraft of 1 and 5 Groups whose departure point from England was the town of Mable-thorpe. The bombers had been warned of the presence of the convoy and the naval escorts had often seen Bomber Command flying out to Germany or coming home again. But, for many of the crews of the ocean-going merchant ships – some of them were new American Liberty ships – these were new conditions. They were in a 'war zone' for the first time. The trouble started when a bomb exploded near H.M.S. *Shear-water*, a corvette whose captain was Lieutenant Nicholas Monsarrat, the author.

Some time during the middle watch, while I was still on the bridge talking to the Navigating Officer, we heard a great many aircraft passing overhead. I took this, as usual, to be one of our big bomber raids on its way to Germany and we did not come to Action Stations. Then, between *Shearwater* and the convoy, there was a flash and a clang and a rain of sparks and a rather large bomb exploded on the surface of the sea, probably about fifty yards away. We prudently lowered our heads below the bridge-rail, to let the bits (if any) go by, then came up for air. I closed up Action Stations but withheld fire; I judged it to be 'one of ours' jettisoning its last bomb as it came back from an earlier raid. We had seen a great many of our bombers struggling home, crippled or short of fuel, during the previous year and I didn't want to make their situation worse.

I made the usual report when I got into Harwich but without too much drama. Even though *Shearwater* was my first command, and cherished accordingly, we owed too much to the R.A.F. for me to want to make a fuss. Just let them get back in safety. If I had thought it was a plane dropping a bomb on its way *out*, I might have been a bit more curt about it.

The report later submitted by the senior naval officer of the convoy states that nine merchant ships had opened fire: seven Liberties and one British and one Dutch tanker. Although the R.A.F. planes immediately fired the correct 'colours of the day', the merchant ships had continued to fire spasmodically for nearly three hours![3]

Who dropped this bomb and why here? The commanders of 1 and 5 Groups had been gradually increasing the bomb-loads of some of their Lancasters throughout the Battle of Hamburg. Squadron records show that the loads of some aircraft were increased by up to 1,000 lb on this night despite the fact that the route to Hamburg and back was sixty miles longer than on earlier raids. Crews whose aircraft suffered mechanical difficulties soon after take-off had orders to fly at least sixty miles out to sea before dumping their loads. No crew reported being in so much trouble that it had to release bombs inside that limit. The bomb may have been released by one of those crews that decided to lighten their load to gain a better performance from their aircraft. There were frequent reports of such unauthorized 'dumpings' over the sea. It is significant that Bomber Command's operational order for this very night should have included the following item under the heading of 'Tactics':

Maintenance of Height. Lancaster aircraft of 1 Group were not to jettison in order to gain extra height.[4]

One R.A.F. man says that his tail gunner, who watched the firing from a distance, believes a bomber was shot down by the naval fire and there were rumours to that effect on R.A.F. airfields the next day but there is no firm evidence that this did happen.

The bombers flew on across the North Sea. For the aircraft of 3 and 8 Groups, much of their flight to the concentration point for the bomber-stream was only fifty miles from the German radar stations on the Dutch coast but, if the local night fighters were up, they made no attacks during this stage of the flight. The next German move, however, represented another step forward in the German recovery from Window. The change was clearly observed by the R.A.F. Listening Service. For years, its German-speaking members had listened in to the conversations between German ground controllers and the night-fighter crews. After the first night in which Window had been used, the R.A.F. listeners had heard the early forms of a running commentary but much of this had been directed at individual night fighters and there had been much return conversation from the night fighters. Now the game was taken a stage further. One German voice was heard giving a much improved form of running commentary, repeating over and over again the details of the height and the progress of the bombers. No call signs to individual aircraft or groups of aircraft were included and the style of the broadcast indicated that no replies were expected from the night fighters.

Some of the various German records that have survived confirm that, on this night, entire *Gruppen* of NJG 3's night fighters were sent up to work free from ground control. Some boxes were probably manned but, for the first time, the major emphasis was now placed on this freelance hunting, making use of the improved form of running commentary. The stormy weather, which would have made orthodox box operations difficult, may have been one factor in bringing in this more flexible system but the improved German tactics on this night showed all the signs of careful preparation. Someone had been doing some hard thinking in the lull of the past few days. German pilots wrote in their log-books that they were on a *Wilde Sau* – Wild Boar – operation but those of their activities on the bombers' route to and from the target were really of the type later to be known as *Zahme Sau* – Tame Boar. In this type of night fighting, the fighters did not receive help from searchlights or the glare of burning cities; they made use of the running commentary to reach the correct area and, then, of their wits and their airborne radar sets to find a bomber target.

The first combats took place soon after the bomber-stream had concentrated, forty miles west of Heligoland, and turned south-east towards its landfall south of the Elbe. There were at least seven encounters before the bomber-stream reached the German coast. One combat was inconclusive. A second resulted in a long fight in which the crews of both aircraft fought with great courage. The bomber concerned was a 10 Squadron Halifax, piloted by Flying Officer J. C. Jenkins, a Welshman, and the fighter was a Junkers 88. The Halifax came from a squadron which had ordered that the mid-upper gunner was the crew member who would release Window and this gun position was empty when the fighter attacked. In a vigorous combat, the young Canadian tail gunner, Flight Sergeant Dick Hurst from Vancouver, scored many hits on the Junkers which was seen to catch fire in both wings but the German pilot persisted in his attacks and his fire also struck home, much of it around Flight Sergeant Hurst's tail turret. The combat ended when the Junkers 88 was seen spiralling slowly down until it disappeared, still apparently on fire, into cloud. The damaged Halifax, which had jettisoned its bombs, flew safely home, its pilot and tail gunner later to be decorated for this combat. The identity of the fighter crew is not known but the Junkers was probably one from 2./NJG 3 which, although damaged, also found its way safely to Wittmundhafen airfield.

The other five combats in this area all had a more final conclusion. Three Lancasters and two Halifaxes were shot down into the sea and there were no survivors. This was a considerable early success for the German defence but it would be wrong to assume that such a rate of success could have been kept up for the remainder of this raid. Three of these five early successes were by acknowledged aces – two by Major Günther Radusch and one by Hauptmann Rudolf Schönert. These two men were both *Gruppe* commanders and highly skilled pilots; other night-fighter crews found great difficulty in using the new system. This type of night fighting might have continued as far as the target area and for much of the bombers' return flight but a new development, provided by nature, was about to cause such difficulties to night fighter and bomber alike that there would be little further contact between these enemies for some time.

There had been cloud over the North Sea all the way from the English coast but the summits of it were rarely higher than 8,000 feet and the bombers had soon climbed through it. Just before the bomber-stream crossed the German coast, however, a strange and, at first, unexplained sight was observed ahead. Great flashes of light lit up a dense and dark mass which towered far above the height at which the bombers were flying. Many of the bomber crews believed this spectacular sight to be the Flak defences of Cuxhaven and Bremerhaven, perhaps with heavy naval guns being used in an anti-aircraft role. A Pathfinder pilot thought that the Germans had brought into action 'a new and terrific weapon'. Some men thought that the cloudy mass that could be seen was smoke billowing from the still burning city of Hamburg. But outside temperatures started to fall sharply and the air became turbulent. The bombers were about to fly into the most violent electrical storm that most of their crews were ever likely to encounter in their lives.

On the outer edge of the storm, the cloud was broken up by huge, sinister rifts and chasms along which the pilots were able to thread a way through the thunderheads, almost continuous lightning revealing the path to follow. But these open spaces eventually disappeared and the heavy bombers plunged into thick cloud. The experience was frightening and dangerous. There were air currents – up, down and sideways – of the most violent strength, flashes of lightning which often struck the bombers, static electricity which played all manner of trick, and the worst danger, ice that could form silently and invisibly but with great swiftness on the outside surfaces of the bombers.

I have never, in all my fifty-four trips, experienced 10/10ths cloud and electric sparks flying everywhere. The ends of my guns had blue streaks flashing off them like a 'witch's broom' about fifty feet long. All the propellers were giant fire wheels and the conductors could not cope. It was the first and only time I have heard thunder – and plenty – whilst flying in a Lancaster. (Flight Lieutenant G. H. Pascoe, 156 Squadron)

It was my first raid and I couldn't be sure what was Flak and what was lightning. The cu-nimbus cloud seemed to be exploding. It was only on my second raid that I realized what real Flak was.

There were sparks on all our guns; they were like angels lit up in a Catholic church. Then, I noticed a great trail of sparks behind my turret, coming right up to the aircraft. I told the pilot that someone was shooting at us. We found out that the wireless operator had left the trailing aerial out. The pilot kicked him in the head – he was sitting just below the pilot's feet – and told him to jettison the aerial. The operator put his hand on the jettison bar but an electric shock kicked him right back up the aircraft as soon as he pressed it. I knew a bit about electricity and suggested that he would do better to use the rubber urine bag. The aerial just dropped away; it seemed to lose its charge as it did so. (Sergeant J. G. McLaughlan, 405 Squadron)

This night was known in the R.A.F. as 'The Night of the Storm' for a long time by those who were on this raid. Even when I came back to the Pacific Theatre, flying from New Guinea, Darwin and Moretai, I never flew in such a storm. (Flying Officer C. R. Johnson, 156 Squadron)

The storm caused many crews to give up. Sometimes the decision was taken quickly – often by the more experienced pilots – bomb-loads were dumped and the bombers returned home to fight again another day. Other crews had the decision forced upon them by the effects of the storm.

I knew something about the inside of cu-nimbus and knew we would have to turn back. The crew, however, had been so jubilant over this being the last trip of their tour that they were going to be sick to death if we aborted so I thought I would prod on for a bit and let them see for themselves that we were not turning back for nothing. This was stupid, especially as I went on further than intended. We entered a boiling cauldron in company with St Elmo and soon I was calling on the rest of the saints to get us out of it. Lightning was flashing all around and one blinding flash shot across the nose, lighting up a most awesome-looking cavern down to our right. We were tossed about almost out of control. Turning, in the accepted sense, was impossible and I had to jink and jerk on to something like the reciprocal, praying all the time that the fins and rudders would not float off and leave us.

The crew were suitably impressed; all I heard on the intercom were several 'Jesuses' from Paddy the bomb aimer. After a lot more hammering and buffeting, we came out of it. (Pilot Officer J. H. Ratcliff, 103 Squadron)

The poor old Halifax was now really struggling and, very soon, the whole airframe seemed to be shuddering and everything started to rattle. At around 15,000 feet, the gallant aircraft finally gave up the ghost and just would not go any higher. By now, icing was extremely severe and all the controls appeared to have seized up. Anyway, the Hally decided it didn't much like the situation and, so, it started to come down again rather too quickly. Indeed, we were in a very steep dive and I suppose that I thought it too low for comfort. We jettisoned and the Halifax did level off. Maybe Tommy managed a minor miracle somehow – he was quite capable of the odd miracle. And so, thankful to be at least still airborne, we returned – greatly shaken and bitterly dejected – to base. (Sergeant O. E. Burger, 77 Squadron)

I have never been as scared in my life and never will be again. I sat there, petrified, then called to the skipper, 'For Christ's sake, get out of this.' He started to climb more steeply but, as the Stirling's ceiling was only 15,000 feet loaded, we reached our maximum height and we were still in cloud. Suddenly, we started icing up. The wings of the kite were a white sheet. Great chunks of ice were flying from the propellers and hitting the fuselage like machine-gun fire. Then the port wing went down and we started dropping like a stone. After what seemed a lifetime, I heard a distant voice whisper, 'Jettison. Jettison.' I have prayed very few times in my life but this occasion was one of them and, thank heaven, someone was listening. (Sergeant C. C. Leeming, 620 Squadron)

Many of the bombers forced to turn back in this way jettisoned their bombs in haphazard manner but others made a definite bombing run on to what they believed to be a useful target after they had emerged from the worst of the storm. Cuxhaven, Bremerhaven, Bremen, Bremervörde, Wilhelmshaven and Heligoland were all bombed in this way. Bremen collected the most bombs – at least twenty loads – and ten people were killed there but its Flak defences shot down a 405 Squadron Halifax. A direct hit on a searchlight position at Cuxhaven killed six German soldiers and one Stirling released its entire load of incendiaries over a ship off the German coast that had dared to open fire at the bomber. 'I bet those guys below wondered what was coming off when they heard that full load whistling down.' Squadron records show that 102 bombers jettisoned their bombs in the sea – some through normal mechanical difficulties but most because of the storm; 106 more jettisoned over some part of Germany before reaching the target area and eighty bombed alternative targets. But just over 400 bombers persisted, ploughing on through the storm and hoping to reach Hamburg.

At least four and possibly five bombers did not survive the storm. A 214 Squadron Stirling, with its lower ceiling, suffered the freezing up of its controls just before crossing the coast. The entire crew baled out into the sea.* A 419 Squadron Halifax developed thick icing on its wings but its mainly Canadian crew voted to press on to the target area which they thought they could see ahead. Only three men managed to bale out when the pilot, Sergeant J. S. Sobin, suddenly found his plane beyond his control. A 115 Squadron Lancaster blew up, probably when struck by lightning, and scattered its wreckage and dead crew members over three German parishes. The other two losses were both caused by the dangerous icing that could develop so quickly when an aircraft flew into the upper levels of a thunderstorm cloud. Fortunate survivors from those two crews can tell their own stories:

The navigator said that we should have been on the target five minutes earlier but could see nothing. The pilot said he would fly

---

* There is an interesting account from a survivor of this plane but its inclusion here would throw this chapter out of balance. It is included later as a separate item.

on one more minute on that course and, then, if there was no sign of the target, he would make one wide circle and, if we couldn't find the target during that, we would drop the bombs and go home.

Half a minute later, we heard the pilot shouting, 'My God! Ice! Jump! For goodness' sake, jump!' Being cautious by nature, I shouted, 'Are we still all right?' I had heard of cases where the rear gunner had jumped too early and the plane had come back without him. There was no reply and, suddenly, there was a horrible crash and I felt that I was spinning round, still in the turret. The weight of the ice on the structure of the fuselage, already damaged by the earlier night-fighter attack and the Flak, had broken the plane up into three pieces. The bomb aimer told me, later, that he reckoned there were about five tons of ice. He had seen that the wings were just like solid square blocks of it. Flying Officer Smyk was a very good pilot and I think that, if the ice had been forming for some time, he would have noticed it. I think it formed in a few seconds. I opened the door of the turret, threw myself back and that is the last I remember until I was only about 150 yards from the ground.

The bomb aimer and the wireless operator were both in the middle of the plane when it broke up and they simply fell out and opened their parachutes. The bomb aimer told me that he had been taken by the Germans to identify the body of the pilot and of the navigator in the front part of the fuselage. He found the pilot still strapped in his seat but the navigator had his parachute on. He thought the navigator had stayed in and tried to help the pilot. They were close friends. (Sergeant A. Jaremko, 300 Squadron)

The other icing loss was that of a Pathfinder Halifax.

All at once, the whole aircraft started shuddering and the back of my turret was blotted out with ice. I turned the turret round and, just for a few seconds, I could see the wings covered with ice and the props were sailing round like white windmills. Then, my view was blotted out again.

The aircraft was losing flying speed and I felt it stall. I got out of the turret quickly to get my 'chute, for I felt we were not going to get out of this, and I was no sooner inside the fuselage when we went into a spin. The G force was very strong; I could not even lift my arm. I was in the centre section at this time and I felt someone kicking to get to the exit but he was pinned down like me. The spin seemed to go on for hours but, then, there was a crash and everything was thrown about.

When I came round, the thing I was most aware of was the silence and I felt very tired and fell asleep, as I thought. I suppose I passed out. When I came round, the second time, it was daylight and I saw that I was sitting in a heap of wreckage and Bert, the engineer, was lying beside me. I could not move but I heard someone talking outside and gave a shout. They were German soldiers and they came and lifted Bert and me out of the remains of the Halifax. I remember cursing them for lifting me by the legs because they were fractured. The soldiers put us down in a field about a hundred yards from the wreckage and I saw that the part I had been in was just the two wings and centre section. The Target Indicators were hanging out and the petrol tanks were right above them. How the lot did not blow up, I'll never know.

Bert was moaning pretty bad and I held his head off the ground. He gave up, finally, and died in my arms. We had drunk quite a lot of beer together, Bert and I, but no more for him and not for me either in the near future. I learned later that the rest of my crew had been killed in the crash, which did not surprise me as the wreckage was scattered across three fields. (Sergeant A. Stephen, 35 Squadron)

The storm area measured at least eighty miles across. It was, of course, the storm which had been seen and reported by the weather-reconnaissance Mosquito the previous evening. The storm conditions reached all the way to Hamburg and they ruined any chance that the remaining bombers might have had of achieving a concentrated bombing attack. Although 423 bombers reported that they had bombed in the Hamburg area, only a small proportion of their bombs could have hit the city.

The attack never achieved the form of a properly conducted Bomber Command raid. The first crews claiming to bomb Hamburg were those of two Canadian Halifaxes which should have been in the second wave of the Main Force bombing ten minutes after Zero Hour. These Canadians bombed thirteen minutes *before* Zero Hour. Many of the Pathfinders did not drop their Target Indicators because of an uncertainty over their position at the time of bombing. The markers that were dropped usually disappeared into cloud although a Bomber Command report on the raid says that green Target Indicators were visible for two short periods totalling twelve minutes during the forty-nine-minute desig-nated bombing period. Skymarkers, the small reserve parachute markers carried by the Pathfinders in case of cloudy weather, were notoriously inaccurate and their use also depended on the marker crews being sure of their positions. Most Main Force aircraft dropped their bombs on dead reckoning or on the glow of fires seen through the clouds. Some steadfast crews remained for up to half an hour in 'the target area', trying to find Hamburg. It was a strange scene – thick cloud, but with deep chasms and valleys lit by flashes of vivid lightning, Flak, searchlights sometimes finding small gaps in the clouds, bombs exploding, the occasional glimpse of a beautiful Target Indicator cascading. One man remembers the scene as 'an exhilarating experience . . . like an inferno in the clouds'. Another says, 'Thunderstorms and aircraft don't mix well at the best of times but fill the storm with Flak, tracer and searchlights – everything but the kitchen sink – and it sure was one hell of an experience.'

Eight bombers were destroyed over that sixty-mile-wide area round Hamburg that could be considered 'the target area' on that night. Two were definitely victims of the Flak, which was taking advantage of the scattered bomber-stream to engage individual targets by radar-predicted fire. One was definitely a fighter victim; a German report says that the wreckage of the fuselage was riddled with bullet holes. The exact cause of the loss of the other five bombers is not known; there were no survivors. The storm may have accounted for some of them although single-engined Wild Boar fighters claimed two victories.

There is evidence available to show where some of the bombs fell. It is clear from German reports, and from the positions at which bombers found themselves when they got reliable 'fixes' on their return flights, that many of those crews which bombed 'Hamburg' by dead reckoning actually bombed well south of the city. A large number of bombs fell into the countryside in the Stade, Buchholz and Lüneburg areas. Very few people were killed by these bombs, most of which fell in fields and woods. It will never be known how many bombers found the true position of Hamburg. Only eleven crews brought back bombing photographs whose position could be identified and the results of these were not of much help, varying as they did between the photograph of a location twenty miles south-west of Hamburg and another which was twenty-seven miles north of the city. The closest photograph to the Aiming Point was that of a 7 Squadron Pathfinder crew. Flight Sergeant D. A. Routen, flying a Stirling, bravely descended to 5,500 feet to place his Target

Indicators three and a half miles north of the Aiming Point.

The reader may remember that Harburg, the town south of Hamburg but officially part of the main city, had been originally chosen as the Aiming Point for the second part of the raid but that this plan had been abandoned. Ironically, Harburg now received many of the bombs intended for Hamburg, although the bombing was never heavy and no concentrated damage was caused. The Hamburg Chief of Police report contains an indignant passage about a fire unit called to a fire at the Noblee & Thorl vegetable-oil works and the neighbouring Phoenix rubber factory, both in the Wilstorfer Strasse in Harburg. The gates of both premises were found to be locked and the night-watchman of the oil works, when roused, even denied there was a fire in his premises. The report passes scathing comment on the absence from both places of the factory fire-fighting teams which should have been on duty. One team was found in a nearby public shelter and the second in a village several kilometres away. Even when these men did arrive, they were accused of standing around in the heavy rain, content to watch the regular firemen put out their fires.

There were many scattered bombing incidents in the main city of Hamburg. There was no recognizable main bombing area and some of the bombs fell into districts which had been destroyed in previous raids. Many fires were started but they were rarely large ones and the fire units, helped by the torrential rain lashing down over the city, soon had them all under control. The biggest fire was at the City Opera House in Altona but, although the auditorium was burnt out, the stage area was saved as also was a large stock of Hamburg's bread ration which had been stored in the building. The Chief of Police's report states that casualties in Hamburg from this raid 'were small', which is another way of saying that his department was still so busy with other work that no effort could be devoted to compiling a casualty list for what was only a minor episode during the battle.

Many R.A.F. crews reported that, after bombing on a dead-reckoning position, they came to an area free of cloud where a considerable raid was taking place. They believed this to be Hamburg but it is more likely that they were watching the partial destruction of Elmshorn, a small town twelve miles north-west of Hamburg. An unconfirmed German report says that events here had started with a flash of lightning striking a house and setting it on fire. It was assumed that the fire had attracted the bombers. Another report, which gives the estimated numbers of the different kinds of R.A.F. bombs dropped on Elmshorn, leads to the conclusion that as many as seventy bombers may have attacked this town. Elmshorn contained many refugees from Hamburg and some of these were probably among the fifty-seven people killed that night. The death toll also included nine prisoners of war although their nationality is not recorded. German reports talk of Elmshorn being '50 per cent destroyed'; it is certain that 254 houses were destroyed and 202 seriously damaged, with four small commercial premises being hit.

R.A.F. bombing caused damage and casualties in a host of other communities that night. Deaths occurred in at least thirteen places outside Hamburg, in an area reaching from Bremen, fifty-five miles south-west of Hamburg, to Kiel, a similar distance to the north. Some of the bombing in this extensive area was that of crews which had deliberately flown off to find an alternative target but much of it was by other crews that had been unable to find Hamburg in the storm.

The last aircraft to bomb in the target area was a Wellington captained by Flight Lieutenant J. C. Morton, of 466 Squadron, whose bomb aimer released his load of incendiaries at 2.55 a.m.

Because of the storm, the return flight of the bomber crews was potentially a dangerous one. Many aircraft were suffering from mechanical problems. The bomber-stream was well scattered and it never managed to close up again; in particular, many crews were well south of their intended position and would not be able to correct this until they started to pick up Gee signals on approaching England. Eleven more bombers were lost during this homeward flight. One of these losses was of a mainly Canadian-crewed Halifax of the Pathfinders which had two failed engines because of the storm. The navigator soon calculated that, because of its gradually failing height, the bomber would never reach England. After polling his crew, the English pilot, Sergeant J. A. Phillips, D.F.M., flew to the southern tip of Sweden and the crew, with varying degrees of enthusiasm, baled out into the night. They all landed safely in farmland near Malmö, from where they proceeded to a mild form of internment at the hands of the neutral Swedes and eventual repatriation to fly with Bomber Command again.

Sergeant Phillips and his crew were lucky. Only one man survived from the other ten bombers lost on the return flight. A Stirling and a Dornier 217 night fighter are believed to have collided in the storm area near the mouth of the River Elbe. One German was injured when the fighter crashed but the Stirling crew, which included three New Zealanders, all died. At least four bombers were attacked as they left the German coast. Three were shot down and the fourth came home with a dead tail gunner. The remaining six bomber victims were shot down in all too familiar circumstances – the bombers straying south of their correct routes and flying through the ground-controlled night-fighter boxes on the Dutch coast which were manned by the experienced crews of NJG 1. Three German pilots – Hauptmann Jabs, Oberleutnant Greiner and Oberfeldwebel Scherfling, all from IV/NJG 1 based at Leeuwarden airfield – easily snapped up these six bombers using the standard box-interception technique. Jabs scored three times, in twenty-two minutes, and Greiner twice. Hermann Greiner, in a letter, expresses surprise that his victims should be attempting to cross 'élite boxes of the German night-fighter force' without the protection of Window. 'It would have been worth their while to have kept a few kilos of these strips of paper as a life insurance.' The truth is that, unless they were deliberately taking short cuts, the crews of these bombers believed themselves to be many miles to the north and they had stopped Windowing some time earlier. One bomber was shot down eighty-five miles south of its designated route! Sergeant Peter Swan, bomb aimer in a 44 Squadron Lancaster shot down into shallow water inside the Frisian Islands, was the only survivor of this last series of blows by the Luftwaffe. After four hours in the water, he was rescued by a small German naval vessel and he remembers the great kindness with which he was treated by the German sailors.

There were two sets of personal coincidences in the deaths of four Canadian airmen in bombers shot down after leaving the German coast. Flying Officer Ernest Kirkham, from

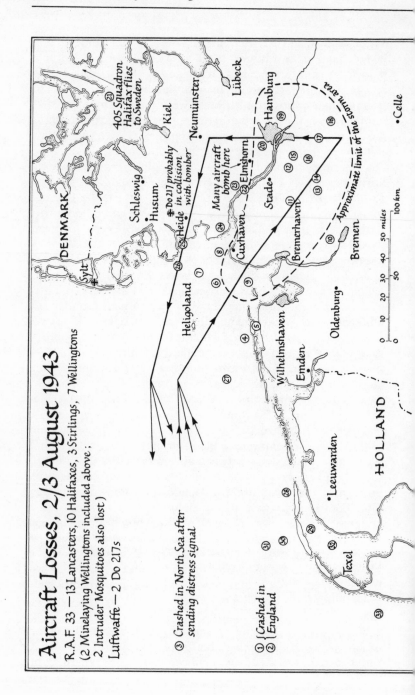

Aircraft Losses, 2/3 August 1943

R.A.F. 33 — 13 Lancasters, 10 Halifaxes, 3 Stirlings, 7 Wellingtons
(2 Minelaying Wellingtons included above;
2 Intruder Mosquitoes also lost)
Luftwaffe — 2 Do 217s

① { Crashed in
② { England

③ Crashed in North Sea after
sending distress signal

405 Squadron
Halifax flies
to Sweden

Do 217 probably
in collision
with bomber

Many aircraft
bomb here

Approximate limit of the storm area

DENMARK

Sylt

Schleswig
Husum
Heide

Kiel

Neumünster

Lübeck

Hamburg

Elmshorn

Stade

Cuxhaven

Bremerhaven

Bremen

Heligoland

Wilhelmshaven

Emden

Oldenburg

Leeuwarden

Texel

HOLLAND

Celle

0   10   20   30   40   50 miles
0   50   100 km

Vancouver, was a navigator in the 44 Squadron Lancaster from which Sergeant Swan survived. His younger brother, Sergeant Thomas Kirkham, was the tail gunner in a 432 Squadron Wellington which also went down into the sea. They were flying their fourth and fifth operations respectively.

Flying Officers Lennie Rogers and Harvey Funkhouser had been school friends in the little industrial town of Port Colborne, Ontario, had been leading members of their high-school football team, had joined the R.C.A.F. within two weeks of each other in 1940, had both trained as pilots, had each been kept back as instructors at the same training airfield in Canada for more than a year, had sailed for England together, had been posted with their newly formed crews to 428 Squadron at Middleton St George on the same day and, on this night, had been making their regulation 'second pilot' trips with two of the squadron's more experienced crews. Like the Kirkham brothers, the two friends both died in the North Sea. The family of Flying Officer Rogers had lost another son over the North Sea four months earlier.

It was probably a Stirling of 75 (New Zealand) Squadron, captained by an English pilot, Sergeant Cyril Bailie, which was the last British bomber victim of the Battle of Hamburg when it was shot down by Hauptmann Jabs twenty-five miles north of Terschelling at 3.51 a.m.

It was a very tired and relieved batch of R.A.F. men who sighted the coast of England in clear weather and prepared to land. The mixed-nationality crew of this Halifax had been arguing about which of them came from the finest country. A Canadian, a New Zealander, an Australian and a Northern Irishman had each had their say.

But the two Englishmen said nothing. They had no need to. All the crew saw the sun rise as we arrived above our Yorkshire base after the rough trip over Germany and must have been thinking, as we taxied to dispersal, 'This is God's country today'. (Flight Sergeant D. E. Girardau, 10 Squadron)

Many crews had difficult return flights because of storm damage to their aircraft but, surprisingly, none of these came down in the sea and there were no serious landing accidents. After they had landed, there was much grumbling among aircrew about the failure of meteorological officers to warn them properly of the storm and a rumour soon started circulating that the weather-reconnaissance Mosquito crew, sent out the previous evening, had not carried out their flight properly. This Pathfinder navigator has recorded his feelings after the raid.

I was tired, cold, depressed and feeling dirty. There was not even the consolation of the traditional tot of rum as our wretched doctor had had it stopped some time previously.

On entering debriefing, there was awaiting us the spruce, alert figure of Air Vice-Marshal Bennett. He was not interested in our trials and tribulations, only why had I said that icing had caused the H2S to fail? I was very irritated and felt with Hotspur when he said:

To see him shine so brisk and smell so sweet,
And talk so like a waiting-gentlewoman
Of guns, and drums, and wounds – God save the mark!

Unlike Hotspur, I kept quiet. My thoughts were undoubtedly unfair but I have never forgotten. (Flight Lieutenant J. Annetts, 35 Squadron)

It had been 75 (New Zealand) Squadron at Mepal who had sent off the first aircraft in the Battle of Hamburg, nine nights earlier. It was the same squadron who greeted the last aircraft to return. Pilot Officer Clifford Logan, an Australian, landed his Stirling safely at 6.30 a.m.*

The final R.A.F. raid in the Battle of Hamburg had been a sour and costly anti-climax for Bomber Command. Total R.A.F. losses for the night had been two aircraft crashed and thirty-three missing, including two Mosquito Intruders and a Wellington minelaying in the River Elbe. In return for this heavy loss of aircraft and aircrew, no serious damage had been caused to Hamburg or any other place in Germany with the exception of the unfortunate town of Elmshorn. The only certain Luftwaffe casualties were the Dornier 217 that had collided with a bomber, another which had been damaged by an Intruder and two Junkers 88s whose crews had suffered landing mishaps because of the stormy weather conditions.

* Pilot Officer Logan and all his crew were killed on 23 September 1943 while raiding Mannheim but the Stirling in which he returned from Hamburg, EE 881, survived the war, serving with 75 Squadron until June 1944 and then with a training unit.

NOTES

1. Public Record Office AIR 14/779.
2. Public Record Office AIR 14/3410.
3. Report of Proceedings, Convoy FS.83, Public Record Office ADM 199/565.
4. Public Record Office AIR 14/391.

18

The Reckoning

Although the R.A.F.'s fourth raid on Hamburg had quite clearly not been a success, Sir Arthur Harris made no attempt to mount another raid to make up for the failure. The Battle of Hamburg was over. It had been R.A.F. Bomber Command that had taken the initiative in planning and preparing this sustained attack on one city and, in the analysis of the results, the costs and the effects of the battle, it is convenient that the R.A.F. operational effort should be studied first. One point is worth repeating. Except for the introduction of Window, the R.A.F. raids on Hamburg were routine ones in every way. Ordinary aircrew, flying the standard aircraft in use at that time, without special training, bombs or tactics, had carried out one of the most dramatic actions of the strategic-bombing war.

A total of 3,091 R.A.F. bomber sorties had been dispatched in the four raids and 2,592 of these had dropped 8,344 tons of bombs in the Hamburg area.

Night	High Explosives	Incendiaries	Total
24–25 July	1,346 tons	938 tons	2,284 tons
27–28 July	1,127 tons	1,199 tons	2,326 tons
29–30 July	1,094 tons	1,224 tons	2,318 tons
2–3 August	676 tons	740 tons	1,416 tons
TOTAL	4,243 tons	4,101 tons	8,344 tons*

* Aircraft believed to have bombed before being shot down have been included but tonnages of Target Indicators and flares, which were added in as 'incendiaries' in Bomber Command figures, are not included.

The results of the raids were both a success and also a justification for – in the technical sense – Area Bombing. Large quantities of those 8,344 tons of bombs did not fall near the designated Aiming Points. In not one of the four nights was there any really concentrated bombing in that area of Hamburg chosen for attack on that night. But, because

Hamburg was such a large city, other areas of it had received the bombs instead. The Battle of Hamburg had been a success because of a long spell of fine flying weather, because of Hamburg's situation near the German coast and on a very wide river which helped the Pathfinders to use their radar sets more profitably, because Sir Arthur Harris was prepared to persevere until a sufficient tonnage of bombs had been dropped and because he applied the strict principle of Area Bombing – that is, that the most densely built-up areas of a large city should be attacked and destroyed by fire. Subsidiary factors were the exceptionally dry weather, which helped to produce the firestorm, and the use of Window which helped the bomber force to arrive at the city and fly over it in relatively unharassed manner. It was very rare for the R.A.F. to find such a favourable set of conditions for night bombing.

The operational success, and the cost of it, had been shared by all of the groups and all of the types of aircraft in Bomber Command as the following tables show.

Group	Sorties	Bombed Hamburg Area (%)		Aircraft Missing (%)	
1	620	521	(84·0)	19	(3·1)
3	493	395	(80·1)	13	(2·6)
4	656	567	(86·4)	18	(2·7)
5	577	512	(88·7)	16	(2·8)
6 (Canadian)	306	238	(77·8)	8	(2·6)
8 (Pathfinder)	439	359	(81·8)	13	(3·0)
TOTAL	3,091	2,592	(83·9)	87	(2·8)

Aircraft Type	Sorties	Bombed Hamburg Area (%)		Missing (%)	
Lancasters	1,369	1,172	(85·6)	39	(2·8)
Halifaxes	971	803	(82·7)	29	(3·0)
Stirlings	468	378	(80·8)	11	(2·4)
Wellingtons	283	239	(84·5)	8	(2·8)
TOTAL	3,091	2,592	(83·9)	87	(2·8)

Of the aircraft which failed to bomb in the Hamburg area, 227 – 7·3 per cent of all sorties dispatched – had to return early because of mechanical troubles and 199 attacked alternative targets or jettisoned their bombs over Germany, mostly during the storm in the last raid. The lower bombing figures for 6 Group should not be held against the Canadians; this was a relatively new group still establishing itself. The best squadron bombing results were obtained by 466 (Australian) Squadron at Leconfield, with all but one of the fifty-five sorties of their faithful old Wellingtons claiming to have bombed the target. There is little to be gained in comparisons between the losses of the different types of aircraft except to say that the lower height at which the Stirlings flew probably gave them more protection from Window. The squadrons suffering the heaviest losses were 102 and 103 Squadrons, which lost five Halifaxes from eighty-six sorties and five Lancasters from 102 sorties respectively. By contrast, nine squadrons went through the four Hamburg raids without loss of any aircraft or crew member. In addition to the eighty-seven aircraft missing, nine other planes – four Stirlings, two Lancasters, two Wellingtons and a Halifax – were written off after either take-off or landing crashes or after suffering severe battle damage. Four more lost aircraft should also be attributed to the Battle of Hamburg. Of the six Wellingtons which had been sent each night to lay mines in the River Elbe while the bombers were raiding Hamburg, one had crashed on take-off and one was missing after crashing in the sea, and two Fighter Command Mosquitoes had been lost in Intruder operations which were in direct support to the Hamburg raids. These further casualties bring the number of R.A.F. aircraft lost to exactly 100 and the number of crews missing to ninety. A total of 552 British and Allied airmen were killed during the R.A.F. night operations of the Battle of Hamburg.* Sixty-five more became prisoners of war and seven were interned in Sweden.

The German defences had not been disgraced, despite the difficulties heaped upon them by Window. The best estimate of the cause of loss of the eighty-seven missing R.A.F. bombers is as follows:

By night-fighter attack	59
By Flak damage	11

* The dead were: United Kingdom, 421; Canadian, 65; Australian, 32; New Zealand, 16; Polish, 7; American, 2; Rhodesian, 2; South African, 2; and one each from Norway, Ceylon, Trinidad, Chile and Argentina.

By Flak and night fighter combined	3
By icing or storm damage	6
By mechanical failure	1
By unknown cause	7

In return, R.A.F. bombers claimed twelve German night fighters destroyed and three more probables. Luftwaffe records confirm the loss of five fighters to bomber action: two Dornier 217s and one Messerschmitt 110 of the conventional night-fighter force and one Focke Wulf 190 and one Messerschmitt 109 of the single-engined Wild Boar force. Three more night fighters – a Dornier 217, a Junkers 88 and a Messerschmitt 110 – were destroyed by Intruders. Only eight German night-fighter aircrew were killed during the Battle of Hamburg.

It is impossible to say exactly how many aircraft and crews had been saved by Window. Bomber Command's average loss against Hamburg in the previous six heavy raids on that city had been 6·1 per cent. If this figure is used, 188 aircraft and crews might have been lost if Window had not been used and the device may thus have saved 101 bombers during the four raids. But this is not a valid conclusion. The increasing number of bombers being pushed through the German night-fighter box system or through the Flak defences of the target area at the time of the Battle of Hamburg would probably have reduced the proportion of aircraft missing to well below the old 6·1 per cent loss rate. The true saving that can be credited to Window was probably between forty and sixty aircraft and crews.

The introduction of Window had, on the face of it, brought this major improvement in Bomber Command's casualty rate but there are some strongly held views in Germany that Window actually brought the R.A.F. more long-term harm than benefit. The development of the countermoves first seen during the Battle of Hamburg – the releasing of fighters from the close confines of the boxes to a freelance role and the provision of a running commentary for those fighters – proceeded apace in coming weeks. Many Luftwaffe men had wanted such changes to take place earlier but it had taken the shock of Window to force the change upon higher commanders. The new tactics, of very loose control and freedom of action for individual night fighters – the so-called *Zahme Sau* or Tame Boar tactics – were very flexible and they soon became successful, particularly when the night fighters were fitted with a new form of airborne radar, the SN-2. Unlike the old *Lichtenstein* radar, this was not affected by Window. Severe losses were inflicted on R.A.F. night bombers during the next nine months by these new tactics. There is certainly some case for saying that, if the R.A.F. had left well alone and not introduced Window, the German commanders might never have abandoned the box system as their principal means of defence and that the R.A.F. losses would ultimately have been less.

It is an interesting and, it must be admitted, a partially valid argument. The unknown factor is how long without the impact made by Window the German commanders would have resisted the pressure by front-line officers to adopt new tactics. But was the Luftwaffe night-fighter force so deplorably led that improvements in tactics would not have come soon anyway? The growing strength of available fighters would have probably forced at least a dual system – the box method and the freelancing one – to be employed and, then, the benefits of the latter should have become obvious. But one never knows in war. The Luftwaffe might not have advanced without the spur of Window and it is possible that Window did cause a greater loss of bombers than it saved. Yet there were other benefits from that device outside the night-fighter versus bomber context. The German Flak never made a complete recovery from the Window setback and Window also became a very useful decoy device, allowing small groups of bombers carrying out spoof raids to appear much more numerous than their actual strength.

Turning to the activities of the American bombers which took part in the Battle of Hamburg, one is immediately forced to the conclusion that, however well intentioned the American effort and interesting their methods, the U.S.A.A.F. role in the Battle of Hamburg was a modest one. Their available strength of heavy bombers was less than half that of the British and, even then, the Americans attempted to attack four targets each day – two in Hamburg and two elsewhere – while the R.A.F. concentrated all their strength at one point. Using only 40 per cent of their available force, the Americans sent 252 Fortresses to Hamburg in two days. Of these, 146 dropped 306 tons of bombs into the city and seventeen bombed elsewhere. Even this modest tonnage might have achieved a major success for the American daylight-bombing methods if they had not had the bad fortune to find all the primary targets on their first raid affected by smoke from the R.A.F. bombing. It is not surprising that the Americans gave up attacking Hamburg for the time being and took themselves off to other targets in Germany. Not the least valuable of the experience gained by the Americans during the Battle of Hamburg was the lesson that, because of such smoke, they should not normally attempt to follow R.A.F. Bomber Command in attacking a target.

The price the Americans paid for their involvement in the Battle of Hamburg was seventeen Fortresses lost – a casualty rate of 6·7 per cent, nearly two and a half times that of the R.A.F. night raids! But the American daylight operations to Hamburg were far less lethal in the proportion of crew members killed in those bombers that were shot down. Forty-six Americans died but 106 survived to become prisoners of war and twenty more were rescued from the sea and brought back to England.

The American formations attacking Hamburg had defended themselves well from German fighter attack. Most of their losses had started with bombers being hit and damaged by Flak, leaving them as stragglers and vulnerable to subsequent fighter attack. Only five of the seventeen losses were due solely to German fighters. American bomber gunners put in claims for forty-three German fighters destroyed. The true figure was probably six, with one German pilot being killed.

In an early chapter of this book, I attempted to show how the Battle of Hamburg would really be a contest between the Allied bomber forces and the civilian population of Hamburg. It is hoped that subsequent chapters will have provided the reader with a description of that contest and it is intended, here, to give no more than a summary of the human casualties and material destruction in the city.

Early rumours put the death toll in Hamburg as 100,000 but this exaggerated figure was soon abandoned and 60,000 was the one more often quoted in early post-war books. But this, too, did not bear the more careful scrutiny that was imposed with the passage of time and it is now accepted that approximately 44,600 civilians died in Hamburg; the bodies of 42,600 were buried but some 2,000 more were never found. To this can be added a figure of about 800 servicemen killed while in the city; the Wehrmacht alone reported 442 men killed or missing. This brings the total death roll to 45,400, but there are elements of estimation in most of the figures used and it might be sufficient to say that 'approximately 45,000' people died. It is probable that 40,000 of these deaths occurred in the firestorm which took place during the second R.A.F. raid. By contrast, less than 1 per cent of the deaths were caused by the two American raids.

Hans Brunswig[1] quotes an interesting report which states that 15,802 of the dead were identified in the following proportions: women, 50 per cent; men, 38 per cent; children, 12 per cent. If this proportion is applied to the total dead, it might be assumed that the fatal casualties were divided as follows: women, 22,500; men, 17,100; and children, 5,400.

A high proportion of the male dead would have been elderly men, above military age. A few of the dead would have been foreign workers, but there are no reports of any foreign-labour camps being seriously hit in the raids. In addition to the dead, 37,214 injured people were taken to dressing stations or hospitals and an unknown further number fled the city without seeking treatment for their injuries.

If comparisons are sought, I would not be the first person to compare Hamburg's death roll of 45,000 to the total of 51,509 civilians killed in the United Kingdom by German bombing during the whole of the Second World War. The number dead in the Battle of Hamburg was only exceeded during the war in Europe by the R.A.F. and American raids on Dresden in February 1945. The only other example of conventional bombing to produce more dead than Hamburg was the U.S.A.A.F. incendiary air attack on Tokyo during the night of 9–10 March 1945 which killed nearly twice as many people as did the six raids of the Battle of Hamburg!

Hamburg's agony in July 1943 was terrible enough without some of the rumours or exaggerations that were later put into print. The worst of these was in 1950 when an Italian author, Curzio Malaparte, devoted ten pages of a book[2] to a gruesome description of how a large number of Hamburg civilians suffering from phosphorus burns sought relief in the waterways of the city. Malaparte told how, as soon as these people emerged from the water, the phosphorus on their skin burst into flame again and the sufferers had to go back into the water. Most of these people had died after one week but several hundred unfortunates survived in half crazed and desperately painful condition. At this time, wrote Malaparte, the area was cleared of civilians. Police and soldiers in boats then went among the wounded, putting them out of their misery by shooting or by smashing in their skulls with oars when the pistol ammunition was exhausted.

The story was repeated ten years later by an American author, Martin Caidin, in his book *The Night Hamburg Died*.[3] Caidin narrows down the scene of this tragedy to the Alster lake and describes the suffering of 'several hundred people' on whom 'particles of phosphorus splattered in a great shower'. He makes no mention of Malaparte's book but writes of his own years of research, of his contacts in Hamburg who 'swear to the authenticity of the story', and to an officer in the United States Army 'who learned that portions of the documents on the aftereffects of the Hamburg attacks were ordered to be destroyed and all references to the surviving victims of phosphorus burns stricken forever from the records'. No German contributors are acknowledged in Caidin's book and the American officer is not named.

In following up this story, I asked many questions on this subject in Hamburg. Several policemen and senior officials were among my contacts, perhaps the one who would have been closest to any such incident being Herr Heinz Bumann, former adjutant to Chief of Police Kehrl. I drew only vehement and shocked denials that anything of the sort ever happened. Hans Brunswig, a senior fire officer in Hamburg at that time who would certainly have known of the incident if it had occurred, also denies this terrible story vigorously in his more recent book, *Feuersturm über Hamburg*. I am pleased to support Brunswig's contention that this incident never occurred.

The report of the Chief of Police carefully lists the destruction of property in his domain. In the administrative city of Hamburg, which included the virtually undamaged township of Harburg, 35,719 (29 per cent) of the 122,323 residential buildings were destroyed and a further 5,666 severely damaged. But, when Harburg is left out of the reckoning and when the number of buildings affected is converted into numbers of 'family-dwelling units', mostly the flats or apartments in which the average Hamburg family lived, the figures for destruction take on a new aspect. The main city had contained 450,800 of these 'dwelling units' and the bombing destroyed no less than 253,400, or 56 per cent, of these. It is small wonder that 900,000 people lost their homes and had to be rehoused somewhere at much expense to Germany's war effort. Churches, museums, libraries, hospitals, schools, theatres and cinemas were all among the 436 public buildings of a non-military nature destroyed or damaged by the bombing.

Some districts of Hamburg had suffered near total destruction. Notable among these were Hammerbrook, Eilbek and Barmbek, which had been hit so hard in the second and third R.A.F. raids. Inhabitants of Hamburg often comment that the R.A.F. bombed the most anti-Nazi areas in the city and spared the most pro-Nazi ones. This comment is partially true. In particular, the wealthy district of Rotherbaum, on the west bank of the Alster and where all the Nazi leaders had their homes and offices, had hardly been touched. 'Very clever', said the Germans. 'The R.A.F. spared the best areas so that the British Army could use the buildings there after the war.' This was not true. Rotherbaum would have been in the centre of the bombing area if the plans for the last two R.A.F. raids had not been affected, firstly by a strong crosswind and then by a storm. The sad fact is that densely populated working areas like Hammerbrook, Billwärder Ausschlag, Barmbek and Altona, which had shown little support for the Nazis, burned particularly well when hit by concentrations of incendiary bombs sometimes intended for other districts.

When one comes to catalogue the commercial and industrial damage caused by the bombing, one meets at least two difficulties. The Chief of Police's report contains long and impressive lists of such premises suffering 'total', 'severe' or 'light' damage and it quotes production losses which are often classed as '100 per cent'. The following résumé of destroyed or damaged premises is based on the report.[4]

Industrial and war-industry firms	580
Warehouses	7
Office buildings	379
Commercial premises (mostly shops etc.)	2,632
Banks, insurance offices etc.	88
Public utility premises	13
Transport premises	13
Public offices	145
Nazi Party offices	112
Military premises	80
Police, fire and civil-defence premises	197
Bridges	12

The first difficulty here is that the report makes no attempt to allocate the damage to individual raids, so that there is no way of telling how effective the American raids were. A second problem is that some of the officials compiling the report may have exaggerated the extent of the damage. For example, the important Blohm & Voss U-boat yard at Steinwerder is classed as being 'severely damaged' and suffering a 70 per cent production loss for a four-month period. When these details were shown to Willy Franzenburg, the works director for that period, he said this was 'rubbish' and that such figures were produced merely to impress Berlin. It should also be borne in mind that a large number of the premises listed were very small ones. The main city of Hamburg, north of the River Elbe, may have been mainly residential but there were large numbers of small workshops of what might be called the 'back-street' variety in those residential areas. It was such premises, destroyed in large numbers by the R.A.F.'s night bombing, that produced such impressive totals of industrial damage in the police report. That is not to say, however, that the cumulative loss of production in such premises did not represent a valuable bonus for the R.A.F. bombing methods. But it is a fact that Hamburg's most important war industries, particularly her U-boat yards, were not seriously damaged. The R.A.F. bombing had never been directed on to the areas in which such industries were situated and the Americans were hampered by smoke and had not yet the numbers of bombers available to achieve the complete destruction of such targets.

But the R.A.F. bombing was meant to achieve indirect rather than direct results. There were other ways of preventing the building of U-boats, for example, than of bombing the slipway on which a U-boat was being built. Preceding chapters have illustrated the general breakdown of life in Hamburg – the destruction of services and communications, the destruction of workers' housing and the killing or putting to flight of the workers themselves. This was the industrial side of the R.A.F.'s offensive. The exact extent of such indirect loss was the subject of much investigation immediately after the war. The United States Strategic Bombing Survey and the smaller British Bombing Survey Unit both did much research in Hamburg. The general conclusion was that the Battle of Hamburg caused a loss of war production equivalent to the normal output of the entire city for 1·8 months of full production. Output returned to 80 per cent of normal within five months but full recovery was never achieved. Taking the production of U-boats, again, as a specific case, it was estimated that between twenty (the American estimate) and twenty-six or twenty-seven U-boats (the British estimate) were never produced because of the July and August 1943 bombing.

The important part about the production losses, whether of U-boats or whatever other type of war material or even of the everyday type of commercial production that a nation needs to sustain itself, was that the Hamburg losses were mainly caused by the indirect methods of the great R.A.F. raids. There are interesting figures available for the number of units of electricity consumed in the city's war industries and for the number of workers reporting at their factories. Electrical consumption in Hamburg's war industry fell by 56·9 per cent in August 1943! The following tables show the numbers of people reporting for work before and after the battle, both in the entire armaments industry of the city and in the Blohm & Voss shipyard.[5]

'Morale effect was, as to material effect, as twenty to one.'[6] So had one of the main claims for strategic bombing often been made by British air leaders before the war. Now, after the greatest blow of the bombing war so far had been struck, how had it affected the morale of the German civilians involved?

After the firestorm

30. This scene may be typical of the conditions in Hamburg streets immediately after the firestorm raid.

31. A large tree apparently uprooted by the force of the firestorm.

32–35. Those who left their shelters in the firestorm.

36 and 37. The recovery of bodies. The lower picture shows the effect of extreme heat on a body in a basement shelter.

The recovery period

38. Messages from relatives left on a lamppost in the devastated area.

39. A good example of that part of Hamburg which was completely destroyed.
Fire has burnt out most of these typically five-storeyed residential blocks
leaving outside walls standing; only a few gaps show where high-explosive
bombs have fallen. This photograph may have been taken in 1944 or even later.

40. The appearance now of one of the four mass graves in the Ohlsdorf cemetery in which the Battle of Hamburg dead were buried. Each grave is 130 metres long and sixteen metres wide and contains up to 10,000 bodies. In the centre of the four graves is the walled memorial to Hamburg's 1939–45 civilian dead. The Hammerbrook and Hamm timber signs are directly in front of the memorial.

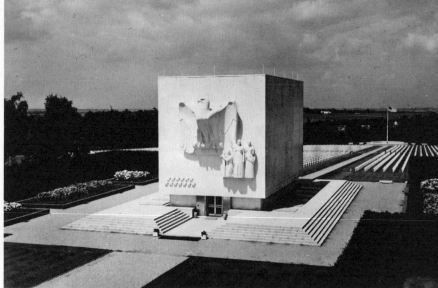

Burial places for Allied airmen of the Battle of Hamburg

△ 41. The British way. The 1939–45 plot of the British Military Cemetery, also in
Ohlsdorf cemetery. Of the 554 R.A.F. men killed in the Battle of Hamburg, 169
are buried here. A further 204 have no known grave and are commemorated on
the Runnymede Memorial for the Missing; the remainder are buried in
cemeteries close to where their aircraft crashed. British war dead always remain
in the countries in which they died.

▽ 42. The American way. America decided that none of her war dead would
be permanently buried in former enemy countries. Those bodies which were
not repatriated to the U.S.A. were thus reburied in cemeteries located in the
countries of their former Allies like the Ardennes cemetery near Liège in
Belgium shown here. Three-fifths of these graves are of dead U.S.A.A.F. men.

Workers in Hamburg's War Industries

	On 30 June 1943	On 1 October 1943	Reduction
German men	297,000	185,000	37·7 per cent
German women	271,000	121,000	55·4 per cent
Foreign men	51,000	20,300	60·2 per cent
Foreign women	15,000	5,000	66·7 per cent
Total	634,000	331,300	47·7 per cent

Workers at the Blohm & Voss Shipyard

Before the raids	9,400
After the firestorm raid	300
On 1 August	1,500
On 1 September	5,000
On 1 October	7,000
On 1 November	7,500

Before examining the effect upon Hamburg's will to carry on the war, it might be of interest to look at the extent of Allied knowledge and expectations. It was obvious, at once, from the reports of bomber crews and from photographic reconnaissance, that exceptionally severe damage had been caused. It took approximately two weeks for more precise information, including the first details of the firestorm, to reach England by means of reports from neutral countries and from various intelligence sources. The news of the firestorm was received 'with some horror' at Bomber Command Headquarters but 'they were strange days and, by the time details came through, the war had moved on and we were doing something else'. The Joint Intelligence Committee (from all three of Britain's armed services) produced a report in September 1943 which attempted to compare the situation in Germany at that time with the conditions of civil disturbance which had helped bring about the German collapse in 1918 and suggesting that there might be a similar breakdown in Germany now.

There was one man on the British side, however, who wanted something more positive to be done. Air Vice-Marshal Donald Bennett, commander of the Pathfinder Group, had been advised by his meteorological staff that the height of the cloud of smoke seen over Hamburg during the firestorm raid must have been caused by fires of 'immense intensity'.

We realized that this was the greatest raid of the war, a far more devastating thing than had ever happened in warfare before. I argued that the whole of the Gestapo grip on the population would have broken down and that the German cities in the north must have panicked with civilians fleeing the cities. Everything must have broken down.

I telephoned various people, asking why can't we take advantage of this in some way? Couldn't we offer immediate peace to Hitler, publicly, or take and hold the key points in northern Germany with parachute troops? Basically, I wanted to force a German surrender on the basis of Hamburg, telling the Germans that we were going on to continue the same treatment on other German cities. But Churchill's unconditional surrender was an obstacle to any such gambit as I was suggesting. But there is no such thing as a really unconditional surrender and that was unfortunate. We should have used that devastation to negotiate for peace. Maybe there was only one chance in twenty of it succeeding but it should have been tried. After all, they did exactly the same to the Japanese after Hiroshima and that worked.

I certainly telephoned Saundby at Bomber Command, the Directorate of Bomber Ops at Air Ministry and Cherwell, Churchill's scientific adviser; he was the main one. But I expect he just smiled and said, 'Yes, I'm sure you're right.' But nothing happened. I think I was just being tolerated.

Whether conditions were ripe for the sort of move that Air Vice-Marshal Bennett was suggesting will be discussed later but it is interesting that Herbert Heinicke, a German soldier stationed in Hamburg at that time, says that a 1,000-man strong transport unit near Fuhlsbüttel Prison, in northern Hamburg, was kept confined to barracks for several days after the worst raid. Herr Heinicke is quite sure that this unit was kept standing by in case the Allied raids were followed up by a seaborne or airborne landing and German troops had to be rushed to the scene of action. He says that other units in the area were kept in the same state of readiness and were not released for recovery and clearance work in Hamburg until it was quite clear that the exceptionally heavy raids were not to be immediately followed up with some kind of attack by Allied troops.

It is true that the raids made a deep impression on many citizens of Hamburg. It would have taken a stout heart not to be drastically affected by the destruction of one's home and possessions and the deaths, in the most pitiful circumstances, of members of families or close neighbours. Many, many people suffered a breakdown in their morale and, for a time, had little thought of loyalty to Hitler, the Nazi Party, or even to their beloved Germany. But any thoughts of open rebellion were usually short-lived and were quickly damped down. The Nazis were absolute masters of the power of propaganda and much thought was given to producing a policy that was a subtle combination of bolstering up the feelings of the civilians with just a hint of the force that could be employed if the civilians did not put their doubts behind them and resume all-out support for Germany's war effort.

The destruction in Hamburg was 'very much regretted' by the authorities but a promise was made: 'Everything will be rebuilt better than ever.' The Press, aware that the attitude of the people of Hamburg would be watched carefully by the remainder of Germany, exhorted those Hamburg people who had fled the city to give the 'correct' impression in their conversations with people outside Hamburg. It was announced that massive reprisal raids were being carried out against cities in England. For example, on 17 August, when the *Hamburg Fremdenblatt* resumed publication after a long gap caused by the raids, it reported that the Luftwaffe had just carried out heavy raids on south-east England and the Midlands and that the industrial city of Lincoln had been 'covered' with bombs. But Lincoln's civil records show that there was no damage at all in the city during the relevant night.

Behind the propaganda was the threat of force. Margot Schulz was the young woman who had watched the flight of the Hamburg bomb victims through the village of Bergedorf.

After the raids, the women used to stand in the street, talking openly against Hitler. The people who had died in the evacuation were still lying there, covered with blankets, waiting to be taken away. The women were saying such things as, 'We want the war to finish. Hitler must be possessed by the devil to allow this thing.' We were absolutely incensed at the horror we had seen. Normally, merely to say that the war was horrible could be treason and you could go to a concentration camp. Now, we were speaking quite openly and nobody took any action. That situation lasted three or four days.

Then came the anticlimax. One morning, a Hamburg newspaper appeared: 'We know what you have been through '– and so on. It was beautifully and sympathetically written. The paper said that it was known that, under stress of these sorrowing times, many things had been said that should not have been said. But, now, the paper said, we had had the opportunity to give vent to our feelings and it was time to return to the honourable position of standing behind our menfolk at the front. That morning, just after the newspapers had appeared, about six lorries appeared in the street. They were full of S.S. men standing rigidly, with rifles showing. They drove slowly up and down the street, not a smile on their faces. It was pure intimidation. We shut up completely after that.

The raids had undoubtedly shocked a large number of Hamburg people and many started to lose that great belief in ultimate victory which had sustained them through previous bad times. But this was not the Germany of 1918. There was no starvation. The German Army was still in firm control of much of its great conquered empire and was far from defeat on the battlefield. The truth is that there was never a chance of any widespread, spontaneous rebellion against the authorities. The destruction and suffering in Hamburg had been terrible but it was confined to one area of Germany and Hamburg's scattered population had neither the power nor the desire to ferment rebellion in the strange places to which many of them had fled. The people of Hamburg – whether still in their own city or in new homes – carried on, stubbornly or sullenly maybe, but their overall morale did not crack. The English experience in bombed cities had been that, provided a community was given firm authority and efficient leadership, that community's morale would hold. The people of Hamburg were given brilliant local leadership and were governed with the firmest of authority.

If anything, the bombing was often counter-productive in terms of morale. The news of what had happened in Hamburg, taken back to their units by thousands of servicemen who were allowed special leave, certainly increased the will to fight on to the end by the German forces. In Hamburg itself, though its people may have been sick at heart at the destruction of homes and the loss of life, they pulled together as they had never done before. 'The inhumanity of this kind of war drew people together. For a while we experienced the aim of the Nazis – a united population.' So writes a young man who did not support the régime and had managed to avoid serving in the Hitler Youth.

But there were others, like Louis Haupt, an ordinary Hamburger who had been a driver on the city's *U-bahn* for seventeen years. Herr Haupt had been bombed out, had suffered the death of his wife and *seven* of his children and had fled to the Sudetenland. This is how he concluded a letter written two weeks after the raids, the letter later being filed in the report of the Chief of Police.

Because I suffered such terrible losses, I asked to be allowed to stay here until the end of the war, so that I can be with my remaining children. I have found a job here with the tramcar company.

I am completely finished and desperate. These losses are too much for me to bear.[7]

NOTES

1. *Feuersturm über Hamburg*, p. 279.
2. Published in Karlsruhe as *Die Haut* (The Skin); first published as *La pelle* (1949).
3. Ballantine Books, 1960, pp. 142–7.
4. Extracts from pp. 64 and 65 of the American translation, pp. 46 and 47 of the original German. The American translation omitted the '2,632 commercial premises'.
5. The first table and the details of power consumption are from the Diary of Rüstungsinspektion X, Bundesarchiv document RW20-10/20; the second table is from the United States Strategic Bombing Survey, Submarine Plant Report No. 2, p. 13.
6. British Official History, Vol. I, p. 86.
7. Appendix 10, p. 98 of the American translation.

19

'Why?'

I have to make this reproach against our enemies of 1939–45; that they directed their attacks quite consciously on to the civilian population. In Hamburg, it was mainly densely populated living areas, with the poorest part of the population and with hardly any industry, which were bombed. It was possible to drop this carpet of bombs over these residential areas because our defences were prevented from operating properly. It was hell on earth. It was obvious that Hitler had to be destroyed, but did this method have to be used? How can people live with such a responsibility on their conscience? (Lady clerk in Hamburg trading firm)*

This book has been about Area Bombing, a form of warfare to which R.A.F. Bomber Command devoted approximately 46 per cent of its wartime effort and which may have taken the lives of 500,000 German civilians at a cost of approximately 25,000 of Bomber Command's fatal casualties. The Battle of Hamburg was an extreme example of success for that form of bombing and, because Hamburg was also an extreme example of a German city target in which the residential areas and industrial areas were completely separated, the battle saw Area Bombing at its most clear-cut. There were hundreds of other Area Bombing raids where these distinctions were not so clear but the objects and methods of the bombing were still the same.

In preparing this book, I corresponded with or had interviews with more than 100 German people, three-quarters of them having been in Hamburg during the time of the bombing in 1943. The lady who wrote the passage quoted at the opening of this chapter is typical of many ordinary German people who questioned me on this subject. Why had Hamburg, a city so close in feeling to England before the war and so anti-Nazi in its politics, been singled out for such terrible treatment? Why had Britain, a supposedly civilized country, deliberately set out to wage war in such a callous and cruel manner? These

---

* Most of the contributions for this chapter were provided after a promise that names would not be published.

questions were asked in a mood of bewilderment, sometimes of disappointment or even anger, even after so many years. They were not easy questions for me to answer properly in the short time that was available (the questions were usually put between the end of one interview and the time for the next appointment).

I would like to offer more carefully prepared views on this complex subject now. I am not the first to deploy arguments in favour of or condemnation of Area Bombing and I will not be the last. But, just as the study of the Battle of Hamburg that has been presented in this book has been partly a personalized one, with ordinary people who were involved telling their own stories, so the answers to the questions will also include a presentation of the attitudes of these ordinary people to the dramatic and historic events in which they were involved. It is clear that many people, on both sides, had little knowledge of the real situation at that time and some still have an incomplete understanding of it even now.

One constraint is vital. The immense value of hindsight must be acknowledged. It is easy, now, to study this subject at leisure but there was little opportunity for leisurely consideration during the war. Decisions had to be made under great pressure. No comment or judgement can now be made without allowance for the period and circumstances in which these events took place. Two further provisos should also be entered at this stage. First, this discussion will not enter, in any depth, into the actual efficiency or success of Area Bombing, still less into other types of operation performed by Bomber Command. I have no dispute with the commonly held – though not unanimous – post-war view that, although Area Bombing made a valuable contribution to the general weakening and defeat of Germany, the cost in British manpower and industrial production and the disappointing results judged Area Bombing to be of doubtful value. As for other types of Bomber Command activities, I would merely restate that superb results were achieved in such operations as those in support of the invasion in 1944, in the precision bombing of transportation and oil targets in Germany in late 1944 and in 1945, in the mining and bombing campaigns against German naval targets, and in the support given to the Resistance groups in the Occupied Countries.

Second, the American role in the strategic-bombing war must also be excluded from this narrow discussion. The main American object was to bomb by day, using visual bomb-aiming methods, those military and industrial targets considered to be acceptable ones to world opinion. It is true that, when their targets were found to be covered by cloud, the Americans sometimes bombed blindly into a general city area, but such bombing was never the main purpose of their operations. A German civilian comment on the Americans is provided by this young man:

The Americans were regarded by us as *soldiers*. Their attacks were during the daytime and were nearly always directed on military targets, even if the civilian population sometimes suffered heavy casualties because of them. They flew in good visibility and risked the aimed fire of our Flak. Hence a certain respect for the 'Amis' as we called them.

It should be stated, however, that, while the Americans behaved with admirable restraint in Europe, and sometimes paid heavily for that restraint, they later practised a very different policy in their bombing of Japan. Because daylight visibility over Japan was rarely good, the American B-29 Superfortresses were turned over to a form of night bombing that was almost an exact copy of the Area Bombing that had been practised by the R.A.F. against Germany. This type of bombing was only carried out during the last five months of war in the Far East but the Japanese cities burnt well and many civilians died in them.

I have said before that it is a complex subject. The pro-German argument will go back to the supposed injustices of the Versailles Treaty of 1919 which took away all her colonies, some of her homeland and bled her so dry by sanctions that she was unable to face the blows of the economic depression that followed the war. Many Germans felt that a new war to correct these injuries was justified. Why did the British have to resort to such an inhuman form of bombing in this new war?

The British answer has its origins in the conditions on the Western Front between 1914 and 1918. Britain's Second World War air leaders had all experienced the horrors of the

Western Front. They believed, with deep passion, that such a form of land warfare, with its stalemate, its battles of attrition and their terrible casualties, must never be repeated. The use of strategic air power to cripple an enemy's means of resistance would produce victory without such a prolonged and costly land campaign. The first chapter of this book described how the opening moves of the Second World War bombing proceeded. British daylight bombing of purely military targets proved too costly and the bombers prepared to change over to night operations. The R.A.F. refrained from bombing any part of mainland Germany for eight months until the Germans invaded France, Holland and Belgium in May 1940. Even when the bombers were released to bomb Germany, their crews were instructed to bomb only legitimate targets of war and they attempted to do this for the next year and a half. It was not until the end of 1941 that it was found that such bombing could not hit these small targets with the navigational and bomb-aiming equipment then available. With that realization, the British faced a most difficult choice: give up the dream of avoiding another 1914 Western Front by strategic bombing, or try a new form of that bombing which might be effective using the limited means available. The decision taken was for Area Bombing.

Yes, it was cruel. Yes, civilians – old people and children quite innocent of any harm done to Britain or her Allies – were certainly going to be killed. Yes, cultural landmarks were going to be destroyed. Yes, terror was meant to be spread the length and breadth of Germany. Yes, it does seem immoral today. But consider two factors which made Area Bombing seem fully justified when it was introduced: the actions already committed by the Germans in other parts of Europe; and the ends that might be achieved if Area Bombing proved successful.

During the period before the R.A.F. turned to Area Bombing, the Wehrmacht, with the full support of the Luftwaffe, had occupied Czechoslovakia, had conquered Poland, France, Holland, Belgium, Denmark, Norway, Yugoslavia and Greece and was deep inside Russia. Given that Germany may have had a grudge against some of these countries because of Versailles – and I only admit there was a case, not fully agreeing with it – given this, what possible harm had such innocent countries as Holland, Belgium, Denmark, Norway, Yugoslavia and Greece done to Germany? The truth is that Germany had carried out a mayhem of military conquest with the purpose of dominating Europe. It was also known that Germany's rule in the vanquished territories was sometimes of the harshest kind.

In the course of their 1940 and 1941 campaigns, the Luft-waffe had killed many a civilian in such places as Warsaw, Rotterdam, Belgrade, Coventry, London and Liverpool. It was very convenient for British propagandists to cite such bombing when their own bombers later started to smash up the German cities but I prefer not to make too much of such bombing in my arguments. The German argument can claim that Warsaw, Rotterdam and Belgrade were tactical attacks in support of the Wehrmacht. I prefer to use the argument that the Wehrmacht had no right to be standing before those cities in the first place. As for the bombing of English cities, the truth is that the German bomber crews were mostly searching for individual factories or dock areas just as the R.A.F. crews were doing over German cities at that time.

And, then, there were the Jews and the concentration camps – possibly unpopular subjects to raise in a book which I hope will be published in Germany but subjects that cannot be left out of the argument. German civilians and servicemen of humble rank may say that they had no knowledge of the extermination of the Jews and the barbarities of the concen-tration camps but information on these subjects had reached Britain. The lower ranks of German society may have been living, at best in a dream world about the glory that Hitler had brought to their country, at worst with doubts about the outcome, but all subject to an oppression which prevented any form of dissension. But every British civilian and serviceman knew, quite clearly, that his country was locked in deadly combat with a power that was led by the most evil of forces. There could be only óne aim – to win the war and to liberate Europe from these forces as quickly and economically as possible. Area Bombing had seemed to be the way ahead in early 1942. Close your eyes to the necessity to hurt civilians and get on with destroying Germany's industrial cities as quickly as possible. The morale of the German civilians will break and production in the factories will fall – not with the factories themselves being bombed but with the city services failing and the workers fleeing, exactly as they were to do in Hamburg. And, if complete breakdown in Germany can be achieved, German collapse and Allied victory will follow. There need be no prolonged land campaign. Why should thousands of Allied soldiers be killed when there was another way? That was the British aim when Area Bombing was introduced in early 1942.

It did not happen. The Battles of the Ruhr and Hamburg were major Area Bombing victories but further successes did not come fast enough to achieve the complete German breakdown that was being sought. The morale of the tough German civilians held, with a little help from the forces of authority. The brilliant organizers of German industry dispersed, rebuilt and improvised faster than the bombers could produce their industrial disruption. It required an eleven-month land campaign in the West to finish off Germany after an even longer period of remorseless meat-grinding on the Russian Front.

But what if Area Bombing had succeeded? The war might have finished one year earlier, with incalculable saving of human life, personal misery and loss of national wealth. Britain and her Allies would certainly have been clear beneficiaries from such an earlier victory and the Germans would probably have come to accept that such an end would have been better than the one they eventually suffered. The tyranny of Hitler would have been lifted from her earlier and she would have been spared the rape by the Russian Army of her eastern provinces.

All this is what the R.A.F. were trying to achieve when they bombed Hamburg in July 1943.

In some ways, Area Bombing was a three-year period of deceit practised upon the British public and on world opinion. It was felt to be necessary that the exact nature of R.A.F. bombing should not be revealed. It could not be concealed that German cities were being hit hard and that residential areas in those cities were receiving many of the bombs, but the impression was usually given that industry was the main target and that any bombing of workers' housing areas was an unavoidable necessity. Charges of 'indiscriminate bombing' were consistently denied. To be fair, only industrial cities were bombed and, as has been said so often, one intention of Area Bombing was to diminish industrial production. The deceit lay in the concealment of the fact that the areas being most heavily bombed were nearly always either city centres or densely populated residential areas, which rarely contained any industry.

The vital links in the dissemination of this view were the press and the radio upon which the public depended for all wartime news. Both were, of course, controlled by the government during this period but the actual method used was the Air Ministry Official Communiqué that was issued after each raid and the press briefings given to aviation journalists by Air Ministry or Bomber Command press officers. The news published never contained outright lies but was a skilful selection of material designed to produce the desired effect. For a typical example, the *Daily Express* referred to the huge tonnages of bombs dropped during the Battle of Hamburg 'on Germany's largest port' and went on to state:

It will be a long time before this is finished and a full count made of all the industrial damage. But it is already known that many important factories, in addition to those previously announced, have been hit and severely damaged. . . . Great damage has been caused to the central and dock quarters, particularly in the Grasbrook, Billwärder Ausschlag and St Georg districts. So, it is clear, that each visit by the R.A.F. is directed at knocking out great sections, making a full pattern that will leave no industrial part immune from the devastation.

The districts named were all on the north bank of the Elbe where, it is true, there were some minor dock areas. There was no mention of the extensive residential areas of Hammerbrook and Barmbek which the R.A.F. already knew had been devastated. Neutral reports that 20,000 or 30,000 people had been killed were dismissed as 'Nazi-inspired stories'.[1] Similarly, a daylight aerial photograph, taken by the R.A.F. and published in the *Illustrated London News* in the same week, does show the edge of the firestorm area but the majority of the picture published consisted of locomotive sheds, railway marshalling yards and some dock quays.

The American Press was much less reticent. An Associated Press report, dated 6 August and syndicated in many American newspapers, may have refuted the idea that the Hamburg raids had been a 'terror' operation or a 'ruthless laboratory test'; the raids had been an attack on 'a prime military target – the nest and center of German submarine production'. But the report went on to refer to the R.A.F.'s destruction of the residential quarters – in contrast to the American precision bombing – saying that the R.A.F. bombing,

ruthless as it may seem to the distant observer, is an integral part of the military attack. Experience has shown that, in other area-bombed cities, the Germans have been able to repair the factories and move the bulk of the civilian population out. This latter, however, was done, not out of humanitarian interest for the comfort and safety of the civilians, but merely as the quickest and cheapest way of providing new houses for the essential workers in the war industries. To prevent that, the wrecking of all housing becomes necessary.

The general public, particularly in Britain, were happy to accept that their bombers were mainly engaged in destroying German industry and it must be said that British people were not too much concerned if workers' housing was bombed at the same time. There was not an excess of sympathy to spare for German civilians at that time. The earlier, well-publicized bombings of Warsaw and Rotterdam, in particular, and of British cities were marvellous gifts to the British propaganda machine. The popular saying was, 'They have sown the wind; they will reap the whirlwind.'

A few, more discerning, people in higher places did suspect that the type of bombing being carried out by the R.A.F. at this time was not of the type being reported in the press. Sir Archibald Sinclair, the Secretary of State for Air, was often pressed to explain what was really happening.

He usually and, on public occasions, invariably, suggested that Bomber Command was aiming at military or industrial installations as, of course, it sometimes was. He did not conceal that severe and sometimes vast damage was done to residential areas but he either implied, or on occasions said, that all this ...as incidental and even regrettable.[2]

Prominent critics of the policy were few. The only politician of note was Lord Salisbury, who persistently pressed Sir Archibald Sinclair on the subject. Liddell Hart, the historian, had earlier urged the use of strategic bombing – his 'indirect approach' which could obviate another Western Front. But in June 1942, after the Thousand-Bomber Raid on Cologne with its R.A.F. claim of so many acres of city destroyed, he wrote in a personal note called *Reflection After Cologne*:

> It will be ironical if the defenders of civilisation depend for victory upon the most barbaric, and unskilled, way of winning a war that the modern world has seen.[3]

It was a perceptive observation to have been made so early in the Area Bombing campaign.

Liddell Hart formed a close association with the person who became the best-known opponent of the R.A.F.'s bombing methods. George Bell was the Church of England Bishop of Chichester. He was a fierce opponent of Nazism but his basic approach to the war was that the entire German nation should not be condemned and punished for the deeds of the Nazi leaders. He particularly objected to Area Bombing. Just after the Battle of Hamburg, he wrote in his *Diocesan Gazette*:

> To bomb cities as cities, deliberately to attack civilians, quite irrespective of whether or not they are actively contributing to the war effort, is a wrong deed, whether done by the Nazi or by ourselves.[4]

Much exception was taken to this public statement by so prominent a person. Bishop Bell was to have preached in his cathedral on 20 September, Battle of Britain Sunday, but his Dean asked him to withdraw. Bell's view, which he continued to express in speeches in the House of Lords, brought him much opposition. The popular press criticized him violently for what they considered to be an unpatriotic stand and for statements that would undermine the morale of R.A.F. aircrews. He received some quiet support from fellow bishops and other minor public figures but none from William Temple, the Archbishop of Canterbury. It is thought that his wartime views on this subject later cost George Bell the appointment to the position of Archbishop of Canterbury when it became vacant.

Those who queried the morality of Area Bombing never received any major public support. The controlled press reports had done their work skilfully and the opinion of the

general public was not receptive to any other view at that
time.

What about the feelings of the men who actually flew to
Germany and dropped the bombs?

All Bomber Command men were volunteers but their
original volunteering had not been for bomber operations,
only for 'flying duties'. It was only after they had completed
their initial training that the R.A.F. had selected them for
duty in Bomber Command. The majority had joined the
R.A.F. because they had a glamorous view of wartime flying;
the public image of the wartime R.A.F. aircrew man was a
high one. Some men had volunteered in preference to com-
pulsory service in the Army or Navy, some for other reasons,
such as revenge after the bombing of their homes or the loss
of relatives to German bombing. But they all shared the general
public hatred of the Nazis and had a desire to achieve an
Allied victory. Whatever else may be said about the aircrew
of Bomber Command, their original motives for volunteering
for the R.A.F. were based on the highest of ideals. Not one in
a hundred would ever have thought that he would become
part of a force that would deliberately and regularly rain
down high explosive and fire on to the homes of ordinary
German families. 'Area Bombing' was a phrase they were
unlikely to have heard until after the war. So these men came
to Bomber Command, partly by chance. It should never be
forgotten that once a man, of whichever side, became subject
to the discipline of an armed service, he ceased to make
decisions about what duties he carried out. His life became as
though subject to a great lottery.

Those men who came to fly Britain's heavy bombers dropped
into a well-established routine. The aircrew were subject to
the same type of Press influence and conditioning as the
general public and what they were told at the briefings about
the targets they were to attack was often as limited and
selective as what the British public were told by the Air
Ministry. The industrial importance and the strength of a
target's defences were always stressed. Thereafter, it was
mostly a question of what coloured Target Indicators the
Pathfinders were using and of other operational details.
Aircrews were rarely told that the Aiming Point and the

ensuing bombing areas had been selected in order to wipe out residential districts. A few hours later, when they were flying over the target, the ground seemed very remote 20,000 feet below. Theirs was a very detached and impersonal form of war. The aircrew knew that many of their bombs must be hitting residential districts but this was all thought to be a necessary part of the main task.

The bomber men's existence was a simple one. 'Obey orders. Do your job as well as you can and hope to survive. Roll on the next leave or the evening out with the other lads in the crew or the girl-friend. Don't worry too much about it. After all, Jerry had started it; let's show him what some real bombing is like. Besides, you might be caught in a burning kite yourself tomorrow night. Civilians? Jerry could have evacuated his cities of women and children if he wanted. This is total war.' That was the general attitude. The majority had no qualms. The average Bomber Command crew member was a young man, rarely older than twenty-five years. In their youth the aircrew had few political or moral attitudes other than the conviction that Hitler had to be beaten. Many idealistic R.A.F. men saw themselves as being on a crusade. One said, 'We felt we were fighting an inhuman philosophy', another, 'We became a force of retribution', and, again, 'There must be such a thing as righteous anger'.

A clear majority of R.A.F. aircrew held the above views. Some modified them after the war but most did not, bearing, stoically, all the criticism of Area Bombing served up by people who had not been so closely involved. I have many statements from such men; this quotation, from a two-tour pilot, can represent this majority opinion.

I did, indeed, think about the types of target attacked but had few qualms, if any. But, having followed the march of the Nazis to war, cheered on by almost every German, and remembering the way in which they acted at Warsaw, Rotterdam, Belgrade, Coventry, London etc., I could only feel that their turn was long overdue! I believe, firmly, that most aircrew felt the same.

I suppose we all mellow somewhat with age but, while war makes less sense as time goes by, I have never regretted the part I played in Bomber Command operations nor have I changed my view that the circumstances prevailing at the time justified area bombing. Even then, I think, we were fully aware that the war was a life-or-death affair, not only for individuals but for the nations involved. Everything that has been written, since, about Hitler's plan for us if we lost, confirms this, since the bomber offensive contributed immensely to our victory.

There was a minority – more sensitive or more thoughtful – who could imagine what was really happening when their bombs went down on a city like Hamburg and, either at the time or later, regretted their part in it. There are no clear-cut divisions. Empire airmen may not always have had the easy conscience of an Englishman from a bombed city. Men who became prisoners of war were sometimes sobered by the sight of what they had helped to achieve. Some navigators were sensitive men who had reservations on the subject. This man was a long-serving Pathfinder navigator.

Area, or town bombing, upset many of the aircrews, myself particularly. I always hated the thought of indiscriminate bombing and always thought of women, children, hospitals and suchlike. But, to whom could you express such doubts? Raids on our cities helped to still the small voice of conscience but it worries me still to this day.

Had the Germans won the war, should we or ought we to have been tried as war criminals? If we believed it morally wrong, should we have spoken out to our squadron commanders and refused to participate? What would have been the result? Court martial!

It would have needed much more courage to have spoken out on this matter than the mere fact of continuing to fly on operations. So no one voiced his reservations but the thoughts live with me to this day.

Men such as this have borne their regrets ever since, a few with the deepest of regrets.

When I volunteered for aircrew, I had a romantic notion of air fighting. I did not foresee the slaughter that ensued. Whatever statesmen and braided air marshals may say and write, it was barbarous in the extreme. 'Whoever harms a hair of one of these little ones . . .' I expect no mercy in the life to come. The teacher told us, clearly. We disobeyed.

There is a third group, the commanders and staff officers who did not fly but who planned the bombing operations. One does not rise to high rank in any service by being too squeamish about casualties, certainly about the casualties of one's enemies. There was undoubtedly a deep sense of service pride in many of these officers, a desire to see the R.A.F. as the leading winners of the war; there was also, among most, the sincere belief that this was the best way to win the war quickly and with the least loss of life to their own side. I asked questions of several such men. My answers varied from this uncompromising comment, 'I always said that the only good Boche was a dead one and I still say that', to this more reasoned answer:

There was a feeling of 'if only we can make this work, it will be a quick way to end the war'. The more quickly the war was ended, the more lives would be saved. This was total war and anything went. I saw a lot of these cities at the end of the war – on the ground and from the air – and, in retrospect, I began to think, 'Oh my God, what have I done taking part in all this?' I remember being appalled at what I saw, feeling that I ought to have a sense of shame and being surprised that I didn't. But I don't think I would be honest if I said that I regretted it now. I still think that what we did was a major factor in bringing about the eventual defeat of Germany. I am sorry that our bombing didn't do it on its own.

German propaganda called them *Terrorflieger*, perhaps not unnaturally – there is little distinction between the bombing of a city's residential areas to produce a breakdown in civilian morale and bombing which spreads terror. One can quickly dispose of the protests made by those senior and influential figures in Germany or by anyone who continued to give full-blooded and active support to the Nazi régime after the early surge of conquest or after the revelation of the savage repression practised on any opponents to the régime, or after it became obvious what was happening to the Jews and many others. Such protests were pure hypocrisy. One suspects that much of the noise made was not a sincere reaction but more a desperate propaganda campaign.

One must sympathize, however, with the understandable reaction of horror to the bombing by the rank and file of German society, whether it be from the civilian population or the humble servicemen. The average German was subject to a ce..sorship of news and a pressure of propaganda far more rigid than in any Allied country. His knowledge of what was being done all over Europe in his name was very limited. One may admire the courage of the few senior personalities who tried to stop Hitler and who usually suffered terribly for their efforts and one can despise the greater number of such elevated people who did nothing, but the ability of the ordinary man to alter events was absolutely non-existent. He, and his family, were caught in a trap between the Allied air forces and the forces of repression in his own country. His dilemma was further compounded by the natural patriotism that most men and women feel for their country when it is in adversity. The history of mankind contains many examples of multitudes of such innocents being put to the sword or dying by slow starvation in siege or blockade. In this case they were bombed and burnt. Bishop Bell of Chichester was right to attempt to separate the ordinary German people from their leaders in the world condemnation and the retribution that followed the turn of the war's tide.

Returning to the citizens of Hamburg in particular, the survivors are often bitter over the bombing of their city and the deaths of so many ordinary people. This former naval officer, who had helped me with an earlier book, refused to send his memories of the time he spent in Hamburg during the bombing.

The period I spent there constitutes the saddest chapter of my life. What was done in Hamburg at that time by the Allied air forces even exceeds anything with which we Germans can be charged. The brutality with which the Hamburg raids were carried out can only be compared with the Dresden raids. People were destroyed in a senseless and brutal way without any effect upon the outcome of the war. There will be hardly anyone who was an eyewitness to these events who will be prepared to talk to you about this because we prefer to forget these events and not hold these things against you.

Here are other views:

No one could understand the British method of waging war; I didn't either. Whoever kills defenceless women and children, *no matter who*, acts inhumanely and in criminal fashion. Hatred was engendered through these terror attacks. We Hamburgers, especially, could not understand the bombing because there had always been strong links between Hamburg and England. In my opinion, we people of Hamburg are a bit English.

I don't agree with the title of your book, 'The Battle of Hamburg'. A battle normally takes place between two groups of soldiers and, surely, the Allied airmen cannot feel proud of having killed tens of thousands of women, children and old people in just a few raids. Our

Flak was manned only by sixteen-year-old boys, eighteen-year-old girls, volunteer Russian prisoners of war and a few soldiers. The air-raid service was mostly made up of men who were over sixty years old and, thus, were too old for front-line fighting. One cannot liken these men to 'soldiers'.

As I was a sixteen-year-old girl who considers it a blessing that I escaped with my life from the inferno, I hope that, in consideration to the thousands of bomb victims, you, as a historian, will give your book a more appropriate title.

But a number of Hamburg people were not surprised at what had happened to their city. There were a few under-standing replies to my standard question on this subject, ranging from the pithy reply of the policeman from Hamburg's dock area, '*Nun haben wir die Scheisse*', which may be politely translated as, 'Now it was our turn to be in trouble', to this comment:

When I was at the home of friends, after being bombed out, some-one said over breakfast, 'This is the punishment for our attack on Coventry', and a teacher colleague of mine, a woman of very noble principles, said to me, later, 'I shouldn't really say this but I felt a wild joy during those heavy British raids. That was the punishment for our crimes against the Jews.' I could only agree with her.

It must be stated that this would be a very exceptional view, not shared by many Germans at that time. German propa-ganda attempted to turn the argument around by saying that the bombing was yet another of Germany's problems caused by the Jews.

Some of the wounds have healed with the passing of the years. Despite what the naval officer predicted, I was received with much politeness and kindness by many ordinary people in Hamburg who had suffered much in 1943. After they had asked their standard question, 'Why?', many of them accepted my explanation if I had time to expound it properly. Their resentment and sadness, now, is often on account of such irreplaceable losses as the destruction of beautiful old buildings and cultural landmarks, although there was sometimes bitter resentment on account of their mistaken but long-held belief that the R.A.F. used large amounts of phosphorus in their bombs or even rained it down in liquid form over Hamburg. Behind these friendly and forgiving people, however, there must be many others who will never forgive and will never want to meet an Englishman however open-minded he tries to be.

So there it was – Area Bombing – a terrible means of waging war but believed at the time to have been necessary and without any reasonable alternative, introduced by the R.A.F. only after all other, more acceptable, means of strategic bombing methods had been found to be unworkable with the tools available at the time. It was an awful means in search of a most desirable end – the swiftest and most economical defeat of an evil philosophy and the liberation of Europe, including, may one say, the liberation of the ordinary people of Germany.

I have presented many views but not my own. Was it justified? I can say, with little difficulty, that the decision to turn the R.A.F.'s heavy bombers on to Area Bombing, early in 1942, was an *understandable* and seemingly *practicable* method of proceeding with the war, given all the circumstances of that time. That decision was still valid eighteen months later, at the time of the Battle of Hamburg, and at any time up to the invasion of France in June 1944. But was it an *acceptable* method of waging war by a country which held itself to be civilized and was seeking to return civilization to the rest of Europe? Even after the post-war years of hindsight, and more than two years of personal study, I cannot decide upon a private answer to that question. I can only try – as I have in previous chapters – to present the background to Area Bombing and a description in detail of one episode in it and now present the views and arguments of other people. It is hoped that this will, at least, provide readers with a better understanding of a subject in which each must answer the moral question for himself.

I will, however, make these additional points. If Area Bombing had toppled Germany before the invasion of France, there would have been a deal less controversy on the subject, just as there has been little argument over the two American atom bombs which knocked Japan out of the war in 1945. Does the fact that the highest ambitions for the R.A.F.'s Area Bombing offensive were not realized mean that it should never have been attempted? It should also be mentioned that since 1945, most of the world has lived in safety and much of it in freedom because of the threat of what nuclear weapons can do to cities. The scale of explosive force used has increased enormously but the principles of the nuclear deterrent are almost identical to those of Area Bombing.

NOTES

1. *Daily Express*, 5 August 1943.
2. British Official History, Vol. III, p. 116.
3. Quoted in *Liddell Hart – A Study of His Military Thought* by Brian Bond (Cassell, 1977), p. 145.
4. Quoted in Ronald Jasper, *George Bell – Bishop of Chichester*, 1967, p. 276.

20

The Aftermath

THE BRIDGE

When, today, after a three and a half week interval, the *Hamburger Fremdenblatt* is published again, we will not look back to the bad days; we will not lament and we will not be despondent but we will direct our thoughts to the future. The history of a great city knows bad times but also times of fortune and progress. And, when the enemy's air terror has set our fortunes so low and has destroyed so much of that which previous generations have created in buildings and culture, we know, nevertheless, that the history of Hamburg will not end in a field of ruins. (An editorial in the *Hamburger Fremdenblatt*, 18 August 1943)

Of course Hamburg survived, but the first few weeks were grim ones. A vast amount of work of the most arduous and harrowing kind had to be carried out immediately after the raids in the continuing heat-wave conditions. There were fears of an epidemic but, so effective were the countermeasures of the authorities, no serious outbreak ever occurred. Men of all kinds laboured hard in Hamburg during those weeks. Special rations of food, alcohol and cigarettes helped to alleviate the dreadful tasks they had to perform.

It should be stated that the central organizing role of Gauleiter Kaufmann and his party officials ensured that a large volume and variety of work was carried out under firm direction, efficiently and with the correct degrees of priority. Although some skilled manpower was sent to the city from outside, Hamburg basically saw itself through this immediate post-raid period under its local leadership and using its local resources. Essential public services were restored; water was the first priority. Vast tonnages of debris were cleared from the streets. The remaining fires were extinguished. Hundreds of unexploded bombs had to be located and defuzed. Much of the preliminary digging and uncovering of these bombs was carried out by convicts from Fuhlsbüttel Prison who volunteered for this work in exchange for the possibility of a partial remission of their sentences. A policeman would wait, standing guard a safe distance away, while the prisoner carried out his dangerous task before the specialist disposal expert came to perform the final defuzing. One policeman asked a prisoner how long he still had to serve in prison. 'Eight days', was the reply. When the policeman congratulated the convict on his imminent release, the convict explained. 'Eight Christmas Days', he meant.

Thousands of dead bodies had to be recovered from the ruins. There has been enough horror in this book without gruesome accounts, of which I have several, from men involved in this work. Much of the work was done by the police, by Wehrmacht men from local units and by 450 inmates from Neuengamme concentration camp who were brought into Hamburg. At first, it was thought by the authorities that the bodies should be burnt, for fear of an epidemic, but this step never became necessary. Instead, the bodies were taken to Hamburg's main cemetery, at Ohlsdorf on the northern edge of the city, where some of the concentration-camp men, assisted by a mechanical excavator, prepared huge mass graves. Lorry after lorry drove up; drivers reported the approximate number of bodies in their loads, watched the remnants of the dead raked out and were given a receipt before driving off to fetch further loads. There was no attempt at identification.

While the work of recovering the dead was being carried out, a two-and-a-half-square-mile part of the firestorm area was prohibited to all but essential workers. Loose bricks were used to construct high walls across the street ends at the edge of this area. The men used to guard the few entrances still needed were from a company of Czechoslovak police who were normally stationed in the Czechoslovak part of the Customs-free harbour. There was much resentment among Hamburg people when they found that these foreign sentries were preventing them reaching the ruins of their own homes. It is possible that the Czechs were employed to free German police or soldiers for more urgent work, but one German soldier, brought in from a barracks near Hamburg to carry out recovery work, believes that the device was a deliberate one so that the sentries could pretend not to understand German, particularly when pressed by soldiers home on compassionate leave. 'A German sentry, who knew all the tricks, would have let any fellow soldier on leave through.' When essential work was completed, the walls were sealed and these areas remained closed, some until the end of the war.

Hamburg received an important visitor soon after the raids. It was not Hitler, although Gauleiter Kaufmann had begged Germany's leader to visit Hamburg and so, too, had Albert Speer who writes:

Hitler's reaction was surly when I asked him to go to Hamburg. He was probably annoyed because he had already been pressed from another quarter (Kaufmann). These approaches did not suit his conception of his elevated position. He gave no reason for his refusals. You could not expect him to be any different when he was in a bad temper.

I regretted that Hitler did not accede to this wish. It would have given an additional boost to the powers of resistance of the people if he had identified himself in some sort of way, like Churchill did, with bomb victims.

The rumour, prevalent in Hamburg at the time, that Hitler had at least flown over the bombed city, was not true and Hitler even refused to see a selected group of Hamburg air-raid workers who went to Berlin!

It was Hermann Goering, leader of the Luftwaffe, who came. Goering had told Gauleiter Kaufmann in a telegram that he had wanted to come immediately after the firestorm but had been needed at Hitler's headquarters. 'I am with you and the much tried population of Hamburg with all my heart', Goering had told Kaufmann on that occasion. Goering did arrive on 6 August, flying into Fuhlsbüttel Airport. He first decorated some young schoolboy gunners at a Flak position at Schwarmenwiek on the Alster and then drove to meet Chief of Police Kehrl at the Hotel Atlantic. From here, Goering went on foot as far as the edge of the firestorm area. He met several groups of civilians and spoke to them, expressing his sympathy for their misfortunes. Goering, dressed in one of his fine uniforms, was constantly greeted with cries of 'Hermann Meier' or 'Well Meier, what have you got to say now?', on account of an earlier rash boast that, if his Luftwaffe could not protect Germany, 'then my name will be Hermann Meier'. There were no arrests.

Later, at a meeting of local leaders at Hamburg's party headquarters, Goering stated that he had to admit that there was no way in which such attacks on cities could be prevented in the foreseeable future. One of those present says:

> After such a statement from the mouth of such an official source, even the most trusting person could not believe in final victory, but no one said anything, then or later. They were good party members and would never have discussed such a statement.

Goering left Hamburg later that day, refusing a helping of his favourite pea soup at the airport restaurant. 'He just wanted to get away from Hamburg.' It is not known whether he had been ordered by Hitler to visit Hamburg but, if the visit was on Goering's own initiative, it was a brave act on Goering's part.

Hamburg passed the remainder of the war with part of its population living as a community in exile. The large-scale evacuation had spread nearly two-thirds of the civilian population through the length and breadth of Germany and even into German communities in Poland and Czechoslovakia. Rail travel was free. Some of the evacuees soon found secure and happy homes with relatives or friends and those who fled only as far as the small towns and villages near Hamburg were also given a warm welcome. Hamburg people were regarded here as neighbours. Those travelling further afield were not always received so kindly. Hamburg people who finished up in southern Germany were often called '*Bombenpack Preussen*' – 'a pack of bombed-out Prussians'. One lady says that 'the farther away we got from cities that had been bombed, the less sympathetic was our reception'. When she attempted to settle in a village in Silesia which was staunchly Nazi, she was told that the Hamburg people should have been proud to sacrifice their homes for the Nazi cause. Generally, the arrival of the Hamburg evacuees disturbed the complacency of many communities which had not yet had any direct contact with the war and, for the first time, the inhabitants of such places became uneasy about the outcome.

A happy story can be told, however, about a Doktor Schmidt, formerly head teacher of the Hammer Gymnasium, the girls' grammar school in Hamm, who settled in the tiny village of Ortenburg, near Vilshofen in a distant eastern corner of Bavaria. Schmidt soon collected two of his former lady teachers and twenty-five pupils and re-created his school. They were a Protestant minority in a Catholic area and, at first, there was little contact with the local community. Doktor Schmidt eventually collected seventy-five Hamm girls and continued teaching them in Bavaria until the end of the war. By then, the villagers had completely changed their attitude; they were particularly impressed with the hard-working attitude of the children from the northern city. Many of the farmers offered to adopt Hamburg children but all of the pupils returned to Hamburg in the autumn of 1945, although some delayed their departure to help get in the harvest.

Life returned to Hamburg soon after the bombings, when approximately half of the evacuees returned before the winter. All available accommodation was packed and many people lived in the basements of ruined houses or in garden sheds on the city's outskirts. Many would live in this manner until the end of the war, although some living accommodation of the Nissen-hut type was constructed later. Factories reopened, commerce resumed, and Hamburg became a living community again in an extraordinarily swift time. That autumn, a near miracle occurred in Hamburg. Trees and bushes that had been burnt in the summer raids suddenly bloomed again, completely out of season. Lilac and chestnut, particularly, produced their 'spring' blossoms. A young telephone operator speaks for many when she says, 'It gave me a feeling of hope to see something beautiful in the terrible conditions of those bombed areas.'

Two other ladies describe this period:

In the ruins, where the basement cellars had defied all the bombs, people were quick off the mark to take possession of any four walls still standing, even if they were half underground. The cellars would soon be cleared of any debris, a ceiling fixed up and windows put in; enough building material was lying around anyway, free for the taking. Having managed to make some sort of living quarters habitable, one would find they were surprisingly comfortable, considering the unusual circumstances; even little rags of curtains adorned the windows. It always struck me that those people were living like 'little moles in their holes' but they were content for the time being. At least they had a makeshift roof over their heads. That was more than lots of other people had. Gradually, the enterprising 'do-it-yourselfers' gathered more bricks and sticks together and built a little more 'on and up' and, like mushrooms, little houses were sprouting out of the ground again.

At that time, one could not, even with the wildest imagination, anticipate that any sort of civilization would ever arise out of the ashes again. (Paula Kühl)

If one thinks back, nowadays, the living conditions after the destruction were really extraordinary. The population became *Kumpels* – 'mates'. We shared everything. One helped the other. Anyone could go alone into the streets and was not robbed or molested. I slept with the door on the ground floor open and nothing happened to me.

Today, it is risky even to go to the *U-bahn*. (Anne-Lies Schmidt)

Hamburg was bombed again, many times, but never as seriously as in that summer of 1943. There was relative calm for nearly a year but, on 18 June 1944, the Americans made the first of seventeen heavy daylight raids carried out between that date and the end of the war. One of the American raids caused the greatest loss of life experienced in Hamburg after the summer of 1943. On 25 October 1944, 455 American bombers set out to bomb three oil refineries in Hamburg but cloud covered their targets and the Americans bombed through this cloud on radar. Most of the bombs fell into the township of Harburg, which had remained relatively undamaged thus far. Much of Harburg was destroyed and 750 people were killed.

The R.A.F. made only one night Area attack in 1944, on the night of 28–29 July. This was carried out by 298 bombers and would have been regarded by Bomber Command as an annual 'revisit' to a city that had ceased to be a profitable target for more frequent attack. The R.A.F. then left Hamburg alone until the last two months of the war when, because the Hamburg shipyards were believed to be producing new types of fast U-boats which could remain below water for long periods and which posed a great threat to Allied shipping, they raided it five times in quick succession.

During the whole of its wartime bombing, Hamburg lost approximately 55,000 civilians killed. This figure approaches the 62,856 Hamburg servicemen who were killed in action or who died of wounds or sickness during the war. The city official who compiled these statistics highlights Hamburg's casualties at home and at the front in the 'total war' of 1939–45 by pointing out that they were three times greater than the entire fatal casualties of the German Army during the Franco-Prussian War of 1870–71.[1]

Coming back to the larger picture of the bombing war, the German leadership was greatly fearful that the British successes at Hamburg would be repeated quickly. If a number of other cities could be devastated in the same way as Hamburg and in a relatively short time, then Germany would probably find herself unable to continue the war and thus give the British bomber leaders the victory they sought. It will never be known whether the final breakdown would have been caused by a collapse in morale or by industrial chaos. But the R.A.F. was not able to follow up the success at Hamburg with an equally successful destruction of even one German city. In the period immediately after Hamburg, Bomber Command's effort was diverted by political orders to raid Italy and by the necessity to attack the German rocket-research centre at Peenemünde, although there soon took place a little-remembered 'battle' involving another large German city, Hannover, with three raids at the end of September and in early October. Of these raids only one was even a moderate success. Bomber Command was still bound by the seemingly inescapable rules of night bombing of that period. If a target was within Oboe range, like the Ruhr was, or if it was a good H2S target near the German coast, like Hamburg, then it could be attacked successfully. Any other target in Germany could not be marked reliably and bombed successfully except in the clearest of visibility. Because Bomber Command would be slaughtered if it flew regularly by moonlight, the Pathfinders had always to contend with the dark, murky, hazy or cloudy conditions of the non-moon periods.

The Battle of Berlin, which was fought that winter, was governed by these rules. This vital contest has been described many times. Sir Arthur Harris claimed that he could 'wreck Berlin from end to end' if the Americans would join in and, later, that he could 'produce a state of devastation by 1 April 1944 in which surrender is inevitable' – this last, using his own bombers after it had become clear that the Americans would not join in. The gallant crews of Bomber Command flew to Berlin sixteen times and to other cities in Germany nineteen times and lost 1,047 of their planes and their crews in doing so. Berlin suffered heavy but not critical damage. The German defences, in particular their night-fighter force using the new Tame Boar interception technique, overcame most of the difficulties posed by Window and the fighters caused most of Bomber Command's severe losses. The climax came on the night of 30–31 March 1944 when Harris unwisely decided to attack Nuremberg, deep in southern Germany, on a moonlit night and the Germans shot down ninety-five out of 782 bombers.*

This is not the place to argue the pros and cons of this fascinating period of the bombing war. It is enough to say that the Battle of Berlin was a costly failure for the R.A.F. and many now assert that it was a mistake to have fought it. Bomber Command should have been spending more effort on improving its target finding, marking and bombing techniques and in attacking smaller cities directly connected with selected industries – the old 'bottleneck industry' argument of the First World War.

The spring and summer of 1944 were to show that the ability to make some of these advances now existed. In this period, Bomber Command was diverted to the support of the invasion of Normandy by attacking German communications and small military targets in France and other German-occupied countries. To the surprise of many people, it was found that a more precise form of bombing was possible when it was necessary to avoid causing casualties to the friendly civilians living around these targets. In particular, a low-level form of target marking, pioneered in 5 Group, opened up immense possibilities. This was probably the most important single development in the part played by the R.A.F. in the bombing war.

Much use of these advances was made when Bomber Command was released from its invasion commitment in the autumn of 1944, but, tragically, a major part of Bomber Command's effort was turned back again to the Area Bombing of German cities at a time when the invasion had been

---

* See *The Nuremberg Raid*, by the same author, which describes this raid and also covers the last year and a half of the bombing war in more detail than is possible here.

successfully completed and when the land conquest of Germany was obviously inevitable within a few months. Although many precision-bombing raids were carried out against German oil and communications targets, city after German city continued to be attacked by the R.A.F. during these months by Area Bombing raids whose methods were little different from the ones employed against Hamburg eighteen months earlier. Bomber Command could provide 1,600 bombers for operations at this time and its destructive power, in the face of a rapidly declining German defence, was immense. Dresden is the name that is best remembered for what must be one of the saddest periods in the bombing war. With due allowance to hindsight, it is realized that, while a case can be made for the earlier use of Area Bombing, there was little justification for its use in the last winter in the war.

By contrast, the American bombing war proceeded in a relatively uncomplicated manner. On 17 August 1943, soon after the Hamburg raids, the Americans carried out the ambitious but risky Schweinfurt–Regensburg raid when they sent 376 Fortresses to key targets deep into southern Germany, for much of the flight without fighter support. The Americans found that the self-defending daylight bomber formation was a myth in the face of determined fighter attack in an operation of such deep penetration. The Luftwaffe celebrated by shooting down sixty of the American bombers. A second attack on Schweinfurt by 320 Fortresses on 14 October produced an equal loss. One must admire the Americans for persisting so staunchly with their doctrine of concentration on selected German industries by daylight attack but the second Schweinfurt operation caused them to give up such deep raids temporarily.

The American doctrine was saved by the appearance of the P-51 Mustang in December 1943. This was a long-range fighter that could accompany the American bombers to almost any target in North West Europe. This was the most important development on the Americans' side of the bombing war and thereafter they never looked back. Their strength grew at an almost unbelievable pace. The Eighth Air Force, which had been able to muster only 323 heavy bombers for the Battle of Hamburg, had, by the end of the war, more than 3,000 operational heavy bombers and 1,300 fighters based in

England and the Mediterranean. Among the many achievements of this aerial armada was the sealing of the fate of the Luftwaffe's day-fighter force and of those night-fighter units which the Germans, in their desperation, used by daylight. The shorter-range R.A.F. fighters shared significantly in this success but the key was the Mustang, which forced the Germans to attack daylight bombers at all stages of a raid and not, as before, only when escorting fighters were absent.*

Hamburg's war came to an end on 3 May 1945, five days before the final collapse of Germany. Hitler had earlier ordered that every town and city in Germany was to be defended against the invading Allied armies. He had also ordered that any party official or military commander who attempted to ignore this order was to be executed. Gauleiter Kaufmann had visited Hitler early in April 1945 and had decided that his leader had now lost all touch with reality. He made plans to save Hamburg. Surrounding himself at all times with a bodyguard of armed students, he ordered that no demolition of vital installations was to be carried out and that, when the first Allied troops arrived, the city was to be surrendered without a fight. By this time, Hitler was dead but Kaufmann was still taking a great personal risk in issuing these orders; there were still Nazi fanatics who would have shot him if they could have reached him.† But Kaufmann's

---

* The operational losses of the heavy bombers of the Eighth Air Force and of R.A.F. Bomber Command were as follows:
R.A.F., September 1939 to May 1945: 8,655 aircraft missing, 50,136 men killed, 9,784 taken prisoner.
U.S.A.A.F., August 1942 to May 1945: 4,301 aircraft missing, 41,844 men killed, missing or taken prisoner.[2]

† Kaufmann does not appear to have received a sentence at the local War Crimes court which the Allies set up at Bergedorf in 1948. He was badly injured in a car crash while being taken to Nuremberg in 1946 and may have been released on health grounds. He died in 1969, well thought of by supporters and opponents alike for his comparatively mild rule in Hamburg, for his leadership during the air raids and for his courage in surrendering the city in 1945 when Germany's cause was clearly lost. Staatssekretär Ahrens, the 'Onkel Baldrian' of the air-raid radio broadcasts, received a four-and-a-half-year sentence. Bürgermeister Krogmann was fined 10,000 marks for failing to do enough to prevent the extermination of Hamburg's Jews and the sending of political prisoners to concentration camps. Chief of Police Kehrl received a four-year sentence

gamble succeeded and, with the cooperation of the local Wehrmacht commander, *Festung Hamburg* – Fortress Hamburg – was spared the horror of artillery bombardment and street fighting.

It was a beautiful May morning and the sun was shining in an azure blue sky. I was awakened about 6 a.m. by a strange, rumbling noise which puzzled me. I jumped out of bed, thinking the bombers were coming back. I dashed out on to my balcony and there it was, the most awe-inspiring sight, never to be forgotten. Rooted to the spot, I just stood and stared. Through the trees I saw the tanks, rolling slowly and peacefully by about 150 feet away from me and the sun gleaming on them. I sighted the first English soldiers, looking out of the turrets, enemies no more and soon to become my friends.

Standing there, gazing at the never-ending line of armoured vehicles, I hardly realized that tears were streaming down my face. Even now, after all these years, tears spring into my eyes when I talk about it; in fact my eyes are wet while I am writing this down.

The young lady who wrote this, Paula Kühl, was later to marry an English soldier. The people of Hamburg were relieved that their final defeat was not at the hands of Russian forces but this day saw the start of a twelve-year British occupation of their city.

Hamburg was rebuilt and is once again a fine, thriving city. The pre-war personal links with Britain were never resumed in their old form, perhaps understandably so after what happened in 1943. The benevolent nature of the British occupation partially restored feelings, although any R.A.F. uniform in Hamburg could be an unpopular sight for many years. The family ties of the pre-war years do not seem to exist in any number now. Hamburg's pattern of trade has altered and there has been a general widening of horizons; America is a more attractive place in which to have a family link now.

There are still many reminders of the war in the ugly concrete *Bunker* shelters that can be seen all over Hamburg, as in every other German city. Sometimes painted to hide their unattractiveness, they are usually used as storehouses or small workshops. They are an embarrassment to the authorities

for his membership of the S.S. having knowledge of the character of that organization.

because they are so strongly constructed that they can only be demolished by using explosives, which is not possible because of the proximity of other buildings. One Hamburg person says, 'We think about them occasionally. We hope that we will not need them any more but it might be that one day we shall be pleased with them again.' One of the massive Flak towers at the Heiligengeistfeld still stands, a hideous thing to have to put up with near the centre of a fine city. The second was demolished at great cost in 1974 and a television mast now stands on the site. By contrast, Gauleiter Kaufmann's fine residence and office overlooking the Alster has been demolished and replaced by a more modern building but the party *Bunker* from which he directed operations during the air raids still exists (in or near the garden of Number 50, Magdalenenstrasse). Not far away, Chief of Police Kehrl's elegant office, in the Milchstrasse, is now a college of music and sculpture.

The Battle of Hamburg is best remembered, not in the rebuilt streets of the firestorm area, but at the four mass graves, laid out in the form of a cross in the beautiful, park-like Ohlsdorf cemetery. Here, in Hamburg's usual sandy soil, are now four raised lawns surrounded by begonias. At the centre of the four arms is a memorial, opened in August 1952, to Hamburg's 55,000 bombing victims. Along the four graves are timber beams bearing the names of Hamburg's wartime districts which suffered from the bombing. The 'Hammerbrook' sign was chosen to stand in the most prominent position, facing the front of the memorial. Some people believe that these signs indicate where people from individual districts were buried. This is not so; the burials were haphazard.

The people of Hamburg believe that Ohlsdorf is the largest cemetery in the world; it contains many other reminders of the war. A quarter of a mile from the mass air-raid graves, there are two plots belonging to the Commonwealth War Graves Commission, with 683 graves of 1914–18 men – prisoners of war who died in northern Germany or sailors washed ashore – and there are 1,443 Second World War graves, half of them being those of R.A.F. men. A total of 169 of the Bomber Command men who died in the Battle of Hamburg are buried here. Near every grave there grows an English rose-bush. Elsewhere there is a plot for German military graves and a memorial to Hamburg's many servicemen missing in Russia. There is a Jewish Memorial and another to the fifty-three Hamburg people who were executed under the Nazi régime between 1933 and the last day of the war. It has been vandalized. There is a mass grave for 140 Russians killed during an American air raid in June 1944, another plot for foreigners – mostly East Europeans – and for Germans without relations in Hamburg, a neat Dutch cemetery, with 350 graves of their countrymen who died as prisoners of war and a memorial to 2,500 more who died at Neuengamme concentration camp.

When I toured Ohlsdorf cemetery, I made this note on my notepad: 'So many dead! So many nations!'

Some participants in the Battle of Hamburg can end these chapters with these random sentiments.

I think that anyone who lived in Hamburg through the entire series of raids and remained sane deserved to spend the remainder of their lives in Paradise.

After all these years, the word 'Hamburg', to me, is still formidable and stands for all the evil of Nazi Germany.

I still think 'Butch' Harris was the greatest commander of the Second World War. He made us all believe in what we were doing and, despite the small chance of survival, very few crews quit.

The Inspector-General of the British Bomber Command who executed such a devilish plan belongs in front of a war crimes court.

We Yanks were asked for what reason we were joining the R.C.A.F. in 1941 before Pearl Harbor. My written reason was, 'to return happiness to the children of Europe'. So, I was saddened whilst flying over the inferno that was Hamburg because I could see that I was bringing death to many German children instead of happiness. After some thought, I concluded that, when caught up in the flow of history, we sometimes must do evil deeds to overcome even greater evil deeds, but I am saddened to this day.

I can honestly say that I was very proud of flying with the greatest Air Force in the world and helping to do my bit in destroying Hitler and his gang. I am sure that most aircrew felt the same way.

And so it was that we all became *Flakhelfer*. We had a great idealism and we were proud to be able to defend our country against our enemies at so young an age. Our eyes were only opened, later, when we realized what a foul game was played with our youth at that time.

The 1943 experiences are still very deeply embedded in my heart and I was and still am proud of the role, even if only minor, which I played in the defence of my beloved Hamburg, which is my native city.

I lost my father, an aunt and two uncles that night in the firestorm. Looking back at it now, I have no reproach for anyone, neither on our side nor the other. It was the world's fate. The war took away seven of my best years. In 1943 I was nineteen years old and it wasn't until 1950 that my mother and I found a home again. Even today, I am afraid of fire.

I was aware that a defeat in battle would mean an end to the way of life we enjoyed in Britain.

After our first Hamburg trip, my navigator and I cycled to Huntingdon and took a boat out on the river. We drifted quietly downstream and Nick said, 'What about those poor sods under those fires.'

I couldn't think of anything to say. We drifted quietly on.

NOTES

1. *Hamburg in Zahlen*, 25 September 1951.
2. Statistics from Air Historical Branch, Ministry of Defence, and Albert F. Simpson Historical Research Center, U.S.A.F. Unfortunately, the American total is not broken down into those killed and those taken prisoner but, as seen in the Battle of Hamburg, the proportion of fatal casualties in their daylight operations was probably lower than that of the R.A.F.

Survivors' Stories

Several particularly interesting accounts of individual experiences during the Battle of Hamburg could not be included in the relevant chapters, usually because the length of those accounts would have upset the balance of the chapters. Extracts from ten such accounts are presented here.

'Shot Down', by Second Lieutenant Rodney W. House, 384th Bomb Group, who was taken prisoner in the first U.S.A.A.F. raid:

When I left the airplane, I estimated our altitude to have been about 16,000 feet. Remembering the words of our Intelligence Officer not to open our parachutes until we could hear sounds on the ground and feel a distinct change in air temperature, I delayed pulling the rip-cord of my parachute until I must have been about 2,000 or 3,000 feet above the ground. I recall that, as I fell, I was on my back and spinning like a seed falling from a tree. I discovered I could stop this motion by crossing my legs thus closing the map pocket on the left leg of my flight suit which was unzipped and open. I also recall that, after falling for some time, it would probably be a good idea to throw away my bale-out oxygen bottle which was strapped to my leg. I very distinctly remember the curious feeling I had when I untied the bottle and threw it to one side only to discover a few minutes later that it was falling in formation with me.

When I hit the ground I grabbed my parachute and threw it in a nearby creek while some ancient farmer stood behind me waving a gun three times as old and twice as big as he and screaming in a strange foreign language that for me the war was over. In those days I was an optimist and I asked in English if perhaps I was in Denmark. At that point I was turned over to a young and very mean-looking individual on horseback carrying a P-38 or Luger, an individual who I gathered was probably home on convalescent leave and whose task it was to take me to a prisoner assembly point.

At this point a curious thing happened. As we went off, I was in front of the horse and he, of course, was at my rear. One of those strange things in one's life happened that perhaps saved my life. I heard a strange grunting sound and, as I slowly turned, I withdrew a package of cigarettes from my pocket to offer one to the horseman and as I looked up the horse's hoofs were pawing the air above my head as though the rider intended to bring the horse down on top of me. When I offered him the cigarette, he reined back the horse and somewhat reluctantly took the cigarette. I tried to look as unafraid and bold as possible (I was not, of course), and I think my deliberate and fearless stance (phoney) impressed the horseman enough to deter him from what I suspect he was about to do.

Shortly thereafter we arrived at a small schoolhouse where there were others assembled and we were all taken in a truck to the wreckage of a downed airplane aboard which all the crewmen were dead and the plane partly burned. I could not identify any of the crew or the aircraft. I ultimately wound up at a Luftwaffe fighter station on the outskirts of Neumünster, where for the next couple of days a constant procession of fighter planes arrived and departed. Along with two or three other captured airmen, we were kept in the base guardhouse after we had been made welcome by a somewhat kindly World War I 'retread' Captain. While in the guardhouse, we were visited by a group of German pilots who seemed quite eager to talk about the air battle and our respective machines and it was here I first learned that German officers salute just like we had seen them do in the movies; that is to say, without headdress, they click their heels and curtly bob their heads. One young flyer did this to me and when I could not resist smiling he became very angry and had to be restrained by his comrades. So much for not believing in what you see in the movies.

'Technical Failure', by Flight Sergeant D. A. Boards, second pilot in a 15 Squadron Stirling on the second R.A.F. raid:

It happened very suddenly although I didn't see it; I was throwing Window out. An engine was on fire and the extinguisher was not working. Flames were going back right past the tailplane. We were well into Germany; the pilot could see some Flak activity at Kiel on the port side. The captain ordered the crew to abandon the aircraft and kept it straight and level to allow them to bale out. Five men went very quickly. I decided not to go straight away but went up to the pilot's position; I think this was because I was a pilot myself and it didn't seem to me that this was a dire emergency. I wanted to have a look and see what was going on.

The pilot put the aircraft into a dive in an attempt to put the fire out. This could be dangerous; our normal advice was not to do this because it might strain and break the wing but it was probably an instinctive action by the pilot, once most of his crew were safe, to try and save the aircraft. I would probably have done the same thing. Then, as I watched the engine burning, only a few feet from the cockpit, the flames died down and all but went out, leaving only a slight glow. We later found out that the oil tank behind the engine had caught fire. It contained thirty-two gallons when full. The feed pipe to the engine had ruptured and the hot engine had ignited the oil. The fuel pipeline had also fractured. I didn't know that the flight engineer was still there. He had done very well to cut off the flow of fuel immediately and we were all lucky that the large fuel tank just behind the engine hadn't caught fire and exploded. We found out that the prop was windmilling; we couldn't feather it and we expected it to come off and tear through the fuselage but it didn't. There was a lot of drag, though.

I suggested to the pilot that we didn't abandon the aircraft but try to get it back. He decided to do this. I went back to the navigator's compartment and looked at his charts. I ignored the winds because they were not particularly strong. I set a straight course for a ditching position 100 miles out in the North Sea. We hoped, at least, that we could get out over the sea, ditch, and be picked up by our side. If we were still O.K. when we reached the ditching position, then we would try for England. Looking back on it, I don't think we had much chance of ditching successfully but both being fairly new to flying, we tended to be optimistic about our chances. The flight engineer said we were O.K. for fuel and had plenty, enough to reach England.

I went back to help the pilot. We were just about maintaining height at 3,000 feet. The two outboard engines were O.K. but the starboard inner's windmilling propeller was screaming like a banshee and the port inner's temperature started to go up with the extra power settings needed to counteract the loss of power and the extra drag on the starboard side. The pilot had to throttle this back and increase power on the two outer engines to compensate.

We never saw any other aircraft and, when we managed to get well out to sea, we laid off a course for the approximate area of Yarmouth. I tried the Gee set but it was a Mark II which neither of us could operate. We took turns in flying because it was such heavy work with the drag and the critical speed for the best fuel consumption. We were doing about 140 m.p.h. instead of the normal 160 m.p.h. We wanted more height so we opened the rear escape hatch and started throwing out guns, ammunition, armour plating, radio equipment – except for the R/T set which we would need when we were landing – seats. The ammunition was the most difficult. Imagine two people over the middle of the North Sea in the middle of the night, handling long belts of ammunition out of trays and throwing them through the hatch without going through ourselves. I hope there were no fishing boats below. We decided to chance the risk of being seen and we put all the interior lights on. There was this 87-feet fuselage lit up; it was like being inside a long, empty bus. We climbed to 3,500 feet and it overjoyed us immensely to think we were going up and not down.

When we approached the English coast, I went down to the bomb aimer's position to look for the shore and I spotted it within two minutes of our estimated landfall time. We came in near Wells on the north coast of Norfolk. It was then just a case of flying down to Mildenhall. We found the beacon and landed normally. The ground crew were very surprised to see only three men get out and we had to put up with a few jokes. The starboard-inner propeller was still turning with its own momentum.

The navigator chart that we used to get back was later displayed in the Briefing Room with this comment, 'If pilots can do this, why can't navigators?'

(The aircraft captain, Flying Officer R. Waugh, received the D.F.C. and Flight Sergeant Boards and the flight engineer, Sergeant F. J. Watson, received D.F.M.s. All three completed their operational tours safely.)

'Interrogation', by Sergeant A. R. Cole, bomb aimer in Flying Officer Waugh's crew:

At first light we were marched off to a small Kriegsmarine depot whose job appeared to be to guard the Kiel Canal. The N.C.O. in charge of our party disappeared into the guardroom leaving us very well taken care of on a sort of parade ground. In due course, a German sailor indicated that I was to follow him to a hut at the far end of the square. When the door was opened, I saw a German naval officer who, as he had two rings, I assumed was the equivalent of a lieutenant. I had been told that if I were captured I should treat enemy officers in the same way as I treated our own. This was a mistake. I entered the room affecting a jauntiness which was almost certainly overdone, as I was not a little apprehensive about my future, assuming I had one. However, with both hands firmly in my trousers pockets I sauntered over to his desk, sat on the corner, and grinned a cheerful 'Good morning'. It became crystal clear that this was not the way to treat a German naval officer, and, when the seemingly obligatory, but more intense, screaming had died down, a young sailor, who had appeared from nowhere and who spoke some English, told me I must stand in front of the desk and answer the officer's questions.

I sensed quickly that my behaviour had given me a moral advantage over my inquisitor, so perhaps the instructions had not been so inappropriate after all. I was afforded some respect and only asked for my name, rank and number. I felt that this was not a sensible moment to disclose the fact that I was only a sergeant and, as I had removed and pocketed my badges at the farmer's cottage, I invented a new rank of 'observer', which seemed to confuse them. I was marched out and left standing on the parade ground for several hours.

'The Rothenburgsort Children's Hospital', by Sister Maria-Luise Wiegand (the hospital was just outside the firestorm area):

I was in a shelter in the basement with a group of about twenty little children, none more than three years old. They were all fast asleep and they slept right through the bombing but the six or seven probationary nurses with me were sighing with anxiety. They sat huddled together, with their heads down in a typical attitude when there is danger above. I had to act like a hen with her chicks with them. The basement was shaking about like a ship and there was no light; even the emergency lighting had gone. I had been in dangerous situations many times. I was born in Indonesia, deep in the jungle. My father was a medical missionary there and I had several dangerous experiences in which I had to act, but this was a situation where I just gave up.

When the raid ended, we behaved just as though we had been trained for such an event, but we hadn't. The senior doctor came down to the basement and told us to leave because the hospital had been hit and was burning. We woke the children up and there was only a little crying from them because they were used to being taken out of the basement after an alarm. We dipped napkins into basins of water and threw these over the babies because of all the glowing embers flying about. We took them all out into the hospital grounds. The fires had caused a storm and the noise of this storm whistling through the broken windows and holes in the hospital was fantastic. The little poplar trees forming the boundary between the hospital and the marshalling yards near by were bent right over by the wind. It was an experience! It was the only time that I wouldn't have wished this upon my enemy.

During the next few hours, parents appeared from all directions and in every manner – on foot, on bicycles, et cetera – in order to take their children. We let anyone go – infectious cases, seriously ill cases – it didn't matter. We were left with 165 children when the children and parents had all gone. The bombed-out people could leave the city but we had to stay with the remaining children.

We became quite exhausted. On one occasion, I was tired out and I lay down on a stretcher. I woke up to find the head midwife sitting on me, cleaning up a baby on her knee. It was an absolute miracle that we survived. We had no casualties except a few children who became ill and a few very tiny babies who had been in oxygen tents when the raid came and these died. And we didn't even have any injured from the bombing except for the smoke from the burning building which hurt our eyes and we had to have drops of cocaine in them.

We received orders to evacuate the hospital. The children were carried by the nurses and the mothers with new-born babies carried them in their arms. We had to go 500 metres to a post office near by where there were buses waiting. They could not get any nearer because of the debris in the streets. They were '*Hamburg Stadt*' buses. We were taken to an orphanage at Reinbek, just outside the city.

'Street Scenes in Hamburg after the Firestorm', by Otto Müller, the police officer in charge of the emergency motor-cycle messenger service:

I was ordered to help collect some phosphor-bomb burn victims at an open place near the corner of the Süderstrasse and the Heiden-kampsweg. There was a bus to take them to a steamer on the Elbe for evacuation but the bus driver was from Hannover and he didn't know the city and we had to lead him by car.

The burnt people were marked with a label round their neck giving their personal details and their degree of burns. I talked to a doctor and he told me that the larger the area of burn, the less pain the people felt but that, when the burns had reached a certain percentage of the body area, death was inevitable. The doctor went through the rows of injured and those with too much area of burn he left behind because there was only room for those with a chance of survival. He was looking for those who were still in pain and these were chosen to be put on the ship. The people being left behind knew that they had no chance. One man dragged himself up my leg to get at my pistol holster – it was simply dreadful. The next day, the place was empty and I hope that these poor people were somehow saved.

On another occasion, I was going through burning streets on my way to Wandsbek when I suddenly saw a young girl. I thought it might even be my own daughter; I had my three children living near by and I had had no chance to see them for several days. I stopped my motor cycle and the girl came running towards me. Her face was black with soot except for two streams of tears which were running down her face. She was dragging her little dead brother behind her; the right side of his face was already scraped smooth. She had been wandering around aimlessly for three days and two nights I think.

This little girl put her hand round my neck and said, 'Dear soldier. Please take us along with you.' I got so angry at this incident that I would have shot any enemy airman who had parachuted down. I also think that any English or American person would have felt the same way. Thank God that I didn't find myself in that position. If I had, I would have ended my life on the gallows.

I took the little girl to a first-aid station.

'The Difficulties of a Night Fighter', by Oberleutnant Joachim Wendtland, a fighter-control officer who flew as an observer in the Messerschmitt 110 of Hauptmann Prinz zur Lippe-Weissenfeld of III/NJG1 on the night of the third R.A.F. raid:

At first we were under the control of Box 2C. The fighter-control officer directed us on to a contact. Then, our radar operator picked up his own contact ahead but we closed on to it very fast and the radar man thought we would ram it. The pilot realized, from the speed of the contact, that it could not be a bomber flying away from us or towards us and must be a little cloud of Window. The pilot held the same course in the hope of following the bundles of Window and finding the bomber dropping them, but the radar operator eventually had to report that he had lost contact. The ground-control officer had kept in touch with his original contact and he directed us again but we had exactly the same experience and remained without a genuine contact.

We were then ordered to freelance and, while we were doing this, I suddenly saw a large violet-blue exhaust flame shooting over our heads. It was only visible for a split second. Unfortunately, I could only react in astonishment at this sighting by saying, 'There! There!' By the time I had given a more detailed description of what I had seen, it was too late for the pilot to follow it up. Because of this, the pilot insisted most vehemently that, in future, I call out without delay, for example, 'Hard turn starboard!' or 'Reverse course!' He told me he would carry out such an order immediately.

After a further long zigzag flight, with the ground-control officer giving details of the bomber-stream and being told of bombers here and there, the pilot suddenly spotted a four-engined aircraft against the northerly twilight at a height of 6,800 metres and about 150 metres in front and above us to the right. It was a visual sighting with no radar. The eight exhaust flames were, in comparison to the ones I had seen earlier, so small and weak in intensity as to be like 3-mm wireless sparks.

The pilot flew after it straight away, positioned himself about eighty metres underneath and matched his speed to that of the bomber. The dark shape of the four-engined aircraft was clearly visible against the sky above us. It was a Lancaster.

The pilot hit its left wing with his first attack and burning pieces of it flew off. The pilot was a little disappointed that the bomber wasn't shot down by this first attack; he had wanted to show me how to hit it between the two engines and finish it off quickly. The Lancaster kept straight and level all the time, without any evasive action.

On his second attack, Prinz zur Lippe used his special method. He slid under the bomber, pulled up the nose suddenly, fired a burst and dropped away quickly in case the bomber blew up. It didn't, although pieces were still falling off it. We attacked again. The bomber still didn't explode; its pilot was trying to reach some low-lying clouds. I didn't see any return fire but we found four bullet holes in one rudder after we landed. I wasn't used to all these manoeuvres. I wasn't strapped in and I kept being pushed down into the floor and then coming up to hit the cockpit roof.

We made one more attack and, this time, his wing started burning after only half a second. We saw the Lancaster go down into a wood near a railway. We started to circle the crash position in the normal manner, so that ground control could fix the position of the success but the radar operator warned the pilot that our petrol was low and we had to leave and land quickly at Stade, actually cutting in front of another fighter that was landing. About fifty metres before we reached the dispersal, the engines cut.

(The Lancaster was a 460 Squadron aircraft with a mixed Australian–English crew on their fourth operation. There were no survivors. It was Prinz zur Lippe-Weissenfeld's forty-third night success. He was killed on 12 March 1944 when 'hedge-hopping' in the Ardennes, being credited with fifty-one successes at the time of his death.)

'Meeting the Germans', by Flight Sergeant F. Fenton of 35 Squadron who landed by parachute near Podendorf, south of Buxtehude, after his Halifax was shot down on the third R.A.F. raid:

I crept under the canopy of a lush green larch tree and found myself in a small haven. With my back to the trunk, I dozed. I awoke with a start. There was a loud clattering very near me. I peered out, my chin on the ground, and saw a heavy farm cart drawing away from me. A young woman was lashing a single bullock furiously. She turned and looked back – it appeared to me, straight into my eyes. She was pretty, slender and looking rather frightened. She needn't have worried. Rape was a long way down my list and I would have forgone the Queen of Sheba for a packet of Players. When she had disappeared, I moved rapidly in the opposite direction. Eventually, I stopped and found another tree. This time I was fully asleep when something woke me and I opened my eyes to see the biggest pistol I

had ever seen. It was in the hand of a tall, corpulent German policeman. He simply said, 'Come, Englishman.'

After that, things became slightly unreal. I sat down in a very
clean farmyard at an iron table covered with a spotless cloth. A
young woman nursing a baby sat opposite me and a very old lady,
cutting runner beans, sat on my right. The latter touched the crown
on my sleeve and said, timidly, 'King?' I nodded and she smiled. A
very old, very clean old man pottered up and said, '*Tommi?*' I
nodded and he smiled and patted my shoulder. He pottered off,
chuckling and saying, '*Tommi? Ja, Tommi.*'

The policeman was visible in the porch of the house and I did not
fancy a large bullet in my spine. I sat quietly. Things up to now had
been very un-Hitler-like! The young woman had obviously been
through this before. In fair English, she asked me if I had a map –
'Silk?' Since it was quite clear that it would soon be found, I gave
her the one in my escape kit unobtrusively. Shielding her actions
from the policeman, she folded it in half and slid it neatly under the
table-cloth. Eventually a car drew up and from it stepped two very
young officers. I did not recognize any specific uniform but they
were not Luftwaffe as far as I could see. They were both extremely
well turned out, neat, clean – almost dandified! Both wore highly
polished riding boots and cavalry breeches. One had a white tunic
which I swear was made of suede or sharkskin. They simply glittered
with smartness. Ignoring me, they approached the young woman,
halted, clicked their heels in unison, bowed and saluted in military
fashion. I thought, 'Christ – I'm in the middle of *The Student Prince*!'

The young woman took it all for granted and accepted their
courtesy with a smile and a slight inclination of the head, baby
notwithstanding. I thought of the map under the table-cloth. Women
are the same the world over.

We drove to what turned out to be the H.Q. of a Flak battery. The
officer in charge was out. I was signed for and duly handed over to a
tough-looking young chap wearing nothing but P.T. shorts and
jackboots. I sat in his office with a sentry in the next office. Two
hours passed slowly. The N.C.O. did nothing at all except arrange
and rearrange five flat cigarettes on an otherwise empty desk. He was
joined by a twin. They faced each other, equally half naked, raised
right arms to full stretch and bellowed, '*Heil Hitler!*' at one another.
Definitely senior N.C.O.s, I calculated. Officers saluted properly
and bowed to ladies in Germany!

'Rescued from the Sea', by Sergeant A. B. Grainger, the
navigator of a 214 Squadron Stirling which crashed into the
sea during the storm in the fourth R.A.F. raid (his pilot was
Sergeant A. A. R. McGarvey):

The mid-upper gunner shouted down that he couldn't see out of his turret; it was icing up. I checked my outside temperature – minus 4 Centigrade! Everything happened very quickly after that. Mac said that the controls were stiff and frozen and he couldn't get the nose down. It seemed to be very soon afterwards that the aircraft appeared to spin. It felt like being in a lift. We were thrown from side to side and had to hold on to something to keep our place. Then the skipper gave the command to bale out. I realized we were still over the sea and I warned everyone to take their dinghies with them. We each had a small, portable dinghy which we clipped on the side of our parachute harness.

Mac was still flying the aircraft but I don't think he was able to do anything with the controls. He checked the boys out, each man reporting as he went. In the end, there was only Mac and I left. We couldn't find our dinghies and we didn't spend too long looking for them; our main concern was to get out of the aircraft. There was a certain amount of panic, let's be honest about it. We knew the plane could only go straight down and, from that height, would go straight in and you wouldn't come up.

We crawled back to the main door, about forty feet. I've no idea how long that took; it seemed like a year. The engines were still running normally. We went out almost together; I was first and Mac right behind me. I pulled my rip-cord and the 'chute opened at once. I knew I was going to land in the water so I kicked off my heavy flying boots and, when I thought I was near the water, I inflated my Mae West by pulling up the little lever opening the CO_2 capsule which blew it up. I saw the aircraft spinning past me and hit the sea. The appearance of the plane was just one of those things that happens in a second and remains with you for ever. There was a splash but it disappeared very quickly.

Then I hit the water and it must have been a fairly gentle landing because I didn't go beneath the surface. I got rid of the parachute harness and parachute and gathered my wits together. I thought the others might be near by and I blew the whistle that we all carried for use in the dark. I heard a call, answering. It was Mac. He shouted, 'Keep on blowing. I'll try and find you.' I'm a very poor swimmer but Mac was an exceptionally strong one. He had played water polo for the Glasgow Police and possibly for Scotland. He soon found me.

He talked about which way we were going to swim. I said we weren't going back, 'It's too far to England', I said. It was only a joke, of course; you know how the English joke. We knew there was land on two sides of us; we could see the searchlights there. We decided to swim towards where we thought the land was closest. I did my dog paddle and, every so often, Mac gave me a pull along. The sea wasn't too rough – a medium swell, no more – but it was very cold. You could feel it striking through your clothes. There were several occasions when I thought I wasn't going to make it. I realized that I was being a burden to him.

There's a gap in my memory here, a period when I can remember nothing. When I came to, dawn had broken; I was lying on my back and Mac was towing me. We could see some light vessels. I had recovered a bit and was able to start swimming myself a bit then. I don't know how long it was – I was in no fit state – before we stopped again. Mac said that he thought the tide had turned against us and we weren't making progress. He said that he was going to leave me and try to reach the nearest light vessel and hope that they would come and pick me up. Before he left me, he took off his Mae West and put it on to my back to give me extra buoyancy and the last I remembered was Mac swimming off. I didn't care when I saw him go; I realized that it was the only chance. He was tired by then and we were both freezing. If he had stayed with me much longer we would both have been lost.

I came to on the deck of a light vessel with Mac pumping me dry. He told me later that he had made the light-vessel crew understand that I was still out there and they sent out a small boat to pick me up. According to Mac, I was unconscious and blowing bubbles.

I was landed on a stretcher; I don't know where. A German naval doctor gave me a thorough examination but the only treatment was some pure golden medicine in an old-fashioned measuring glass which I drank. Then, I was placed on a bed with no blankets. The orderlies brought a half cylindrical wooden cover with rows of light bulbs facing inwards for heat treatment. I don't remember any more.

I have no idea what happened to the rest of the crew; Mac and I were the only survivors. There is no doubt about it that he saved my life. I filled in a full report about what he had done and sent it through the Swiss authorities and, after the war, he was awarded the George Medal.

'Letters from Heaven', by Margot Schulz, who lived at Bergedorf, eight kilometres south-east of Hamburg:

The air was full of pieces of partially burnt paper and we played this game of reaching up and catching these pieces of paper to see what they were. It was like a black snowstorm. A person might say, 'Look, I've got half a mark note.' Someone else would say, 'This was a love letter.' My sister found half a birth certificate.

You didn't play the game all the time but, when you were outside, hanging out the washing or suchlike, you would just reach up and catch a piece. This went on for many days.

'Back to Work', by Wilma Rathjens, who worked in the U-boat yard of Howaldtswerke as a canteen assistant:

The workers were given a lot of encouragement to return to work immediately after the raids. They were given beer, cigarettes and butter for their families, all free. The strict rationing system for food broke down and ration books did not need to be shown nor were the coupons cut out. I felt this to be a deliberate move to encourage people to stay in the city and return to work.

I remember that on the first day and for several days afterwards, the naval band from the nearby U-boat training unit came and played for us at lunch-time. They played all the forbidden tunes like 'Tiger Rag'.

About three weeks later, Doenitz and some staff officers came to encourage our workers. Some of them received the *Verdienstkreuz* decoration. I was given 244 marks [about £24 or 100 U.S. dollars] and a large box of sweets because I had started back to work on the first day after the bombing of the yard. Other girls received money and sweets but in proportion to how soon they had started back.

Order of Battle of R.A.F. Bomber Command, 24 July 1943

1 GROUP
(Air Vice-Marshal E. A. B. Rice)
H.Q. Bawtry Hall

Unit	Airfield	Type of Aircraft
12 Squadron	Wickenby	Lancaster
100 Squadron	Grimsby	Lancaster
101 Squadron	Ludford Magna	Lancaster
103 Squadron	Elsham Wolds	Lancaster
166 Squadron	Kirmington	Wellington
300 (Polish) Squadron	Ingham	Wellington
305 (Polish) Squadron	Ingham	Wellington
460 (R.A.A.F.) Squadron	Binbrook	Lancaster

3 GROUP
(Air Vice-Marshal R. Harrison)
H.Q. Exning, Newmarket

Unit	Airfield	Type of Aircraft
15 Squadron	Mildenhall	Stirling
75 (New Zealand) Squadron	Mepal	Stirling
90 Squadron	West Wickham	Stirling
115 Squadron	East Wretham*	Lancaster Mark II
149 Squadron	Lakenheath	Stirling
214 Squadron	Chedburgh	Stirling
218 Squadron	Downham Market	Stirling
620 Squadron	Chedburgh	Stirling

* Renamed Wratting Common in August 1943.

Unit	Airfield	Type of Aircraft
Special Operations:		
138 Squadron	Tempsford	Halifax
161 Squadron	Tempsford	Halifax, Hudson, Havoc, Lysander
192 Squadron	Feltwell	Halifax, Wellington, Mosquito
Non-operational:		
196 Squadron	Witchford	Converting from
199 Squadron	Lakenheath	Wellington to Stirling

4 GROUP
(Air Vice-Marshal C. R. Carr)
H.Q. Heslington Hall, York

10 Squadron	Melbourne	Halifax
51 Squadron	Snaith	Halifax
76 Squadron	Holme-on-Spalding-Moor	Halifax
77 Squadron	Elvington	Halifax
78 Squadron	Breighton	Halifax
102 Squadron	Pocklington	Halifax
158 Squadron	Lissett	Halifax
466 (R.A.A.F.) Squadron	Leconfield	Wellington

5 GROUP
(Air Vice-Marshal Hon. R. Cochrane)
H.Q. Morton Hall, Swinderby

9 Squadron	Bardney	Lancaster
44 (Rhodesia) Squadron	Dunholme Lodge	Lancaster
49 Squadron	Fiskerton	Lancaster
50 Squadron	Skellingthorpe	Lancaster
57 Squadron	Scampton	Lancaster
61 Squadron	Syerston	Lancaster
106 Squadron	Syerston	Lancaster
207 Squadron	Langar	Lancaster
467 (R.A.A.F.) Squadron	Bottesford	Lancaster
617 Squadron	Scampton	Lancaster
619 Squadron	Woodhall Spa	Lancaster

6 (CANADIAN) GROUP
(Air Vice-Marshal G. E. Brookes)
H.Q. Allerton Park Castle, Knaresborough

Unit	Airfield	Type of Aircraft
408 Squadron	Leeming	Halifax
419 Squadron	Middleton St George	Halifax
427 Squadron	Leeming	Halifax
428 Squadron	Middleton St George	Halifax
429 Squadron	East Moor	Wellington
432 Squadron	Skipton-on-Swale	Wellington

Non-operational:

426 Squadron	Linton-on-Ouse	⎰ Converting from
431 Squadron	Tholthorpe	⎱ Wellington to Halifax
434 Squadron	Tholthorpe	Halifax

(new squadron, not yet ready for operations)

8 (PATHFINDER) GROUP
(Air Vice-Marshal D. C. T. Bennett)
H.Q. Castle Hill House, Huntingdon

7 Squadron	Oakington	Stirling, Lancaster
35 Squadron	Graveley	Halifax
83 Squadron	Wyton	Lancaster
97 Squadron	Bourn	Lancaster
105 Squadron	Marham	Oboe Mosquito
109 Squadron	Marham	Oboe Mosquito
139 Squadron	Wyton	Mosquito
156 Squadron	Warboys	Lancaster
405 (R.C.A.F.) Squadron	Gransden Lodge	Halifax
1409 (Meteorological) Flight	Wyton	Mosquito

Fighter Command squadrons engaged in Intruder operations:

10 GROUP

307 (Polish) Squadron	Fairwood Common	Mosquito
456 (R.A.A.F.) Squadron	Middle Wallop	Mosquito

11 GROUP

157 Squadron	Hunsdon	Mosquito
418 (R.C.A.F.) Squadron	Ford	Mosquito
605 Squadron	Castle Camps	Mosquito

Unit	Airfield	Type of Aircraft
12 GROUP		
25 Squadron	Church Fenton	Mosquito
141 Squadron	Wittering	Beaufighter
410 (R.C.A.F.) Squadron	Coleby Grange	Mosquito

Order of Battle
of American Heavy Bombers

Units in VIII Bomber Command, U.S. Eighth Air Force, 24 July 1943

1st BOMBARDMENT WING
(Brigadier-General Frank A. Armstrong)
H.Q. Brampton Grange, Huntingdon

Unit	Airfield	Type of Aircraft
91st Bomb Group	Bassingbourn	Boeing B-17
92nd Bomb Group	Alconbury	Boeing B-17
303rd Bomb Group	Molesworth	Boeing B-17
305th Bomb Group	Chelveston	Boeing B-17
306th Bomb Group	Thurleigh	Boeing B-17
351st Bomb Group	Polebrook	Boeing B-17
379th Bomb Group	Kimbolton	Boeing B-17
381st Bomb Group	Ridgewell	Boeing B-17
384th Bomb Group	Grafton Underwood	Boeing B-17

4th BOMBARDMENT WING
(Colonel Curtis E. LeMay)
H.Q. Elveden Hall, Thetford

94th Bomb Group	Bury St Edmunds	Boeing B-17
95th Bomb Group	Horham	Boeing B-17
96th Bomb Group	Snetterton Heath	Boeing B-17
100th Bomb Group	Thorpe Abbots	Boeing B-17
385th Bomb Group	Great Ashfield	Boeing B-17
388th Bomb Group	Knettishall	Boeing B-17

The recently arrived 390th Bomb Group, at Framlingham, was not yet operational.

On 13 September 1943, the 1st and 4th Bombardment Wings were redesignated the 1st and 3rd Bombardment Divisions.

Order of Battle
of Luftwaffe Fighters

Units in the West from Denmark to Northern France, 24 July 1943

Because Luftwaffe fighter units – particularly the day fighters – were frequently moved and, because of the lack of reliable documents, it is difficult to present a completely accurate Order of Battle for a particular day. It is believed that the night-fighter units listed below are accurate but there are uncertainties about the locations of some day-fighter units. The following points should be noted:

1. The '*Stab*' was a small *Geschwader* headquarters flight.

2. Only a unit's main airfields are listed; there were numerous small detachments. Similarly, only a unit's principal aircraft types are listed.

3. Abbreviations for aircraft makes are used as follows: Me – Messerschmitt, Ju – Junkers, Do – Dornier, Fw – Focke-Wulf. It should be stated that the German abbreviation for the Messerschmitt 109 and 110 was Bf (Bayerische Flugzeugwerke) but the 'Me' commonly used in English will be used here.

1 JAGDDIVISION
(Generalmajor von Döring)
H.Q. Deelen, Holland

Unit	Airfield	Type of Aircraft
Night Fighters:		
Stab NJG 1	Deelen	⎫
I/NGJ 1	Venlo	⎪
II/NJG 1	St Trond	⎬ Me110
III/NJG 1	Twenthe	⎪
IV/NJG 1	Leeuwarden	⎭
Day Fighters:		
Stab JG 1	Deelen	Me109, Fw190
I/JG 1	Deelen	Fw190
II/JG 1	Woensdrecht, Schiphol	Fw190
III/JG 1	Leeuwarden	Me109

Unit	Airfield	Type of Aircraft
I/JG26	Grimbergen, Wevelghem	Fw190
III/JG54	Schiphol	Me109

2 JAGDDIVISION
(Generalleutnant Schwabedissen)
H.Q. Stade

Unit	Airfield	Type of Aircraft
Stab NJG3	Stade	
I/NJG3	Vechta, Wittmundhafen	Do217, Ju88, Me110
II/NJG3	Schleswig, Westerland	Do217, Ju88, Me110
III/NJG3	Lüneburg, Wunstorf, Stade	Me110
IV/NJG3	Grove, Kastrup	Do217, Ju88
NJ-Kommando 190	Aalborg	Fw190
Stab JG11	Jever	Fw190
I/JG11	Husum	Fw190
II/JG11	Jever	Me109
III/JG11	Oldenburg	Me109
10 Staffel/JG11	Aalborg	Fw190
Jagdstaffel Heligoland	Heligoland	Me109
III/JG26	Nordholz	Me109, Fw190

3 JAGDDIVISION
(Generalmajor W. Junck)
H.Q. Metz

Unit	Airfield	Type of Aircraft
Stab NJG4	Metz	⎫
I/NJG4	Florennes	⎬ Do217, Me110
II/NJG4	St Dizier	⎪
III/NJG4	Juvincourt	⎭
Stab JG26	Lille Nord	Fw190
II/JG26	Vitry-en-Artois	Fw190

(Many other *Gruppen* of JG2, 27 and 54 are not listed, because they were too far from any Battle of Hamburg supporting operations.)

4 JAGDDIVISION
(Generalmajor J. Huth)
H.Q. Döberitz, Berlin

Unit	*Airfield*	*Type of Aircraft*
Stab NJG5	Döberitz	
I/NJG5	Stendal, Volkenrode	
II/NJG5	Parchim, Greifswald	Me110
III/NJG5	Werneuchen, Kolberg, Greifswald	

5 JAGDDIVISION
(Oberst H. von Bülow-Bothekamp)
H.Q. Schleissheim, Munich

IV/NJG4	Finthen (Mainz)	Me110

(This *Geschwadwe* – the Wild Boar unit – was not part of a division mence the building up of a new *Geschwader*.)

SUNDRY NIGHT-FIGHTER UNITS

Stab JG300	Hangelar (Bonn)	Me109, Fw190
I/JG300	Hangelar (Bonn)	Me109, Fw190
II/JG300	Rheine	Fw190
III/JG300	Oldenburg	Me109

(This *Geschwader* – the Wild Boar unit – was not part of a division at this time.)

Parts of NJG2, recently returned from Italy, were refitting and retraining at Gilze Rijen in Holland but were not yet operational.

R.A.F. Group and Squadron Performances and Casualties

This appendix is both a statistical record of the part played by each group and squadron in the four night raids of the Battle of Hamburg and a listing of every R.A.F. aircraft lost in those raids.

To enable fair comparisons to be made between units, crews which bombed specific alternative targets in Germany when their aircraft were forced to turn back because of technical difficulty are included in the 'bombed' totals; so too are two crews which reached Hamburg but found their bomb-release mechanisms to be defective. The six Wellingtons sent each night to drop mines in the River Elbe near Hamburg are also included in the 'dispatched' and 'bombed' totals. Damaged aircraft and men wounded are not listed because some squadrons did not record such details.

Individual aircraft lost are identified by their manufacturer's serial number and the crew by the captain's name. Ranks used include posthumous promotions. All but three of the captains of bombers shot down or lost over Germany and the sea were killed; only F/Sgt Wilkens of 156 Squadron, Sgt Davie of 158 Squadron and Sgt McGarvey of 214 Squadron survived. The experience in operations (ops) flown of each lost crew has been added.

The number 'down' given to each lost bomber, e.g. '11th down on 2nd raid' for the first entry of 12 Squadron, corresponds to the number on the appropriate map in the text. The numbering has normally been done in the order of crash locations along the route and may not always represent the time order of crashes. The cause of a bomber's loss has been given in most cases. This reconstruction is the best possible and is considered reliable in most cases although it should be emphasized that the positions on the maps of some of the bombers lost over the sea must sometimes be approximate.

There may be some omissions in the sections giving details of which crews shot down German fighters since only those claims which are confirmed by reliable German documents have been listed.

The following abbreviations for ranks are used here and in subsequent sections:

R.A.F.: Wing Commander – W/Cdr, Squadron Leader – S/Ldr, Flight Lieutenant – F/Lt, Flying Officer – F/O, Pilot Officer –

P/O, Warrant Officer – W.O., Flight Sergeant – F/Sgt, Sergeant – Sgt.
Luftwaffe: Major – Maj., Hauptmann – Hptm., Oberleutnant – Oblt, Leutnant – Lt, Oberfeldwebel – Ofw., Feldwebel – Fw., Unteroffizier – Uffz.

NO. 1 GROUP

632 sorties – 473 Lancasters and 159 Wellingtons – dispatched, 564 crews bombed. 14 Lancasters and 6 Wellingtons missing, 3 other Wellingtons written off after crashes. 126 men killed, 4 prisoners.

12 Squadron, Wickenby. 92 Lancaster sorties, 78 bombed, 2 missing.

Lancaster EE142 (W.O. W. Salthouse), 11th down on 2nd raid, probably by Me110 of Ofw. Schmale, I/NJG3. 6 killed, 1 prisoner. Crew on 13th op.

Lancaster DV224 (F/O S. Norris), 19th down on 4th raid, probably by Hamburg Flak. 7 killed. Crew on 2nd op.

100 Squadron, Grimsby. 89 Lancaster sorties, 78 bombed, 3 missing.

Lancaster EE169 (W.O. R. Gafford), 16th or 17th down on 2nd raid by either Ofw. Kubisch, rear gunner in Me110 of Maj. Lent, IV/NJG1, or by Ju88 of Lt Stock, IV/NJG3 (see also Lancaster ED708 of 106 Squadron with which this incident is interchangeable). 7 killed. Crew on 12th op.

2 men killed in crew of F/Sgt E. L. Pickles during combat with fighter on 3rd raid.

Lancaster ED705 (F/Lt R. R. Howgill), 7th down on 4th raid, by fighter attack. 7 killed. Crew on 18th op.

Lancaster EE688 (W.O. A. R. Wilden, D.F.C.), 28th down on 4th raid, probably by Me110 of Oblt Greiner, IV/NJG1. 7 killed. Crew on 21st op.

101 Squadron, Ludford Magna. 92 Lancaster sorties, 85 bombed, 1 missing.

Lancaster JA863 (F/Sgt D. P. P. Hurst), 7th down on 2nd raid, probably by Me109 of Maj. Herrmann, Stab/JG300. 7 killed. Crew on 6th op.

103 Squadron, Elsham Wolds. 102 Lancaster sorties, 89 bombed, 5 missing.

Lancaster ED389 (W.O. G. E. B. Hardman), 1st down on 1st raid, probably by Me110 of Hptm. Sigmund, IV/NJG1. 7 killed. Crew on 17th op.

Lancaster JA866 (F/Sgt R. A. Moore), 2nd down on 1st raid by Me110 of Oblt Drünkler, I/NJG5. 7 killed. Crew on 6th op.

Lancaster ED878 (W.O. F. F. O'Hanlon), 12th down on 1st raid, probably by Me110 of Oblt Greiner IV/NJG1. 7 killed. Crew on 13th op.

Lancaster ED645 (W.O. J. S. Stoneman), 17th down on 4th raid, cause unknown. 7 killed. Crew on 19th op.

Lancaster ED922 (W.O. R. Dash), 22nd down on 4th raid, cause unknown. 7 killed. Crew on 14th op.

166 Squadron, Kirmington. 72 Wellington sorties, 60 bombed, 4 missing and 1 written off after crashing.

Wellington HX314 (W.O. G. Ashplant, C.G.M.), 8th down on 1st raid by Hamburg Flak. 5 killed. Crew on 22nd op.

Wellington HE810 (P/O E. G. Birbeck), 18th down on 3rd raid, cause unknown. 5 killed. Crew on 4th op.

Wellington HF455 (W.O. J. A. C. Newman), 2nd down on 4th raid when it crashed soon after take-off. No casualties.

Wellington HE578 (W.O. R. R. Burton), 3rd down on 4th raid, probably because of technical difficulties. Distress signals received. 5 killed. Crew on 14th op.

Wellington HF464 (Sgt H. Nash), 29th down on 4th raid by Me110 of Oblt Greiner, IV/NJG1. 5 killed. Crew on 7th op.

300 (Polish) Squadron, Ingham. 57 Wellington sorties, 53 bombed, 1 missing and 1 written off after crashing.

Wellington HE807 (F/Lt J. Spychla), 1st down on 4th raid, crashed near Worksop after take-off. No casualties.

Wellington HF605 (F/O W. Smyk), 14th down on 4th raid through icing but after earlier fighter attack and Flak damage. 2 killed, 3 prisoners. Crew on 8th op.

305 (Polish) Squadron, Ingham. 30 Wellington sorties, 26 bombed, 1 missing and 1 written off after crashing.

Wellington HF472 (Sgt S. Grzeskowiak), 13th down on 1st raid, crash-landed at Trusthorpe, Lincs, returning from raid short of fuel. No casualties.

Wellington HZ467 (F/Sgt S. Grzeskowiak), 23rd down on 4th raid, cause unknown. 5 killed. Mixed crew but pilot on 2nd op.

460 (Australian) Squadron, Binbrook. 98 Lancaster sorties, 95 bombed, 3 missing.

Lancaster W4987 (Sgt A. G. Ashley), 11th down on 1st raid, by Cuxhaven Flak. 7 killed. Crew on 5th op.

Lancaster JA689 (F/Sgt H. L. Fuhrmann), 17th down on 3rd raid, probably by Fw190 of Uffz. Lövenich, II/JG300. 7 killed. Crew on 8th op.

Lancaster ED525 (F/O A. J. Johnson), 28th down on 3rd raid by Me110 of Hptm. Prinz zur Lippe-Weissenfeld, III/NJG1. 7 killed. Crew on 4th op., some of a second tour.

NO. 3 GROUP

493 sorties – 431 Stirlings and 62 Lancasters – dispatched, 407 crews bombed. 10 Stirlings and 3 Lancasters missing, 3 other Stirlings written off after crashes or battle damage. 81 men killed, 19 prisoners. 1 confirmed Me110 destroyed.

15 Squadron, Mildenhall. 72 Stirling sorties, 60 bombed, 1 missing and 2 total losses after crashing.

5 men prisoners from crew of F/O R. Waugh when ordered to bale out in technical difficulty on 2nd raid but the aircraft recovered and returned to base.

Stirling EH893 (F/Lt J. R. Childs), 9th down on 2nd raid when damaged by Hamburg Flak and then attacked by Me110 of Uffz. Loeschner, III/NJG3. 7 killed, 1 prisoner. Crew on 14th op.

Stirling EF437 (Sgt V. Jackson), 19th down on 2nd raid when crash-landed short of petrol at Mildenhall. No casualties.

Stirling EF339 (F/O G. Bould), 2nd down on 3rd raid when crash-landed at Coltishall. No casualties.

75 (New Zealand) Squadron, Mepal. 79 Stirling sorties, 66 bombed, 3 missing.

Stirling EE890 (Sgt H. Nicol), 6th down on 1st raid, probably by Me110 of Fw. Meissner, II/NJG3. 4 killed, 3 prisoners. Mixed crew, 5/10 ops.

Stirling BF577 (F/Sgt J. A. Couper), 24th down on 4th raid, possibly after collision with Do217 of Fw. Krauter, II/NJG3. 7 killed. Crew on 2nd op.

Stirling EH928 (Sgt C. Bailie), 31st down on 4th raid by Me110 of Hptm. Jabs, IV/NJG1. 8 killed. Crew on 15th op.

90 Squadron, West Wickham. 68 Stirling sorties, 56 bombed, 1 written off after crash. No aircrew casualties. 1 Me110 destroyed by crew of F/O W. Day on 3rd raid.

Stirling BK693 (P/O R. Whitworth), 20th down on 2nd raid after Flak damage, crash-landing at Stradishall.

115 Squadron, East Wretham. 62 Lancaster Mk II sorties, 51 bombed, 3 missing.

Lancaster DS673 (Sgt R. W. Bennett), 5th down on 4th raid, probably by Ju88 of Ofw. Heitmann, I/NJG3. 7 killed. Crew on 9th op.

Lancaster DS629 (F/Sgt C. Button), 6th down on 4th raid, probably by fighter attack. 7 killed. Crew on 9th op.

Lancaster DS715 (P/O R. J. Mosen), 16th down on 4th raid, probably struck by lightning. 7 killed. Crew on 4th op.

149 Squadron, Lakenheath. 61 Stirling sorties, 55 bombed. No aircraft or aircrew casualties.

214 Squadron, Chedburgh. 40 Stirling sorties, 31 bombed, 3 missing.
Stirling EE902 (P/O R. W. Belshaw, D.F.M.), 10th down on 1st raid by fighter attack. 6 killed, 2 prisoners. Crew on 16th op.
Stirling EF407 (F/O H. P. Shann), 29th down on 3rd raid, probably by fighter attack. 7 killed. Crew on 1st and 2nd ops.
Stirling EF409 (Sgt A. A. R. McGarvey), 9th down on 4th raid by icing. 5 killed, 2 prisoners. Crew on 3rd op.

218 Squadron, Downham Market. 74 Stirling sorties, 57 bombed, 3 missing.
Stirling BF567 (W/Cdr D. T. Saville, D.S.O., D.F.C.), 7th down on 1st raid by fighter attack. 7 killed, 1 prisoner. Most of crew on 9th operation of 2nd tour.
Stirling EE825 (Sgt J. Clark), 16th down on 3rd raid, probably by Hamburg Flak. 7 killed. Crew on 3rd op.
Stirling BF578 (Sgt R. Pickard), 24th down on 3rd raid, damaged by Hamburg Flak and then attacked by Me110 of Uffz. Rohlfing, III/NJG3. 2 killed, 5 prisoners. Crew on 2nd op.

620 Squadron, Chedburgh. 37 Stirling sorties, 31 bombed. No aircraft or aircrew casualties.

192 Squadron, Feltwell. 13 sorties – 6 Wellingtons, 4 Mosquitoes, 3 Halifaxes – dispatched on radio-countermeasures operations, flying with the Main Force to the Hamburg area. 11 operated successfully. No aircraft or aircrew casualties.

NO. 4 GROUP

662 sorties – 601 Halifaxes and 61 Wellingtons – dispatched, 578 crews bombed. 18 Halifaxes missing, 1 Halifax written off after crash. 110 men killed, 20 prisoners. 1 confirmed Do217 destroyed.

10 Squadron, Melbourne. 84 Halifax sorties, 77 bombed. No aircraft or aircrew casualties.

51 Squadron, Snaith. 87 Halifax sorties, 71 bombed, 3 missing. 1 Do217 destroyed by crew of Sgt A. Fletcher on 1st raid.
Halifax HR940 (Sgt W. J. Murray), 4th down on 1st raid by Ju88 of Oblt Köberich, IV/NJG3. 7 killed. Crew on 2nd op.
Halifax JD309 (Sgt A. Fletcher), 7th down on 3rd raid by fighter attack. 7 killed. Crew on 4th op.
Halifax HR859 (W.O. E. R. Sklarchuk), 8th down on 4th raid, probably by Me110 of Maj. Radusch, II/NJG3. 7 killed. Crew on 5th op.

76 Squadron, Holme-on-Spalding-Moor. 91 Halifax sorties, 75 bombed, 3 missing, 1 written off after crash.

Halifax DK187 (F/O G. Such), 3rd down on 1st raid by fighter attack. 7 killed. Crew on 14th op.

Halifax DK188 (F/Sgt W. E. Elder), 18th down on 2nd raid, crash-landing at Shipdham after fighter combat. 1 man killed in the combat.

Halifax EB244 (Sgt A. R. Biercke), 27th down on 3rd raid by Hamburg Flak damage and then attacked by fighter. 2 killed, 5 prisoners. Crew on 3rd op.

Halifax EB249 (F/O S. I. Dillon), 11th down on 4th raid, probably by fighter attack. 7 killed. Crew on 6th op.

77 Squadron, Elvington. 73 Halifax sorties, 68 bombed, 1 missing.

Halifax JB956 (F/Sgt G. H. Sutton), 11th down on 3rd raid, probably by (believed) Do217 of Oblt Raht, II/NJG3. 8 killed. Crew on 11th op.

78 Squadron, Breighton. 84 Halifax sorties, 68 bombed, 3 missing.

Halifax JD148 (Sgt L. E. Maidment), 14th down on 2nd raid by Wilhelmshaven Flak. 2 killed, 1 died of wounds, 4 prisoners. Crew on 3rd op.

Halifax JD252 (Sgt R. Snape), 3rd down on 3rd raid, probably by technical failure. 7 killed. Crew on 4th op.

Halifax JD798 (F/Sgt F. Fraser), 14th down on 3rd raid, probably by Hamburg Flak. 7 killed. Crew on 6th op.

102 Squadron, Pocklington. 86 Halifax sorties, 75 bombed, 5 missing.

Halifax JD316 (F/Lt T. Bakewell), 9th down on 1st raid by fighter attack. 8 killed. Crew on 11th op.

Halifax JD150 (Sgt G. H. Brown), 4th down on 2nd raid by Me110 of Fw. Meissner, II/NJG3. 7 killed. Crew on 3rd op.

Halifax JB864 (F/O G. M. Clarke), 6th down on 2nd raid by fighter attack. 4 killed, 3 prisoners. Crew on 3rd op.

Halifax HR711 (Sgt J. S. Gaston), 6th down on 3rd raid by fighter attack. 7 killed. Crew on 3rd op.

Halifax W7883 (F/Sgt T. A. Macquarie), 12th down on 3rd raid, probably by Do217 of Lt Sachsenberg, II/NJG3. 7 killed. Crew on 1st op.

158 Squadron, Lissett. 96 Halifax sorties, 86 bombed, 3 missing.

Halifax HR914 (Sgt W. H. Bolam), 5th down on 1st raid by Me110 of Lt Böttinger, II/NJG3. 7 killed. Crew on 1st op.

Halifax JD277 (F/Sgt N. R. MacDonald), 10th down on 3rd raid, probably by Do217 of Oblt Raht, II/NJG3. 6 killed, 1 prisoner. Crew on 15th op.

Halifax HR751 (Sgt C. K. Davie), 20th down on 4th raid by Hamburg Flak. 1 killed, 6 prisoners. Crew on 4th op.

466 (Australian) Squadron, Leconfield. 61 Wellington sorties, 58 bombed. No aircraft or aircrew casualties.

NO. 5 GROUP

577 Lancaster sorties dispatched, 3 recalled, 518 crews bombed. 16 Lancasters missing, 1 written off after crash. 109 men killed, 6 prisoners. 2 confirmed German fighters destroyed.

9 Squadron, Bardney. 68 Lancaster sorties, 3 recalled, 61 bombed, 2 missing.

Lancaster JA692 (F/Lt C. W. Fox), 15th down on 3rd raid, probably by Hamburg Flak. 8 killed. Crew on 17th op.

Lancaster ED493 (Sgt D. Mackenzie), 33rd down on 4th raid, probably by Me110 of Ofw. Scherfling, IV/NJG1. 7 killed. Crew on 7th op.

44 (Rhodesia) Squadron, Dunholme Lodge. 51 Lancaster sorties, 46 bombed, 1 missing.

Lancaster W4778 (Sgt A. R. Moffatt), 32nd down on 4th raid, probably by Me110 of Hptm. Jabs, IV/NJG1. 6 killed, 1 prisoner. Crew on 4th op.

49 Squadron, Fiskerton. 59 Lancaster sorties, 53 bombed. No aircraft or aircrew casualties.

50 Squadron, Skellingthorpe. 47 Lancaster sorties, 37 bombed, 1 missing, 1 written off after crash.

Lancaster R5687 (F/Sgt N. P. I. Castells), 13th down on 2nd raid by Bremerhaven Flak. 7 killed. Crew on 2nd op.

Lancaster ED468 (Sgt E. W. A. Clarke) crashed on take-off and burnt out. No serious casualties.

57 Squadron, Scampton. 63 Lancaster sorties, 57 bombed, 3 missing.

Lancaster ED616 (F/Sgt G. A. N. Parker), 25th down on 3rd raid by Hamburg Flak. 7 killed. Crew on 7th op.

Lancaster ED931 (F/Sgt E. F. Allbright), 26th down on 3rd raid by fighter attack. 6 killed, 1 prisoner. Crew on 21st op.

Lancaster JA696 (F/Sgt A. C. Browning), 15th down on 4th raid, cause unknown. 7 killed. Crew on 1st op.

61 Squadron, Syerston. 63 Lancaster sorties, 55 bombed, 3 missing.

Lancaster ED782 (P/O J. M. Phillips), 5th down on 3rd raid by fighter attack. 7 killed. Crew on 23rd op.

Lancaster JA873 (F/Lt B. M. Laing), 18th down on 4th raid by fighter attack. 8 killed. Crew on 13th op.

Lancaster W5000 (F/O R. Lyon), 27th down on 4th raid, probably by Ju88 of Lt Leube, I/NJG3. 7 killed. Crew on 4th op.

106 Squadron, Syerston. 58 Lancaster sorties, 51 bombed, 2 missing.

Lancaster ED303 (Sgt E. G. McLeod), 8th down on 2nd raid, probably by fighter attack. 7 killed. Crew on 2nd op.

Lancaster ED708 (F/Sgt J. B. Charters), 16th or 17th down on 2nd raid (see Lancaster EE169 of 100 Squadron with which this incident is interchangeable). 7 killed. Crew on 8th op.

207 Squadron, Langar. 48 Lancaster sorties, 45 bombed, 1 missing.

Lancaster W4962 (F/O C. Burne), 12th down on 2nd raid by Me110 of maj. Ehle, II/NJG1. 5 killed, 2 prisoners. Crew on 2nd op.

467 (Australian) Squadron, Bottesford. 64 Lancaster sorties, 59 bombed, 3 missing. 1 Me109 and 1 Fw190 destroyed by crews of Lancasters 'D' and 'Y' on 3rd raid but squadron records do not identify the crews concerned.

Lancaster W5003 (P/O J. L. Carrington), 2nd down on 2nd raid by fighter attack. 5 killed, 2 prisoners. Crew on 12th op.

Lancaster W4946 (P/O J. T. Buchanan), 15th down on 2nd raid, probably by Me110 of Hptm. Jabs, IV/NJG1. 7 killed. Crew on 1st op.

Lancaster ED534 (F/Sgt R. W. Park), 13th down on 3rd raid, probably by fighter attack. 7 killed. Crew on 1st op.

1 man killed in crew of P/O D. Symonds during combat with fighter on 4th raid.

619 Squadron, Woodhall Spa. 56 Lancaster sorties, 54 bombed. No aircraft or aircrew casualties.

NO. 6 (CANADIAN) GROUP

312 sorties – 225 Halifaxes and 87 Wellingtons – dispatched, 250 crews bombed. 5 Halifaxes and 3 Wellingtons missing. 43 men killed, 11 prisoners.

408 (Goose) Squadron, Leeming. 52 Halifax sorties, 45 bombed, 1 missing.

Halifax DT749 (F/Lt C. C. Stovel, D.F.C.), 5th down on 2nd raid, probably by Do217 of Lt Sachsenberg, II/NJG3. 5 killed, 3 prisoners. Crew on last of combined Coastal Command and Bomber Command tour of 42 ops.

1 man prisoner from crew of Sgt J. D. Harvey when aircraft in a spin during storm on 4th raid; aircraft recovered and returned to base.

419 (Moose) Squadron, Middleton St George. 56 Halifax sorties, 43 bombed, 1 missing.

Halifax DT798 (Sgt J. S. Sobin), 13th down on 4th raid by icing. 4 killed, 3 prisoners. Crew on 4th op.

427 (Lion) Squadron, Leeming. 55 Halifax sorties, 46 bombed. No aircraft or aircrew casualties.

428 (Ghost) Squadron, Middleton St George. 62 Halifax sorties, 50 bombed, 3 missing.

Halifax DK239 (Sgt D. H. Bates), 19th down on 3rd raid by fighter attack. 6 killed, 1 prisoner. Crew on 2nd op.

Halifax EB212 (P/O V. T. Sylvester), 26th down on 4th raid, cause unknown. 8 killed. Crew on 28th op.

Halifax EB274 (W.O. M. Chepil), 30th down on 4th raid, probably by Me110 of Hptm. Jabs, IV/NJG1. 8 killed. Crew on 17th op.

429 (Bison) Squadron, East Moor. 50 Wellington sorties, 42 bombed, 1 missing.

Wellington JA114 (W/Cdr J. A. Piddington), 3rd down on 2nd raid by fighter attack. 3 killed, 2 prisoners. Crew on 3rd op. of 2nd tour.

432 (Leaside) Squadron, Skipton-on-Swale. 37 Wellington sorties, 24 bombed, 2 missing.

Wellington LN294 (W/Cdr H. W. Kerby), 20th down on 3rd raid by fighter attack. 4 killed, 1 prisoner. Most of crew on 5th op. of 2nd tour but W/Cdr Kerby had done two previous Fighter Command tours.

Wellington HE906 (P/O D. R. C. McDonald), 25th down on 4th raid, probably by fighter action. 5 killed. Crew on 5th op.

NO. 8 (PATHFINDER) GROUP

439 sorties – 257 Lancasters, 145 Halifaxes, 37 Stirlings – dispatched, 386 crews bombed. 6 Lancasters, 6 Halifaxes and 1 Stirling missing, 1 Lancaster and 1 Stirling written off after crashes. 79 men killed, 5 prisoners, 7 interned.

7 Squadron, Oakington. 78 sorties – 41 Lancasters and 37 Stirlings – 67 bombed, 1 Stirling missing and 1 written off.

Stirling EF369 (P/O G. R. Woodward), 21st down on 2nd raid, written off after crash-landing at Oakington. No casualties.

Stirling EF364 (F/O A. L. Forbes), 4th down on 3rd raid by fighter attack. 7 killed. Crew on 9th op., possibly more ops on a previous squadron.

35 Squadron, Graveley. 86 Halifax sorties, 71 bombed, 3 missing.

Halifax HR815 (F/Lt H. C. Pexton), 21st down on 3rd raid by Hamburg Flak and finished off by fighter. 5 killed, 2 prisoners. Crew on 17th op.

Halifax HR906 (F/Sgt R. Spooner), 22nd down on 3rd raid by fighter action. 6 killed, 1 prisoner. Crew on 6th op., possibly more ops on a previous squadron.

Halifax HR863 (P/O E. Solomon), 12th down on 4th raid by icing. 6 killed, 1 prisoner. Crew on 16th op.

83 Squadron, Wyton. 57 Lancaster sorties, 56 bombed, 1 written off after crash.

Lancaster R5625 (P/O K. A. King), crash-landed at Sibson after Flak damage over Hamburg. No casualties.

97 Squadron, Bourn. 76 Lancaster sorties, 74 bombed, 2 missing.

Lancaster EE172 (F/O C. Shnier), 23rd down on 3rd raid by fighter attack. 7 killed. Crew on 28th op.

Lancaster ED862 (P/O D. J. Marks, D.F.M.), 30th down on 3rd raid, probably by Me110 of Maj. Lent, IV/NJG1. 7 killed. Crew on 30th op.

156 Squadron, Warboys. 83 Lancaster sorties, 73 bombed, 4 missing.

Lancaster JA709 (F/O L. R. Crampton), 1st down on 2nd raid by fighter attack. 7 killed. Crew on 20th op.

Lancaster EE178 (F/Sgt C. W. Wilkens), 10th down on 2nd raid by fighter attack. 6 killed, 1 prisoner. Crew on 19th op.

Lancaster ED598 (F/Lt B. F. Smith, D.F.C.), 8th down on 3rd raid by fighter attack. 7 killed. Crew on 14th op., some of a second tour.

Lancaster ED822 (F/Sgt M. T. Hall), 9th down on 3rd raid by fighter attack. 7 killed. Crew on 1st op.

405 (Vancouver) Squadron R.C.A.F., Gransden Lodge. 59 Halifax sorties, 45 bombed, 3 missing.

Halifax HR917 (F/Lt H. W. J. Dare), 4th down on 4th raid probably by Do217 of Hptm. Schönert, II/NJG5. 7 killed. Crew on 1st op., possibly more on a previous squadron.

Halifax HR849 (Sgt A. F. Gregory), 10th down on 4th raid by Bremen Flak. 7 killed. Crew on 5th op.

Halifax HR871 (Sgt J. A. Phillips, D.F.M.), 21st down on 4th raid by storm damage. 7 interned. Crew on 21st op.

139 Squadron, Wyton. This squadron dispatched 34 Mosquito bomber sorties in connection with the Battle of Hamburg either by bombing Hamburg on nights when there were no major raids or by carrying out diversionary operations in northern Germany while the Main Force was attacking Hamburg. 25 sorties operated as ordered and 6 bombed alternative targets. No aircraft or aircrew casualties.

1409 (Meteorological) Flight, Oakington. 8 Mosquito sorties carried out in connection with the Battle of Hamburg. No aircraft or aircrew casualties.

FIGHTER COMMAND INTRUDER OPERATIONS

25 Squadron, Church Fenton. 9 Mosquito sorties, 1 confirmed German fighter destroyed by crew of F/Lt E. R. F. Cooke on 1st raid. 1 Mosquito missing.

Mosquito DD748 (F/Lt E. R. F. Cooke) lost on 3rd raid by technical failure. 2 killed.

141 Squadron, Wittering. 20 Beaufighter sorties. No successes, no losses.

157 Squadron, Hunsdon. 6 Mosquito sorties. No successes, 1 Mosquito missing.

Mosquito HJ820 (F/O J. O. Tanner) lost on 4th raid, shot down by Hannover Flak. 2 killed.

307 (Polish) Squadron, Fairwood Common. 3 Mosquito sorties. No successes, no losses.

410 (Canadian) Squadron, Coleby Grange. 8 Mosquito sorties. No successes, no losses.

418 (Canadian) Squadron, Ford. 20 Mosquito sorties dispatched. 1 confirmed Do217 written off after being hit by crew of S/Ldr Moran on 4th raid. No losses.

456 (Australian) Squadron, Middle Wallop. 6 Mosquito sorties. No successes, no losses.

605 Squadron, Castle Camps. 20 Mosquito sorties. 1 confirmed Me110 destroyed by crew of F/O A. G. Woods on 3rd raid. 1 Mosquito missing.

Mosquito —— (F/O/ A. V. Aylott) lost on 4th raid, cause unknown. Presumed crashed in sea. 2 killed.

541 and 542 Squadrons, Benson. These squadrons carried out 5 Spitfire photographic reconnaissance sorties to Hamburg without loss.

U.S.A.A.F. Bomb Group
Performances and Casualties

This appendix only covers the American daylight raids on Hamburg on 25 and 26 July 1943. It should be remembered that a much greater U.S.A.A.F. effort than this was devoted to attacking other targets in Germany during the period of the Battle of Hamburg.

Not included in 'sorties' are those B-17s which took off as 'air spares' but which were not required and were released. All sorties were by B-17s. The numbering of shot-down aircraft follows the numbering in Maps 7 and 8. Because most shot-down B-17s were attacked by more than one German fighter and because most shot-down German fighters were hit by fire from more than one B-17, no attempt will be made here to credit either type of success to individual German pilots or B-17 crews.

91 Bomb Group, Bassingbourn. 39 sorties, 29 bombed, 3 missing.

B-17 42-29813 (2nd Lt Marshall L. Pilert) 324th Squadron, 13th down on 1st raid by Flak damage and fighter attack. 1 killed, 9 prisoners. Mixed crew on 1st and 4th missions.

B-17 42-3031 (Lt James W. Rendall Jr) 324th Squadron, 1st down on 2nd raid by Flak damage and fighter attack. 4 killed, 6 prisoners. Crew – unknown number of missions.

B-17 42-42709 (Lt Jack A. Hargis) 322nd Squadron, 2nd down on 2nd raid after damage by fighter attack. Ditched in North Sea off English coast. 10 rescued. Crew on 2nd mission.

303rd Bomb Group, Molesworth. 40 sorties, 34 bombed, 1 missing.

B-17 42-29606 (Lt John A. Van Wie, killed) 360th Squadron, 4th down on 1st raid by Flak damage and fighter attack. 4 killed, 6 prisoners. Crew on 21st mission.

351st Bomb Group, Polebrook. 44 sorties, 32 bombed, 1 missing.

B-17 42-3272 (Lt Edwin S. Boyd) 511th Squadron, 8th down on 1st raid by engine failure and fighter attack. 6 killed, 4 prisoners. Crew – unknown number of missions.

379th Bomb Group, Kimbolton. 40 sorties, 19 bombed Hamburg and 1 an alternative target. 19 aborted after failure to join combat wing.

B-17 42-23175 (Lt Frank A. Hildebrandt) 524th Squadron, 1st

down in 1st raid by fighter attack. 10 prisoners. Crew on 8th/9th mission.

B-17 42-5917 (2nd Lt Philip A. Mohr) 524th Squadron, 3rd down on 1st raid by fighter attack. 4 killed, 6 prisoners. Crew on approx. 3rd mission.

Lt Willis C. Carlisle Jr, pilot of 524th Squadron, killed when his B-17 attacked by fighter on 1st raid.

381st Bomb Group, Ridgewell. 41 sorties, 14 bombed Heide as an alternative on 1st raid, 16 bombed Hamburg on 2nd raid, 3 missing.

B-17 42-30013 (Lt William R. Moore) 532nd Squadron, 9th down on 1st raid by Hamburg Flak. 4 killed, 6 prisoners. Crew on 7th mission.

B-17 42-29976 (Lt Jack H. Owen) 532nd Squadron, 10th down on 1st raid by Flak damage and fighter attack. 10 prisoners. Crew on 8th mission.

B-17 42-30153 (Capt. Joe E. Alexander) 532nd Squadron, 14th down on 1st raid after Flak damage. Crash-landed at Südmoor, near Aurich. 10 prisoners. Crew on 4th/6th mission.

Lt Sidney Novell, a navigator on his first mission, killed when his B-17 damaged by Flak on 2nd raid.

384th Bomb Group, Grafton Underwood. 41 sorties, 17 bombed, 20 aborted after failure to join combat wing, 7 missing.

B-17 42-3122 (2nd Lt Ralph J. Hall) 545th Squadron, 2nd down on 1st raid by mechanical difficulty and fighter attack. 10 prisoners. Crew on 6th mission.

B-17 42-3069 (Lt Gordon J. Hankinson) 544th Squadron, 5th down on 1st raid by Flak damage and fighter attack. 10 prisoners. Crew on 3rd mission.

B-17 42-3024 (2nd Lt P. J. Ward) 544th Squadron, 6th down on 1st raid by Flak damage and fighter attack. 7 killed, 3 prisoners. Crew on 2nd mission.

B-17 42-3088 (Lt Clarence R. Christman, killed) 544th Squadron, 7th down on 1st raid by fighter attack. 5 killed, 5 prisoners. Crew on approx. 3rd mission.

B-17 42-29670 (Lt Kelmer J. Hall) 544th Squadron, 11th down on 1st raid by Flak damage and fighter attack. 2 killed, 8 prisoners. Crew on 2nd mission.

B-17 42-3075 (Lt John M. Hegewald) 544th Squadron, 12th down on 1st raid by Flak damage and fighter attack. 7 killed, 3 prisoners. Crew on 1st mission.

B-17 42-5883 (Lt Thomas J. Estes) 544th Squadron, 15th down on 1st raid by fighter attack. 10 rescued by Danish fishing boat.

R.A.F. Group and Squadron Performances and Casualties

This appendix is both a statistical record of the part played by each group and squadron in the four night raids of the Battle of Hamburg and a listing of every R.A.F. aircraft lost in those raids.

To enable fair comparisons to be made between units, crews which bombed specific alternative targets in Germany when their aircraft were forced to turn back because of technical difficulty are included in the 'bombed' totals; so too are two crews which reached Hamburg but found their bomb-release mechanisms to be defective. The six Wellingtons sent each night to drop mines in the River Elbe near Hamburg are also included in the 'dispatched' and 'bombed' totals. Damaged aircraft and men wounded are not listed because some squadrons did not record such details.

Individual aircraft lost are identified by their manufacturer's serial number and the crew by the captain's name. Ranks used include posthumous promotions. All but three of the captains of bombers shot down or lost over Germany and the sea were killed; only F/Sgt Wilkens of 156 Squadron, Sgt Davie of 158 Squadron and Sgt McGarvey of 214 Squadron survived. The experience in operations (ops) flown of each lost crew has been added.

The number 'down' given to each lost bomber, e.g. '11th down on 2nd raid' for the first entry of 12 Squadron, corresponds to the number on the appropriate map in the text. The numbering has normally been done in the order of crash locations along the route and may not always represent the time order of crashes. The cause of a bomber's loss has been given in most cases. This reconstruction is the best possible and is considered reliable in most cases although it should be emphasized that the positions on the maps of some of the bombers lost over the sea must sometimes be approximate.

There may be some omissions in the sections giving details of which crews shot down German fighters since only those claims which are confirmed by reliable German documents have been listed.

The following abbreviations for ranks are used here and in subsequent sections:

R.A.F.: Wing Commander – W/Cdr, Squadron Leader – S/Ldr, Flight Lieutenant – F/Lt, Flying Officer – F/O, Pilot Officer –

North Sea by B-17s of 303rd Bomb Group on 1st U.S. raid. 2 prisoners.

Totals of NJG1: 15 R.A.F. bombers and 1 B-17 shot down, 1 night fighter lost.

1/NJG3, Vechta and Wittmundhafen
Successes: 2 R.A.F. bombers – 1 4-engined bomber by Lt Leube; 1 Lancaster by Ofw. Schmale.

Own aircraft lost:
Me110G-4 5468 (pilot not known) crashed at Stukenborg, near Vechta, probably after combat with Stirling of 90 Squadron on 3rd raid. Crew unhurt.

II/NJG3, Schleswig and Westerland
Successes: 16 R.A.F. bombers – 1 Lancaster, 1 Halifax, 1 Stirling, 1 Wellington by Maj. G. Radusch; 1 unidentified bomber by Hptm. W. Elstermann; 2 Halifaxes, 1 Lancaster by Oblt G. Raht; 1 4-engined bomber by Lt Böttinger; 1 4-engined bomber by Lt Führer; 3 4-engined bombers by Lt G. Sachsenberg; 1 4-engined bomber by Ofw. Heitmann; 1 Stirling, 1 Halifax by Fw. H. Meissner.

Own aircraft lost:
Ju88C6 360334 (Lt W. Töpfer) shot down into sea off Sylt by Mosquito of 25 Squadron on 1st raid. 2 men killed.

Do217N 1414 (Ofw. W. Ziegler) crashed near Flensburg, probably after combat with Halifax of 51 Squadron on 1st raid. 2 men killed.

Do217 1493 (Hptm. H. Baer) crash-landed near Westerland airfield after being hit by a Mosquito of 418 Squadron, possibly by one of the Mosquito's bombs, on 4th raid. Crew wounded.

Do217N 1419 (Fw. Krauter) crashed at Wiemerstedt, 10 km north of Heide, possibly after collision with a bomber.

III/NJG3, Lüneburg, Wunstorf and Stade
Successes: 3 R.A.F. bombers – 1 Lancaster by Ofw. W. Kurrek; 1 4-engined bomber by Uffz. Löschner; 1 Stirling by Uffz. W. Rohlfing.

Own aircraft lost:
Me110G-4 6277 (Ofw. W. Kurrek) shot down near Lüneburg airfield by Mosquito of 605 Squadron on 3rd raid. 2 men killed.

IV/NJG3, Grove and Kastrup
Successes: 2 R.A.F. bombers – 1 Halifax by Oblt G. Köberich; 1 4-engined bomber by Lt H. Stock. No losses.

Totals for NJG3: 23 R.A.F. bombers shot down, 6 night fighters lost.

NJG5
This *Geschwader* was not directly engaged in the Battle of Hamburg, being held back to cover Berlin, but some of its more experienced

crews were either temporarily attached to more forward *Gruppen* or operated from forward airfields on certain nights. In this way Oblt E. Drünkler of I/NJG5 and Hptm. R. Schönert of II/NJG5 shot down 1 4-engined bomber and 1 Halifax respectively. No losses were suffered.

Stab JG300, Bonn
Successes: 2 Lancasters by Maj. H. Herrmann. No losses.

I/JG300, Bonn
Successes: 3 R.A.F. bombers – 2 4-engined bombers by Ofw. Lönnecker; 1 4-engined bomber by Fw. W. Rullkötter. No losses.

II/JG300, Rheine
Successes: 1 Lancaster by Uffz. H. Lövenich.
   Own aircraft lost:
   1 Fw190 (Hptm. F. Angermann) shot down over Hamburg (probably St Pauli) by Lancaster of 467 Squadron on 3rd raid. Pilot killed.

III/JG300, Oldenburg
Successes: no details.
   Own aircraft lost:
   1 Me109 (Uffz. H. Fritz) shot down near Oldenburg by Lancaster of 467 Squadron on 3rd raid. Pilot killed.

Lt F. Rübsam of JG300, but *Gruppe* unknown, also shot down 1 4-engined bomber.

Totals for JG300: 7 R.A.F. bombers shot down (probably several more but no reliable details). 2 night fighters lost.

PART TWO. DAY-FIGHTER UNITS

(All 'raids' mentioned below are U.S.A.A.F. operations to Hamburg on 25 and 26 July 1943.)

I/JG1, Deelen
Successes: 4 B-17s – 2 by Oblt Engleder, 2 by Uffz. Kunze. No losses.

II/JG1, Woensdrecht and Schiphol
Possibly in action but no details.

III/JG1, Leeuwarden
Success: 1 B-17 by Maj. K.-H. Leesmann.
   Own aircraft lost:
   Me109G-6 207 (Maj. K.-H. Leesmann) shot down on 1st raid by unknown American bomb group.

I/JG11, Husum
Success: 1 B-17 by Fw. Spreckels. No losses. (This *Gruppe* also claimed 3 B-17s on the Hannover raid of 26 July.)

II/JG 11, Jever
Claimed 6 B-17s on 1st raid by Hptm. G. Specht, Oblt G. Sommer, Lt Rose, Lt W. Gloerfeld, Lt Hondt and Fw. M. Hauptmann.

Own aircraft lost on 1st raid:

Me109G-6 20026 (Lt W. Gloerfeld) collided with stabilizer of B-17 of 379th Bomb Group and crashed near Bliedersdorf, near Buxtehude. Pilot wounded.

Me109G-1 14147 (Lt E. Kämpf) possibly shot down by B-17 of 303rd Bomb Group, crashed near Itzehoe. Pilot wounded.

Me109G-1 14125 (Uffz. W. Riedmann) shot down by B-17, crashed Sauensiek, 10 km south-west of Buxtehude. Pilot wounded.

(This *Gruppe* also claimed 3 B-17s and lost 3 Me109s against the Hannover raid of 26 July.)

III/JG 11, Oldenburg
Successes: 2 B-17s by Oblt H. Frey. No losses.

Jagdstaffel Heligoland
Success: 1 B-17 by Oblt König. No losses.

III/JG 26, Nordholz
No details of successes. Own aircraft lost: Me109G-6 16447 (pilot not known) crash-landed at Stade after combat. Pilot unhurt.

Acknowledgements

I am particularly grateful to the following men and women who participated in various ways in the Battle of Hamburg. It is only the generous and willing help of these people that has made it possible for me to produce this book in the particular form I always wished for it.

BRITISH, EMPIRE AND ALLIED AIRCREW*

7 Squadron: P/O H. W. Bacon, F/Lt S. Baker, F/Sgt F. R. Cox, P/O R. H. Dean, Sgt W. B. Hawkins, W.O. C. Thornhill. *9 Squadron:* Sgt D. N. Bennett, W/Cdr P. Burnett, Sgt J. Gaskell, F/Lt G. F. Robertson, Sgt P. A. S. Twinn. *10 Squadron:* F/Sgt W. Booth, F/Lt R. H. Brookbanks, Sgt G. Culverhouse, S/Ldr A. I. S. Debenham, F/Sgt C. R. Farrar, F/Sgt A. L. Fuller, F/Sgt D. E. Girardau, Sgt J. Gray, Sgt R. N. Hurst, Sgt H. T. Mogridge, P/O G. Stevens, S/Ldr J. F. Sutton, Sgt J. D. Whiteman. *12 Squadron:* Sgt F. A. Attwood, Sgt E. Brooks, P/O R. Clarke, Sgt J. A. L. Currie, Sgt A. C. Farmer, Sgt T. H. Franklin, S/Ldr A. J. Heyworth, Sgt C. W. Lanham, Sgt T. Matthews, F/Lt J. N. Rowland, F/O W. F. Snell, F/Lt V. Wood. *15 Squadron:* F/Sgt D. A. Boards, Sgt A. R. Cole, P/O G. W. Gabel, F/O E. H. W. Harrison, F/Sgt J. A. Hughes, W.O. E. Hurley, F/Sgt K. G. Pollard, Sgt T. V. W. Rigby, F/O J. Vaughan. *25 Squadron:* F/O V. H. Linthune. *35 Squadron:* F/Lt J. Annetts, F/Sgt R. E. Bates, F/Lt R. B. Berwick, Sgt W. C. Campbell, Capt. J. K. Christie, S/Ldr E. K. Creswell, F/Lt A. J. F. Davidson, F/Sgt F. Fenton, F/O C. A. Hewlett, P/O L. E. N. Lahey, F/Sgt N. J. Matich, P/O W. J. Simpson, Sgt A. Stephen, Sgt C. G. Weldon, F/Lt G. R. Whitten. *44 Squadron:* F/Sgt R. A. C. Hellier, F/O R. H. Marshall, F/Sgt H. E. Palmer, Sgt C. R. Snell, F/Sgt Q. F. Snow, Sgt P. L. Swan. *49 Squadron:* Sgt C. M. Chamberlain, Sgt J. E. Hudson, F/O D. Jones, Sgt T. J. Page, Sgt N. D. Panter, Sgt R. W. Petty, Sgt O. Roberts, Sgt C. Wiltshire. *50 Squadron:* F/O I. D. Bolton, F/Sgt M. M. Cole, P/O D. A. Duncan. *51 Squadron:* Sgt E. Brookes, F/Sgt M. C. Foster, F/O F. P. C. Garland, F/Sgt H. M. George, Sgt W. G. Hart, Sgt A. R. Jordan, Sgt T. Nelson, Sgt D. W. Thomp-

* Abbreviations not used earlier: Air Commodore – Air Cdre, Group Captain – Gp Capt. All ranks are those held at the time of the Hamburg raids.

son. *57 Squadron:* F/O F. Crowther, Sgt T. Davies, Sgt S. H. Guy, P/O W. E. McCrea, Sgt J. Murray, F/Sgt J. Sheriff, P/O R. J. Sherrett. *61 Squadron:* F/O G. Aley, F/O J. H. Dyer, Sgt E. F. Gardiner, Sgt R. F. Lewin, Sgt P. B. Smith, F/3gt A. E. Wilson. *75 Squadron:* Sgt S. A. Longman, F/O E. J. Mansell, Sgt J. L. Mitchell. *76 Squadron:* Sgt S. H. Bates, Sgt A. W. Davis, F/Sgt W. E. Elder, Sgt E. Freeman, Sgt F. A. Newton, F/Sgt K. R. Parry, F/Lt W. F. Readhead, Sgt V. A. Thompson, F/Sgt H. D. Weaver. *77 Squadron:* F/O M. R. Ashman, Sgt D. Brown, Sgt O. E. Burger, Sgt B. Hallam, Sgt E. C. Honey, Sgt R. A. K. Lawrence, P/O E. G. McClorry, Sgt A. G. S. McCulloch, F/Sgt D. F. Thorn. *78 Squadron:* Sgt A. E. Beswick, F/Sgt D. G. Cumming, F/Lt A. Forsdike, F/O J. E. Kelt, Sub-Lieutenant J. M. Robertson R.N.V.R., F/Sgt B. J. Rudge, Sgt J. Sowter. *83 Squadron:* F/Sgt F. J. Chadwick, Sgt H. Coles, F/Sgt J. A. Cook, F/Sgt E. Cummings, Sgt P. L. T. Lewis, S/Ldr N. H. Scrivener, W/Cdr J. H. Searby, W/Cdr W. H. Shaw, F/Sgt J. W. Slaughter. *90 Squadron:* P/O D. Beaton, Sgt A. R. Clarke, F/O W. S. Day, Sgt P. Foolkes, Sgt K. G. Forester, Sgt S. Guyon, F/Lt G. W. Ingram, F/Sgt C. Keefe, F/Sgt C. A. Mitchinson, Sgt J. G. Morris, P/O J. Pattinson, F/Sgt A. J. Rhodes, Sgt C. N. Searle, Sgt R. W. Siddons, P/O R. A. Whitworth. *97 Squadron:* Sgt C. S. Chatten, F/Lt W. I. Covington, P/O S. R. Dawson, F/Sgt G. F. Gower, W.O. W. H. Layne, S/Ldr E. E. Rodley. *100 Squadron:* F/O W. Bentley, Sgt E. J. Clark, W.O. J. R. Clark, F/Sgt G. W. Cooke, Sgt W. L. Couzins, F/O L. W. Crum, W.O. D. G. Edwards, F/Sgt W. G. Green, Sgt C. Gregory. *101 Squadron:* F/Lt W. D. Austin, Sgt P. G. Davys, Sgt D. Geall, Sgt R. B. Hooper, W.O. P. A. F. Johnson, F/Sgt J. W. Lawrence, F/Sgt E. M. McAlister, F/Lt R. L. L. McCullough, Sgt T. C. Marchant, F/Sgt E. S. Moore, Sgt R. Schofield, F/Sgt K. Thompson, Sgt E. A. Walters, Sgt G. G. Whittle. *102 Squadron:* F/O F. R. Booth, Sgt R. Learmond, Sgt W. M. McArter, F/Sgt R. G. Pharo, Sgt F. W. Powell, P/O W. J. Slater, Sgt R. J. Twine, F/Lt A. C. Walters, F/Lt J. W. Ward, Sgt H. Williams. *103 Squadron:* F/Sgt C. W. Annis, Sgt N. H. Bolt, Sgt B. R. Bound, Sgt S. D. Clewer, F/O J. A. Day, F/O E. J. Densley, W.O. S. F. Gage, F/Sgt P. W. Lees, Sgt J. H. McFarlane, Sgt D. S. Potter, P/O J. H. Ratcliff, Sgt T. D. G. Teare, F/O G. Wood. *106 Squadron:* Sgt R. P. Castleman, F/Sgt J. Dacey, F/Sgt S. V. Grimes, Sgt W. P. Haig, Sgt W. F. Tookey. *115 Squadron:* Sgt E. Albone, Sgt F. H. Eaglestone, Sgt D. W. N. Franklin, F/Sgt A. Howell, Sgt G. R. Mooney, W.O. E. H. Noxon, Sgt R. Stewart, F/Sgt I. J. Williamson. *139 Squadron:* F/Lt R. A. V. Crampton, Sgt J. Marshallsay, F/Sgt V. J. C. Miles, Sgt C. R. T. Mottershead, F/Sgt E. R. Perry. *156 Squadron:* Sgt G. D. Aitken, Sgt A. L. Barlow, W.O. P. A. Coldham, F/Sgt J. E. Foley, F/O C. R. Johnson, F/Lt G. L. Mandeno, F/Sgt G. H. Pascoe,

F/Sgt J. C. Ross, S/Ldr D. H. Thomas, F/Sgt C. W. Wilkins. *157 Squadron:* F/Lt H. E. Tappin. *158 Squadron:* Sgt A. Bierton, W.O. C. R. Buckland, Sgt J. Cotter, Sgt C. K. Davie, Sgt A. M. Glendenning, P/O W. Holden, F/O L. C. Kemp, Sgt T. Kennedy, Sgt J. M. Lally, P/O L. D. Leicester, Sgt J. Loudoun, P/O W. C. L. McKay, Sgt W. N. Patterson, Sgt D. A. Robinson, F/O T. Smart, F/O G. V. Smith, Sgt A. K. Snell, Sgt N. H. Stimson, Sgt R. Thurston, Sgt A. K. Young. *166 Squadron:* Sgt P. R. Chambers, Sgt D. A. Collins. *192 Squadron:* P/O F. Baldwin, F/O R. V. Broad, Sgt E. G. Sharpe, F/O R. J. K. Turner. *207 Squadron:* F/Lt D. M. Balme, F/O R. O. P. Beatty, P/O W. H. Benton, Sgt K. R. Blundell, Sgt R. E. C. Buck, Sgt A. Cordon, F/Sgt S. Craig, F/Lt J. F. Grime, P/O K. Newby, Sgt H. Pettie. *214 Squadron:* F/Sgt A. Boyd, Sgt W. L. Clements, Sgt R. Conolly, F/O K. E. W. Evans, Sgt A. B. Grainer, Sgt K. J. Hovers, F/O F. Lee, W/Cdr D. J. McGlinn. *218 Squadron:* F/Sgt J. C. Allan, Sgt B. Anderson, Sgt S. A. Bain, F/O H. C. Eyre, F/Sgt E. J. Insull. *300 Squadron:* Sgt N. B. Garnowski, Sgt A. Jaremko, F/Sgt T. J. Markowski, F/O P. P. Stachowski, F/Lt R. Stadtmuller. *305 Squadron:* F/O Z. Bobinski, F/O J. Dziedzik, F/Sgt H. Ignatowski, W.O. M. Kosmalski, F/O L. S. Lewicki, Sgt J. Madracki.* *405 Squadron:* Sgt R. A. Andrews, P/O H. Gowan, Sgt W. H. King, Sgt L. D. Kohnke, Sgt J. G. McLaughlan, F/Sgt G. W. Mainprize, Sgt J. H. Rogers. *408 Squadron:* P/O J. E. Bemister, P/O G. J. Richardson. *419 Squadron:* W/Cdr M. M. Fleming, Sgt E. R. Kirkham, Sgt J. M. Mahoney, P/O J. Sibalis, F/O J. A. Westland. *427 Squadron:* P/O E. A. Johnson, P/O G. S. Schellenberg, P/O L. Vogan. *428 Squadron:* P/O N. M. Bush, Sgt P. Demcoe, P/O H. Dernick, S/Ldr J. M. Forman. *429 Squadron:* Sgt G. D. Allester, P/O K. A. Craig, P/O F. C. Edmunds, P/O G. Fitzgerald, F/O J. W. Kerr, F/Lt G. F. Pentony. *432 Squadron:* Sgt G. W. Hodges, Sgt E. Judkins, Sgt J. H. Smith. *460 Squadron:* Sgt H. L. Britton, Sgt C. J. Challis, F/Sgt A. G. Elwing, F/O A. Flett, Sgt E. F. Groom, Sgt I. C. Heath, Sgt W. G. Lamb, F/Sgt A. E. Llewellyn, F/Sgt D. B. Moodie, Sgt P. W. Moore, F/Sgt M. R. Nash, F/Sgt G. J. Oakshott, F/Sgt A. J. O'Brien, P/O T. E. Osborn, F/O/ J. E. C. Radcliffe, P/O H. T. Scott, F/O K. L. Shephard, Sgt B. Treacy, F/Sgt R. S. Webster. *466 Squadron:* F/O D. F. Bateman, Sgt F. B. Black, F/Sgt G. B. Coombes, F/Sgt J. Evans, Sgt D. Green, Sgt A. L. McMorron, F/Sgt K. M. Mansell, P/O E. A. Miles. *467 Squadron:* Sgt S. Bethell, Sgt W. Booth, F/Sgt S. Bray, Sgt E. C. Brookes, Sgt W. G. Calderhead, Sgt C. H. Hawton, Sgt F. W. A. Hendry, Sgt F. G. Miller, Sgt G. Niblett, Sgt H. E. Twitchett, P/O J. H. Whiting. *605 Squadron:* F/O A. G. Woods.

---

* Sgt Madracki's contribution came in the form of a diary. He was killed in a raid on Stettin on 29–30 August 1944.

619 Squadron: S/Ldr R. G. Churcher, Sgt F. E. Gostling, F/Sgt R. A. Knights, Sgt H. N. Knilans. *620 Squadron:* F/O W. Goodall, F/O P. S. Hobbs, Sgt C. C. Leeming, Sgt S. D. Slade, F/O E. Walker. *1409 (Meteorological) Flight:* F/O N. W. F. Green, F/Lt G. H. T. Hatton, F/O A. F. Pethick.

The following contributors also flew as bomber-crew members on one of the Hamburg raids: Air Cdre A. M. Wray, commander No. 12 Base; Gp Capts H. I. Cozens, H. I. Edwards, V.C., S. C. Elworthy, station commanders at Ingham, Binbrook and Waddington; Major T. F. S. Southgate, No. 4 Group Flak Liaison Officer.

COMMANDERS AND STAFFS ETC.

Air Ministry: Air Cdre S. O. Bufton, Director of Bomber Operations.
Bomber Command Headquarters: Air Marshal Sir Arthur Harris, W/Cdr W. I. C. Inness, S/Ldr F. A. B. Fawssett.
8 Group Headquarters: Air Vice-Marshal D. C. T. Bennett, Gp Capt. C. D. C. Boyce, S/Ldr H. W. Lees.
H.M.S. Shearwater (in Coastal Convoy FS.83): Lt N. J. T. Monsarrat (died August 1979).
36 Air–Sea Rescue Unit: P/O K. G. Muir.

U.S.A.A.F. AIRCREW*

91st Bomb Group: Maj. D. G. Alford, T/Sgt J. Allen, 2nd Lt L. J. Connors, 2nd Lt E. L. Goelz, S/Sgt C. A. Gundersen, 2nd Lt C. N. Smith, Lt E. P. Winslow. *303rd Bomb Group:* T/Sgt H. E. Hernan, 2nd Lt J. D. Walsh. *351st Bomb Group:* Maj. C. F. Ball, Maj. E. Ledoux, Lt B. Schohan, Lt C. B. Stackhouse, Lt L. P. Stover. *379th Bomb Group:* 2nd Lt A. E. Batick. *381st Bomb Group:* S/Sgt G. H. Orin, Lt J. H. Owen, S/Sgt K. K. Rector, Capt. G. G. Shackley, 2nd Lt J. H. Wemmer. *384th Bomb Group:* 2nd Lt J. E. Armstrong, 2nd Lt C. C. Carlin, T/Sgt H. J. Cocklin, Lt H. L. Cromwell, Lt D. H. Davis (died February 1978), T/Sgt A. W. Detrick (died October 1978), 2nd Lt W. B. Dillon, 2nd Lt G. L. Doubet, Lt T. J. Estes, 2nd Lt P. H. Gordy, Lt K. J. Hall, Lt R. J. Hall, S/Sgt C. Hammock, 2nd Lt R. W. House, T/Sgt W. L. House, T/Sgt E. R. Keathley, T/Sgt B. Landrum, 2nd Lt W. F. McGeehan, T/Sgt D. W. Marshall, S/Sgt L. J. Reandeau, S/Sgt R. C. Smiley.

COMMANDERS AND STAFFS

Maj.-Gen. I. C. Eaker, commander 8th Army Air Force; Lt-Col G. W. Jones, H.Q. VIII Bomber Command.

* Abbreviations not used earlier: Major – Maj., Technical Sergeant – T/Sgt, Staff Sergeant – S/Sgt.

THE PEOPLE OF HAMBURG

Altona: Friedel Behnke, Hanni Paulsen (now Polte), Ilse Schrader.
Barmbek: Elli Kellner, Kaete Kirchner (now Enoch), Bruno Koclajda,
Bruno Lauritzen, Elli Nawroski (now Müller), Helene Sydow (now
Nöhring). *Billbrook:* Gertraude Voss. *Borgfelde:* Rolf Witt. *Dulsberg:*
Otto Müller, Helmut Wilkens. *Eilbek:* Hildegard Jäh, Anne-Kaete
Seiffarth. *Eimsbüttel:* Heinrich Capell, Siegfried Franz, Elsbeth Tisch.
Eppendorf: Hans Maass. *Freihafen:* Martin Wolff. *Fuhlsbüttel:* Willy
Franzenburg, Frieda and Hermann Kröger. *Hamm and Hammerbrook:*
Marie Brand, Herbert Brecht, Käte Hoffmeister (now Schäfer),
Werner Karotka, Traute Koch, August Koopmann, Helga von
Luck, Arthur Lüneburg, Maria Mai, Elfriede Mucke, Frieda Nolze,
Ingeborg Reifkogel, Ilse Rose, Ingeborg Scheffel, W. Völckers,
Fernanda Weist. *Harburg:* Anne-Lies Schmidt. *Harvestehude:* Heinz
Bumann, Hermann Matthies, Otti and Ernst Schwarze. *Neustadt:*
Anna Hinrichsen, Otto Mahncke, Rosa Todt. *Othmarschen:* Andreas
Jacobsen. *Ottensen:* Waldemar Schmielau. *Rothenburgsort:* Maria-
Luise Wiegand. *Rotherbaum:* Irmgard Schlöttig (now Finnern).
St Georg: Louise Schäfer (now Harcus). *St Pauli:* Werner Broddeck,
Inge Bube (now Heitmann). *Wandsbek:* Paula Kühl (now Alexander),
Karl-Heinz Alfeis, Hertha and Hermann Frank, Margot Jahnke
(now Hoffmann). *Wilhelmsburg:* Wilma Rathjens (now Schermer).
Winterhude: Dieter and Hans John, Alma Zeiher.

In addition to the above, a 1943 fireman named 'Karl', another
fireman and his wife, and a harbour policeman all provided contributions but would not allow their names to be published.

Military and Naval Personnel in Hamburg
Lt Hermann Bock, Uffz. Friedrich Dierkes, Obergefreiter Herbert
Heinicke, Lt Dr Walter Luth, Obergefreiter Hans Nielsen, Uffz.
Arnold Schwenn, Oblt Max Siegmann, Kapitän Herbert Wichmann.

Flak Helpers
Traugott Bauer-Schlichtegroll, Hans-Jürgen Handtmann, Albert
Hartung, Walter Stapelfeldt.

Polish Workers in Hamburg
Irena Chmiel (now Zlotnicka), Zygmunt Skowronski.

Villages near Hamburg
Bergedorf: Margot Schulz (now Clark). *Hamersen:* Wilhelm Meinke,
Heinrich Weisker.

Contributor Dr Hans Enoch was forced to leave Hamburg in 1938
and Professor Dr Gerhard Rose was a consultant in hygiene to the
Luftwaffe sent to Hamburg immediately after the 1943 raids.

LUFTWAFFE AIRCREW

Night-Fighter Units
III/NJG1: Uffz. Rolf Angersbach. *IV/NJG1:* Uffz. Friedrich Abromeit, Oblt Ernst-Georg Drünkler, Oblt Eberhard Gardiewski, Oblt Hermann Greiner, Hptm. Hans-Joachim Jabs. *I/NJG2:* Uffz. Heinrich Scholl. *I/NJG3:* Feld. Heinz Moritz, Uffz. Eberhard Scheve, Uffz. Hans-Georg Schierholz, Oblt Paul Zorner. *II/NJG3:* Uffz. Josef Krinner, Uffz. Otto Kutzner, Uffz. Hubert Prommer. *III/NJG3:* Lt Hans Raum. *IV/NJG3:* Uffz. Walter Heidenreich. *II/NJG5:* Lt Peter Spoden, Lt Rudolf Thun. *III/NJG5:* Lt Günther Wolf. Oblt Joachim Wendtland, of Luftnachrichten Regt 202, flew on a night-fighter sortie with a Me110 of III/NJG1. Uffz. Erich Handke, a radar operator of IV/NJG1, did not fly against the Hamburg raids but provided a copy of a very useful diary.

Day-Fighter Unit
II/JG11: Lt Wolfgang Gloerfeld.

COMMANDERS AND STAFFS

General Josef Kammhuber, commander XII Fliegerkorps; Maj. Wolfgang Falck, staff of *General der Nachtjagd;* Hptm. Walter Knickmeier, Stab/NJG1.

GERMAN GOVERNMENT

Reichsminister Albert Speer.

PERSONAL ACKNOWLEDGEMENTS

I have received valuable help from many other individuals and from various organizations. Five people deserve special mention.

I would never have been able to assemble so much vital German material for this book were it not for the diligent and friendly cooperation of Emil Nonnenmacher of Eppstein/Taunus and Norbert Krüger of Essen. I thank Emil Nonnenmacher for his valuable help in many ways, in particular for his expert advice on all night-fighter matters and for making available to me relevant details from his own archive material – as yet unpublished – as well as a great number of other details from a special collection built up over more than twenty-five years by his colleague, Hans Ring. Norbert Krüger, an expert on the civil side of the bombing war and on the German Flak, also gave freely of his private archive material besides helping in many other ways; in particular he was a fine travelling companion and interpreter during an interviewing visit to Hamburg and North Germany.

In England I owe a great debt to two friends who volunteered to do the bulk of my London research. Patrick Mahoney of Chadwell Heath carried out the first phase of an extensive Public Record Office search and Chris Everitt of Eton Wick carried out all the secondary research when the Record Office moved from Chancery Lane to Kew. The fifth of this 'first wave' of helpers is my wife, Mary, who has spent many hours checking my typescript and drawing the preliminary maps, all with the utmost care and diligence.

My regular typist, Janet Mountain of Swineshead, has handled the extensive correspondence and two drafts of a long manuscript with a skill and willingness which is appreciated as much as ever.

I also give my thanks to many other people who have helped me in a voluntary capacity and in many different ways. It is only pressure of space which forces me to marshal their names by alphabetical list and by their country of residence, as follows:

In England: Elizabeth and Malcolm Downie, Annemarie Lamb, Ted Sylvester and Alan Taylor of Boston, Bill Chorley of Ottery St Mary, Tom Cushing of Little Snoring, J. N. De Gruchy of Blandford Forum, Roger Freeman of Dedham, Rob Forbes-Morgan of London S W 16, Mick Gibson of Higham Ferrers, Aileen Glossop (formerly L.A.C.W. Walker of R.A.F. Bardney) of Nottingham, Brian Goulding of Nottingham, Peter Harris of Chelmsford, Richard Harrison of York, Mike Hodgson of Mareham le Fen, Adrian Liddell Hart of Stroud, Neville Mackinder of Finchley, George Moore of Woodhall Spa (Chief of the Lincolnshire Fire Brigade), Peter Middlebrook of Worcester, Peter Pountney of Grimsby, J. Rutkiewicz of Hounslow and Flight Lieutenant Jack Stewart of the R.A.F.

In the U.S.A.: Paul Chryst of Pottstown, Pa (and the 91st Bomb Group Association), Michael Kernan of Washington, Al Garfold and family of Pittsburgh, Dr Geoffrey Giles of Yale, Brigadier-General Frederick Maxwell of Arlington and T. Paxton Sherwood of York, Pa (and the 381st Bomb Group Association).

In Germany: Horst Diener of Dortmund, Hans Hermann Lohse of Elmshorn, Hans Meckel and Detlev Seifarth of Hamburg and Herbert Scholl of Schliersee.

In New Zealand: John Barton of Auckland and Peter Strugnell of R.N.Z.A.F. Base Ohakea.

In Australia: Godfrey Ball of Brisbane.

I would like to thank Sir Freddie Laker for making it possible for ordinary people like me to fly the Atlantic at reasonable cost.

I have also received valuable assistance from many organizations, this help often going well beyond what might be considered a standard service. I wish to thank them all:

In England: the Association of Jewish Refugees, the Bomber Command Association, the Boston Branch of Lincolnshire Libraries, the College Library of R.A.F. Cranwell, the Imperial War Museum (particularly Mike Willis and David Nash), Lloyd's Register of Shipping, the Meteorological Office at Bracknell, the Air Historical Branch, the Hydrographic Department and Departments AR8b, AR9a and OS9a of the Ministry of Defence, the Pathfinder Association, the Polish Air Force Association, the Public Record Office (particularly Mr F. Lambert) and the Royal Air Force Museum at Hendon.

In the U.S.A.: the American Battle Monuments Commission (particularly Colonel William Ryan), the National Personnel Records Center, the Office of Civil Defense (James W. Kerr) and, of the U.S.A.F., the 1361st Audiovisual Squadron (Dana Bell) and the Albert F. Simpson Historical Research Center.

In Germany: the Deutsche Dienststelle, the Gemeinschaft der Jagdflieger, the Textarchiv of the *Hamburger Abendblatt* and, particularly, the Hamburg Staatsarchiv (Claus Stukenbrock).

In Canada: the Department of Veterans' Affairs, the Public Archives and the R.C.A.F. P.O.W. Association (Don Morrison).

In Australia: the Department of Defence Air Force Records.

In New Zealand: Secretary of Defence – Records.

In my search for ex-B-17 crew members in the highly mobile society of the United States, I was given assistance by the municipal authorities of the following communities: the Chief of Police at Coos Bay (Dan Arthur) and the Mayor's Offices at Des Moines, Great Bend, Houston, Lansing and Tupper Lake. I also received valuable and friendly help from Mrs Shirly Therrien of the City of Port Colborne, Canada and the Commune of Aabenraa, Denmark.

I acknowledge the permission of the Controller of H.M. Stationery Office to quote from the British Official History and from Crown copyright documents in the Public Record Office.

I am pleased to record my thanks to the following newspapers and magazines which published my appeals for participants in the Battle of Hamburg:

United Kingdom: *Daily Telegraph, Evening News* (London), *Birmingham Post, Grimsby Evening Telegraph, Lincolnshire Standard, Lincolnshire Echo, Polish Daily, Nottingham Evening Post, Western Morning News. Air Mail, Air Pictorial, R.A.F. News, Royal British Legion Journal, Royal United Service Institute Journal.*

U.S.A.: *New York Times Book Review, Washington Post Review of Literature. AOPA Pilot, Air Force Magazine, Air Force Times, Aviation Week and Space Technology, Friendly Times* (United Airlines), *TWA Skyliner, 8th Air Force News.*

Germany: *Hamburger Abendblatt. Aerokurier, Flugrevue-Flugwelt, Jägerblatt, Luftwaffen-Revue.*

Australia: *The Australian, The Herald, The Mercury, The Sunday Mail, The Sunday Times, Queensland Courier Mail, Reveille.*

Canada: *Calgary Herald, Edmonton Journal, Ottawa Journal, Victoria Colonist, Vancouver Sun, Winnipeg Free Press. Canadian Flight, Canadian Forces, Sentinel, Royal Canadian Legion.*

New Zealand: *Dunedin Evening Star, New Zealand Herald, The Dominion, The Press.*

Bibliography

OFFICIAL HISTORIES

Webster, Sir Charles, and Frankland, Noble, *The Strategic Air Offensive against Germany, 1939–1945*, H.M.S.O., 1961.

Craven, W. F., and Cate, J. L., *The Army Air Forces in World War II*, Univ. of Chicago Press, 1948–58.

Hamburg Polizeipräsident Report, unpublished but translations available through the National Technical Information Service, U.S. Department of Commerce, Springfield, Va, and Microinfo Ltd, Alton, Hants.

Hamburg, Senate of the City of, *Die Jüdischen Opfer des Nationalsozialismus in Hamburg*, Hamburg, 1965.

OTHER WORKS

Bekker, Cajus, *The Luftwaffe War Diaries*, Macdonald, 1968.

Bond, Horatio, *Fire and the Air War*, National Fire Protection Association, Boston, Mass., 1946.

Bowman, Martin W., *Fields of Little America*, Wensum Books (Norwich), 1977.

Boyle, Andrew, *Trenchard – Man of Vision*, Collins, 1967.

Brunswig, Hans, *Feuersturm über Hamburg*, Motorbuch Verlag, Stuttgart, 1978.

Freeman, Roger A., *The Mighty Eighth*, Macdonald, London, and Doubleday, New York, 1970.

Harris, Sir Arthur, *Bomber Offensive*, Collins, 1947.

Jaspar, Ronald C. D., *George Bell – Bishop of Chichester*, Oxford Univ. Press, 1967.

Jones, Neville, *The Origins of Strategic Bombing*, William Kimber, 1973.

Lenton, H. T., *German Submarines*, Macdonald, 1965.

Lochner, Louis P., *The Goebbels Diaries*, Hamish Hamilton, 1948.

Price, Alfred, *Instruments of Darkness*, Macdonald & Jane's, 1977.

Reitlinger, Gerald, *The Final Solution*, Vallentine, Mitchell, 1953.

Rumpf, Hans, *The Bombing of Germany*, Frederick Muller, 1963.

Saundby, Sir Robert, *Air Bombardment*, Chatto & Windus, 1961.

Speer, Albert, *Inside the Third Reich*, Weidenfeld & Nicolson, 1970.

Index

The city of Hamburg has not been indexed but its constituent districts and surrounding villages have been listed under 'Hamburg'. Passing references to aircraft or technical devices of frequently mentioned types are not indexed, particularly in the 'action' chapters, Chapters 7–17. Individual units and airfields in Appendixes 1–3 and airmen in Appendixes 4–6 have not been indexed.